EPIGRAPHIA ZEYLANICA

BEING

LITHIC AND OTHER INSCRIPTIONS OF CEYLON

EPIGRAPHIA ZEYLANICA

BEING

LITHIC AND OTHER INSCRIPTIONS OF CEYLON

EDITED AND TRANSLATED BY

H. W. CODRINGTON
AND
S. PARANAVITANA

IN FOUR VOLUMES
1904-1934

VOL. IV
1933 - 1934

GYAN

Published by

Gyan Publishing House
5, Ansari Road
Daryaganj, New Delhi-110002
Phone: 011-47034999, 9811692060
E-mail: books@gyanbooks.com

Distribution Network
gyanbooks.com
India, USA, Canada, UK, Australia, France

ISBN : 978-81-212-3351-4 (Set)
ISBN : 978-81-212-4990-4 (PB)
First Published, London, 1934

2nd Impression 2020

Printed at: Gyan Press, Delhi.

ARCHAEOLOGICAL SURVEY OF CEYLON

EPIGRAPHIA ZEYLANICA

BEING

LITHIC AND OTHER INSCRIPTIONS OF CEYLON

EDITED AND TRANSLATED

BY

H. W. CODRINGTON
CEYLON CIVIL SERVICE
[*Retired*]

and

S. PARANAVITANA
EPIGRAPHICAL ASSISTANT TO THE
ARCHAEOLOGICAL COMMISSIONER

LONDON
PUBLISHED FOR THE GOVERNMENT OF CEYLON BY HUMPHREY MILFORD
OXFORD UNIVERSITY PRESS, AMEN HOUSE, E.C.
PRINTED IN GREAT BRITAIN
1934

ERRATA

(for Parts 2 and 3)

Page 68, line 24, *for* 1164 *read* 1114.

,, 78, line 29, *for* වියල *read* වියළ.

,, 80, line 10, *for* viyala *read* viyaḷa.

,, 158, line 26, *for* viṣa-dahara *read* viṣ[ā]da-hara.

,, 168, line 7, *for* the burning poison of mental transgression *read* who removes sinfulness and affliction of mind.

,, 168, *delete* footnote 2.

No. 1. SAṀGAMU VIHĀRA ROCK-INSCRIPTION.

By S. PARANAVITANA.

AT Saṁgamuva, a village about two miles to the north-east of Gokarälla in the Häṭahaya Kōraḷē of the Kuruṇāgala District, there is a low, rocky hill on which are to be seen the remains of an ancient Buddhist monastery. The neighbouring tank, Mäddekäṭiya-väva, when full, approaches almost to the foot of the hill on the eastern side, along which ran the old path leading to the shrines and monastic dwellings. A series of steps, numbering over a hundred, cut on the bare side of the rock, leads one to a plateau, about ten acres in extent, on which are an old *stūpa* now reduced to a low mound of debris, and a few stumps of rough stone pillars marking the sites of old monastic buildings. The modern *vihāra* is also in this area; and near the entrance to it are some architectural fragments, to wit, a guardstone, a moonstone, and a stone slab with a symbol resembling the old Brāhmī *śa* carved on it. From this plateau, rough stone steps lead to a shrine, dating from the Kandyan period, built in a cave near the top of the hill. This shrine is now undergoing renovation; and a new wall, built about five years ago, partly conceals a pre-Christian Brāhmī inscription[1] incised on the drip-ledge of the cave. In the vicinity of this shrine, a gigantic rock boulder, under which was another, more spacious cave, has tumbled down at an unknown period, damaging the Brāhmī inscription[2] on its drip-ledge. There are four more caves at the site: two near the shrine, one at the foot of the hill close to the tank and the last, the most spacious one at the site, about 100 yards to the south of the shrine.

On a flat rock near the modern *vihāra* are fragments of several inscriptions (*A.S.I.* Nos. 732-742) which, from the script, may be ascribed to the period between the fifth and seventh centuries. One of these contains the name 'Goṇagiri'; but the fragmentary nature of the record does not permit us to conclude that this was the ancient name of the place.

At the top of the flight of rock-cut steps mentioned above, to the left as one ascends the hill, an area measuring 4 ft. 4 in. by 3 ft. 0½ in. has been made into a raised and smoothed panel by chiselling away the rock surface around it; and, on this, the record dealt with in the present paper has been incised.

---

[1] What is now visible of this inscription reads:—*Parumaka Citagutaha bariya parumaka* . . . . .

[2] The remaining letters of this inscription read:—*Bata Śabanaśa* . . . . *laśa puta Ma* . . . . . .

This, along with the other epigraphs at the place, was copied for the first time by the present writer in 1931 [1].

Eighteen lines of the record are now visible and, after the last line, the dressed surface of the rock has room for four more lines; but no indications of any writing are now to be seen here. Owing to the fact that the record is engraved on a rock which is open on all sides to the weather and liable continually to be trodden by people going up and down the hill, it has suffered considerably. Lines 13–16 only are completely legible, the others being more or less damaged. Line 17 is completely illegible and, of lines 8–10, only a few letters can be made out, making it impossible to have a connected reading of this part of the record.

The **letters**, regularly incised, are, on an average, 2 in. in height. They belong to the **script** of the twelfth century and call for no remarks in particular. The last four lines of the document consist of a Sanskrit verse in the *Vasantatilaka* metre, of which the third *päda* is completely, and the fourth more than half, damaged. The rest of the record is in Sinhalese which also contains a considerable number of Sanskrit *tatsamas* as is usual in the Sinhalese writings of this period. As regards **orthography**, it may be noted that conjoint letters are used in writing such Sinhalese words as *karamha* (l. 5) and *mäkuvamha* (l. 14), whereas in *vamha* (ll. 3–4), the *virāma* sign is used. The cerebral *ḷ* occurs in the Sanskrit word *akṣarāḷi*, though in classical Sanskrit this letter is absent. This peculiarity is also noticed in Sanskrit documents written in the Grantha script of South India.

As regards **grammar**, the use of the verbal forms of the present tense, e.g. *nokaramha* (l. 5) *mäkuvamha* and *vüvamha* (l. 14), to express the future tense, is noteworthy.

The **contents** tell us about an alliance between **Gajabāhu** and **Parākramabāhu**; and, as such, the record is of exceptional historical importance. We have no difficulty in identifying the two princes as Gajabāhu II and Parākramabāhu I. The script of the record is that of the period to which these two princes belong; and, moreover, there was only one occasion when a Gajabāhu was a contemporary of a Parākramabāhu. The document also tells us that the two princes were related to each other as maternal cousins or brothers-in-law; and this fact agrees with the statements of the chronicles regarding the relationship between Gajabāhu II and Parākramabāhu I.

---

[1] See *A. S. C. Annual Report* for 1930–31, p. 5.

The document is briefly worded; and, in it, the princes speak in the first person. After introducing themselves by name, they at once, and without any formalities, come to the subject-matter of the agreement. By its first clause, they promise that, till the ends of their lives, they will not wage war against each other. The second clause is not completely preserved; but we are in no doubt regarding what it dealt with. By it, the two princes come to an agreement that the possessions of the one who would be the first to pass away will become the property of the survivor. The third clause is almost completely illegible and we, therefore, cannot speak about it with any confidence. By the fourth and last clause of the treaty, the two princes declare that a king who is an enemy of one of them, is an enemy of both, i.e. they enter into an offensive and defensive alliance. Imprecations against themselves if they act contrary to this agreement are then followed by a benedictary verse in Sanskrit of which nearly half is obliterated.

Turning now to the *Mahāvaṁsa*, in which the events of this period are narrated with a wealth of detail, we read, in the seventieth chapter of that chronicle, how Parākramabāhu, after consolidating his position in the principality of the Dakkhiṇadesa to which he succeeded on the death of his uncle Kittisirimegha, undertook a campaign against his cousin Gajabāhu II, with the object of making himself the sole master of Laṁkā. In the various encounters which took place during the course of this campaign, Parākramabāhu's generals have always the advantage over the troops of Gajabāhu and the latter's capital, Poḷonnaruva, itself falls into the invader's hands. Gajabāhu then solicits the help of Mānābharaṇa, the ruler of Rohaṇa, who readily comes on the scene and, instead of succouring Gajabāhu, schemes for his own aggrandizement.

Seeing this new danger, Gajabāhu appeals to Parākramabāhu for protection; and the latter, who had recovered from his temporary reverses at the hands of the Rohaṇa troops, recaptures Poḷonnaruva and becomes virtually the master of the Rājaraṭṭha. At this stage, the monks intervene and bring about a reconciliation between the two cousins. Parākramabāhu restores the dominions of Gajabāhu and himself retires to his province. Gajabāhu, on his part, now definitely takes the side of Parākramabāhu and not only refuses to listen to Mānābharaṇa's advances for an alliance; but, moreover, he makes Parākramabāhu the heir to his kingdom and has this fact engraved on a stone tablet at the Maṇḍalagiri Vihāra[1]. Doubtless we have, in the present inscription,

[1] *Mv.* lxxi, vv. 1–5.

a copy of the treaty entered into, on this occasion, by Gajabāhu II and Parākramabāhu I. Perhaps, it was another copy of the same document that Gajabāhu caused to be engraved at the Maṇḍalagiri Vihāra.

The last named place, now known as Mäḍirigiriya, is situated in the Tamankaḍuva District of the North-Central Province. The site was explored by the Archaeological Survey in 1897 and 1907, when two inscriptions of the tenth century were discovered [1]; but the inscription of Gajabāhu II, mentioned in the *Mahāvaṁsa*, has not come to light. Mr. Harry Storey, who visited the site in 1924, looked for this inscription; but, instead, he found a duplicate of the pillar inscription discovered in 1897 [2]. The site, which is very extensive, is in dense forest and some of the remains are yet buried in the debris. Gajabāhu's inscription, which must have been either identical with the present document or, at least, must have had many points in common with it, may, therefore, be yet discovered.

Comparing the *Mahāvaṁsa* account with the present document, there appear to be certain discrepancies between the two. The chronicle would have us believe that the settlement arrived at, on this occasion, between the two princes, was all to the advantage of Parākramabāhu and that Gajabāhu, as befitting a vanquished monarch, humbled himself in the presence of the former. It mentions the fact that Gajabāhu bequeathed his kingdom to Parākramabāhu; but does not indicate at all that this as well as the other conditions of the peace were reciprocal. Moreover, in this document, Gajabāhu's name is mentioned first, showing that his antagonist had conceded him precedence in rank.

These discrepancies may be due to the bias which the author of this part of the *Mahāvaṁsa* had in favour of Parākramabāhu; but, on the other hand, they are more apparent than real. The treaty is, in reality, to the advantage of Parākramabāhu. We must not forget that Gajabāhu, nominally at least, was Parākramabāhu's overlord and, had he not been worsted in warfare, he would not have treated his younger rival as an equal in status as he does in this document. The second clause, by which, apparently, each of the contracting parties makes the other his heir, becomes, in effect, the leaving of his kingdom by Gajabāhu to Parākramabāhu who was very much the younger of the two.

---

[1] See *A.S.C. Annual Report* for 1897, p. 7 and the *Annual Report* for 1907, pp. 30-32. For the inscriptions see *E. Z.* Vol. II, pp. 25-33.

[2] *Ceylon Antiquary and Literary Register*, vol. x, pp. 67-87.

in the ordinary course of events, there was very little probability that Parākramabāhu would predecease Gajabāhu for the latter to benefit by this agreement.

By consenting to forgo the opportunity of capturing the Poḷonnaruva throne when he was able to do so by force of arms and waiting to succeed to it in this manner, Parākramabāhu has shown much political sagacity. At that time, there were several other princes who could show a claim as good or better than that of Parākramabāhu to the overlordship of the Rājaraṭṭha[1]; and, had Parākramabāhu at once taken possession of the throne when Gajabāhu was vanquished, he would have been considered, by many of his contemporaries, as a usurper. By this treaty, Parākramabāhu established a legitimate claim, above those of his rivals, to the territories under Gajabāhu's rule. It may, of course, be questioned whether, according to the Sinhalese law of succession, Gajabāhu could, in this manner, will away his kingdom.

The last clause is, apparently, directed against Mānābharaṇa, the ruler of Rohaṇa. He, too, had ambitions similar to those of Parākramabāhu and was the latter's chief obstacle in his way to the throne of Poḷonnaruva. As Parākramabāhu had learned by his experience in the campaign that he had just brought to a successful end, Mānābharaṇa's troops were not to be despised and a combination of the forces of Rohaṇa and Rājaraṭṭha would possibly have become too powerful for him to resist. By this treaty, Parākramabāhu isolated Mānābharaṇa and prevented the possibility of such a combination. The statement in the *Mahāvaṁsa* (ch. lxxi, v. 2) that Gajabāhu refused to listen to Mānābharaṇa's advances for an alliance, shows that he, on his part, faithfully observed the provisions of this treaty. Thus, we see that though, on the face of it, the treaty appears as advantageous to Gajabāhu as to Parākramabāhu, on a deeper study of it, we find that the latter was the person who stood to gain by it in reality. The document must have been worded in this manner in order to spare the feelings of the humiliated old monarch and the person who drafted it appears to have been a master in the somewhat Machiavellian diplomacy of the times. It may also be of interest to note that the occurrence of the technical terms *vigraha* and *sandhāna* proves that the document was drawn up by one familiar with the Arthaśāstra, the Indian science of politics.

---

[1] Gajabāhu had two brothers, Mahinda and Aṇikaṅga, who had a better claim to the throne of Poḷonnaruva than that of Parākramabāhu. Mānābharaṇa, the ruler of Rohaṇa, had as much right to the sovereignty as Parākramabāhu.

One other question that may arise is the reason why this document was engraved at the Saṁgamu Vihāra. We do not know what the place was called in mediaeval times; but, though it was within the territories under Parākramabāhu's rule before he became sole monarch of the island, there is nothing to prove that the place was close to his residence, even temporarily. Equally inexplicable is the reason why Gajabāhu, on his part, went to the Maṇḍalagiri Vihāra to register his version of the agreement, instead of doing so at his capital, Poḷonnaruva. If a conjecture be permissible, we may surmise that Maṇḍalagiri Vihāra and the Saṁgamu Vihāra were the residences of the principal monks who, on either side, exerted themselves to bring about a reconciliation between the contending rulers. Perhaps, the documents were engraved on stone at the instance of the monks who considered such a step necessary to ensure the faithful observance, by both parties, of the agreement entered into.

TEXT.

1 [ස්වස්ති] [||*] ශ්‍රී මහාසම්මතපරම්පරා
2 [යෙන්] නොපිරිහී ආ සත්‍යධනවූ ගජ
3 බා[හු ප]රාක්‍රමබාහු දෙසුරුබඩු වම්
4 හ [||*] [අ]ප කළ සන්ධානයට ජීවිතාන්ත
5 දක්වා විග්‍රහයක් නොකරම්හ [||*] ඔවූ
6 නොවූත් අයාමෙහි පළඹවූ කෙනකුන්
7 ගෙ .. .. පසුවූවත් අත්පත්
8 (වන්න) .. .. එක්කෙනකුන් ..
9 (වැ) මෙ .. .. .. [රා]ජ්‍ය වි[ලුප්ත] වන නියායෙ
10 ත් .. .. [අප] දෙදෙනා කෙරෙන්
11 එක්කෙනකු[න්හට] සතුරුවූ රජදරුකෙ
12 නෙක් ඇත් නම් දෙදෙනාට මැ සතුරන [||*] මෙ
13 ට විරුධයක් කළමො නම් තුඹුරුවන් ආඥ
14 මැකුවම්හ [||*] නරකයෙන් මුක්ත නොවූවම්හ [||*]
15 අ චන්ද්‍රතාරමවතාජ්ජගදක්ෂරාළි
16 රෙෂා පරාස්ඛනයොරනයොරනන්‍යම් [|*]
17 – – ⏑ – ⏑ ⏑ ⏑ – ⏑ ⏑ – ⏑ – –
18 සෙනහාද්‍රිතා ⏑ ⏑ ⏑ – ⏑ ⏑ – ⏑ තා – [||*]

TRANSCRIPT.

1 [Svasti] [||*] Śrī-Mahāsammata-paramparā-
2 [-yen] no-pirihī ā satya-dhana-vū **Gaja-**

Saligama Vihara Rock-Inscription

Scale about [illegible] inches to [illegible] feet

3 **bā[hu Pa]rākramabāhu** de-sūrubaḍu vam-
4 -ha [॥*] [A]pa kaḷa sandhānayaṭa jīvitānta
5 dakvā vigrahayak no-karamha [॥*] Ovu-
6 -n≠ovun ayāmehi paḷamu-vū kenakun-
7 ge .. .. pasuvūvan at-pat
8 (vanna) .. .. ek-kenakun ..
9 -(vä) me .. .. [rā]jya vi[lup]ta vana niyāye-
10 -n .. .. [apa] de-denā keren
11 ek-kenaku[nhaṭa] saturu-vū raja-daru-ke-
12 -nek ät nam de-denāṭa mä saturaha [॥*] Me-
13 -ṭa viruddhayak kaḷamo nam tunuruvan ājñā
14 mäkuvamha [॥*] Narakayen mukta no-vūvamha [॥*]
15 Ā candra-tāram≠avatāj≠jagad≠akṣar≠āḷi-
16 -r≠eṣā parārttha-dhanayor≠anayor≠ananyam [।*]
17 – – ᴗ – ᴗ ᴗ ᴗ – ᴗ ᴗ – ᴗ – –
18 sneh≠ārddratām ᴗ ᴗ ᴗ – ᴗ ᴗ – tā- [॥*]

TRANSLATION.

[Lines 1–4] Hail! We are the two brothers-in-law [1], **Gajabāhu** and **Parākramabāhu,** who have come down in unbroken succession from the lineage of the illustrious Mahāsammata, and to whom truth is a treasure.

[Lines 4–14] According to the treaty that we have contracted, we shall not, till the ends of our lives, wage war [against each other]. Of each other ...... of the one who will be the first to pass away ...... possession of the one who will survive [2] .... of one ..... so that the kingdom may be destroyed .... If there be any kings who are enemies to either of the two of us, they are enemies to both of us. Were we to do anything contrary to this [agreement], we shall

---

[1] *Sūru-baḍu* is a variant form of *suhuru-baḍu* which is found in Sinhalese literary works (e.g. the *Nikāya Saṅgraha*, Colombo edition of 1890, p. 28) and means 'brother-in-law'. For the explanation of the word, see my note 'Gajabāhu and Mahallakanāga: their relationship' in *J. R. A. S., C. B.*, vol. xxx, pp. 452–454. According to the Sinhalese system of kinship, the same term is used to denote the relationship of maternal cousin and brother-in-law (see Mr. Hocart's 'Indo-European Kinship System' in *C. J. Sc. G*, vol. i, p. 185); the term *suhuru-baḍu* or *sūru-baḍu* may, therefore, also mean 'maternal cousin'. Parākramabāhu was the son of the sister of Gajabāhu's father; and a sister of Parākramabāhu was given in marriage to Gajabāhu. So the princes may either be called cousins or brothers-in-law.

[2] *Pasuvūvan*:—Literally 'the one who shall be the later' (to die).

be as if we had transgressed the command of the Three Gems[1]. We shall [also] never be delivered from hell.

[Lines 15–18] May this writing[2] protect the world so long as the Moon and the Stars endure; [May] the union[3] of these two, whose wealth is for the good of others, ... suffused with love ......

No. 2. THE GAḌALĀḌEṆIYA INSCRIPTION OF SĒNĀSAMMATA VIKRAMA BĀHU.

By H. W. CODRINGTON.

THIS inscription is cut on the rock immediately below the record of the monk Dharmmakīrtti, the founder of Gaḍalāḍeṇiya Vihārē, dated in the third year of Bhuvanaika Bāhu IV. It is followed by an epigraph dated the first of the waning moon of Nikini in the Buddhist year 2054 (1511 A.D.) in the reign of a king, whose name almost certainly is Jayavīra. A copy of our inscription exists on palm leaf and has been used in this edition.

The record is dated in the eighth year of **Sēnāsammata Vikrama Bāhu cakravartti,** who, as we have seen while discussing the Palkumbura copper plate (*E.Z.*, Vol. III, pp. 240–247), was the founder of Kandy as a capital. The Kobbākaḍuva Vihārē *sannasa*, now extant only in a copy, is dated in the thirty-seventh year of this king. The Galgānē Vihārē *tuḍupata* and that of Kuṭṭaṅgal Vihārē or Vēravaḷa, otherwise known as Radāgoḍa Vihārē, both also existing only in copies, are dated on the eighth of the waxing moon of Vesak, 2052 A.B. (1510 A.D.), but give no regnal year. As the inscription immediately following the present epigraph belongs to another reign and is dated in Nikini of 2054 A.B. (1511 A.D.), Vikrama Bāhu must have ceased to rule at some date between April 16, 1510 and August 10, 1511. If his thirty-seventh year was 'expired', he came to the throne at the latest in 1474 or 1475, and we may not be far wrong in placing his accession about the same time as that of Bhuvanaika Bāhu VI, which took place in 2015 A.B. (1472–3 A.D.)[4]. This Kōṭṭē king's Dädigama inscription[5] of the month of Poson in the year following the eighth or 1480–1 A.D.

---

[1] *Tunuruvan* = P. *Ratanattaya.* The Buddha, the Dhamma and the Saṅgha.

[2] *Akṣarāḷi* :—Literally 'a row or series of letters'.

[3] *Ananyam* :—Literally 'the absence of difference'.

[4] *Buduguṇa Alaṅkāraya*, and Araṁkälē documents, published by Sir D. B. Jayatilaka in the *Svadeśa Mitrayā* of July 27 and August 3, 1924.

[5] *E. Z.*, Vol. III, pp 278–286.

rehearses the terms of an amnesty given on the suppression of the *Siṁhaḷa saṅgē*, 'Sinhalese war', to the people of the Four Korales, who feared that punishment would ensue 'when the affair in the Uḍa-raṭa has also been settled'. It is tempting to connect the rebellion, which clearly affected the greater part of the Kandyan kingdom and was suppressed according to our record by the month of Il in Vikrama Bāhu's eighth year, with this 'Sinhalese war', and to suppose that the settlement of 'the affair' (*kāriya*) in the Hill Country was the reduction of the Kandyan king's refractory subjects to order. Vikrama Bāhu, if we may trust the *Rājaratnākaya*, was of the same clan as the Kōṭṭē monarch [1].

Tradition tells us of Vikrama Bāhu, the founder of Kandy, that there was no king of the Hill Country and that the state elephant, let loose to find one, discovered a young prince with his mother at Asgiriya in Mātalē District. In Kandy his mother founded the Talagahamula Vihārē on Mount Airy as well as a dēvālē and pansala; the Geḍigē Vihārē was built over her ashes by her son, the king. Asgiri Vihārē was named after his mother's village. Tradition further attributes to one and the same king the building of Geḍigē Vihārē and of Pōya Maḷuva.

According to the *Mahāvaṁsa* one Vīra Vikrama became king in Kandy in 2085 A.B. (1542–3 A.D.). This portion of the Pāli chronicle is quite late and is based on the *Rājaratnākaraya*, itself a work of no great authority. Now, the name Vīra Vikrama nowhere appears in the *Rājaratnākaraya*; from the allusive epithets applied to the king his name may have been Vīra Vikrama or Vikrama Bāhu. The story of his reign is preceded by a lengthy account of the princess Mayurāvatī, who was born of a peahen's egg, and of the origin of the Meheṇavara-vaṁsa. The king himself is said to have been the 'grandson' (*munubura*) of the great king Jayamahalēna Savulu Parākrama Bāhu, descended from the princess Mayurāvatī on the one side, and of the great king Vikrama Bāhu of the Meheṇavara-vaṁsa on the other. He came to the throne in 'Kaṭupulla bada Seṅkhaṇḍa nam Śrīvarddhana-pura', which was his by birthright (*janma-pravēṇi*). He conquered his enemies, Sinhalese and Tamil. He placed bodily relics of

[1] In view of the evidence supplied by the Dädigama epigraph the *Siṁhaḷa peraḷiya* of the *Rājāvaliya*, which affected the country between the Kaḷugaṅga and the Valavē under the leadership of Śrīvarddhana Patirāja and Kūragama Himi and which was suppressed by Ambulugala Raja and the army of the Four Kōraḷēs, cannot have been the whole of the movement. A rebellion in the same area in 1476 under Goruci, which was also suppressed by Bhuvanaika Bāhu's brother, is mentioned in the Pegu Kalyāṇi inscription. Perhaps the rebellion extended over several years. To have merited the name of the 'Sinhalese war' or 'rebellion' it must have been widespread. The eighth year of our present record possibly may be 'expired', in which case it corresponds with the year following the eighth of Bhuvanaika Bāhu VI.

Buddha near his city, made a great *vehera* with stone pillars by it, and built a two-storied Uposatha enclosure, the reference being to the dāgāba and the Pōya Maḷuva close to Malvattē Vihārē. Among other good works, he constructed a new Mahā Vihārē for the Great Elder, learned in the Three Piṭakas, who came from abroad with thirty-five monks. This Great Elder was Dharmmakīrtti, who reformed the Saṁgha and held an ordination in the Mahavāligaṅga; tradition has that he was of Pōya Maḷuva. The king also went on pilgrimage to Adam's Peak and Mahyaṅgaṇa, and made offerings to the Tooth Relic of Buddha and to Bentoṭa Vihārē, where was enshrined the Tooth Relic of Mahā Kāśyapa. Between the first king of Ceylon, Vijaya, and this king were 250 anointed sovereigns, an impossible figure.

In spite of the absence of any explicit mention of Asgiri Vihārē, I think that there can be little doubt that this king is identical with Vikrama Bāhu, the traditional founder of Kandy as a capital. In my article on the Palkuṁbura copper plate [1] we have seen that the date 2085 A.B. cannot be correct, for according to the Nātha Dēvālē record of the end of that year the reigning king was Śrī Jayavīra Mahā-väḍa-vun-täna. It may be noted that this erroneous date does not stand alone in the *Rājaratnākaraya*. A few sentences before, this work assigns the year 1929 A.B. (1386–7 A.D.) to the reign of Bhuvanaika Bāhu VI.

Further details are supplied by the *Siduruvāṇā Kaḍaim-pota*, a short account of the great Baṇḍāras who ruled much of the present Kandy District in the Gampola period. The coronation of Bhuvanaika Bāhu (V) is mentioned. Seemingly after this the turbulence of the Baṇḍāras was brought to an end by Vikrama Bāhu. He migrated from Gaṅga-śrī-pura (Gampola) to Pērādeṇi-pura, and thence to the plot of land (*bhūmiya*), where dwelt Seṅkhaṇḍa. There on the *Vijaya-bhūmi-bhāga*, 'having suppressed the troubles', he made his capital. The Baṇḍāras were deprived of their umbrellas and shields and were given *mudali* titles. In other words they ceased to be semi-independent princes. The selection of the *Vijaya-bhūmi-bhāga* as the site of the palace in Kandy is said by legend to have been due to a hunted hare turning on and chasing its pursuers. The *Siduruvāṇā Kaḍaim-pota*, however, seems to connect the name with the suppression of the Baṇḍāras.

The title 'Sēnāsammata' itself to some extent confirms the tradition of the finding of the prince in the absence of any king in the Hill Country, and the length of the reign, at least of thirty-six years, indicates that the king came to

[1] *E. Z.*, Vol. III, pp. 240–247.

the throne in his youth. In other documents his full name is given as Siri Saṅgabō Śrī Sēnāsammata Vikrama Bāhu. He apparently was only of the Mehenavara clan on his mother's side.

The **script** of our record does not differ in any very marked degree from that of the Gaḍalādeṇiya slab pillar; it definitely is anterior to the middle of the sixteenth century. The orthography is poor. The Malayalam ന, found as early as the Hapugastänna inscription of Parākrama Bāhu V, is used throughout for න.

The **contents** promise that no loss of life shall be inflicted on the people of certain provinces named, forming, if not the whole, at least a considerable part of the Kandyan kingdom of the time, and provide that the heriot or *maḷāraya* of those who have fallen in warfare or in the elephant hunt shall, in the absence of an heir, be devoted to the restoration of vihārēs in disrepair. The name Aṭasiyapattuva applied to Mātalē is unknown elsewhere. Pansiyapattuva, where distinct from Dumbara, roughly equals the present Uḍa Dumbara and Vēṇḍaruva. Goḍa-raṭa has now disappeared, but is found in the *Maha Kaḍaim-pota* between Maturaṭa and Pasgam-raṭa. The Laṁkātilaka inscription of Vikrama Bāhu III speaks of Paṭṭiyagama in Goḍa-raṭa; it was, therefore, identical with part of Lower Hēvāhäṭē. 'Aṭapeḍiya' appears in the *Daṁbadeṇi Asna*[1], but in connection with Kotmalē. Mahatoṭa can hardly be Māntōḍḍam, the Mahātittha of the *Mahāvaṁsa*[2], as no provinces on that side of the Island are mentioned and we know that the Adikāriya of Nuvarakalāviya was under Kōṭṭē; rather it must be Couto's Periyaturai, which he places between Trincomalee and 'the point of Jafanapatão' (Dec. V, lib. 1, cap. 5). The *Maha Kaḍaim-pota* mentions a 'Māvaṭu-raṭa' on the border of Ruhuṇa in Pihiṭi-raṭa, and also defines Ruhuṇa as lying between the Kaḷugaṅga, the Mahaväligaṅga in Kotmalē, the limits of Māyā-raṭa, and the Mahaväligaṅga in Māvaṭu-raṭa in the Pihiṭi country.

The **Yāpābhaṇḍāra** of our inscription appears to have been a personage of importance, apparently next in dignity to the king. His name is of some interest, as the *Siduruvāṇā Kaḍaim-pota* mentions a Baṇḍāra of the name in Gangoḍa and another in Unaṁbuva. Further a Yāpā Raja or Maharaja occurs in tradition. Bound up with the Colombo Museum *Rājavaṁsa* (M 4) are a few leaves giving the story of Mädagama Dēvālē in Sabaragamuva. On the last day of Äsaḷa in Śaka 1304 (1382 A.D) a Brahman staying at Mädagama had a dream revealing the presence of a weapon of the god Kandasāmi. The dēvālē was

---

[1] *Aṭabāge mura pirissa vaga pirissa Kotmalē Aṭapeḷiyē* (var. *Aṭapeḍiyē*) *väddōya polu-väddōya mas-väddōya.*

[2] Sinh. *Mahavuṭu, Māvaṭu.*

established and the fact reported to 'Sūryya Maharaja who united Laṁkā under one canopy'. About 200 years later Sūryya Maharaja's 'third grandson' the king of Sītāvaka and Yāpā Raja twice went to war without success. The third time the two kings fought at Ōpanākē Māliyaddē-vela and the king of Sītāvaka was beaten. Peace was made, the boundary between the kingdoms being fixed at the Pērās-āḷa, and Yāpā went to the throne of Uḍa-kaṭṭuva or the Hill Country. In the proceedings of the Board of Commissioners, 1821, an ola report of Mahavaḷatännē Disāva gives the history of Uggal Alutnuvara Dēvālē. It was built by Sūriya Maharaja and afterwards endowed by Yāpā Maharaja; Rāsiṁha Maharaja also made offerings. Yāpā Maharaja, if these stories be not mythical, thus lived before Rājasiṁha I (1554–1593 A.D.)[1].

The word *pajuruvan* appears to be unknown elsewhere. The reading is certain. It is very tentatively suggested that it is derived from Skt. *pajra*, 'fat; wealthy, rich; powerful, strong', and means the 'great men'. 'Princes' suits the context, but the termination *-vahansē* is attached to *mudalivarun* in the Vīgulavatta inscription of Vikrama Bāhu III.

With *ät-vagē*, 'elephant hunt', may be compared *vaga paṅgu vasam*, the service holdings of the elephant department in Ūva.

The *maḷāraya*, later *marāḷaya*, or heriot is well known in India and Ceylon. In the Island one third of the movables of the deceased escheated to the Crown if he left sons, and the whole if he left none[2]. Knox says:

'Whensoever any man dies, that hath a stock of Cattel, immediately out thence must be paid a Bull and a Cow with a Calf, and a Male and Female Buffalo, which tax they call Marral' (*Historical Relation of Ceylon*, pt. II, chap. iv; cf. *ib.*, chap. v), and:

'Lands of Inheritance which belong to Women are exempted from paying Heriots to the King' (*ib.*, pt. III, chap. vii).

The impost was abolished by Kīrttiśrī (1747–82 A.D.), but on one occasion at least was enforced by the last king of Kandy. The provision in the present document was to secure merit for the deceased as well as for the king.

---

[1] Mr. Paranavitana writes to me: 'On the exterior of the walls of a cave shrine, now abandoned, at Mäṭiyaṅganē in the Daṁbadeṇi Hatpattu, there are paintings of gods with their names written below. In addition to such well-known deities as Brahma, Viṣṇu, Skanda, etc., we have here a figure of a deity labelled Yāpā-bhanḍāra. He holds a katty in one hand. The shrine appears to be at least two centuries old. Of course we cannot be certain that the deified Yāpā-bhanḍāra was the same as the person of that name mentioned in this inscription.'

[2] *Documentos Remettidos da India*, ii, p. 136, letter from the king of 3 January, 1612. See also *Foral*, fol. 169, 172.

Śakradumahādi in line 10 is meant for *Śakra Brahmādi.* There is no doubt as to the reading. Mr. Paranavitana writes: 'The *akṣara* read as *ḍu* has some resemblance to the Grantha *bra*. As conjoint consonants are sometimes written so that they are not joined to each other, I would prefer to read this as *Śakra Bramhādi.*'

The name **Sanhas Sivattā Nāyinārun,** who attested our document, also appears in the Alutnuvara amnesty record, in the Vannipola grant of the year following the twentieth, and in the Kobbākaḍuva Vihārē *sannasa* of the thirty-seventh year, all of Sēnāsammata Vikrama Bāhu. It does not follow that one and the same person is referred to. In the Galgānē Vihārē and the Kuṭṭaṅgal Vihārē grants of 2052 A.B. (1510 A.D.) the attestor was Sanhas Sivattēva Kala Perumāl and 'Sannissiwatte Kulapperumal'; the last mentioned document exists only in an English translation.

TEXT.

1 (ස්වස්ති) ප්‍රශස්ත [මහා] සම්මත පරම්පරානුයා(ත සූ)රිය වංශානිජාත **සේනා සම්මත වික්‍රම** [බාහු චක්‍රව]ර්ති

2 ස්වාමීන්[වහ]න්සේට අටවනු ගිල අව (ස)තවක සිදුරුවාතා දෙනුවර බලවිට සරසියපතනුව [1] මා[තලය]

3 අටසියප[තනුව දූ]ම්බර ප(න්)සියපතනුව ගො(ඩ)රට මතුරට ඌව අටපෙඩිය සොරම්බර වෙල

4 අසස කොත්මලෙ ගංපළ දෙලොස්බගේ [2] [බූ](ලත්)[ග]ම මගතොට තිරුකු නාමලය මඩ

5 ක(ල)[පුව ඇ]තුළු[ව මෙ කී සෑම]යෙහි උතතම් මධම[අ]ධම කනිෂටෙදි [3] වනු [4] පජු(රුවන්) පවති[නා] සේ

6 නා[වි](හෙ)න් කෙනකුන්ට **වික්‍රම** බාහු මහරජ්ජුරුවන් **ශාපාභණ්ඩාර** රජදරු භණ්ඩාර ඇ

7 තුළුවූ පජුරුවන්වහන්සේලා වසින් [5] පාණ [6] හානි ණො [7] කරවනු නො ක [රනු](වත් සේවා)ක[ම]

8 සි වැටූණු කෙනකුන් හා ඇත්වගේ දූව වැටනු [8] කෙනකුනුගේ මළාරයට ගිම් කෙනෙක්

9 ණෑතුව [9] තිබේ නම් ජරාවාසව තිබෙන විහාර කැරවීමට පුදනුවත් තුනු රුවන්ගේ ආඥය

---

[1] For සාරසියපතනුව.
[2] For දෙලොස්බාගේ.
[3] For කනිෂ්ඨාදී.
[4] Probably for මතු.
[5] For විසින්.
[6] For ප්‍රාණ.
[7] For නො.
[8] For වැටුණු.
[9] For නැතුව.

10 දළදා පාත්‍ර ධතුන්[1]වහන්සේගේ ආඥය ශක්‍රඩුමහාදි[2] තිස් තුන් කොටියක් දෙවියන්

11 ගේ ආඥය උත්පලවර්ණ සුමන විභීෂණ ෂන්මුඛාදි සතර වරම් දෙවියන[3] ගේ ආඥය

12 මණිකාන්තාවගේ ආඥය පත්තිනි දෙවියන්ගේ ආඥය මෙ කී ආඥ කියා වදාළ මෙ

13 (හව)රි(න්) මේ ශිලාලෙඛ්‍යය කොටවා දුන් බවට [සංඝ]ස් සිවතනා නායි නාරුම්භ

TRANSCRIPT.

1 (Svasti) praśasta [Mahā] Sammata paramparānuyā(ta Sū)riya vaṁśābhijāta **Sēnāsammata Vikrama** [**Bāhu** cakrava]rtti

2 svāmīn-[vaha]nsē-ṭa aṭavanu Hila ava (sa)tavaka Siduruvānā De-nuvara Balaviṭa Sarasiyapattuva[4] Mā[talaya]

3 Aṭasiyapa[ttuva Du]mbara Pa(n)siyapattuva Go(ḍa)raṭa Maturaṭa Ūva Aṭapeḍiya Sorambara Vela-

4 assa Kotmale Gaṁpaḷa Doḷosbagē[5] [Bu](lat)[ga]ma Mahatoṭa Tirukunāmalaya Mañḍa-

5 ka(la)[puva ä]tuḷu[va me kī sāma]yehi uttama maddhama [a]dhama kaniṣṭadi[6] catu[7] paju(ruvan) pavati[nā] sē-

6 nā[va-](ge)n kenakun-ṭa **Vikrama Bāhu** maharajjuruvan **Yāpābhaṇḍāra** raja-daru bhanḍāra ä-

7 tuḷu-vū pajuruvan-vahansēlā vasin[8] pāṇa[9] hāni ṇo[10] karavanu no ka[ranu-](vat sēvā)ka[me-]

8 yi väṭuṇu kenakun hā ät-vagē duva väṭanu[11] kenakunu-gē maḷāraya-ṭa himi kenek

9 ṇätuva[12] tibē-nam jarāvāsa-va tibena vihāra käravīma-ṭa pudanu-vat Tunuruvan-gē ājñāya

10 Daḷadā Pātra dhatūn[13]-vahansē-gē ājñāya Śakraḍumahādi[14] tis tun koṭiyak deviyan-

---

[1] For ධාතුන්. The ධ as written is almost indistinguishable from ය.

[2] *Sic.*

[3] For දෙවියන්.

[4] For *Sārasiyapattuva*.

[5] For *Doḷosbāge*.

[6] For *kaniṣṭhādi*.

[7] Probably for *matu*.

[8] For *visin*.

[9] For *prāṇa*.

[10] For *no*.

[11] For *väṭuṇu*.

[12] For *nätuva*

[13] For *dhātun*. The *dh* as written is almost indistinguishable from *ya*.

[14] *Sic.*

The Gaḍalādeṇiya Inscription of Sēnāsammata Vikrama Bāhu

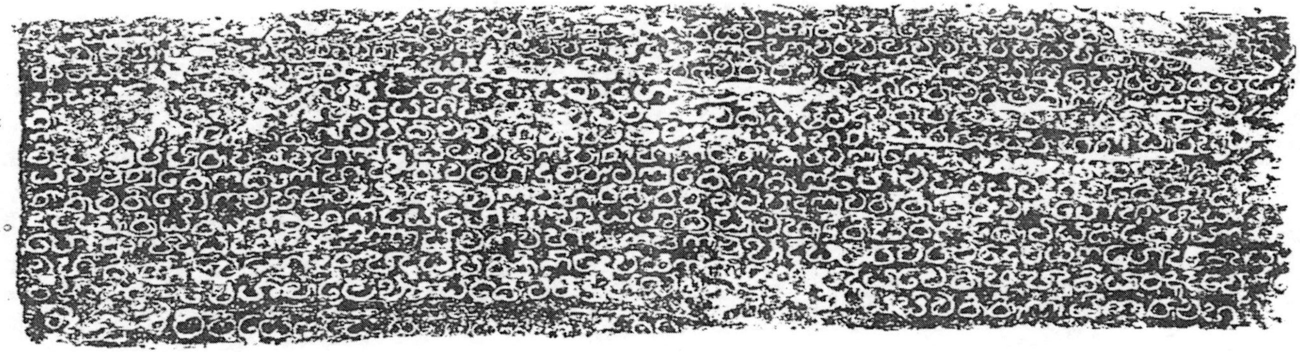

Scale about ¾ inch to 1 foot

11 gē ājñāya Utpalavarnna Sumana Vibhīṣana Ṣanmukhādī satara varam deviyana[1]-ge ājñāya

12 Mahīkāntāva-gē ājñāya Pattini deviyan-gē ājñāya me kī ājñā kiyā vadāḷa me-

13 (h)e(va)ri(n) me śilālekhyaya koṭavā dun bava-ṭa [**Sanha**]**s Sivattā Nāyinārumha**

TRANSLATION.

Hail! On the seventh of the waning moon of Hila in the eighth year of His Majesty the Sovereign Lord **Sēnāsammata Vikrama Bāhu,** born of the race of the Sun in lineal descent from the famous Mahā Sammata (it was decreed as follows):—

On no one, high, middling, low, or lowest, and the rest, of the host, in which the great men shall continue hereafter, of Siduruvānā De-nuvara, Balaviṭa, Sārasiyapattuva, Mātalē Aṭasiyapattuva, Dumbara Pansiyapattuva, Goḍa-raṭa, Maturaṭa, Ūva, Aṭapeḍiya, Sorambara, Vela-assa, Kotmalē, Gampaḷa Doḷosbāgē, Bulatgama, Mahatoṭa, Trincomalee, Batticaloa, of all this aforesaid region, shall loss of life be caused to be inflicted or be inflicted by the great king **Vikrama Bāhu, Yāpābhaṇḍāra,** the bhaṇḍāra the king's son, and the other great men. And should there be no owner for the heriot of any one who shall have fallen in warfare and in the elephant hunt, (this heriot) shall be offered for the restoration of vihārēs which are out of repair.

This is the command of the Three Gems; this is the command of the Tooth and Bowl Relics; this is the command of Śakra, (Brahma) and the rest of the thirty-three *koṭi* of gods; this is the command of the four guardian gods Utpalavarnna, Sumana, Vibhīṣana, Ṣanmukha, and the rest; this is the command of Mahīkāntāva; this is the command of the goddess Pattini.

To the effect that this stone inscription has been cut and given in obedience to the royal order setting forth (as sanctions) these aforesaid commands I, **Sanhas Sivattā Nāyinārun,** (do certify).

---

[1] For *deviyan*.

NOTE.—For the early kings of Kandy see 'Some Documents of Vikrama Bāhu', *J.R.A.S., Ceylon Branch,* XXXII, pp. 64 ff., and 'Notes on the Kandyan Dynasty in the fifteenth and sixteenth Centuries', *Ceylon Literary Register,* II (1932), pp. 289 ff., 343 ff.

No. 3. THE GADALĀDENIYA SLAB-PILLAR INSCRIPTIONS.

By H. W. CODRINGTON.

THIS slab pillar now stands outside the main entrance of the Gaḍalādeṇiya Vihārē, a foundation of the fourteenth century situated in Uḍunuvara of Kandy District; it was set up in its present position by Mr. H. C. P. Bell, Archaeological Commissioner, who found it inside the temple. It is inscribed on all four faces. On the front of the slab is a record of the fifth year of king **Siri Sañgabō Śrī Jayavīra Parākrama Bāhu** granting an amnesty to **Mēṇavara Tuṇayan,** nephew of the *āpā* **Parākrama Bāhu of Doḍamvela,** and the people of the Five Countries, on the reduction of the Hill Country then recently effected before the Coronation Festival held on the twelfth of the bright half of Vesak. This is preceded on one of the narrow sides by the word *Siddhi* engraved beneath the sun and moon, a *cakra* and conch shell. On the reverse of the slab, continued on the other narrow side, is the undertaking of the rebels to be faithful to His Majesty; their leader is here called Mēnavara Tuṇayārun.

The **script** definitely is posterior in date to that of the Maḍavaḷa record of the year following the forty-sixth of Parākrama Bāhu VI. It differs but little from that of the Gaḍalādeṇiya rock inscriptions of the eighth year of Sēnāsammata Vikrama Bāhu and of 2054 A.B. (1511 A.D.) in the reign of Jayavīra.

The **identity of the grantor of the amnesty,** Jayavīra Parākrama Bāhu, is doubtful. The fact that, if the reading be correct, the king 'came to our country after raising one canopy of dominion over Tri Siṁhaḷa', and also that he swore to the amnesty in the presence of the Tooth Relic, then undoubtedly at Kōṭṭē, proves that he was not merely a ruler of the Hill Country. It may, therefore, be taken as certain that he was a Kōṭṭē sovereign. If we confine ourselves to kings with *Vīra* or *Jayavīra* in their names, there are two to whom our inscription can be attributed, Vīra Parākrama Bāhu, who according to the *Rājāvaliya* followed Parākrama Bāhu VI, and Vīra Parākrama Bāhu VIII, the brother and ultimate successor of Bhuvanaika Bāhu VI.

As shown in my article on the Oruvaḷa copper plate (*E.Z.*, Vol. III, pp. 51 ff.), Parākrama Bāhu VI died about 1467. From the *Buduguṇa Alaṅkāraya* and the Araṁkälē palm leaf records we know that Bhuvanaika Bāhu VI came to the throne in 2015 A.B. (1472–3 A.D.). There are, therefore, some five years to be accounted for. The history of this interval differs in the authorities. According to the *Rājāvaliya* Vīra Parākrama Bāhu, the grandson of Parākrama Bāhu VI, was speedily dethroned and put to death by Bhuvanaika Bāhu VI. The version of this chronicle used by Valentyn styles him Jayavīra Parākrama Bāhu and gives him a reign of seven years, confusing him with Bhuvanaika Bāhu VI, who is omitted. Queyroz also calls him 'Javira-Paracrama-Bau' or 'Javira', but, as usual with this author, assigns to him an impossible number of years. The *Rājaratnākaraya*, however, places between Parākrama Bāhu VI and Bhuvanaika Bāhu VI a king Jaya Bāhu, and the eighteenth century *Mahāvaṁsa*, which for this period commonly is based on this work, follows suit. Couto, who had reliable information, has a very different account and gives two kings, namely 'Maha Pracura Mabago' or 'Javira', who reigned 'a few years', and his idiot son, who remained on the throne for two years until replaced at the request of his aunt the regent by Bhuvanaika Bāhu VI (Dec. V, book I, chap. 5).

The existence of Jaya Bāhu seems to be proved by the Mädagoḍa Vihārē copper plate of the year following the third of Siri Saṅgabō Śrī Sakalakalā Sarvajña Paṇḍita Jaya Bāhu (registered N.W.P., 683). This purports to have been given at Yāpāpaṭana in Pihiṭi-rajaya to Vīdāgama Maitri Mahanetpāmula Maha Tera Sāmi. He was the tutor of Phussadeva Sumaṅgala Sāmi, the recipient of the grant of 2021 A.B. (1479 A.D.), rehearsed in the Araṁkälē records already mentioned. This grant of 2021 A.B., however, speaks of Mädagoḍa as having been given to Phussadeva Sumaṅgala. The Mädagoḍa plate has not been examined critically. But the copy shows the usual Kōṭṭē style, and the existing plate, even should it turn out to be of comparatively modern workmanship, probably reproduces a genuine document. Couto may be right in stating that there were two kings between Parākrama Bāhu VI and Bhuvanaika Bāhu VI. If this was the case, both may have dated their accession from the same year, as did the first two Gampola kings and Parākrama Bāhu IX and Vijaya Bāhu VII.

Parākrama Bāhu VIII is styled Vīra Parākrama Bāhu by the *Rājaratnākaraya* and the *Mahāvaṁsa*, and also by the *Rājāvaliya*, Valentyn, and Queyroz. Couto calls him 'Javira Pracura Mabago', that is Jayavīra Parākrama Bāhu. But the Kuḍumirissa inscription of the tenth year of Siri Saṅgabō Śrī Parākrama Bāhu confirms a grant to Brahmans by his 'father the great king', a grant spoken of at the end of the record as the original *sanhasa* given in the time of Śrī Parākrama Bāhu Väḍa-un-tän. The Kudumirissa king almost certainly is Parākrama Bāhu VIII. The Oruvaḷa copper plate, which we have assigned to this king, also gives the same name. The Siri Saṅgabō Śrī Jayavīra Parākrama Bāhu of the present document, therefore, may not be the brother of Bhuvanaika

Bāhu VI. A stronger objection to such an identification is that Sēnāsammata Vikrama Bāhu, who reigned at least for thirty-six years, came to the throne before Parākrama Bāhu VIII, and there is no record of his subjection to Kōṭṭē; he uses the title *cakravartti.* Of the two Vīra or Jayavīra Parākrama Bāhus the first is to be preferred. The record thus may belong to the year 1471–2. But this attribution hardly agrees with Couto's account of the idiot king.

If, however, the attempt to identify the king of our inscriptions with any known Jayavīra or Vīra Parākrama Bāhu of Kōṭṭē be abandoned, we are left with Paṇḍita Parākrama Bāhu VII and Dharmma Parākrama Bāhu IX. The first of these two seems to have sat on the throne but a short while and is ruled out, as control of the Hill Country is precluded by the reign of Vikrama Bāhu of Kandy. Of the second the *Rājāvaliya* says (ed. B. Gunasekara):—

'The king of Kotte having heard that the prince then ruling in the hill-country had ascended the throne and made a proclamation by beat of tom-tom, and in open defiance withheld payment of tribute, sent for prince Sri Rajasinha who was at Menikkadawara, and entrusted the army to him. He himself encamped in the Four Korales, and sent his brother-in-law Kirawelle Ralahami with an army, who encamped in Yatinuwara and took possession of Kunukohupitiya. But the king of the hill-country obtained peace by sending three lacs of *paṇam* and two elephants, and his own daughter to boot for a wife. . . . .

'Not many days after this, the king of the hill-country raised a rebellion in the Four Korales. Dharma Parakrama Bahu having heard of this, committed the army to his younger brother Sakalakala Walla of Udugampola, and sent him to seize the hill-country. Accordingly, Sakalakala Walla encamped in the heart of Yatinuwara. The king of the hill-country came to meet him, and, in token of homage, sent a pearl umbrella, a conch, and shield, and a neck ornament. Sakalakala Walla took the end of the said ornament and tied his beautiful feet with it. Then he put it on the neck of Ekanayaka Mudali, warning him by way of rebuke, "Act not thus again"; and having come to the city of Jayawardhana, presented himself before king Dharma Parakrama Bahu, and returned to his own city Udugampola[1].'

Parākrama Bāhu IX according to the Kälaṇiya inscription of his nineteenth

[1] Better, 'At that time the king of Kōṭṭē having heard that the prince (*raja*) ruling the Hill Country'. 'He himself' from the context is Rājasiṁha. For 'brother-in-law', read 'brother' (*sahōdara*), and for 'his own daughter', 'a daughter of his'. In the second paragraph 'the king of the hill-country' is not in the Sinhalese. 'A conch and shield' (*hak paliha*) should be rendered 'a conch (coloured) shield'. This and the pearl umbrella were ensigns of royalty.

year came to the throne in 2051 A.B. (1508–9 A.D.). The Dondra record of his brother Vijaya Bāhu VII (*A.I.C.*, no. 163) gives that king's accession year as Śaka 1432, normally equal to 1510–11 A.D. Vijaya Bāhu's Uḍugampola copper plate (*ib.*, no. 172) is dated in the year following the eighth on the fifteenth of the dark half of Poson on the occasion of a solar eclipse. There were eclipses on the required date in 1517 and 1518; the last is said not to have been visible in Ceylon. The Poson of the ninth year, therefore, was that of 1517, and consequently the Śaka year 1432 must be 'current'. This Śaka year, 1431 'expired', began on March 27 and the Buddhist year 2051 ended on May 4, 1509. The two brothers thus came to the throne on some day between these two dates. According to Barros (II, iii, 1; *JRAS.*, *Ceylon Branch*, XIX, no. 59, p. 366) in September or October, 1508, their father, Parākrama Bāhu VIII, was very ill, and it may have been this sickness which led him to raise his sons to the royal dignity. The death of the old king was reported to the king of Portugal by Albuquerque on November 15, 1513 (*Alguns Documentos*, p. 297).

If Jayavīra Parākrama Bāhu be Parākrama Bāhu IX, the date of the amnesty will fall on September 30, 1513. Mēṇavara Tuṇayan may or may not be the prince who was ruling the Kandyan provinces as Jayavīra in 2054 A.B. (1511 A.D.). In his Gaḍalādeṇiya epigraph of that year Jayavīra is styled 'great king'. His namesake of the Nātha Dēvālē inscriptions of 1543 calls himself *Mahā Väḍa-vun-täna*, *Āsthāna*, or *Maha Āsthana*. The change of style from the *cakravartti* of Vikrama Bāhu is noteworthy. Perhaps it resulted from Parākrama Bāhu's reduction of the Hill Country at least to a semblance of submission to Kōṭṭē. There seems to be no ground for objecting to this identification of the Kōṭṭē king in the script, which is not very different from that of the epigraph of 2054 A.B. Against it is the fact that Dharmma Parākrama Bāhu IX is styled Siri Saṅgabō Śrī Parākrama Bāhu in his Kälaṇiya inscription. On the whole, however, in spite of the difficulty caused by the name, I am inclined to identify the grantor of the amnesty with this king rather than with an earlier ruler of Kōṭṭē. The reduction of the Hill Country is recorded in the *Rājāvaliya*, and further the date of the coronation given in the inscription fits in perfectly with the limits fixed above for the accession, namely March 27 and May 4, 1509. In that year the twelfth of the bright half of Vesak fell on May 1.

The general contents of the inscriptions have been indicated. The Meheṇavara clan, to which the principal beneficiary of the amnesty belonged, was that branch of the royal family descended from the ex-nun (*meheṇi*) Sunandā by her marriage with Bodhigupta, one of the seven Maurya princes who brought the

Bō tree to Ceylon. Another, Sumitra, the Jaya Maha Lē, was the ancestor claimed by the kings of Kōṭṭē.

The enumeration of the 'Five Countries' in our first record differs from that prevalent in later times. The De-nuvara of Gampaḷa Siduruvāṇā is the later Uḍunuvara and Yaṭinuvara, but probably included the present Uḍapalāta, which from its name seems at one time to have formed part of the first named of these two divisions; the Gaṅgapalāta, Mädapalāta, and Kaňdupalāta still remain. Baḷaviṭa is the modern Hārispattuva and part, if not the whole, of Tumpanē. Pansiyapattuva is Dumbara, In modern times the 'Five Countries' were De-nuvara (Uḍunuvara and Yaṭinuvara), Tumpanē, Hārispattuva, Dumbara, and Hēvāhäṭē.

Of interest is the rehearsal of the royal prerogatives which, it is evident, the rebel prince had usurped. Unfortunately the text is far from being satisfactory. The first, if the reading be correct, can only be ඇත් වෙළෙඳාම, 'trading in elephants', always a royal right; the second, as deciphered by Mr. Paranavitana, also refers to elephants; the third, fourth, and fifth are not in doubt. The mention of striking fanams appears to be unique in the lithic records of Ceylon. For the history of the fanam in the Island in the middle ages, see *Ceylon Coins and Currency*, pp. 80, 81, 254.

The reading ශක්තිවූ පංණතට in C, line 33, is clear. Better sense would have been given by ශක්තිවූ පමංණට, 'to the extent or best of our strength'. In C, lines 35, 36, the reading seems fairly certain in view of the phrase..... *kara-vū kenaku-ṭa patak basak vat minissun kenakun vat no härä* on slab B of the amnesty inscription of Sēnāsammata Vikrama Bāhu at Alutnuvara.

With the 'commands' of the Three Gems, of the Tooth and Bowl Relics, and of the gods, may be compared the following curious sentence occurring in the proceedings of the Raṭa Sabhāva, the ancient Sinhalese court still held in the North Central Province:—

Siṁhaḷē maha-rajjuruvan-gē Koḷaṁba maha-rajjuruvan-gē ran kaḍuvē ran oṭunnē aṇa dannavānam tahanami.... Nuvaravävē Kumārasiṁha Mudiyansē-gē toppi haḷuvē aṇa dannavānam tahanami...devenivatva tunvenivatva tahanami tahanami tahanami.

'If you know the command of the golden sword and of the golden crown of the great king of Siṁhaḷē, of the great king of Colombo, it is forbidden.... If you know the command of the hat of Nuvaravävē Kumārasiṁha Mudiyansē [the Vanniyār], it is forbidden; .... A second time, a third time it is forbidden, it is forbidden, it is forbidden.'

As will be seen the formula has been interpolated with a reference to the Governor of Ceylon; I have omitted the references to the Government Agent and to the Raṭēmahatmayā.

The god Boksal is Däḍimuṇḍa Dēvatā Baṇḍāra Deviyō of Alutnuvara. The 'four guardian divine great kings' are those of the *divya-loka*, namely Dhṛtarāṣṭra, Virūḍha, Virūpākṣa, and Vaiśravaṇa. Those of Ceylon are Viṣṇu, Saman, Vibhīṣaṇa and Skandha or Kataragam Deviyō.

TEXT.

I.

A.

සිධි

B.

ස්වස්ති ප්‍රශස්ත
මහා සම්මත පරම්පරා
නුයාත සූර්‍ය්‍ය වංශෝත්
භූත මහාරාජාධිරාජ
ශ්‍රීමත් සිරි සඟබෝ
ශ්‍රී ජයවීර පරාක්‍රම බාහු
චක්‍රවර්ති ස්වාමීන්වහ
න්සේට පස්වනු වප පුර
පැළවිය දෙඩම්වෙල පරා
ක්‍රම බාහු ඈපාණන්ගේ
බෑනා මේණවර තුණයන් හා
ගම්පල සිදුරුවාණ දෙ
නුවර බලවිට මාතලය
පන්සියපත්තුව ඌව
ඇතුළුවූ පස්රට වාස
ය කරන බොහෝ ජන
යාත් මෙවත් වෙසග පු
ර දෙලොස්වක සවර්ණා
භිෂෙක මගල්‍යයට ප
ළමුව කළ දික්විජයෙහි
දි භය පත්වැ අභය දෑ
න ඉල්වා සිටිනා හෙයින්
ඉදිරියේ දවස මේ යථො
ක්ත ජනපදයෙහි උත්

තම මධ්‍යමාධම සිය
ලු මනුෂ්‍යයන්ට අක්‍ෂී
හානි අඟහානි ජීවිත
හානි නො කරනු නො කර
වනුව තුනුරුවන්ගේ
ආඥය දළදා පාත්‍ර ධා
තුන්වහන්සෙගේ ආ
ඥය ශක්‍ර බ්‍රහ්ම විෂ්ණු
මහෙශ්වරාදිවූ දෙවිය
න්ගේ ආඥය කියා දළදා
සාමීන්ගේ සම්මුඛයෙහි
දී සත්‍යප්‍රතිඥ කොටැ
ලියා දෙන්නේයයි වදාළ
මෙහෙවරන් මේ ශිලාලෙ
ඛ්‍යය ලියා දුන් බවට

II.

A

ස්වස්ති **සිරි සඟබෝ**
ශ්‍රී **ජයවීර පරාක්‍රම** බාහු
චක්‍රවර්ති ස්වාමීන්වහන්සේට
පස්වනු වප පුර පැළවිය දෙ
(ඩම්)වෙල **පරාක්‍රම** බාහු ඈපාණ
න් බැත **මේණවර තුණයාරුන්**
ඇතුළුවූ (ඇම) දෙනම්හ අ
පටත් රට සේනාවටත් අභ
ය දුන ශිලාලෙඛ්‍ය කරවා
දෙවා වදාළ ත්‍රි(සිංහළ)යට එ
කාතපත්‍රවැ අ(ප රට[1])ට ප්‍රාප්ත
ජයවීර පරාක්‍රම (බාහු) මහා
රාජොත්තමයාණන්(ව)හන්
සේට අප (හා) රට සේනාව වි
සින් විරුධ නො වී එකාන්ත (පක්‍ෂ)
වැ පවතිනුවත් වැඩ උන් තැන
ට විපක්‍ෂ රජ යුවරජ ඈපා
මාපා සිටු සෙනෙවිරත් අදි
කාර ඇතුළුවූ තවර තරම්

The Gaḍalādeṇiya Slab-Pillar Inscriptions

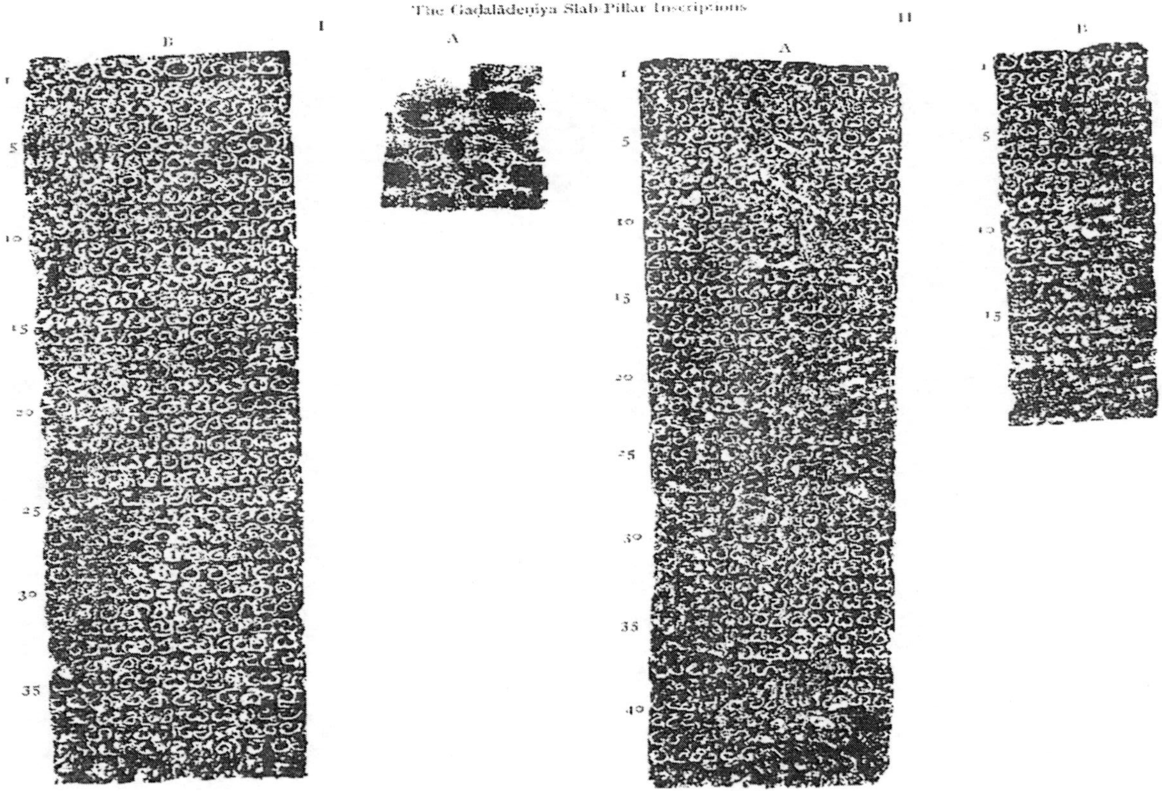

කෙනකුන්වත් (පක්‍ෂ) නො ව
නුවත් වැඩ උන්(තැනට) එකා
න්ත පක්‍ෂ කෙනකුන්ට විප
ක්‍ෂ නො වනුවත් (.. ත් වෙළ)[2]
ඳාම ඇතු(ත් නැග) [ඒ]ම[1] පණ
ම් ගස්වීම පටබැඳවීම ආ
කර කැ(ර)වීම .. .. (ද) .. (දිය)
නො කරනුවත් .. ත් .. ..
.. ඔවුන් .. (ය)ත් (කැඳව .. ..)
ගමන් ක(ර)වනුවත් සම්(ම)
(ත)යක්[1] පැමිණි්විට අප අ
(පෙ ක්)ස්වකම්ට [ර]ට[1] සමුදාව
කැඳවා ගෙන ගොස් එ කියන
[කාරි]ය[1] ශක්තිවූ පණිතට සා
[දා][1] දෙනුවත් විපරිතයකට
[කෙ](නකු)ට පතැක් බසක් මි
[නි](ස්සු)න් කෙනකුන් ගමන්
නො කරවනුවන් අදගස
වරදවා ආ ගි(ය) කෙනකුන්
නො (සි)ටුවා ගමන් කරවනු
වද තුනුරුවන්ගේ ආඥය
දළදා පාත්‍ර ධාතුන්ව[හ]න්සේ
ගේ ආඥය (ශක්‍ර බ්‍ර)හම
විෂ්ණු මහෙශ්වරාදි දේ[ද]

B.

වියන්ගේ ආ
ඥය කිඟිරළි
උප්පුල්වන් සමන්
බොක්සල් ස්ක
න්ධ විභීෂණාදි
දෙවියන්ගේ ආ
ඥය සතර වර
ම් දෙවි ම(හරජ)
දරුවන්(ගේ) ආ
ඥව කි(යා) මේ
සත්‍ය(ප්‍රතිඥා) ශි

ලාලෙඛ්‍යය ලි
යවා දුන් (බ)ව(ට)
.. ..
මේණ(වර) [තුණ](යා)රුන්[1]
පෙරු(මාළන් ව)
මිහ .. ..
.. ..

TRANSCRIPT.

I.

A.

Siddhi

B.

Svasti praśasta
Mahā Sammata paramparā-
nuyāta Sūryya-vaṁśōt-
bhūta mahārājādhirāja
Śrīmat **Siri Saṅgabō**
Śrī Jayavīra Parākrama Bāhu
cakravartti svāmīnvaha-
nsē-ṭa pasvanu Vapa pura
päḷaviya **Doḍamvela Parā-**
krama Bāhu āpāṇan-gē
bāna **Mēṇavara Tuṇayan** hā
Gampaḷa Siduruvāṇā De-
nuvara Baḷaviṭa Mātalaya
Pansiyapattuva Ūva
ätuḷu-vū pas-raṭa vāsa-
ya karana bohō jana-
yāt mevan Vesaga pu-
ra doḷosvaka svarṇṇā-
bhiṣeka maṅgalyaya-ṭa pa-
ḷamuva kaḷa dik-vijayehi-
di bhaya pat-vä abhaya dā-
na ilvā siṭinā-heyin
idiriyē davasa me yatho-
kta janapadayehi ut-
tama maddhyamādhama siya-
lu manuṣyayan-ṭa arttha-
hāni aṅga-hāni jīvita-
hāni no karanu no kara-
vanuva Tunu-ruvan-gē
ājñāya Daḷadā Pātra dhā-
tunvahanse-gē ā-
jñāya Śakra Brahma Viṣṇu
Maheśvarādi-vū deviya-
n-gē ājñāya kiyā Daḷadā-
sāmīn-gē sammukhayehi-
di satya-pratijñā koṭā
liyā dennēyayi vadāḷa
mehevarin mē śilā-le-
khyaya liyā dun bava-ṭa

---

[1] **A** 11, පරට; 24, ඇතුන් නැග[ඒ]ම; 29, 30, සම්(මත)යන්; 30, 31, අ(ෙප ෙ)ස්වකාමට රට; 33, [කාරි]ය; 34, [දා]; **B** 15, are as read by Mr. S. Paranavitana.

[2] Doubtful.

II.

A.

Svasti **Siri Saṅgabō Śrī Jayavīra Parākrama Bāhu** cakravartti svāmīnvahansē-ṭa pasvanu Vapa pura päḷaviya **Do- (ḍam)vela Parākrama Bāhu ā-** pāṇa- n bāna **Mēṇavara Tuṇayārun** ätuḷu-vū (äma) denamha a- pa-ṭat raṭa sēnāva-ṭat abha- ya dāna śilā-lekhya karavā devā vadāḷa Tri (Siṁhaḷa)ya-ṭa e- kātapatra-vä a(pa raṭa-[1])ṭa prāpta **Jayavīra Parākrama (Bāhu)** mahā- rājottamayāṇan (va)han- sē-ṭa apa (hā) raṭa sēnāva vi- sin viruddha no vī ekānta (pakṣa-) vä pavatinuvat Väḍa-un-täna- ṭa vipakṣa raja yuvaraja āpā māpā siṭu senevirat adi- kāra ätuḷu-vū kavara taram kenakun-ṭat (pakṣa) no va- nuvat Väḍa-un-(täna-ṭa) ekā- nta pakṣa kenakun-ṭa vipa- kṣa no vanuvat (.. t veḷa-)[2] ñdāma ätu(n näga-)[ē]ma[1] paṇa- m gasvīma paṭabäñdavīma ā- kara kä(ra)vīma .. .. (da) .. (diya) no karanuvat .. t .. .. .. ovun .. (ya)t (käñdava .. ..) gaman ka(ra)vanuvat sam(ma-) (ta)yak[1] päminị-viṭa apa a- (p)e s(ē)vakama-ṭa (ra)ṭa[1] samu- dāva käñdavā gena gos e kiyana [kāri]ya[1] ṣakti-vū paṇata-ṭa sā- [dā][1] denuvat viparītayaka-ṭa [ke](naku)-ṭa patāk basak mi- [ni](ssu)n kenakun gaman no karavanuvat adahasa varadavā ā gi(ya) kenakun no (si)ṭuvā gaman karavanu- va-da Tunu-ruvan-gē ājñāya Daḷadā Pātra dhātunva[han]sē- gē ājñāya (Śakra Bra)hma Viṣṇu Maheśvarādi [d]e-

B.

viyan-gē ā- jñāya Kihiräḷi- Upulvan Saman Boksal Ska- ndha Vibhiṣaṇādi deviyan-gē ā- jñāya satara vara- m devi ma(haraja-) daruvan-(gē) ā- jñāva ki(yā) mē satya-(pratijñā-) śi- lā-lekhyaya li- yavā dun (ba)va-(ṭa) .. .. **Mēṇa(vara) [Tuṇa](yā)run**[1] **Peru(māḷun** va-) mha .. ..

---

[1] A 11, *pa raṭa*; 24, *ätun näga[ē]ma*; 29, 30, *sam(mata)yak*; 30, 31, *a(p)e s(ē)vakama-ṭa raṭa*; 33, [*kāri*]*ya*; 34, [*dā*]; B 15, are as read by Mr. S. Paranavitana.

[2] Doubtful.

TRANSLATION.

I.

Prosperity! Hail! On the first of the waxing moon of Vap in the fifth year of His Majesty the Sovereign Lord **Śrīmat Siri Saṅgabō Śrī Jayavīra Parākrama Bāhu,** the great king sprung from the race of the Sun in lineal descent from the famous Mahā Sammata.

Whereas **Mōṇavara Tuṇayan,** nephew of the *āpā* **Doḍamvela Parākrama Bāhu,** and the great multitude dwelling in the Five Countries, (to wit) De-nuvara of Gampaḷa Siduruvāṇā, Baḷaviṭa, Mātalē, Pansiyapattuva, and Ūva, asked for the grant of an amnesty having been put in fear on the subjugation of the realm effected before the Golden Anointing (Coronation) Festival on the twelfth of the waxing moon of this Vesak just past, (His Majesty) faithfully promised in the presence of the Tooth Relic that henceforth loss of property or of limb or of life should not be inflicted or caused to be inflicted upon the people in this aforesaid country, all whether great or middling or small, setting forth that such is the command of the Three Gems, the command of the Tooth and Bowl Relics, the command of Śakra, Brahma, Viṣṇu, Maheśvara and the rest of the gods, and he ordered that (this) should be written and given.

In obedience thereto (it is certified) that this stone record has been written and given.

II.

Hail! On the first of the waxing moon of Vap in the fifth year of His Majesty the Sovereign Lord **Siri Saṅgabō Śrī Jayavīra Parākrama Bāhu.** We are **Mōṇavara Tuṇayārun,** nephew of the *āpā* **Doḍamvela Parākrama Bāhu,** and all the other (chiefs). Stone records of amnesty having been drawn up and given to us and to the host of the country by His Majesty, who came to our country after raising one canopy of dominion over Tri Siṁhaḷa, on the part of ourselves and of the host of the country (we undertake as follows):—

We will not resist the great king **Jayayīra Parākrāma Bāhu,** but will be entirely on his side; we will not be on the side of any one, whether king, sub-king, prince, heir-apparent, grandee, commander-in-chief, or adigar, who is opposed to His Majesty; we will not oppose any who are entirely on the side of His Majesty; we will not do [the following acts, viz.]? trading in elephants, riding on elephants, striking fanams, conferring titles, digging for precious stones, ... and the like

. . . . . having summoned them we will send them (for duty). When an edict is brought we will summon the host of the country and go with it on our service and carry out that aforesaid business in obedience to the mighty command. We will not send either word or letter or any men to any one for a rebellion; should any one come or go frustrating (this rebellious) intention, we will not detain him but will send him on his way.

(This is) to the effect that, setting forth that such is the command of the Three Gems, the command of the Tooth and Bowl Relics, the command of Śakra, Brahma, Viṣṇu, Maheśvara and the other gods, the command of Kihirāḷi-Upulvan, Saman, Boksal, Skandha, Vibhīṣaṇa and the other gods, the command of the four guardian divine (? great kings), we have caused to be written and have given this stone record of faithful promise.

. . . .

I am Mēṇavara [Tuṇa]yārun Perumāl.

. . . .

No. 4. THE KANDY NĀTHA DĒVĀLĒ INSCRIPTIONS.

By H. W. Codrington.

THE inscriptions here discussed are cut out on eight stones forming part of the western wall of the Nātha Dēvālē in Kandy; five stones are in one row and three in the next. The first record is complete. The text reads straight across stones A and B, and is continued first on C and then on D. The fifth stone, E, of the top row contains part of another epigraph. Immediately beneath this are two smaller stones, F and G. These two with another, H, to their right present a consecutive text. There is missing one inscribed stone, if not more. The temple authorities have not improved the condition of the record by the use of cement wash and paint. The estampage reproduced is that recently made by the Archaeological Department. It has been carefully checked with the original. Use also has been made of photographs of an older estampage, supplied to me by the kindness of Mr. H. C. P. Bell, retired Archaeological Commissioner.

I.

The first epigraph is dated on the tenth of the dark half of Bak in the Buddhist year 2085 (30 March, 1543), and records the grant of various concessions by the king **Śrī Jayavīra Mahā Väḍa-vun-tāna** to the people of Dumbara, Pansiyapattuva, Mātalē, and Ūva Tunkiṁda, and of the village Alutgama for their services in an attack by the Portuguese on the Hill Country. The identity of this king has been discussed in the paper on the Palkuṁbura copper plate (*E.Z.* Vol. III, pp. 240 ff.). The present inscription chiefly is of value in giving us the correct name of the ruler who was on the throne of Kandy in 2085 A.B., as this year, according to tradition, marks the accession of Vikrama Bāhu, the founder of that city as the capital. We have already seen that this date in all probability was derived from the record now published, engraved as it is on a temple the foundation of which was attributed to this Vikrama Bāhu. A shrine of the god Nātha in Senkaḍagala or Kandy is mentioned in the Sagama inscription of the reign of Bhuvanaika Bāhu V. This shrine, if identical in site with the present dēvālē, quite possibly was rebuilt by Vikrama Bāhu. The existing building, however, as it stands, cannot be his, for the wall, on which our inscriptions are cut, evidently has been rebuilt, and at least one stone of the second epigraph lost in the process.

The **script** calls for no comments. It is of use for purposes of comparison with that of the Gaḍalādeṇiya record of Sēnāsammata Vikrama Bāhu. The document is not the work of a scholar.

The **date** was read as 2085 many years ago, when the inscription was in a better condition. The *akṣara* හ of දහස් is quite clear, and there is only room for two *akṣaras* between the ස් and the unmistakable පස්වසු on stone B. From the arrival of the Portuguese in Ceylon up to the expulsion of the earlier Kandyan dynasty by Rājasiṁha I there are only three dates requiring two *akṣaras*, namely the Buddhist years 2065 (හැට), 2085 (අසූ), and 2095 (අනූ). Between these the question must be settled in favour of 2085 by the remains of the second *akṣara* සූ on the stone and in the older estampage.

Mē (*sa*) .. .. *raṭavala*. There is space only for two *akṣaras*, the last of which from the traces remaining seems to have been *ra*. The defective word, therefore, may be *satara*, 'of these four countries'. Pansiyapattuva often is used almost as a synonym of Dumbara. If this be the case here, only three countries are mentioned. But many Kandyan palm leaf registers differentiate between Dumbara and Pansiyapattuva, this last corresponding with the present Uḍa Dumbara, Vēṇḍaruva, and Palispattuva. 'The remaining two countries' spoken of later are Siduruvāṇā Denuvara and Baḷaviṭa. The 'Five Countries above the mountains' were these two with Dumbara, Mātalē, and Ūva (cf. the Gaḍalādeṇiya slab-pillar inscription of Jayavīra Parākrama Bāhu).

The word *Paraṁgi*, 'Frank', occurs here seemingly for the first time in Sinhalese literature. Which attack by the Portuguese on the Kandyan country accompanied by local rebellion is referred to is unknown. Nuno Alvarez Pereira was attached to the Court of Kandy from July 1542 and there is no indication of hostilities in the documents published by Schurhammer (*Ceylon*, Schurhammer and Voretzsch, Leipzig, 1928) between Pereira's arrival and the date of the inscription. Fr. S. G. Perera, S.J., writes to me:—

'I suppose the "disturbance made by the Portuguese" must be some petty affair dignified into an incursion and defeat of the Portuguese. In 1543 February Nuno Alvares Pereira set out from Kandy with a Captain and 2000 men to meet the Portuguese Factor Amaro Mendez who had come to Trincomalee with Miguel Ferreira at the King's request (Schurhammer, pp. 175-6). Pereira met with some opposition from the "ladram que sosegua aquela terra"; and Miguel Ferreira and the Factor went away. It is perhaps this incident that has been magnified into an expulsion of the Portuguese. At least I do not know of any other before March 1543, which can even bear a semblance of a "disturbance by the Portuguese"; unless perhaps an attack by Mayadunne or Bhuvaneka Bahu was believed to have been instigated by the Portuguese.'

Fr. Perera's supposition may be right, for the countries most favoured by the present edict are those from which the people would have been called out for service towards Trincomalee. The remaining two countries; Siduruvāṇā Denuvara and Baḷaviṭa, would be exposed to an attack from the side of Colombo.

Viyadama, literally 'expenses', here clearly mean the supplies to the royal household. *Näṅgi-avurudu-kada* presumably is the *kat rājakariya* or pingo duty; a pingo load of sweets and the like, now known as *peṇum kada*, 'appearance pingo', is still presented to landlords at the New Year. The hybrid Sinhalese and Tamil term *ājña-murittu-daḍa* or fine for breaking orders is now unknown; perhaps it may be the same as *hiṅga-kāsi*, the money paid for default of personal service.

The sentence *pisiya pera-vā atana iḍam-batut* is difficult. The *iḍama* or *iḍam-ge* was the official guest house of the *gama-rāḷa*, whose duty it was to entertain chiefs on circuit therein, and to supply them with *aḍukku* or cooked provisions; here, as it is mentioned in connexion with supplies to the royal household, it must mean the king's resting-place, later known as *gaman-maligāva*, 'journey palace'. The word *atana* usually means 'there', 'in that place'; if this is the case in this sentence, it must be understood to refer to the countries and village mentioned, a somewhat forced meaning. If, however, we can take it as the Sinhalese equivalent of *āsthāna*, qualifying *iḍam*, that is 'the royal resting places', the sense is somewhat better. *Pera-vā* can hardly be *peravā*, 'having wrapped up or covered'. The word occurs in the phrase *me vak pera-vā*, 'up to this time', in the *Nikāya Saṅgraha* and elsewhere. Clough gives *vā* as a particle of comparison, 'as', 'like', 'so'; *pera-vā* thus could mean 'as before'. *Pisiya* may be the conditional mood of *pisanavā*, 'should one cook' (Mudaliyar A. M. Gunasekara's *Sinhalese Grammar*, p. 249), or 'that which is cooked'. If the first be correct, *pera-vā* will have to be understood in the sense 'as before' qualifying *iḍam-batut*; if the second, it will go with *pisiya*, 'up to and including what is cooked', that is the cooking, but in this case the whole phrase is superfluous as *bat* is cooked as opposed to uncooked rice. And it may be doubted whether *pisiya* can bear the meaning 'cooking'.

The *liyannō* were the minor headmen; *liyana-rāla* was so used in certain provinces until recent times. *Balu-parageri-as-maḍala* must be identical with the later *Kukkan-maḍuva*, *Sudu-harak-pantiya*, and *As-pantiya*, the Departments of the Hunting Dogs, of the White (foreign) Cattle, and of the Horses. The first named department, as being contrary to the principles of Buddhism, was abolished by Kīrttiśrī and its people turned into a military body, the *Maḍuvē ättō*.

Peraḷi-koṭa de-piṭa at .. karavā. The missing *akṣara* almost certainly is ම or ව. I have read this tentatively as මේ, *mē*, the contracted form of මෙහෙ, *mehe*, 'work'.

II.

As already stated, the second inscription is defective. It deals, among other things, with the *nila paňḍuru* or money presents on appointment to office and with the *maḷaraya* or heriot. *Deya* on slab E has been taken not as 'thing' but as *dēya*, 'what is proper to be given', which suits the preceding words. *Ekaḷosayi* may have reference to some monetary denomination such as *ridī* or *paṇam*, larins or fanams.

The Tunkiňda of Ūva, of course, is Uḍukiňda, Mädakiňda and Yaṭikiňda. Mädakiňda no longer exists, but is found in the Kandyan and early British documents.

The king here is styled Āsthāna or Mahā Āsthāna. The title was in common use in the sixteenth century; in later Kandyan times it seems to have been restricted to the king's brother.

TEXT.

I.

A, B.

1 ශ්‍රී බුධ වර්ෂයෙන් (දෙද)හ(ස්) [අ](සූ) පස්වනු බග අව දසවක
2 උඩරටට පරංගී(න් ෙ)[කරෙ]වූ වියවුලවූ තැන් දුම්බර ප(න්)
3 සියපත්නුව මානලෙ උව [නුන්කි]ද අලුත්ගම(න්) [ල]න්දන් **ජයවීර**
4 **මහා වැඩවුන්නෙන**ට මේ (ස) .. .. රටවල කුඩා මහත් සේනාව
5 පරංගීන්ටත් කොටා බොහෝ ප(ක්ෂපා)තව සිටි නිසා මෙ කියන සේනා වගෙන්
6 රජගෙට ගන්නා වියදමින් නැගි අවුරුදු කදත් අඟුඹුරිත්නුදඩත් පිසිය පෙරවා අතන •
7 ඉඩම් බතුත් ඇර සෙසු දෙරටට ගමටත් රටට ඇරි රදලටවත් කොරළයාට ලිය(න්)
8 නත්වට්ත් බ(ලූ) පරගෙරි අස්මඩලට අගයක් නො දෙන්වත් ගිය රදල කෙනකු

C.

1 (න්)ව කෝරළයානුට
2 එක දවසකට සාල් නු
3 නෙ බත් ඇර අමුනු බතක් නො කන්
4 වත් අමුනු අගයක් නො ගන්වත් **ජයවීර**
5 **වැඩවුන්නෙන**ට පෙරළි කොට දෙපිට අත් ..
6 (ක)රවා සිටි එකෙක් ඇත්නම් උගෙන් රජ
7 ගෙට ගන්නා ඇම වියදම්ම ගන්වත් වැඩවූන්
8 තැන ආඥ පවතිනා තෙක් මෙ අස්න රග
9 ට පවතිනා පණිතට සක් (ඇම) සතර වරම් දෙවි

D.

1 යන් ඇනුළුවූ සියලු හිස් (නුන් කො)
2 පියන් දෙවියන් දෙස්කොට කු(ඩා ම)හ
3 ත් සේනාවට මේ සිලාලෙඛ්‍යය ෙ
4 කාටාවා දුන් බවට **ශ්‍රීජයවීර** ම
5 **හා වැඩවුන්නැන** වම්හ

---

[1] Traces of ම or ව; perhaps මේ.

II.

E.

1 උව තුන්කිඳට
2 ඇතුළුවූ කුඩා මහත් සේනාවට
3 **ජයවීර අස්ථාන** පවත්වා දෙන තැ
4 න්ම නම් නිල කත් ත ..[1] ..[2] සෙසු දෙය
5 ඇර නිල පඬුරු එකලොසයි මළාර

F, G, H.

1 නනි[3] සරස් (ඇ)නි එකොස් මළෙ නම් උහෙන් එ ක(මට)
2 රජගෙට ගන්ටත් **ජයවීර මහා අස්ථාන** ආඥ
3 මේ රගට පැවති බව දැනගැන්ම යහපති

TRANSCRIPT.

A, B.

1 Śrī Buddha varṣayen (de-da)ha(s) [a](sū) pasvanu Baga ava dasavaka
2 Uḍa-raṭa-ṭa Paraṁgī(n) [kere-]vū viyavula-vū tän Dumbara Pa(n-)
3 siyapattuva Mātale Uva [Tunki]ňda Alutgama(t) [l]atdan **Jayavīra**
4 **Mahā Väḍa-vun-tena-**ṭa mē (sa) .. .. raṭavala kuḍā mahat sēnāva
5 Paraṁgīn-ṭat koṭā bohō pa(kṣapā)ta-va siṭi nisā me kiyana sēnāvagen
6 raja-ge-ṭa gannā viyadamin näňgi-avurudu kadat ājñā-murittu daḍat pisiya pera-vā atana
7 iḍam batut ära sesu de-raṭa-ṭa gama-ṭat raṭa-ṭa äri radala-ṭa-vaṭ koraḷayā-ṭa liya(n-)
8 nan-ṭa-vat ba(lu)-parageri-as-maḍala-ṭa agayak no denṭat giya radala kenaku-

C.

1 (n-)ṭa kōraḷayāku-ṭa
2 eka davasaka-ṭa sāl tu-
3 ne bat ära amutu batak no kan-
4 ṭat amutu agayak no ganṭat **Jayavīra**
5 **Väḍa-vun-tena-**ṭa peraḷi-koṭa de-piṭa at ..[4]
6 (ka)ravā siṭi ekek ät-nam u-gen raja-
7 ge-ṭa gannā ,äma viyadam-ma ganṭat Väḍa-vun-
8 täna ājñā pavatinā tek me asna raňga-
9 ṭa pavatinā paṇata-ṭa Sak (äma) satara varam devi-

---

[1] නී or තී. [2] ළේ, ළි, or ළ. [3] Or නැනි, or නැති.

[4] Traces of *m* or *v*; perhaps *mē*.

I

A

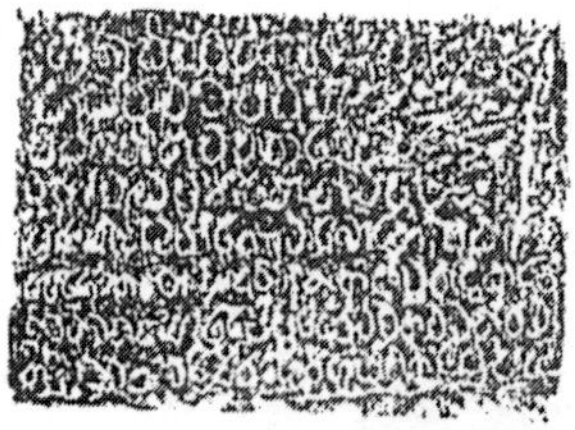

B

C

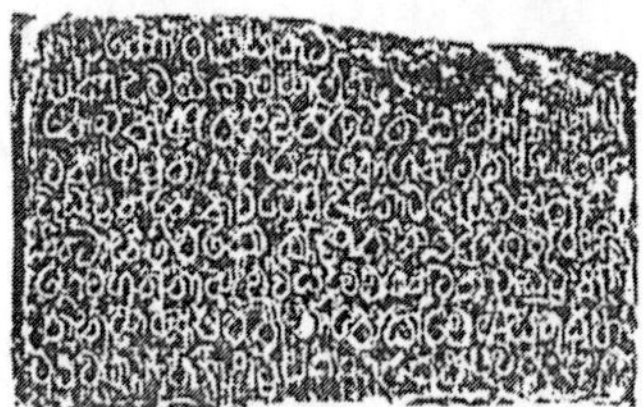

D

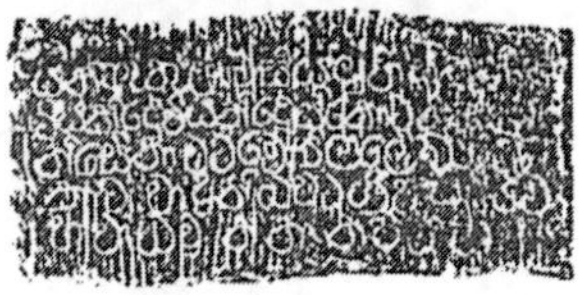

II

E

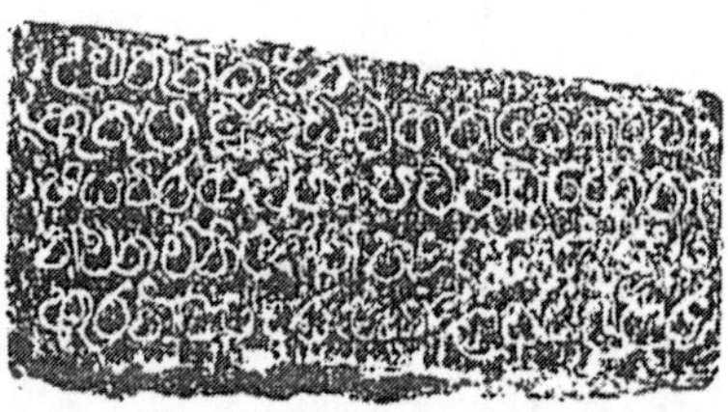

F

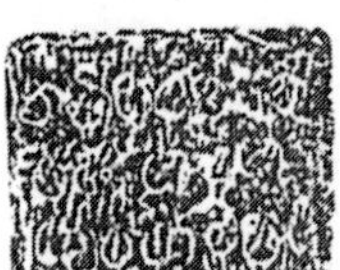

G

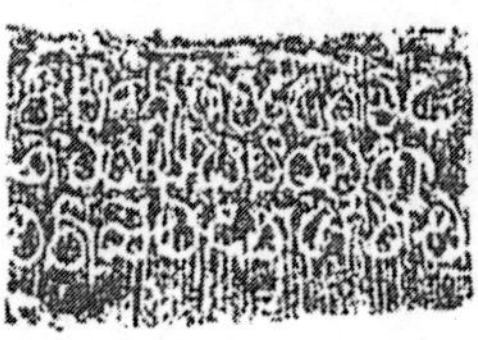

H

Scales — I, about [illegible] inch to 1 foot; II, about 1 inch to 1 foot

D.

1 yan ätuḷu-vū siyalu tis (tun ko-)
2 ṭiyak deviyan des-koṭa ku(ḍā ma)ha-
3 t sēnāva-ṭa mē silā-lekhyaya
4 koṭāvā dun bava-ṭa **Śrī Jayavīra Ma-**
5 **hā Väḍa-vun-täna** vamha

II.

E.

1 Uva Tunkiňda-ṭa
2 ätuḷu-vū kuḍā mahat sēnāva-ṭa
3 **Jayavīra Āsthāna** pavatvā dena tä-
4 nma nam nila kat ta ..[1]•..[2] sesu deya
5 ära nila paňḍuru ekaḷosayi maḷāra-

F, G, H.

1 nani [3] sarak (ä)ti ekek maḷe nam u-gen e ka(maṭa)
2 raja-ge-ṭa ganṭat **Jayavīra Mahā Asthāna** ājñā
3 mē raňga-ṭa pävati bava dänagänma yahapati

TRANSLATION.

I.

A, B, C, D.

On the tenth of the waning moon of Bak in the year of Buddha 2085. Because, when there was a disturbance made by the Portuguese against the Hill Country, the governors of Dumbara, Pansiyapattuva, Mātalē, Ūva Tunkiňda, and Alutgama, (and) the host, small and great, of these (four) countries, having beaten the Portuguese, were very loyal to **Jayavīra Mahā Väḍa-vun-tena,** from the supplies taken for the king's house from this aforesaid host there shall be remitted the New Year pingo, the fine for infringing orders, and, should food be cooked, the supplies of cooked rice for the royal resting places as heretofore.

For the remaining two countries and the village neither to the chief sent to (govern) the division nor to the *kōraḷayā* and the minor headmen shall any money be paid for the departments of the hunting dogs, the foreign cattle, and the horses. Except the cooked rice (equal to) three (parts of) uncooked rice a day for any chief or *kōraḷayā* who has gone (on circuit), no new (contribution of) cooked rice shall be eaten, no new (contribution of) money shall be taken.

[1] *ni* or *ti*. [2] *l*, *li*, or *la*. [3] Or *näni*, or *näti*.

If there be any one who has rebelled against **Jayavīra Väḍa-vun-tena** or who has (worked) for both sides, from him shall be taken for the king's house all and every one of the (usual) supplies.

To the command, which is to endure according to this edict so long as the order of Majesty shall endure, I, **Śrī Jayavīra Mahā Väḍa-vun-tāna,** (certify) that I have called to witness all the thirty-three *koṭi* of gods including Śakra and all the four guardian gods and have caused to be inscribed this stone record and have given it to the host, small and great.

II.

E.

1. To the Tunkiňda of Uva . . . .
2. to the host, small and great, including . . . .
3. established and given by **Jayavīra Āsthāna** . . . .
4. titles, offices, ? pingos, ... (and) the remaining things proper to be given
5. except . . . . . . the money presents for offices, 11 ; the heriot . . .

F, G, H.

If any one dies having cattle they shall be taken from him for the king's house for that business. It is well to know that the commands of **Jayavīra Mahā Āsthāna** are to this effect.

No. 5. POḶONNARUVA: COUNCIL CHAMBER PILLAR-INSCRIPTION.

By S. PARANAVITANA.

THE sub-joined record is engraved on the four sides of a pillar, broken into two nearly equal pieces, which are now joined together and preserved in the Archaeological Museum at Anurādhapura. It was discovered in the vicinity of Niśśaṁka Malla's Council Chamber on the embankment of the Tōpāväva at Poḷonnaruva; and has been noticed in the *Annual Report of the Archaeological Survey of Ceylon* for 1909, p. 39. The base of the pillar and its capital, if it had one, have both been broken off; and it seems to have served some architectural purpose, possibly as a tread in a flight of steps[1]. The two pieces of the pillar now

[1] An inscribed pillar serves a similar purpose in the pavilion popularly known as the Rajamāligāva in the Citadel at Poḷonnaruva.

stand together to a height of 5 ft. 9 in.; and the sides are 11½ and 8 in in breadth. Owing to the rough usage the pillar has been subjected to, the ends and the edges are considerably wasted and some chips are missing at the fractures. The pillar has also suffered to some extent from its exposure to the weather; and the writing on the upper part of side A, the greater part of side C, and a few lines at the top of sides B and D are, therefore, deciphered with some difficulty. Nevertheless a reasonably full and accurate reading of the whole text is possible with the aid of two other fragmentary inscriptions, to be noticed later, whose contents are very similar to those of the present epigraph.

The **letters,** engraved fairly deep, vary in size from 1½ to 2 inches. The **script,** which is somewhat cursive in type, is Sinhalese of about the ninth, or early tenth, century. The *akṣaras-pa* and *ga* can hardly be distinguished, respectively, from *ṭa* and *ha*. The following **orthographical** peculiarities may also be noted:—*Kämbur* in A l. 25 is obviously the same as the familiar word *kumbur*; but it is not certain whether this is actually a variant form or a clerical error. *Munumbuvan* (B ll. 4–5) is evidently the same as *munumburan*, the genitive plural of *munumbur*. The loss of *r* in this nominal form is noteworthy; but, again, there is the possibility of a clerical error. The termination *ä* in Doti Valaknä (B ll. 11–12) is strange; from the analogy of similar names in mediaeval documents, one would have expected the form Valaknā. *Päḷa* (B l. 21) occurs in other documents as *pāḷa*[1].

The language presents several points of interest. We have, in the present epigraph, a number of words which are not found in other records of the period. *Pupak* (A l. 21) and *sud-hiṅgur* (B l. 22) help us to determine the correct etymology of the modern words *puvak* and *siddiṅguru*, of which these forms, respectively, are the prototypes. *Arigiya* in A ll. 16–17 is, most probably, derived from Skt. *ārakṣya*; and the change of *k* to *g* in this word is noteworthy. *Punapunä* A l. 18) is taken to be the same as Skt. *punaḥ-punaḥ*, P. *punappunaṁ*. *Aṭiyän* in C l. 27 has the instrumental singular termination *än*, instead of the usual *en*; a parallel form is *väḷän* in the pillar inscription of Mahinda V[2]. The record also contains certain words of which the meaning is either doubtful or altogether obscure. These will be discussed in the footnotes attached to the translation. The passive verbal form *devanu labamha* (C ll. 26–27) is also worthy of note, as such forms, though very common in the later stages of the language, are rare in the period to which

[1] See *E. Z.* Vol I, p. 133; Vol. II, pp. 110, 233, 286, and 288, and Vol. III, p. 193.
[2] See below p. 60.

this epigraph belongs. That part of the document coming on side B lacks clearness in its syntax; for instance, the gerund *vaḷandā* in ll. 8–9 is superfluous as the finite verb *vaḷandanu* occurs at the end of this clause.

The **date** given in the record is the fourth year of a king referred to by his *viruda* title of **Abhaya Salamevan.** Mr. Bell [1] has identified this monarch with **Kassapa V** (*circa* 908–918); but, as we have no other data, except the form of the script, to decide this point, we cannot be quite certain. Palaeographically, the record may be ascribed to **Dappula V** (*circa* 918–930) or Kassapa V, both of whom had this *viruda* title; but there is no other evidence which would help us to determine the question as to which of these two monarchs the Abhaya Salamevan of this inscription has to be identified with.

The record is concerned with the grant of immunites to certain lands held by an individual, whose name is not clearly legible, as a *pamaṇu* (freehold) on condition of paying, annually, one *päḷa* of dried ginger to a hospital founded by **Doti Valaknä.** The paying of a small quit-rent by holders of freehold land to a religious or charitable institution was a custom not infrequently met with in mediaeval Ceylon [2].

We have numerous examples of edicts, granting immunities to estates, belonging to religious institutions, and, sometimes, to private individuals, in mediaeval Ceylon; and they are all written in the same style [3]. In fact, in the ninth and tenth centuries, a formula in which such documents were worded, seems to have been in use. There are, of course, many variations in detail; but, in the main, all these grants of immunities were drawn up according to a stereotyped model. They open with the date in the regnal year of the reigning monarch and, after giving the names of the land and the institution or person concerned, mention the order delivered, with the consent of the Council, by the king or the heir-apparent, as the case may be, granting the immunities specified. Then follow the names of the officials who were deputed to proclaim the edict in the village concerned and the details of the immunities, such as the dues from which the land was exempted, or the officials whose entry to the estate in question was forbidden. Sometimes, the names of the officials who proclaimed the edict follow the details regarding the immunities. Such edicts are referred to, in the documents themselves, as *attaṇi*, *pärahär*, *attäṇi-pärahär*, *abhaya* or *samvatā*.

---

[1] *A. S. C. Annual Report* for 1909, p. 39.

[2] For instance, see the Nāgama Pillar-Inscription (*E. Z.*, Vol. II, No. 4) and the Rambāva Slab-Inscription (*ibid.*, No. 12).

[3] See *E. Z.*, Vol. I, Nos. 11–13, 16 and 17; Vol. II, Nos. 1–12 and Vol. III, Nos. 5 and 28.

The present document departs almost entirely from this model. The order is not delivered by the king, nor by the heir-apparent; but by some dignitary whose personal name, but not his official title, is given. No mention is made of the Council (*sabhā*). The order is addressed to certain officials, two of whom, the administrators of the districts in which the lands concerned were situated, are referred to by their personal names. The other minor officials are merely referred to by the names of their offices; and all these functionaries are exhorted to protect the lands in question. Then follow the details regarding the tenure of the land and the immunities to which it was entitled. After this occurs the statement that the pillar was set up, at the request of the first-named of the officials to whom the order was addressed, so that the notice of kings may be received and the land may become a *pamaṇu* (free-hold). The regnal year and the date are given towards the end of the document which is referred to, not by any of the technical terms above mentioned, but by *arak* 'protection'.

Only two other inscriptions of this type—both of them fragmentary—are so far known to me. One of these is from Rajamahavihāra at Vihāregama in the Dam̆badeṇi Hatpattu of the Kuruṇāgala District; and the other has been found at a place named Mäda-Ulpota in Gan̆gala Pallēsiya Pattuva, Mātalē East. These two inscriptions, though not of much interest in themselves, were of some help in arriving at the correct reading in certain places of the present record where the writing is not clearly legible; and, for purposes of comparison, I have, therefore, taken them as the subject of the next two articles.

The document throws some light on the economic conditions of Ceylon in the ninth and tenth centuries. We have already mentioned that the owner of the land had annually to pay one *päḷā* of ginger, as quit-rent, to a hospital. The ginger was to be measured by a particular *lahassa* (modern Sinhalese *lāha*) which held four *aḍmanā*. This statement shows that there were, in the tenth century, various *lahasu* measures of different capacities. The same conclusion can be arrived at from the Badulla pillar inscription which also mentions a particular *lahasu* measure, but without giving its capacity[1]. Even at the present day, in different parts of Ceylon, the grain measures, though bearing the same designation, vary in capacity.

If the owner of the land failed to supply the ginger as specified, he was required to give, in lieu of it, one *huna* of gold computed at the rate of one *aka* for each *lahassa*. It may reasonably be assumed that the gold given in lieu of the

---

[1] *E. Z.*, Vol. III, p. 79.

ginger was the market value of the commodity then prevailing. But it is somewhat difficult to utilize this information for comparing the price of this commodity in the ninth century with that prevailing now, as we are not certain that the mediaeval *lahassa* is of the same capacity as the modern *lāha*. This statement also proves that the number of *lahasu* in a *pāla* was the same as that of *akas* in a *huna*. As the systems of weights and measures which were current in Ceylon at this period are not well ascertained, the data supplied by the present epigraph cannot, however, be utilized with certainty. Three valuable notes dealing with these questions, kindly supplied by Mr. Codrington, have been appended to this paper and I do not, therefore, propose to discuss them here.

Mahamal Bud (Mahāmalla Buddha), who issued the order embodied in this document, is referred to without mentioning his official position; but from the fact that he issued orders to the governors of two districts, we can infer that he held a very high position in the administration of the state. An inscription discovered in 1931 in a garden near the Malvatu Oya, within the municipal limits of Anurādhapura, is concerned with the grant of immunities to certain lands held as *pamuṇu* in the family of Mahamal Bud. This record is also dated in the reign of a king named Abā Salamevan and it is possible that it refers to the same Mahamal Bud figuring in the present epigraph. **Diyavällä Kasbā** who, in addition to the governorship of the district called Maharaṭ, also held the office of *muk-hi* [1], figures in the fragmentary pillar inscription from Mäda-Ulpota, in the same capacity as he does in this record. It is at his representation that the order was issued, and, therefore, his position is similar to that of the officer called the *vijñapti* in Indian documents. **Hivaḷä Agbo,** the other official mentioned in this inscription, is not otherwise known.

As regards the **geographical names** occurring in this document, **Maharaṭ,** which is evidently the name of a district, seems to be the same as the **Mahāraṭṭha** mentioned in the *Mahāvaṁsa* (chap. lxxii, vv. 141, 163, 190 and 199). It figures in the chronicle in the account of Parākramabāhu I's campaign against Gajabāhu II; and from the trend of the narrative, it seems to have been the country adjoining the Kalāväva. If the original site of the present inscription was anywhere near Poḷonnaruva—as it is natural to believe, because the builders who utilized the pillar would not have taken the trouble to transport it from a very great distance—the territory included in the Mahāraṭṭha seems to have extended from the Kalāväva to the neighbourhood of Poḷonnaruva. We may, however,

---

[1] The exact meaning of this term is not known. See below p. 45, footnote 12.

surmise that the original site of the pillar was very near the eastern boundary of that district, as the order was addressed to the governors of both that district as well as the adjoining one. This was evidently due to the fact that the two lands affected by the order were in two different districts. It is natural to believe that two properties belonging to the same person and forming the subject of the same document were situated not far from each other, and therefore it follows that they were near the very confines of the respective districts in which they were included.

Maharaṭ was included in a *danaviya* called **(Giri)vaḍunnā,** not known from other sources. A *danaviya*, therefore, was a territorial division larger than a *raṭa*

TEXT.

A.

1 මහමල් බු
2 දුනු වපනින්
3 (ගිරි)වඩුන්නා ද
4 නවියෙහි ම
5 හරච් ලද් දිය
6 වැල්ලැ කස්
7 බාසගු ඉසා
8 වෙතරවලද් ගි
9 වලැ අග්බො
10 යගු ඉසා කුළ
11 සම්අරුබ් පිට
12 ත්සම්අරු
13 බ්කැමියන්
14 ඉසා සෙ[පු ර]
15 ද්කොල්කැමි·
16 යන් ඉසා අ
17 රිගිය පුතු
18 පුතාපුතා [||*] නො
19 ප රටගි වූ දෙ
20 සෙණක් ගු
21 ළුපුපන් කොට
22 ගැමැ දෙමෙළ්කැ
23 බැල්ල ඉසා
24 මහරැකැසෙ
25 කැම්බුජ් කඩ
26 මජ් ඉසා වෙගි
27 .. .. .. වූ මහ

B.

1 (වෙද්)නා
2 (රක් නු)මා
3 ඉසා මෙක්
4 නු දරුවු
5 [නු]ම්බුවන්
6 ඉසා පර
7 පුරෙන් නො
8 නොරා වළ
9 නූ පොලි
10 ය බැනූ
11 දෙනි වල
12 ක්නැ කළු
13 වෙදහල
14 ට හඩුරැ
15 දු හඩුරැදු
16 [පතා බද්]
17 දට සාර්
18 අඹමනා
19 ගන්නා ල
20 හපුයෙන්

21 එක්පැලක්
22 සුද්ගිගු
23 ර් දි වළඤ්නු
24 කොට් ඉසා
25 සුද්ගිගු
26 ර් නොදිය
27 හුණ එක්
28 ලගසුව
29 කට් එක්

C.

1 අකක් රත්
2 හුනක් දෙනු
3 කො[illegible] ඉසා
4 මෙ ගමැ දෙ[කැ]
5 බැල්ලට් [කැ]
6 මබුර්කඩව
7 රට් වූ වි[යවූ
8 ලක්] ඇත ස
9 බායෙ ගිඤ්
10 න සම්දරුව
11 ත් සාහා (පසි)
12 ඤ්වත්නා ඉසා
13 නුත්නකයැ
14 කැබැලි ගනු
15 ත් කැබැලි ග
16 ත්නා ඉසා
17 මෙයට් මඟ්
18 ශිව පියගි
19 ව මෙලාත්ගි
20 පෙරෙනාට්වූ ර
21 ද්කොල්කැමි
22 යත් නොවදනා
23 ඉසා පමණු
24 වන සෙය් මි
25 පල් නුවනක්
26 දෙවනු ලබම්
27 හ අටියැත්
28 මෙ අරක් මූ
29 ක්ගිකම් කර්
30 න දිසවැල්ලැ

D.

1 [කස්බා]
2 අඩුද්
3 අප් පූ
4 රට්ගි දූ
5 ත්වියෙත්
6 අප් .. ..
7 වා .. .. කැ
8 මෙක්නු
9 නියම්
10 න් මෙ කනු
11 කො[ට්] අ[ශ]
12 ශ සල
13 මෙවන් ම
14 [පුර්මූකා]
15 සතරව
16 න ගවුරු
17 දුයෙහි
18 වෙසග්
19 සඳ් පුත්
20 මස්හි තෙ
21 ලෙස්වක්
22 දවස් වදාල
23 මින[॥*]මෙ දව
24 ස් පිටින්
25 මෙක්නු තැ
26 න මිනිසුන්
27 වැදූ සග
28 (ත්) කුබුර්

Poḷonnaruva: Council Chamber Pillar-Inscription

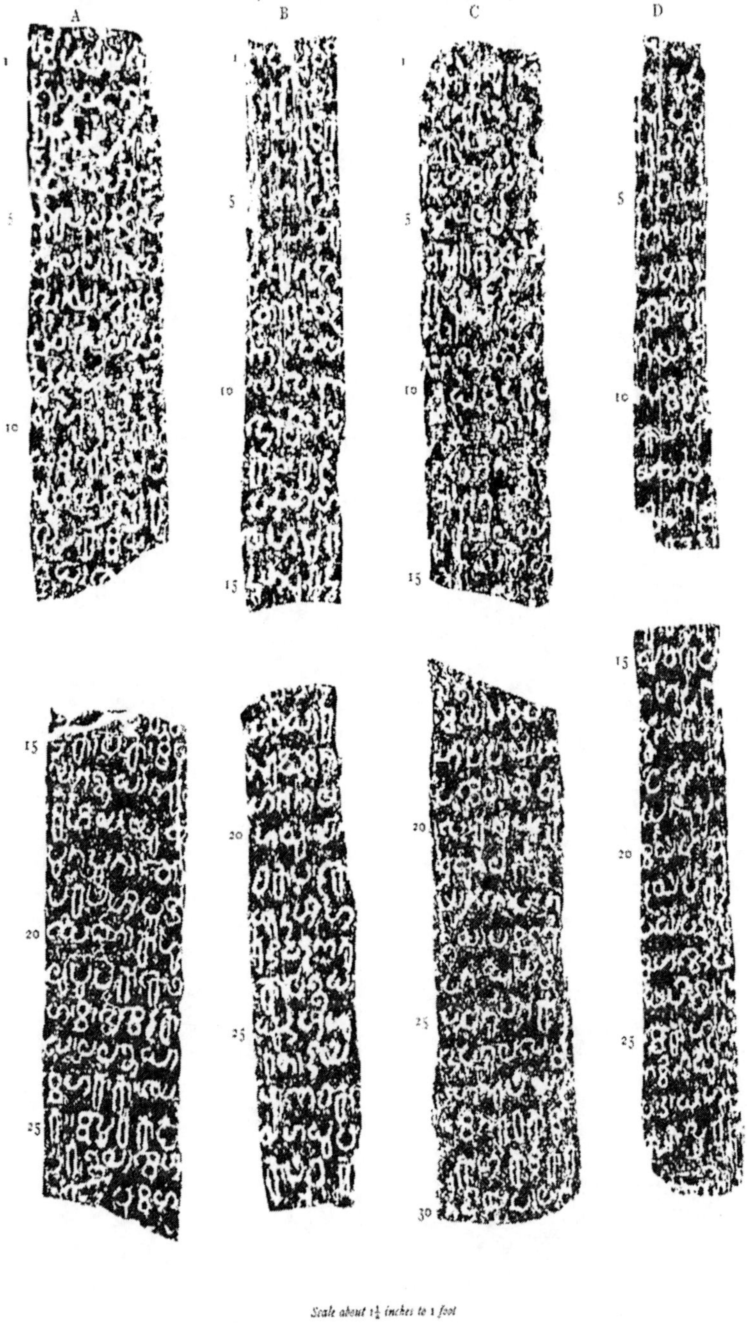

Scale about 1½ inches to 1 foot

TRANSCRIPT.

A.

1 **Mahamal Bu-**
2 -**dā**hu vajanin
3 (**Giri**)**vaḍunnā**-da-
4 -naviyehi **Ma-**
5 -**haraṭ**-lad **Diya-**
6 **vallä Kas-**
7 **bā**yahu isā
8 v(e)ta-raṭ-lad **Hi-**
9 -**vaḷä Agbo-**
10 -yahu isā kuḷa-[1]
11 sam-arub piṭa-
12 -t-sam-aru-
13 -b-kämiyan
14 isā se[su-ra]-
15 -d-kol-kämi-
16 -yan isā a-
17 -rigiya yutu
18 punapunā [||*] To-
19 -pa raṭ-hi vū de-
20 seṇāk hu-
21 -lu-pupak **Koṭ-**
22 **gämā** Demeḷ-kä-
23 -bälla isā
24 **Maharäkāye**
25 **Kāmbur-kaḍa-**
26 -**var** isā mehi
27 .. .. .. vū maha-[2]

B.

1 (ved)nā
2 (**Rak** tu)mā
3 isā mek-
4 -hu daru-mu-
5 -[nu]mbuvan
6 isā para-
7 -puren no-
8 torā vaḷa-
9 -ndā pol[i]-
10 -ya bändä
11 **Doti Vala**
12 -**knä**[3] kaḷa
13 vedahala-
14 -ṭ havuru-
15 -du havurudu
16 [patā bad]-[4]
17 -daṭ sär-
18 aḍ-manā
19 gannā la-
20 -hasuyen
21 ek-päḷak
22 sud-hiṅgu-
23 -r di vaḷandanu
24 koṭ isā
25 sud-hiṅgu-
26 -r no-diya-
27 huṇa ek-
28 lahasuva-
29 -kaṭ ek-

---

[1] The letter *ku* is not quite clear; but the reading given above is supported by the Vihāregama inscription, below p. 53.

[2] This letter can also be read as '*ga*'.

[3] Can be read as *Palaknä* also.

[4] Though the letters of this line are for the most part destroyed, the reading given is fairly certain.

C.

1 akak ran
2 hunak denu
3 ḳoṭ isā
4 me gamä de-[kä]-
5 -bällaṭ [Kā]-
6 -mbur-kaḍava-
7 -raṭ vū vi[yavu-
8 -lak] äta sa-
9 -bāye hind-
10 -na sam-daruva-
11 -n sāhā (pasi)-
12 -ndvannā isā
13 tun-nakayä
14 käbäli ganu-
15 -t käbäli ga-
16 -nnā isā
17 meyaṭ maṅg-
18 giva piyag[i]-
19 -va melātti
20 perenāṭṭu ra-
21 -d-kol-kämi-
22 -yan novadanā
23 isā pamaṇu
24 vana sey mi-
25 pal nuvanak
26 devanu labam-
27 -ha aṭiyän
28 me arak mu-
29 -k-hi- kam kar-
30 -na **Diyavällä**

D.

1 [**Kasbā**][1]
2 avud
3 ap pu-
4 -raṭ-hi dä-
5 -nviyen
6 ap .. ..
7 -vā .. .. kä[2]
8 mek-hu
9 niyami-
10 -n me kanu
11 koṭ **A**[**bha**-]
12 -**ya Sala**-
13 **mevan** ma-
14 -[purmukā]
15 satara-va-
16 -na havuru-
17 -duyehi
18 Vesag-
19 sand pun-
20 mas-hi te-
21 -ḷesvak
22 davas vadāḷa-
23 -mha [॥*] Me dava-
24 -s piṭin[3]
25 mek-hu tä-
26 -na minisun
27 vädä saga-
28 -(t) kubur[4]

---

[1] Compare the Mäda-Ulpota inscription, below p. 57.

[2] No connected reading of lines D 6–7 is possible.

[3] May also be *pivin*.

[4] No traces of writing are visible after line 28: but the Mäda-Ulpota record shows that this inscription did not end here.

TRANSLATION.

[Lines A 1–18]. By the command of **Mahamal Bud**[1]. By **Diyävälla Kasbā**[2] who has received [the governorship of] the district of **Maharaṭ**[3] in the province of **(Giri)vaḍunnā**[4], and by **Hivaḷā Agbo**[5], who has received [the governorship of] the adjoining district, and by the officers called the *kuḷa-sam-arub* and *piṭat-sam-arub*[6], and by the other officers of the royal household, [this] should be protected again and again.

---

[1] P. *Mahāmalla Buddha*. In this name, *Mahāmalla* is obviously a *viruda* title for which see *E.Z.*, Vol. III, p. 199.

[2] *Kasbā* = P. *Kassapa*, Skt. *Kāśyapa*. *Diyavälla* is a place name.

[3] With the expressions *Maharaṭ-lad* and *veta-raṭ-lad*, it may be interesting to compare modern expressions like *raṭa läbī karavana*, which are used in referring to officials like Raṭēmahatmayās.

[4] *Girivaḍunnā* :—If this reading is correct, the name is equivalent to P. *Girivaḍḍhamāna*.

[5] [illegible] = P. *Aggabodhi*. *Hivaḷa* is the name of a village.

[6] *Kuḷa-sam-arub* and *piṭat-sam-arub* which, obviously, are the designations of some minor officials, have here been met with for the first time. The same two classes of officials are referred to, in the Vihāregama inscription, by the slightly different terms *kuḷat-sam-arub* and *piṭas-samun*. The Mäda-Upota pillar has *piṭassam-arub* and, in the missing portion of that record, the other term too must have occurred. From the contexts in which they occur in the three records, it is clear that these terms refer to two classes of government officers. All the documents in which these officials are mentioned together are concerned with the grant of *pamuṇu* lands to private individuals and from the fact that they are expressly named while the other classes of royal officers are referred to in a general way, we may presume that they had an intimate connexion with this branch of the administration of the government. An officer called a *piṭassam* is mentioned in the Mihintalē tablets of Mahinda IV in company with another styled *raj-ge upāni kämi* (*E. Z.*, Vol. I, p. 95). Both these officials were given a certain allowance from the income of the monastery and, therefore, we may be justified in presuming that they were servants of the monastery. But the second named officer, from his title itself, appears to have had some connexion with the palace as well. It is a well-known fact that certain functionaries were common both to the monasteries and to the royal palace. The term *piṭassamu*, occurring in the Mihintaḷē inscription, has not been satisfactorily explained. Dr. Wickremasinghe renders it conjecturally by 'one who arranges outside affairs' (*E. Z.*, Vol. I, p. 108, n. 9). In both these terms, the essential element appears to be *atsam* or *assam* which also occurs in other names of monastery officials mentioned in the Mihintaḷē tablets, to wit, *veher-atsam*, *karaṇḍu-atsamu*, *dāge-atsam*, and *dummal-assam*. An earlier form of *atsam*, namely, *atasama*, occurs in a fragmentary inscription at Puvarasankuḷam near Mihintaḷē. Various suggestions have been put forward for the interpretation of *atsamu*. Müller, deriving it from Skt. *hasta* + *sam*, renders it by 'receiver of revenues'; Mudaliyar B. Gunasekara by 'sealing' and Dr. Wickremasinghe by 'keeper'. None of these interpretations, however, has anything to recommend it. In *piṭat-sam-arub*, *piṭat* means 'outer'; therefore, in the term used in juxtaposition with it, namely, *kuḷat-sam-arub*, *kuḷat* may mean 'interior', though I do not know of any place where the word is found used in this sense, nor any etymological reasons for this meaning. *Arub*, the last element of these two compounds, is also obscure both in meaning and etymology. It is doubtful whether it is the same as *arub*, equivalent to Pāḷi *ārāma*, occurring in the Mihintaḷē tablets (*E. Z.*, Vol. I, p. 92).

[Lines A 19-C 3]. The Tamil allotment[1], comprising of two *seṇās*[2] of *hulu*[3] and areca-palms[4] in [the village of] **Koṭgam** and **Kāmbur-kaḍavar** in[5] [the village of] **Maharakāya** . . . . . in this . . . shall be enjoyed in [their] lineage, without cessation[6], by His Worship (Mahavednā) **Rak**[7] and the children and grandchildren of this [personage]. The same shall be rented [to yield] interest[8] and one *pāḷa*[9] of dried ginger[10] [measured] by a *lahasu*[9] taking four *aḍmanā*[9]

---

[1] *Demeḷa-käbälla* :—See *E. Z.*, Vol. III, p. 143.

[2] For the explanation of this word, see *E. Z.*, Vol. III, p. 143.

[3] Fenugreek, *trigonella foenum graecum*. See *E. Z.*, Vol. III, p. 140, n. 4 and p. 143.

[4] *Pupak* :—This word is a compound of *pu* (Skt. *pūga*) 'areca-nut' and *pak* which, in literary Sinhalese, means 'fruit' and is probably derived from Skt. *pakva* 'ripe', used in a secondary sense to denote 'ripe fruit or nut' and later extended in meaning to express 'fruit' or 'nut' in general. See Geiger, *E. S.*, *s.v.* The modern equivalent of *pupak* is *puvak* which Geiger derives from *pūga*, but is at a difficulty to account for *ak*. The form preserved in this epigraph helps us to understand the correct etymology of the modern Sinhalese word *puvak*.

[5] *Kāmbur-kaḍavar* is evidently the name of a land. *Kāmbur*, however, appears to be a variant form of, or a clerical error for, the familiar word *kumbur*. The name is repeated on side C; but, as the first letter is not legible, we are not able to test the correctness of the form occurring here. The word *kaḍavar* is possibly the earlier form of *kaḍavara* occurring in the fourteenth-century rock-inscription at Gaḍalādeṇiya, in the phrase *kumburu biju . . . . muṇak hā gam-kaḍavara ekek*. Here the word appears to mean 'share'. *Kaḍa* is perhaps equivalent to Skt. *khaṇḍa* 'piece'; but no conjecture is possible as to the meaning of *vara*. *Kāmbur-kaḍavar* may, if the first member of the compound be taken as equivalent to *kumbur*, be interpreted as 'share of a field'.

[6] The occurrence of the gerund *vaḷandā* in B ll. 8–9, interrupts the smooth flow of the order of words in the sentence. It is unnecessary, as the finite verb *vaḷandanu* at the end of this sentence refers to this as well as the other clauses.

[7] The reading *mahavednā* is very doubtful. *Mahavednā* 'the Chief Physician' occurs in the *Nikāya Saṅgraha* as one of the principal functionaries of the state under Parākramabāhu I. The cognate title of *Suḷuvedanā* 'the Junior Physician' is found in an inscription of the reign of Parākramabāhu I, found at Anurādhapura. But the word has not been met with in any other document of the tenth century. *Rak* = P. *Rakkha*.

[8] *Poliya bändä* :—*Poli* 'interest' occurs very commonly in the modern language and is connected with the Tamil root *poli*, 'to increase'. *Bändä*, literally, 'having tied' may mean 'having rented or mortgaged'. It may be conjectured that the holder of the land, in order to ensure the regular payment of the dues to the hospital, was requested to rent out as much of the land as would be necessary for this purpose.

[9] About these terms of capacity, see Mr. Codrington's notes appended to this paper.

[10] *Sud-hiṅgur* = Skt. *śuddha śṛṅgavera*, P. *suddha siṅgivera*. In modern Sinhalese, the phrase *suddha karanavā* has the meaning of 'cleaning' or 'removing the husk', of cereals, &c. *Sud* might also be the same as the modern Sinhalese *sudu* 'white'. Thus *sud-hiṅgur* may mean 'prepared or cleaned ginger' or 'white ginger'. *Sud-hiṅgur* is undoubtedly the earlier form of *siddiṅguru* which is the term by which the Skt. *nāgara* is translated in Sinhalese books on medicine. I have, therefore, treated it as having the same meaning as Skt. *nāgara* and translated it by 'dried ginger'.

should be given year after year as rent to the hospital founded by **Doti Valaknä**[1]. Should it not be possible to give the dried ginger, [as specified], a *huna*[2] of gold, [computed at the rate of] one *aka* for one *lahasu* of ginger, should be given in lieu of it.

[Lines C 3–23]. Should there be any dispute in connexion with the Tamil allotment[3] of this village or the *kämbur-kaḍavar*, the gentlemen[4] who sit in the assembly shall arbitrate and settle the same. *Käbäli*[5] shall be taken [from these lands] if *käbäli* be taken from [the lands belonging to] the three fraternities[6]. The officers of the royal household, such as *magiva*, *pegiva*[7], *melätti*[8] and *perenāṭṭu*[9] are not to enter this [estate].

[Lines C 23–D 23]. With the desire that we shall be noticed[10] by kings in order that [this estate] may become a *pamaṇu*[11], and as **Diyavällä Kasbā** who performs the office of *muk-hi*[12] came and notified in our presence[13] . . . . .[14] this

---

[1] *Doti Valaknä*:—*Doti* = P. *Joti*, frequently met with as a personal name. *Valaknä* is obviously a title; but its significance is not clear and it has also not been met with elsewhere.

[2] For these terms, see Mr. Codrington's notes appended to this article.

[3] *Dekābälla*:—It is quite clear from the context that the names of the lands given in A ll. 21–26 are repeated in C ll. 4–7. In place of the word *Demaḷa-käbälla* in the earlier part of the record, *dekäbälla* is substituted here. We can, therefore, be almost certain that these two words are synonymous. In fact, *dekäbälla* seems to be nothing more than an abbreviated form of *demeḷ-käbälla*. The compound word *dekäbäli-laduvan* occurs in the slab-inscription near the Stone Canoe in the Citadel at Anurādhapura (*E.Z.*, Vol. I, No. 8), where it has been translated by Dr. Wickremasinghe as 'the recipients of two allotments'.

[4] *Sam-daruvan*:—See *E.Z.*, Vol. III, p. 88.

[5] See *E.Z.*, Vol. III, p. 277, n. 9.

[6] *Tun-nakaya* (P. *Nikāyattaya*, the three fraternities) were the Mahāvihāra, the Abhayagiri, and the Jetavana sects of monks.

[7] For these two terms, see *E.Z.*, Vol. III, p. 146.

[8] See *E.Z.*, Vol. III, p. 110.

[9] *Ibid.*, p. 145.

[10] Literally, 'we shall be caused to be given an eye by kings', if the reading *mipal nuvanak devanu labamha* be correct. The reading as well as the translation offered of this phrase are not beyond doubt.[1]

[11] For this word, which is usually spelt *pamuṇu*, see *E.Z.*, Vol. III, p. 276, n. 3.

[12] This word has not been found elsewhere; but from the context it is clear that it is the name of an office, though we do not know exactly what its nature was. *Muk-hi* may be derived from Skt. *mukhya*, in which case, it means 'chief'. In South Indian documents, *mugam* (Skt. *mukham*) means the 'word of the king' and the officer, whose duty it was to note down the verbal orders of the king, was called *mugaveṭṭi*, an official title which was, in the slightly different forms of *mukaveṭṭi* and *mohoṭṭi*, also current in Ceylon during the fifteenth and sixteenth centuries. *Muk-hi* in this record is perhaps the precursor of *mukaveṭṭi* of later times. This supposition is strengthened by the fact that it was on the representation of Diyavällä Kasbā, who performed the office of *muk-hi*, that the order embodied in this document was issued. Probably it was the royal consent which was communicated by Diyavällä Kasbā.

[13] *Puraṭ-hi* is also not known from any other document. I have taken *puraṭ* to be derived from *puras* or *purasthāt*.

[14] No reading, which would give any sense, of lines. D 6–7 is possible, though most of the letters are clear.

pillar was set up by the order of this [Diyavällä Kasbā][1], and we delivered these [regulations of] protection[2] on the thirteenth day of the bright half of the month of Vesag[3] in the fourth year of His Majesty **Abhaya Salamevan**[4].

[Lines D 23–28]. After[5] this day, the field .... men from the place of this [person], having come[6] .....

APPENDIX.

NOTES ON THE HUNA AND GRAIN MEASURES.

By H. W. Codrington.

I. I understand the text to mean that the grantee was to pay yearly 1 *pāḷa* of white ginger measured by a *lahassa* of 4 *aḍmanās*, or, in default, 1 *huna*, that is, 1 *aka* of gold for each *lahassa*.

The modern Table of grain measures is:—

pata	*hunḍuva*	*näḷiya*	*laha*	*timba*	*pāḷa*	*amuṇa*
640	320	160	40	10	4	1

Twenty *amuṇas* make 1 *yāḷa*.

This Table, however, does not represent actual practice; the number of *patas* or single handfuls in the *näḷiya* varies, as does the number of *näḷi* in the *laha*. There is also a small and a large *laha*. In some places it is ten of the small which make a *pāḷa*, in others ten of the large. The *timba* and the *pāḷa* are considered to be fixed as the tenth and quarter of the *amuṇa*; each is divided into so many *lahas*, the number varying with their size.

Moggallāna's *Abhidhānappadīpikā* gives the following Table:—

kuḍuba, pasata	*pattha*	*āḷhaka*	*doṇa*	*mānikā*	*khāri*	*vāha*
20,480	5,120	1,280	320	80	20	1

He also gives a few other details. Thus, another name for the *āḷhaka* is the *tumba*, for the *pattha* the *nāḷī*, and for the *vāha* the *sakaṭa*, which last is etymologically the equivalent

---

[1] It is not clear from the context to whom *mek-hu* refers. I have assumed that it refers to Diyavällä Kasbā, as his name precedes this word. But this gives rise to a difficulty. The sentence can then be interpreted to mean that the pillar was set up by Mahamal Bud on the orders of Diyavällä Kasbā. The opening clause of the document makes it quite clear that Mahamal Bud was a higher official than Diyavällä Kasbā, for the former issues orders to the latter. In order to avoid this difficulty, I have, though in a somewhat forced manner, taken this part of the record to mean that the actual setting up of the pillar was executed at the orders of Diyavällä Kasbā, while the regulations embodied in the document were according to the command of Mahamal Budā, who speaks in the first person, in the opening words of the document.

[2] *Arak* = Skt. *ārakṣā*.

[3] P. *Vesākha*, Skt. *Vaiśākha*. The second Sinhalese month, April–May.

[4] P. *Silāmeghavaṇṇa*.

[5] *Piṭin*, literally 'outside'.

[6] The exact purport of the clause contained in ll. D 23–28 is not clear as the reading, in some places, is not certain. The same clause occurs in the Mäda-Ulpota inscription with the addition of some more words, not clearly legible, after *kubur* with which the present record seems to end. Perhaps, this epigraph also contained the additional words found in that inscription.

of the Sinhalese *yāḷa.* Further, 10 *doṇa* are said to make 1 *ammaṇa*, and 10 *ammaṇas* 1 *kumbha.*

Moggallāna's Table is based on Pāli authorities and does not agree with the Sinhalese. That part of it, however, dealing with the *pasata* or single handful and the next two denominations is common also to the Cōḷa, Malabar, and Kandyan Tables; above the *pattha* or *nāḷi* all differ. Combining Moggallāna's figures, where the others are in agreement, with his supplementary material, and including the *doṇa*, which corresponds with the Sinhalese *tiṁba*, we get :—

pasata	*pattha* or *nāḷi*	*āḷhaka* or *tumba*	*doṇa*	*ammaṇa*
640	160	40	10	1

His information touching the *ammaṇa* doubtless is from Sinhalese usage, as the number of single handfuls in it agrees with the modern Table. The *pāḷa* is absent, but it occurs as the fourth of the *amuṇa* in Niśśaṁka Malla's inscriptions.

The Mihintalē Tablets mention the *näḷiya*, the *aḍmanā*, and the *pata.* In one place we find 1 *aḍmanā* 2 *patas*, in another 2 *aḍmanās* (the highest given), and once the *näḷiya*, but not in connexion with the other denominations. More than 2 *patas* are never mentioned, and it is fairly certain that 4 *patas* equal the *aḍmanā.*

Combining the Mihintalē data with those supplied by the present inscription, we find :—

4 *patas* = 1 *aḍmanā*

16 *patas* = 4 *aḍmanā* = 1 *lahassa.*

The *lahassa* thus equals the modern *laha*, and the *aḍmanā* the ordinary *näḷiya*, the *nālī* of Moggallāna.

The *lahassa* is still in use in Jaffna in the Tamil form of *lāccam*, that is *lāssa*, as a measure of superficial area. In the Peninsula 4 *cuṇḍu* make 1 *kottu* or *paḍi* (seer), and 2 seers of paddy seed are required to sow one *lāccam* of ground. If the *lāccam* be restored to its place in the Table of grain measures we get:—

8 *cuṇḍu* = 2 *paḍi* = 1 *lāccam.*

The number of *cuṇḍu* in the *lāccam* thus agrees with the number of *huṇḍu* in the *laha.*

II. It is evident from the present inscription that, as 1 *aka* is to the *huna*, so 1 *lahassa* is to the *pāḷa.* We may consider the *huna* as a weight and as a coin.

The *huna* as a weight is given in the *Yogārṇava* of the reign of Bhuvanaika Bāhu I and in subsequent Tables as the equivalent of 3 *kaḷaňdas* or 24 *akas.* Moggallāna, on the other hand, makes 1 *suvaṇṇa* equal to 5 *dharaṇas* (*kaḷaňdas*) or 40 *akkhas* (*akas*). A *huna* of 24 *akas* implies a *pāḷa* of 96 *aḍmanās*, and a *huna* of 40 *akas* a *pāḷa* of 160 *aḍmanās.* Both these figures are far in excess of the value of the *pāḷa*, 640 *patas*, that is, 160 *aḍmanās*, making the *amuṇa* both in Moggallāna and the modern Tables. We need not further consider the *huna* as a weight.

In inscriptions the *huna* occurs but rarely :—

(1) 19 Sena II (*Ceylon Coins and Currency*, p. 197), *dasa hunak ran*, ten *hunas* of gold.

(2) 9 Udaya I (*ibid.*), *pas hunak ran*, five *hunas* of gold.

(3) ? Kassapa IV (*ibid.*), *eka huna de äkakä mal*, one *huna* two *akas* (? worth of) flowers.

(4) Mr. Paranavitana supplies a fourth instance dating from about the sixth century, namely :—*eka saya huna kavaṇa* one hundred *huna ka*[*ha*]*vaṇa.* This occurs on a step leading to a shrine in the Northern Dāgäba area near 'Burrows' Pavilion'. Mr. Paranavitana

compares the formation of *huna ka[ha]vaṇa* with that of *mala-kahavaṇa*, *dama-kahavaṇa*, already known from inscriptions.

Examples (1) and (2) may refer to bullion; (3) may refer to bullion or coin; (4) certainly must mean coin.

It may be noted that the word *huna* is spelt with the dental ණ. But as *sunu*, 'lime', is also so spelt in *E.Z.*, Vol. I, p. 97, though derived from Skt. *cūrṇṇa*, there is no difficulty in tracing *huna* to *suvarṇṇa*. That this is the correct etymology is rendered more than probable by the names of the weight corresponding to the *huna* in the cognate Tables. Thus in the Malabar 3 *kaḷañcu* make 1 *kārṣam*, in the old Tamil 2 *kaḷañju* make 1 *kaisu*, and in the *Gaṇita Sāra Saṅgraha* for gold 2 *dharaṇas* are equal to 1 *karṣa*. Moggallāna's value of the *suvaṇṇa* has been given above. *Karṣa* and *suvarṇṇa* are synonyms.

From the analogy of the Tamil *poṉ* and Canarese *honnu* 'gold', it may be argued that *huna* was a synonym for the *kahavaṇuva* coin. But the *Mahāvaṁsa Ṭīkā* calls this coin *hirañña*, and this is in accordance with the usual practice of the commentators, who render the Pāli *hirañña* by *kahavuṇu* and *suvaṇṇa* by *rat-rana*, 'red gold', that is fine gold bullion (*Ceylon Coins and Currency*, pp. 52, 188, 254). In spite of this, the expression *huna-ka[ha]-vaṇa* in the sixth-century inscription coupled with *soṇṇa-kahāpaṇa* in *Mahāvaṁsa*, lxxxi, 45, though much later in date than the epigraph now under discussion, inclines me to think that the *huna* was the largest gold coin of the period or a coin of account of the same value. This gold coin was 8 *akas* in weight. Accordingly, the *pāḷa* of the present document should contain 8 *lahassas* or 32 *aḍmanās*. This is two *lahas* short of the modern *pāḷa*. But if by the converse process of reasoning we work back from the existing measure, we arrive at a *huna* of 10 *akas*, and no coin of this weight is known.

Thus, the most likely solution of the problem presented by the inscription seems to be one by which the *huna* is a coin and not a weight, and the *pāḷa* not the modern one of 10 *lahas*, but rather one of 8 *lahassas*. There is no direct evidence for such a *pāḷa*, but the analogy of small and large *näḷi* and *lahas* and the great variation in measure now in use make its existence not impossible. The *bara*, the equivalent of this hypothetical *pāḷa*, is mentioned in the following Note.

III. The relation of the *aḍmanā*, 'half *manāva*', to the *näḷiya* in the Mihintalē Tablets is obscure. Rhys Davids surmised that the two were identical, and Moggallāna's Table supports this view. But the fact that both are mentioned in the same inscription makes this identification doubtful. A solution of the problem, perhaps, is to be found in the existence at the present day of two *näḷi*, the ordinary measure of the name, and the *hambā-* or *baṇḍāra-näḷiya*, 'royal *näḷiya*', in use in temples.

The first mentioned *näḷiya* according to the Tables should consist of 4 *patas*, but in practice varies greatly. The *baṇḍāra-näḷiya* in general usage is slightly in excess of the ordinary *näḷiya*. Thus in Vavuniya District it is of 10 single handfuls against the usual 7, and at Dambulla of 6 against 4; in Lower Dumbara it is said by some to be 1½ times the ordinary *näḷiya* of 3 handfuls, by others to be of 5 handfuls of a big man.

Also in the temples is the *baṇḍāra-kuruṇiya*. This seems to be a variety of the larger *laha*, *kuruṇiya* in some parts of the country being a synonym of *laha*.[1] In Lower Dumbara

[1] The difference between the *laha* and the *kuruṇiya* is in the shape of the measure. The former a wooden plate, the latter a pot-like vessel, as is also the *näḷiya*.

it is said to be of 9 *näḷi*; it is not connected in the popular mind with any definite number of *baṇḍāra-näḷi*.

The silver *näḷiya*, of the Daḷadā Māligāva, as tested in my presence, contains 8 single handfuls.[1] It is known simply as *näḷiya*, though double the ordinary measure of this name in the Tables. Four make a *baṇḍāra-kuruṇiya*, and 16 the *bara*, 'burden' or head-load'. This *kuruṇiya* is identical with the old Cōḷa *kuruṇi* or *marakkāl*.

But anciently there was also a *näḷiya* of 4 *aḍmanās*, witness the *Dampiyā aṭuvā sannaya*:—'aḍḍha-nāli mattaṁ, aḍa-näḷiyak matu—de aḍamanāk matuyayi sēyi' (ed. Sir D. B. Jayatilaka, p. 100).[2] This *näḷiya* of 16 handfuls thus is equal to the *lahassa* of our inscription; it may be the Mihintalē measure.

We thus find three distinct *näḷi*, of 4 handfuls, of 16 handfuls, and an intermediate one represented by the Māligāva silver *näḷiya* and the different *baṇḍāra-näḷi*. The smallest, agreeing as it does with the South Indian, may be the 'Tamil', and the largest the 'Sinhalese' *nāḷī* of the *Vinayattha Mañjūsa* (*Kaṅkhāvitaraṇī Tikā*, Colombo, 1912, p. 174). The Māligāva *näḷiya*, being a double *aḍmanā*, seems really to be an old *manāva*. A measure of this name still exists in the Low Country, and according to the Tables is half the usual *näḷiya*. But its contents in handfuls may well have varied with the *näḷiya*.

The following Table of early mediaeval grain measures is put forward tentatively. The figures in heavy type are those obtained from the Mihintalē Tablets, the present inscription, the *Dampiyā aṭuvā sannaya*, and the Māligāva. The hypothetical *pāḷa* of 8 *lahassas* has been included. The division of the *amuṇa* into 5 instead of 4 *pāḷas* is required by its value of 640 *paṭas* given both by Moggallāna and by the modern Tables.

pata	*aḍmanā* *nāḷī*	? *manāva* (Māligāva *näḷiya*)	*näḷiya* *lahassa*[3]	(*baṇḍāra-kuruṇiya*)	*doṇa* (*timba*)	*pāḷa* (*bara*)	*amuṇa*
4	**1**						
8	**2**	**1**					
16	**4**	2	**1**				
32	8	**4**	**2**	**1**			
64	16	8	4	**2**	1		
128	32	**16**	8	4	**2**	**1**	
640	160	80	40	20	10	5	**1**

Support for the above Table is given by the mediaeval *kiriya* and its fractions, once employed for measuring paddy land. The *kiriya* was equated with 4 *amuṇas* and was divided into 4 *pā* or quarters, 20 *massas*, and 80 *käṇas*, on the same principle as the *kahāpaṇa*. The *pā*, therefore, was the *amuṇa*, the *massa* the *pāḷa* of 8 *lahassas*, and the *käṇa* the *baṇḍāra-kuruṇiya*. We must, however, await further light from inscriptions before this Table can be fixed with absolute certainty.

[1] This is the exact capacity of the official Maldivian *näḷiya* of 4 *lāhi* (Sinh. *huṇḍu*).

[2] I am indebted for this reference to Mr. S. Parinavitana.

[3] See p. 48, note 1.

No. 6. VIHĀREGAMA PILLAR-INSCRIPTION.

By S. PARANAVITANA.

AT Vihāregama, in the Uḍukaha Kōraḷē West of the Daṁbadeṇi Hatpattu in the Kuruṇāgala District, there is an ancient monastery now known as Rajamaha Vihāra. The site, which is on a low hill, has been restored in recent times. The remains include some caves, one of which has a Brāhmī inscription[1] of pre-Christian date, a ruined shrine with pillars of the Poḷonnaruva style, and various architectural fragments now displaced and utilized in modern works. A flight of rough stone steps leads to the top of the hill; and, at the bottom of this, to the right, is now placed the upper half of an inscribed pillar[2] with *kalasa*-shaped capital. It is said to have been removed, several decades ago, to its present site from a neighbouring *chena*; but nobody was able to tell me exactly from where.

The preserved portion of the pillar measures, without the capital, 10½ in. by 10 in. by 2 ft. 7½ in. in height. The first five lines of side A are badly worn and the whole of side B, except the first six lines, is altogether illegible. After the fifth line on side D occur four symbols which are usually found at the close of pillar inscriptions of the ninth and tenth centuries; but the record does not appear to have ended here. Possibly, the remaining part of the sentence was inscribed below these symbols on the missing portion of the pillar. Horizontal lines are drawn, roughly parallel to one another, at an average distance of 6¼ inches, on three sides of the pillar; and in the spaces thus formed are written three or four lines of writing, according to the size of the letters which, on an average, are 1½ inches in height.

The script may be ascribed to the first half of the tenth century and shows forms more developed than in the record dealt with in the foregoing article. The writing is regular and uniform and there is nothing regarding it calling for special attention. As regards grammar, the only point to be noted is the form *munuburavun* in B l. 3 which may be compared with *munubuvan* in the Poḷonnaruva Council Chamber pillar-inscription. This word is the genitive plural of *munu-*

[1] *A. S. I.* No. 659, see *C. J. Sc. G*, vol. ii, p. 211.

[2] *A. S. I.* No. 660, see *C. J. Sc. G*, vol. ii, p. 211. The two records were copied, for the first time, by the writer in 1931.

buru and the regular form would be *munuburan* or *munuburuvan.* The word *nind* in C l. 4 has not been found in any other document of the period.

The record is **dated** in the ninth year of an unnamed king who was the elder brother or cousin (*bā*) of the heir-apparent (*mahapā*), also unnamed, by whom the edict was issued. Palaeographically, the epigraph ought to be assigned to a reign between Kassapa IV and Mahinda V and, in order to identify the monarch, we have to select a ruler of this period whose reign extended for nine years or more and whose *mahapā* was related to him as a younger brother or cousin. In this period, Kassapa V, Dappula V, Sena III, Mahinda IV and Sena V, had reigns extending to nine years or more. In the reign of Kassapa V, the *mahapā* was Dappula whose relationship to the former is not stated. But I have elsewhere[1] shown that Dappula could possibly have been a son of Udaya I; and, if this be correct, he was a younger cousin of Kassapa V, and could have referred to the latter as *bā*. In the reign of Dappula V, the heir-apparent was Udaya (III) who, it is certain, was not the former's younger brother or cousin[2]. In Sena III's reign, the *mahapā* was Udaya (II) who, from the Velmilla inscription[3], is known to have been a son of Kassapa IV. If the statement in the *Pūjāvalī* that Sena III was a brother of Udaya II and if the parentage of the latter suggested by me in *E. Z.* III, p. 141, be accepted, these two princes were not related in the manner given by the present record. Mahinda IV, who had a son of his as the heir-apparent, is out of the question. Sena V had a younger brother of his own as *mahapā*. Thus, our epigraph may belong to **Kassapa V** or **Sena V**. We are unable, at present, to be more exact; but the earlier monarch appears to be the likelier candidate.

The **object** of the record was to register the gift of a land, the name of which is not preserved, to a person named **Niligalu Bud,** and the immunities granted thereto. In style, the document closely resembles the Poḷonnaruva Council Chamber pillar-inscription, many words and phrases being peculiar to both. Of the officers instrumental in proclaiming the edict, the name is preserved of one only and he is not known to us from other documents.

---

[1] *E. Z.*, Vol. III, p. 142.

[2] See the Puliyaṉkuḷam slab-inscription (*E. Z.*, Vol. I, pp. 182–190) and *E. Z.*, Vol. III, pp. 141–142.

[3] *E. Z.*, Vol. III, p. 296.

TEXT.

A.

1 .. ..
2 ම .. ..
3 .. ..
4 ත් .. ..
5 .. .. ක
6 න් ඉසා වෙ
7 ල්වැස්ස
8 න් ඉසා රට්
9 ලදුවන් ඉ
10 සා කුලත්ස
11 ම්අරුබ් පිට
12 ස්සමුත් ඉ
13 සා සෙපු
14 රද්කොල්කැ
15 මියන් ඉසා
16 අරියිය පු
17 තු පුනපුනා [॥*]
18 තොප රට්හි
19 ආවූ සතර්
20 සෙණක්
.. ..

B.

1 **ලිගලු බුද්**
2 නුමා ඉසා මෙ
3 කු දරුමුනුබු
4 රවුන් ඉසා ප
5 රපුරෙන් නො
6 තොරා වලඤ
.. ..

C.

1 කොට් ඉසා
2 මෙ ගැම්හි ගෙ
3 ල්කුලි දෙමෙ
4 ල්කුලි නිඤ්
5 කොට් ඉසා
6 මෙ ගම්ට් මඟ්
7 යිව පෙහිව
8 මෙලාට්සින්
9 රද්කොල්කැ
10 මියන් නො ව
11 දනා කොට්
12 ඉසා සෙපු
13 ගැම්හි කැ
14 බැලි ගනුත්
15 මෙ ගැම්හි
16 කැබැලි නො
17 ගන්නා කොට්
18 ඉසා බැවත්
19 හිමියන් වහ
20 න්සෙ නවවන
21 හවුරුදුයෙහි
22 මහපාණන්
23 වහන්සෙ ව
.. ..

D.

1 වර කුඩසලා
2 එරා ඉසා මෙනු
3 වක් දෙනමො
4 එක්සෙ වැ ණි
5 **ලිගලු බුද්** හට් මෙ
.. ..

Vihāregama Pillar Inscription

Scale about ⅞ inch to 1 foot

Māda-Uḷpota Pillar-Inscription

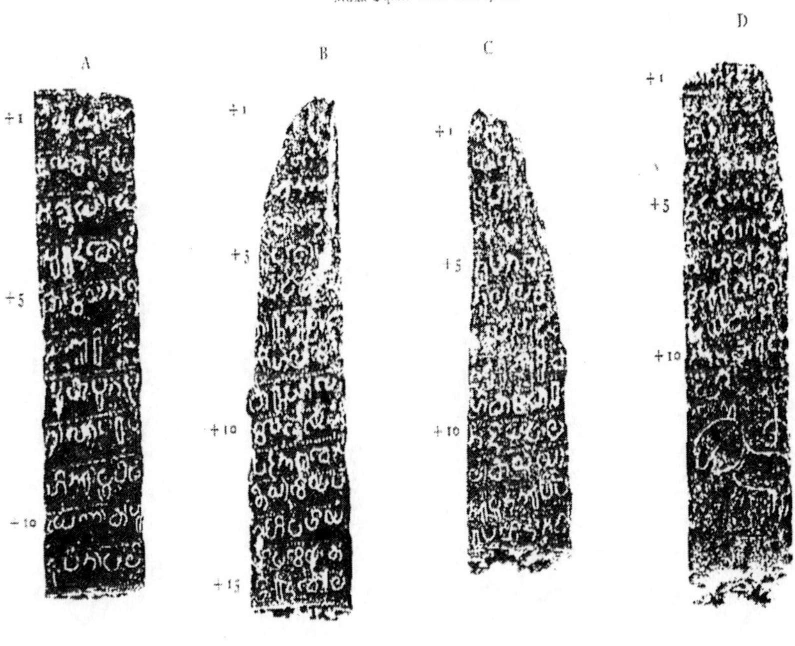

Scale about 1⅞ inches to 1 foot

TRANSCRIPT.

A.

1 .. ..
2 ma .. ..
3 .. . .
4 n .. ..
5 .. .. ka-
6 -n isā ve-
7 -ḷ-vässa-
8 -n isā raṭ-
9 laduvan i-
10 -sā kuḷat-sa-
11 -m-arub piṭa-
12 -ssamun i-
13 -sā sesu-
14 -radkol-kä-
15 -miyan isā
16 arigiya yu-
17 -tu punapunā [ı*]
18 Topa raṭ-hi
19 ävū satar-
20 seṇāk
.. ..

B.

1 -**ligalu Bud**
2 tumā isā me-
3 -ku daru-munubu-
4 -ravun isā pa-
5 -rapuren no-
6 torā vaḷandā
.. ..

C.

1 koṭ isā
2 me gämhi he-
3 -ḷ-kulī deme-
4 -ḷ-kulī nind
5 koṭ isā
6 me gamaṭ maṅg-
7 giva pegiva
8 melāṭsin
9 rad-kol-kä-
10 -miyan no-va-
11 -danā koṭ
12 isā sesu-
13 gämhi kä-
14 -bäli ganut
15 me gämhi
16 käbäli no-
17 gannā koṭ
18 isā bā-vat-
19 himiyan vaha-
20 -nse navavana
21 havurudyehi
22 mahapāṇan
23 vahanse va
.. ..

D.

1 vara **Kuḍasalā**
2 **Erā** isā metu-
3 -vāk denamo
4 ekse vä **Ni-**
5 -**ligalu Bud**-haṭ me
.. ..

TRANSLATION.

. . . . by the *vel-vässan*[1], and the governors of districts[2] and the *kuḷat-sam-arub*, the *piṭassam-arub*[3] and the other officers of the royal household, this should be protected again and again . . . . . . which is in your districts and which comprises of four *seṇās*[4] of . . . . His Worship **Niligalu Bud**[5] and his children and grandchildren should enjoy (this) in their lineage without interruption . . . . and having . . . . and having made the *heḷ-kulī* and *demeḷ-kulī*[6] proprietary[7] (to this estate itself) and having made the *maṅg-giva, piya-giva,*[8] *meläṭsi*[9] and other officers of the royal household not to enter this estate and having made the *käbäli*[10] to be not levied from this estate[11] even if *käbäli* be levied from other estates, as it was ordered by His Highness, the *mahapā*, in the ninth year of His Majesty, the King, his elder brother[12] . . . . the aforesaid persons including . . . . and **Kuḍasalā Erā**, having come together, to **Niligalu Bud**, this . . . .

No. 7. MÄDA-ULPOTA PILLAR-INSCRIPTION.

By S. Paranavitana.

ABOUT three years ago, the lower portion of an inscribed pillar was unearthed in the paddy field at Mäda-Ulpota, an abandoned village in the Gaṅgala Uḍasiya Pattuva of the Mātaḷē District. It now stands in a *chena* adjoining the field and the inscription on it was copied by the present writer in July, 1932. Without taking into account the base of the pillar, which was buried below the

[1] By this term is meant, most probably, a class of agricultural officers. It also occurs in the Buddhannehäla pillar inscription, *E.Z.*, Vol. I, p. 197.

[2] *Raṭ-laduvan*, see *E.Z.*, Vol. III, p. 111.

[3] For these two terms, see above, p. 43, n. 6.

[4] See *E.Z.*, Vol. III, p. 143.

[5] P. *Nīlagalla Buddha*.

[6] These two terms occur also in the Īripinniyāva pillar-inscription (*E. Z.*, Vol. I, p. 168). Two kinds of imposts levied respectively on the Sinhalese and Tamil inhabitants of the country are probably to be understood by these two technical terms.

[7] *Nind*:—This is undoubtedly the earlier form of *ninda* in the modern word *ninda-gama*. In the Kandyan land tenure system, a *ninda* village or field was one held in exclusive possession. The word *nind* is probably derived from Skt. *nija* 'one's own', cf. the Bengali *nij*, a word which denotes the demesne lands of a landlord (*J.R.A.S.* for 1929, p. 90).

[8] For these two terms, see *E. Z.*, Vol. III, p. 146.

[9] See *E. Z.*, Vol. III, p. 110.

[10] *Ibid.*, p. 277, n. 9.

[11] For the interpretation of *gam* as 'estate', see *E. Z.*, Vol. III, p. 276, n. 1.

[12] The word *bä* may also mean an elder paternal cousin.

ground, the preserved portion measures $8\frac{1}{2}$ in. square by 3 ft. in height. Sides A and D have each eleven lines of writing preserved, side B fifteen and C thirteen. The figure of a dog is engraved below the last line on side D.

The writing is between parallel lines three inches apart from one another. The **letters** average $1\frac{1}{2}$ in. in size. Lines + 1 to + 7 of side B and + 1 and + 2 of side C are wholly or partly illegible; the rest of the writing on this fragment is fairly well preserved. The **script** may be assigned to the first half of the tenth, or the closing decades of the ninth, century. It shows more developed forms than the script of the Poḷonnaruva Council Chamber pillar-inscription; but the two records cannot be separated from each other by a considerable number of years, as Diyavälla Kasbā figures in both in the same capacity.

The name of the king in whose reign the document was **dated** has not been preserved. The **object** of the epigraph was the grant of immunities to a land which was situated in a village called **Panāväli** and which, apparently, was set apart for the benefit of the servitors at the Council Hall (*attaṇi-hala*). Owing to the fragmentary nature of the record, we are not in a position to ascertain further details regarding the grant.

In **style**, the document resembles the Poḷonnaruva Council Chamber pillar-inscription and it enables us to settle one or two doubtful points in the reading of that record. Therefore, this fragment is published here though not of much interest in itself.

TEXT[1].

A.

+ 1 ටස්සම්අ
+ 2 රැඹිකැමිය
+ 3 ග් ඉසා සෙ
+ 4 සු රද්කොල්
+ 5 කැමියන් ඉ
+ 6 සා අරිගිය
+ 7 යුතු පුනපු
+ 8 නා[॥*] තොප රට
+ 9 ගි ආවු එක්
+ 10 සෙණක් හු
+ 11 **ලූ පනාවැලි**

B.

+ 1 .. ..
+ 2 .. ..
+ 3 .. .. (ගත්නා)
+ 4 .. කොට දෙ .. ..
+ 5 .. ට තො .. ..
+ 6 ට වැ (ම)
+ 7 .. රු අත්(නා)
+ 8 ණීහල මෙහෙ
+ 9 කරැවත් බ
+ 10 ඹබදෙයෙන්
+ 11 වළඤනු කොට
+ 12 ඉසා මෙයට
+ 13 මගිව පිය
+ 14 ගිව මෙලාත්
+ 15 නි රද්කොල්

[1] See Plate 6, facing p. 52.

C.

+ 1 .. ..
+ 2 .. ..
+ 3 ටි පමණු [ව]
+ 4 න සෙය් [මිපල්]
+ 5 නුවනක් [දෙ]
+ 6 නු ලබම්[හ]
+ 7 අපියැන් [මෙ]
+ 8 අරක් මුක්
+ 9 ගිකම් කර
+ 10 න දිශවැල්
+ 11 ලැ කස්බා
+ 12 අවුද් අප පු
+ 13 රටිගි දුන්මි

D.

+ 1 සඳ් පුන්ම
+ 2 ස්ගි දසප
+ 3 ක් දවස් ව
+ 4 දළම්හ [॥*] මෙ
+ 5 දවස් පිටි
+ 6 ත් මෙකුන් වැදූ
+ 7 සගත් කු
+ 8 ඹුර්(ගි) නො
+ 9 .. .. තැන්
+ 10 (ක)ම් කරව
+ 11 පි [॥*]

TRANSCRIPT.

A.

+ 1 -ṭassam-a-
+ 2 -rub-kämiya-
+ 3 -n isā se-
+ 4 -su-rad-kol-
+ 5 kämiyan i-
+ 6 -sā arigiya
+ 7 yutu punapu-
+ 8 -nā[॥*] Topa raṭ-
+ 9 -hi āvū ek-
+ 10 seṇāk hu-
+ 11 -lu **Panāväli**

B.

+ 1 .. ..
+ 2 .. ..
+ 3 .. (gannā)
+ 4 .. koṭ de .. ..
+ 5 .. ṭ to .. ..
+ 6 -ṭ vä (ma)
+ 7 .. ru at(tā)-
+ 8 -ṇi-hala mehe-
+ 9 karuvan ba-
+ 10 -mbadeyen
+ 11 vaḷandanu koṭ
+ 12 isā meyaṭ
+ 13 maṅgiva piya-
+ 14 giva melāt-
+ 15 -ti rad-kol-

C.

+ 1 .. ..
+ 2 .. ..
+ 3 -ṭ pamaṇu [va-]
+ 4 -na sey [mipal]
+ 5 nuvanak [de-]
+ 6 -nu [1] labam[ha]
+ 7 aṭiyän [me]
+ 8 arak muk-
+ 9 -hi-kam kara-
+ 10 -na **Diyaväl-**
+ 11 **-lä Kasbā**
+ 12 avud apa pu-
+ 13 -raṭ-hi dänvi-

D.

+ 1 sand pun-ma-
+ 2 -shi dasapa-
+ 3 -k davas va-
+ 4 -dāḷamha [|*] Me
+ 5 davas piṭi-
+ 6 -n mekun vädä [2]
+ 7 sagat ku-
+ 8 -mbur(hi) no
+ 9 .. .. tän
+ 10 (ka)m karava-
+ 11 -yi [3] [|*]

TRANSLATION.

. . . . by the officers called [*pi*]*ṭassam-arub* [4] and by the other officers of the royal household, [this] should be protected again and again. [The village] **Panāväli** which is in your district and which comprises of one *seṇā* [5] of *hulu* [6] . . . . should be enjoyed, unreservedly [7], by the survitors at the Council Hall [8]. To this [estate], *maṅgiva, piyagiva* [9], *melāṭsi* [10] and the other

---

[1] The Poḷonnaruva Council Chamber pillar-inscription has *devanu labamha* in place of *denu labamha* of this record. See above, p. 40.

[2] The Poḷonnaruva inscription has *mekhu tänä minisun vädä.*

[3] With ll. D+4–11 of this pillar, compare ll. D 23–28 of the Poḷonnaruva record. It is a pity that this particular passage in both these epigraphs is not well preserved and a correct reading of it is, therefore, not possible.

[4] See above, p. 43, n. 6.

[5] See *E.Z.*, Vol. III, p. 143.

[6] *Ibid.*, Vol. III, p. 143.

[7] *Bambadeyen* :—For the explanation of this word, see below, p. 67, n. 5.

[8] *Attāṇi-hala* is probably derived from Skt. *āsthāna-śālā.* This compound, which has not been met with before, seems to support Dr. Wickremasinghe's suggestion (*E.Z.*, Vol. I, p. 161, n. 8) that *attāṇi* in the oft-recurring word *attāṇi-pärahär*, in the mediaeval Sinhalese inscriptions, means 'assembly' or 'council'. See below, p. 66, n. 3.

[9] For these two terms, see *E.Z.*, Vol. III, p. 146.

[10] See *E.Z.*, Vol. III, p. 110.

officers of the royal household are not to enter . . . . With the desire that we shall be noticed by kings, so that this estate may become a *pamaṇu* and as **Diyävalla Kasbā** who performs the office of *muk-hi* came and notified in our presence[1] . . . . we ordered . . . . . on the tenth day of the bright half of the month of . . . . . . After[2] this day, the field . . . .[3] this person having entered . . . .[4]

---

[1] Ll. C+3–13 of this record are identical with ll. C 23–D 5 of the Poḷonnaruva Council Chamber pillar-inscription. Compare the translation and notes relating to this part of that record.

[2] *Pitin* :—See above, p. 46, n. 5.

[3] The meaning of the word *sagat* occurring after *kumbur* in l. D+7 is not quite clear.

[4] For the passage occurring in ll. D+4–11, compare above, p. 46, n. 6.

No. 8. POLONNARUVA PILLAR-INSCRIPTION OF MAHINDA V

By S. Paranavitana.

THIS pillar was discovered at the eastern porch of the Quadrangle at Polonnaruva and is now preserved in the Archaeological Museum at Anurādhapura. Its base and its capital are both missing and it seems to have been utilized as a lintel, for on one side are two square mortice holes, which were obviously intended for fitting it to the two door-jambs. Its present dimensions are 8 in. by 7 in. by 5 ft. in height.

The epigraph, which covers all the four faces of the pillar, has been included as No. 42 in the list of inscriptions, copied between 1901 and 1905, appended to the *Annual Report of the Archaeological Survey of Ceylon* for 1905 (p. 40). An eye-copy of it, prepared under the supervision of Mr. Bell, is also preserved in the Office of the Archaeological Commissioner. I edit the epigraph from the original stone.

The **letters**, which are very shallowly incised between parallel lines, each $1\frac{7}{8}$ in. apart from one another, are, on an average, an inch in height. Owing to the rough treatment that the pillar has undergone, the writing is in a very bad state of preservation. Excepting some letters in lines 16–19, side A is fairly well preserved; and, on the second face, lines 2 and 6 are partly, and lines 18–20 completely, illegible. The third face has been badly damaged in cutting the two mortice holes; and of this side, lines 7–28 are almost completely obliterated. The fourth side is also considerably worn, but the writing can be deciphered without much difficulty. Sides A and B each contain 32 lines of writing. How many lines there were on side C cannot be definitely ascertained, though it may be conjectured that it also had the same number as sides A and B. Side D has nine lines of writing and the figures of the sun, the moon, a monk's fan, a scythe, a crow and a dog.

The script is Sinhalese of the tenth century and agrees, almost in every detail, with that of the inscriptions of Mahinda IV[1]. The introductory part of the document is written in a very florid style. Some of the phrases used here are also found in a fragmentary inscription, from Raṇava in the Nuvarakalāviya District,

[1] See the Mihintaḷē Tablets (*E. Z.*, Vol. I, plates 14 and 15) and the slab-inscription near the Stone Canoe at Anurādhapura (*E. Z.*, Vol. I, plate 16).

belonging to the reign of a king named Abhā Salamevan, who, from the form of the script employed, may be identified with Dappula V or Kassapa V[1]. As regards **orthography** and **grammar,** the present document is in keeping with the standard of the period; nevertheless, attention may be drawn to the following words:—*Vuṭunu* (Skt. *veṣṭana*), in A ll. 7-8, is generally found in literature as *voṭunu*; the forms *vuṭun* and *vuṭunä* (locative singular), however, are found in the 'Jetavanārāma' Slab inscription (No. 1) attributed to Mahinda IV[2]. For *väḷän* in A l. 9, see my remarks on this word in the Kataragama pillar inscription[3]. As regards the instrumental singular termination in this word, the form *pähän*, occurring in the phrase *sivipähän vana-aturu hobavamin*, in the *Dharmmapradīpikā*[4], may be compared. *Pīmen* in A l. 10 is the instrumental singular of *pīm* which is a variant form of *piyum* (Skt. *padma*) found in the standard Sinhalese dialect. The form occurring in our record, though earlier in date, shows more advanced phonetic decay, than *piyum*. *Äsäḷä* in A ll. 25–26 is found more commonly in the form of *Äseḷä*.

The record is **dated** in the second year of a king styled **Sirisaṅgbo** who has been identified by Mr. Bell with **Mahinda IV** (954–970 A.D.)[5]; but from the names of the parents of this king given in the epigraph, the identification becomes untenable. The mother of Sirisaṅgbo of the present record is called **Saṅgā-räjna** and his father is said to have been **Mihind-maha[rad]**. The reading *maha-radun* in the name of Sirisaṅgbo's father is, of course, conjectural, the last three *akṣaras* being too much weathered to be deciphered with certainty. The only other possible reading to be substituted for *maha-radun* is *maha-pāṇan*; but, if we adopt this reading, we cannot reconcile the data gathered from this record with other well-established facts. During the tenth century, to which this record should be ascribed on palaeographical grounds, there was only one king, with the throne name of Sirisaṅgbo, whose father was a prince named Mihind Mahayā (or Mahapā). This was Udaya II[6]; but his mother was named Kitā-räjna, whereas the mother of the Sirisaṅgbo of this record was Saṅgā. The two cannot, therefore, be considered identical. Thus we have to reject the possible

---

[1] This inscription is yet unpublished. See *A.S.C. Annual Report* for 1895, p. 9.

[2] *E. Z.*, Vol. I, pp. 222 and 223.

[3] See *E. Z.*, Vol. III, p. 220.

[4] Colombo Edition of 1915, p. 273.

[5] *A.S.C. Annual Report* for 1905, p. 40.

[6] *E. Z.*, Vol. I, p. 183. Udaya III, who was also a Sirisaṅgbo, has been taken by Dr. Wickremasinghe to be a son of Mihind Mahayā (see *E. Z.*, Vol. III, p. 20). But see the Velmilla inscription, *E. Z.*, Vol. III, pp. 294–302.

alternative reading *mahapāṇan* and adopt the reading *maharadun*. The only monarch named Mihind (Mahinda) who could have been a father of a tenth-century king was the fourth of that name. Mahinda III flourished towards the end of the eighth century and a son of his is, therefore, out of consideration. Two sons of Mahinda IV, namely, Sena V (971–981 A.D.) and Mahinda V (981–1017 A.D.), reigned after him; but the first mentioned was a Salamevan[1] and cannot, therefore, be identified with the Sirisaṅgbo of this record. Hence, it is only with **Mahinda V,** who, from the order of succession, was entitled to the *viruda* name **of** Sirisaṅgbo, that the author of the present epigraph can be identified.

As regards Saṅgārājna, the mother of Sirisaṅgbo (Mahinda V) and wife of Mihindmaharad (Mahinda IV), it may be stated that, according to the *Mahavaṁsa*, Mahinda IV espoused a princess of the **Kāliṅga** royal family; and by her he had two sons[2], one of whom, according to the explicit statement of the chronicle[3], was Sena V. The *Mahāvaṁsa* does not give the name of the other son of the Kāliṅga princess, nor does it state who the mother of the third son of Mahinda was. Dr. Wickremasinghe assumes that prince Udaya, who was the *yuvarāja* of Sena V, but, for some unknown reason, did not succeed him on the throne, was the second son of Mahinda IV from the Kāliṅga princess, and that Mahinda V was a son of a princess Kitti, another consort of Mahinda IV[4]. Mr. John Still, on the other hand, takes Kitti to be the same as the Kāliṅga princess and assumes that she was the mother of all the known children of Mahinda IV[5]. Prof. Geiger seems to be of the same opinion as Mr. Still[6]. From this inscription, it becomes clear that the mother of Mahinda V was not Kitti; but we cannot be quite certain whether Saṅgā was the same as the Kāliṅga princess or was a wife of Mahinda IV not mentioned in the chronicles. If A l. 18 of this record has been correctly read, Mahinda V claims to belong to the Kāliṅga stock; and as none of his ancestors professes to belong to this royal family, we may conjecture that it was through his mother that he traced his descent from the Kāliṅga lineage[7]. If so, Saṅgā, the mother of Mahinda V, may be considered the same as the Kāliṅga princess whom Mahinda IV espoused. And as it is

---

[1] See *Cūḷavaṁsa*, English translation, Pt. I, p. 185, n. 5.

[2] *Mhv.* liv. 9–11.

[3] *Ibid.*, v. 57.

[4] See Genealogical Tree facing p. 59 of *E. Z.*, Vol. II.

[5] *Index to the Mahāvaṁsa*, Genealogical Tree No. 5.

[6] *Cūḷavaṁsa*, English translation, Pt. I, p. 356.

[7] For the custom of sons being regarded as of the same stock as that of their mothers, see *C. J. Sc. (G.)*, vol. ii, pp. 235–240.

expressly stated that this princess bore only two sons, one of whom was Sena V, and as the second son can reasonably be identified with Mahinda V, prince Udaya, the third son of Mahinda IV, must have been born of Kitti or some other princess not mentioned in the chronicles.

In contrast to the fulsome eulogies bestowed on Mahinda V in the present epigraph, he appears from the chronicles to have been a weak and incapable ruler. A certain tragic interest attaches to his name as the last of the long line of Anurādhapura kings. In the thirty-sixth year of his inglorious reign, the armies of the great Coḷa king Rājarāja swept over his kindgdom; he himself with his queen and his treasures fell into the invader's hands and had to pay the penalty of his inefficient rule by ending his days as a captive at the Coḷa court[1].

The epigraph is a grant of immunities to land in the village of **Muhundnaru,** in the Eastern Quarter, belonging to a *pirivena*, of which the name is obliterated, in the monastery called **Mahamevnā Tisaram.** The names of the officers who were instrumental in promulgating this edict cannot all be made out. **Vaṭrak Kasbā Äraksamaṇa,** the name of one of the *ājñaptis*, also occurs in the Äṭavīragollāva Pillar-Inscription attributed to Dappula V[2]; but it is doubtful whether both inscriptions refer to the same person, for the Äṭavīragollāva pillar is fifty-three years earlier in date than the present epigraph.

TEXT.

A.

1 [සි]රිබර්කැන්කු
2 ලකොත් ඔකාවස්
3 පරදූරෙන් බ[ට
4 ල]ත්දිවිපොළොයො
5 න් පරපුරෙන් ශ්‍රී
6 මිවූ නාගදෙවුදෙ
7 විබම්බූන් වුටු
8 නුමැණමෙ බමර
9 වැළැත් හෙති සර
10 ණපිමෙන් ලකුළු
11 [ෙ]ලාපිළිසරණමු
12 නිකුනිපත් සැහැ
13 කුලකෙව්ලු සූදෙ
14 නාපරදූරෙන් ආ
15 ලත්නිරඤ්කිරි[ළ්]
16 කුළ්ගි තෙද්ගිනි
17 න් දූවි පවර් ..
18 .. කා[ලිඟු]කුලකෙ[ා
19 න්] මිහින්මහ[ර
20 දුන්] වහන්[සෙ
21 ට] සහාරජ්න
22 කුසැ දුනු පිහිස
23 ග්බොමහරජ්හු
24 සත් ලැඟු දෙවන

---

[1] See *Mhv.*, chap. lv.

[2] *E.Z.*, Vol. II, p. 48.

25 හවුරුදුයෙහි ඈ
26 සැළැ අව අටව
27 ක් දවස් වැඳැ වද,
28 ළ එක්තැන්සම්යෙ
29 ත් අන්තාණිකාඤු
30 ගිඤ්වත්නටි නි
31 ල්ගොන්නා අග්
32 බොනාවන් වරැ [ව]

B.

1 න මෛකාප්පර්
2 මහ .. ..
3 ඉසා දම්ගමු
4 ඕවිම් ඉසා ම
5 හකිලිගම් නි
6 .. .. ම් ඉසා මූ
7 වරක් කස්[බා]
8 අරක්සමණ
9 න් වරැ කුඩිස
10 ලා මහතැම් ස
11 ග්ගඩි ඉසා [මෙ]
12 නුවක් දෙනමො
13 වැදූ වජාළ එක්
14 තැන්සම්යෙන්
15 මහමෙවිනා [නි]
16 සර[ම්] රජ්[ම
17 ග]වෙහෙරගි ..
18 .. ..
19 .. ..
20 .. .. [ප]
21 රිවෙත්ගි .. ..
22 පැදුම්පස්හි
23 මුහුඥ්නරැ[වෙන්]
24 බහාලු පස්ප
25 යලැ සතර්සී
26 මායෙන් ඇතුළ්
27 [පූ]තාන් තැ[න]ට
28 [ම]හ්[ග]ව් ප[ය]ගි
29 ව් නොවද්නා ඉ
30 සා මෙලා[ට]ඩි ර
31 [ද්කොල්]කැ[මිය
32 න් නොවද්නා] ඉසා

C.

1 වැරි පෙරෙනාටටි
2 යම් නොවද[නා*] ඉසා
3 දෙරුවනැ දෙකම්
4 තැන් නොවද්නා ඉ
5 සා ගැල්ගොන් මිවූ
6 න් නොගන්නා ඉසා
7–28 * * * * * *
29 [කිලිග්ගම්] .. ..
30 දෙවිම් ඉසා [වම]
31 රක් කස්බා [අ]ර
32 ක්සමණන් වරැ

D.

1 [කුඩි]සලා සඟ්
2 [හය් ඇතුළ] මෙ
3 නුවාක් දෙනමො
4 [වැඳැ] වදාළ එ
5 ක්තැන්සම්යෙ
6 න් මෙ අත්තාණි
7 කාඤු පෙරැගැ
8 ර් බමබදෙ[යෙ]
9 න් දු[න්]මහයි [॥*]

TRANSCRIPT.

A.

1 [Si]ribar-kät-ku-
2 -la-kot Okāvas-
3 parapuren ba[ṭa
4 La]kdiv-poḷo-yo-
5 -n parapuren hi-
6 -mi-vū nā-gadevu-de-
7 -vi-bambun vuṭu-
8 -nu-mäṇa-me bamara-
9 väḷän hebi sara-
10 -ṇa-pīmen lakuḷu
11 lo-piḷisaraṇa-mu-
12 -nindun=ipat Sähä-
13 kula-kevlu Sudo-
14 -nā-parapuren ā
15 Lak-nirind-kiri[ḷ]-
16 kuḷhi ted-gini-
17 -n dävi pavar ..
18 .. **Ka**[**liṅgu**]**-kula**-k[o-
19 -t] **Mihind-maha**[**ra-**
20 **-dun**] vahan[se-
21 -ṭa] **Saṅgā-räjna**
22 kusä dunu **Sirisa-**
23 **-ṅgbo**-maharaj-hu
24 sat läṅgu devana
25 havuruduyehi **Ä-**
26 **-säḷä** ava aṭava-
27 -k davas vändä vadā-
28 -ḷa ek-tän-samiye-
29 -n attāṇi-kaṇu
30 hindvannaṭ **Ni-**
31 **-lgonnā Ag-**
32 **-bonāvan** varä [va]-

B.

1 -na Mekāppar
2 **Maha** .. ..
3 isā **Damgamu**
4 **Sivim** isā **Ma-**
5 **-hakiliṅgam Ni-**
6 .. .. **m** isā **Va-**
7 **-ṭrak Kas**[**bā**]
8 **Araksamaṇa-**
9 **-n** varä **Kuḍsa-**
10 **-lā-vatkāmi Sa-**
11 **-ṅghayi** isā [m]e-
12 -tuvak denamo
13 vädā vajāḷa ek-
14 tän-samiyen
15 **Mahamevnā** [**Ti**]-
16 **-sara**[**m**] raj-[ma-
17 -ha]-veherhi ..
18 .. ..
19 .. ..
20 .. .. [p]i-
21 -rivenhi .. ..
22 pädum-pas-hi
23 **Muh**[**u**]**ndnaru**[ven]
24 bahālū pas-pa-
25 -yalä satar-sī-
26 -māyen ätuḷ-
27 [vū]tāk tä[na]ṭ
28 [ma]ng-[gi]v pi[ya]-gi-
29 -v no-vadnā i-
30 -sā melā[ṭ]si ra-
31 -[d-kol]-kä[miya-
32 -n no-vadnā] isā

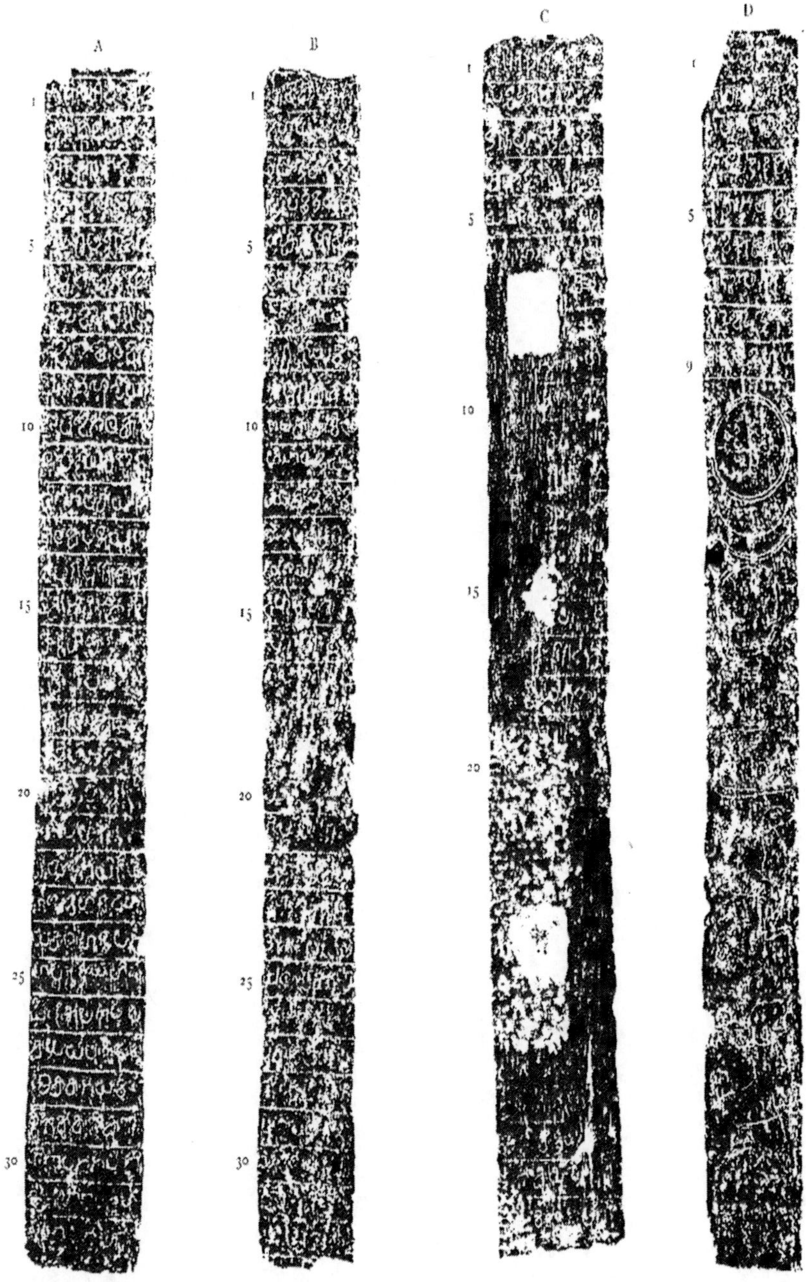

Scale about 1¾ inches to 1 foot

C.

1 väri perenāṭṭi-
2 -yam no-vad [nā*] isā
3 deruvanā dekam-
4 tän no-vadnā i-
5 -sā gäl-gon mivu-
6 -n no-gannā isā
7–28 *Illegible*
29 **[Kiliṅg-gam]** .. ..
30 **Devim** isā [**Vaṭ**]-
31 **rak Kasbā** [**A**]**ra-**
32 **-ksamaṇan** varä

D.

1 [**Kuḍ**]**salā Saṅg-**
2 -[**hay** ätuḷu] me-
3 -tuvāk denamo
4 [vändä] vadāḷa e-
5 -k-tän-samiye-
6 -n me attaṇi-
7 kaṇu perähä-
8 -r bamba-de[ye]-
9 -n du[n]mahayi[u*]

TRANSLATION.

[Lines A 1-27]. On the eighth day of the waxing moon in the month of **Äsäḷ**[1] in the second year after the raising of the umbrella [of dominion] by the great king **Sirisaṅgbo**[2] who is descended from the lineage of Okāvas[3], the pinnacle of the very illustrious *kṣatriya* race; who is, by[right of] descent, the lord of the young damsel, the land of Lakdiv[4]; who has come in succession from Sudonā[5], the banner of the Sähä[6] race in which was born the Chief of the Sages[7], the Refuge of the World, who is adorned with [a pair of] lotuses, which are his two feet, made beauteous by swarms of bees, which are the jewels on the diadems of *nāgas*[8], *gandharvas*[8], gods and *brahmas*[8]; who, by the fire of his majesty caused burning on mountain peaks which are the crowns of the [other] kings of Laṅkā[9]; who is the pinnacle of the **Kāliṅga** royal house; and who was born unto the great king **Mihind**[10] in the womb of queen **Saṅgā**[11].

---

[1] Skt. *Āṣāḍha*, June-July. [2] P. *Siri Saṅghabodhi*. [3] P. *Okkāka*, Skt. *Ikṣvāku*.

[4] P. *Laṅkādīpa*, Skt. *Laṅkādvīpa*, i.e. the island of Ceylon.

[5] P. *Suddhodana*. The name of the Buddha's father.

[6] P. *Sākya* or *Sakka*. Skt. *Śākya*.

[7] *Munindu* = Skt. *munindra*, P. *muninda*, a name of the Buddha.

[8] Different classes of supernatural beings.

[9] *Lak-nirind-kiriḷ-kuḷhi ted-ginin dävi*:—Though this phrase is not quite well preserved on the stone, the reading is beyond doubt as it is supported by a fragmentary pillar inscription from Bayava in the Dēvamädi Hatpattu of the Kuruṇägala District, the relevant part of which reads '*Sähä-kula-kevulu Sudonā-parapuren ā Lak-nirind-kiriḷ-kuḷhi ted-ginin dävi pavar Sirisaṅgbo rad-haṭ dā Saṅgā-räjna kusä dunu Abhā Salamevan maharad-hu.* But, though I have given the literal translation of this phrase, its appropriateness here is not quite obvious, and the metaphor used is unusual.

[10] P *Mahinda*. [11] P. *Saṅghā*.

[Lines A 27–C 6]. In accordance with the decree of unanimous assent[1] declared, after making salutations[2] [to the king], that an edictal pillar[3] should be set up, I, **Maha** . . . . . . and I, **Damgamu Siva** and I, **Mahakiliṅgam Ni** . . . . Members of the Bodyguard, [all] in the service of **Nilgonnā Agbonā**; and **Kuḍsalā-vatkämi Saṅghay,** in the service of **Vaṭrak Kasbā Araksamaṇa**—We all of us—in accordance with the decree of unanimous assent declared after making salutations [to the king, order] that in regard to all those lands included within the four boundaries of the five *payalas*[4] from **Muhundnaruva**[5] in the Eastern Quarter given to the . . . . . . *pirivena* in the great royal monastery of **Mahamevnā Tisaram**[6], [the said lands] are, not to be entered by *maṅggiv*[7] and *piyagiv*,[7] not to be entered by *melaṭsi*[8] and other officers of the royal

---

[1] *Ek-tän-samiyen*:—The exact meaning of this word still remains obscure. For this tentative rendering see *E.Z.*, Vol. III, p. 107.

[2] *Vändä vaḍāla*:—This phrase, which occurs thrice in the present record, is also found in the Mäḍirigiriya Pillar-Inscription of Kassapa V (*E. Z.*, Vol. II, p. 31), and the Bilibāva Pillar-Inscription of the same king (*E. Z.*, Vol. II, p. 42). It also occurs in the Aṁbagamuva Rock-Inscription of Vijayabāhu I as *pā vändä ä*. From these phrases, it appears that when the officers delivered the royal order to the messengers, they bowed down to the king. For similar customs in Kandyan times, see *Pybus's Mission to Kandy*, Colombo, 1862, p. 58.

[3] The word *attäṇi-kaṇu* is of frequent occurrence in inscriptions of the ninth and tenth centuries. Dr. Wickremasinghe derives the word *attäṇi* from Skt. *āsthāna* 'assembly' or 'council' (*E. Z.*, Vol. I, p. 161, n. 8) and this seems to be supported by the phrase *attäṇi-hala mehekaruvan* occurring in a fragmentary inscription at Mäda Ulpota (see above, p. 56). The word *attäṇi* also occurs frequently in the compound *attäṇi-pärahär* 'immunities granted by the Council'. *Attäṇi-kaṇu* is probably a shortened form of *attäṇi-pärahär-kaṇu* 'the pillar (on which is written) the immunities granted by the Council'.

[4] The word *payala* is often found in inscriptions of this period. See Index to *E. Z.*, Vol. II, for references. It appears to have been a term of land measurement; but it is doubtful whether it is connected with the form *päla*.

[5] A fragmentary pillar of Sena I (see *E. Z.*, Vol. III, pp. 291–294) from Poḷonnaruva mentions a village named Muhundehigama which may perhaps be the same as Muhundnaru (P. *Samuddanagara*) of our inscription. A village named Muhunnaruggāma is mentioned in the *Mahāvaṁsa* (Ch. lviii v. 42); but as this was in the Southern Quarter, it was different from the village mentioned here.

[6] P. *Mahāmeghavana Tissārama*. This monastery is also mentioned in the 'Vessagiriya' slab inscription of Mahinda IV (*E. Z.*, Vol. I, p. 33). It appears to be another name of the well-known Mahāvihāra at Anurādhapura which was established by king Devānampiya Tissa in the garden named Mahāmeghavana. Dr. Wickremasinghe equates *mevnā* with *meghavaṇṇa*; but the latter assumes the form of *mevan* in mediaeval Sinhalese (cf. *Salamevan* for *Silāmeghavaṇṇa*) and the garden called Mahāmeghavana is referred to, in Sinhalese literature, as Mahamevnā (see *Pūjāvaliya*, Colombo, 1922, p. 666).

[7] See *E. Z.*, Vol. III, p. 146.

[8] See *E. Z.*, Vol. III, p. 110. The interpretation of *melāṭsi* and its variant forms suggested there is supported by the occurrence, in North-Indian inscriptions, of the word *uparikara* as the name of

household[1], not to be entered by *väri*[2] and *perenäṭṭiyam*[3], not to be entered by *deruväna*[4] and *dekamtän*[4]; that carts, oxen and buffaloes are not to be impressed.

. . . .

[Lines C 29–D 9]. We, all of us, [namely], ... I. **Kiliṅggam Devu** . . . . and **Kuḍsalā Saṅghay** in the service of **Vaṭrak Kasbā Araksamaṇa**, gave these immunities as a *brahmadeya*[5] gift in the form of an edictal pillar, in accordance with [the decree] of unanimous assent declared after saluting [the king].

No. 9. POḶONNARUVA: FRAGMENTARY SLAB-INSCRIPTION OF SUNDARA-MAHĀDEVĪ.

By S. PARANAVITANA.

NEAR the Royal Palace at Poḷonnaruva, there are the remains of a *maṇḍapa* which is built on a platform in three tiers faced with sculptured slabs of stone.[6] This edifice, which has been identified by Mr. A. M. Hocart with the Rājaveśyā-bhujaṅga-maṇḍapa, mentioned in the *Mahāvaṁsa* as built by Parākramabāhu I, was conserved by the Archaeological Department in 1931; and, in the course of the work, it was found that the builders of this structure had

some kind of impost. (See *Journal of the Bihar and Orissa Research Society*, vol. xvi, p. 78.) Skt. *uparikara* and Tamil *mēlāṭsi* are of the same meaning (*upari* = *mēl* 'above' and *kara* = *āṭsi* 'tax') and one may actually be a translation of the other.

[1] The compound *melāṭsi-radkol kämiyan* can also be translated as 'officers of the royal household called the *melāṭsi*'.

[2] See *E. Z.*, Vol. I, p. 53, n. 7. [3] See *E. Z.*, Vol. III, p. 144. [4] See *E. Z.*, Vol. III, p. 143.

[5] *Bambadeyen* or *bambadesen*:—See *E.Z.*, Vol. III, p. 191, n. 12. For the meaning of this word, which is the same as Pāli *brahmadeyya*, the following passages from Buddhaghosa's *Sumaṅgalavilāsinī*, the Commentary to the *Dīgha Nikāya*, will be helpful. *Brahmadeyyan ti seṭṭhadeyyaṁ, chattaṁ ussāpetvā rāja-saṁkhepe bhuñjitabban ti attho* (P.T.S. Edition, Part I, p. 246). 'A *brahmadeyya* is a most excellent gift; it means that (what is granted) should be enjoyed in royal manner having the umbrella (of possession) raised.' As an alternative explanation Buddhaghosa adds:—*Brahmadeyyan ti seṭṭhadeyyaṁ yathā dinnaṁ na puna gahetabbaṁ hoti nissaṭṭhaṁ pariccattaṁ evaṁ dinnaṁ ti attho.*' 'A *brahmadeyya* means an excellent gift; what is given is not to be taken back; it is given up and renounced; what is given in this manner is meant.' A *brahmadeyya* gift, according to this explanation, appears to be a gift over which the donor renounces any sort of future claim.

[6] For descriptions of this building see *A. S. C. Annual Report* for 1905, pp. 3-5; for 1930-31, pp. 7-8 and *A. S. C. Memoirs*, vol. ii, p. 3.

utilized several earlier inscribed stones for the steps, mouldings, and coping stones [1]. At the same time, evidence was found, which, while confirming Mr. Hocart's hypothesis concerning the identity of this edifice, also proves that it had been repaired, and its original design materially altered, at a later period, probably during the reign of Parākramabāhu II. It is therefore not certain whether these inscribed stones were used in the building when it was first constructed or when it was restored later. The fragmentary record which forms the subject of the present paper is inscribed on a slab used for the coping on the eastern side of the lowest of the three tiers of this platform.

The slab measures 5 ft. 1 in. by 2 ft.; and originally one face of it was inscribed all over and must have contained about 45 lines of writing. Only about one-sixth of the record, consisting of its first seven lines, is now preserved, the rest having been effaced, perhaps wilfully, when the slab was utilized for its present purpose. Even in the preserved portion, some letters of the first two lines are illegible, while lines 3-7 are fairly clear. The **letters**, which have been rather shallowly incised, are about ¾ in. in size. The **script** is of the twelfth century and contains nothing worthy of particular mention. The **orthography** calls for no remarks; and, as regards **grammar**, the gerund *kopā*, from the root *kup*, is noteworthy as it has not been found elsewhere.

The preserved part of the record is not enough to determine what its purport was. The first two lines contain a Pāli stanza eulogizing a *thera* named **Ānanda**; and the next five lines introduce us to **Sundaramahādevī**, the queen of **Vikramabāhu I** (1116-1137 A.D.) who was the son of **Vijayabāhu I** (1058-1164 A.D.). The only other epigraph mentioning this princess, who came from Kāliṅga, is the inscription in a cave at Diṁbulāgala in the Tamankaḍuva District [2]. The present record, so far as the preserved portion goes, does not contain anything which we do not already know about these rulers and the queen.

The *thera* named Ānanda, mentioned in the opening Pāli verse, is described as a great dignitary of the Buddhist Church in Ceylon. He is called 'a banner raised aloft in the land of Laṁkā' and is said to have had some connexion with the Buddhist Church of Tambaraṭṭha as well as that of the Coḷa country; but, as the full text of the verse in question cannot be made out, we cannot say precisely what this connexion was.

---

[1] A preliminary account of these inscriptions will be found in *C. J. Sc.* (*G.*), vol. ii, pp. 186 and 208-209.

[2] *E. Z.*, Vol. II, pp. 184-189 and 194-202.

Tambaraṭṭha was the country from which Parākramabāhu II, as stated in the *Mahavaṁsa* [1], invited a Buddhist monk of saintly character, named Dhammakitti. Professor Geiger is of opinion that this Tambaraṭṭha was a district of South India [2]; but there are facts which go against this identification. In Sinhalese writings, like the *Pūjāvalī* [3], the country from which the elder Dhammakitti came to Ceylon is called Tamaliṅgamu. The Sinhalese chronicles also state that Candrabhānu, the Jāvaka king who twice invaded Ceylon during the reign of Parākramabāhu II, and was on both occasions repelled, was a king of Tamaliṅgamu [4]. The Pāli chronicle *Hatthavanagalla-vihara-vaṁsa* [5], on the other hand, states that Candrabhānu's country was called Tambaliṅga (Skt. *Tāmraliṅga*). Therefore it is clear that the Sinhalese *Tamaliṅgamu* and the Pāli *Tambaraṭṭha* and *Tambaliṅga* were names of one and the same region. The country called Mādamaliṅgam, mentioned in the inscriptions of Rājendra Coḷa [6] as one of the territories which submitted to his arms, also appears to be the same as Tamaliṅgamu of the Sinhalese writings. *Mā* in the Tamil name means 'great', and is found prefixed to the names of countries and towns, as, for instance, in Mā-pappālam for Pappālam (Papphāla of the *Mahāvaṁsa*) [7]. In Rājendra-Coḷa's inscriptions, Mādamaliṅgam is mentioned along with the names of other countries in Indo-China and the Malay Peninsula, and its location must also be looked for in that area.

Now, Monsieur G. Coedés published in 1918 an inscription in incorrect Sanskrit, found at a place named Jaiya in the Malay Peninsula, and dated in the Kaliyuga year 4332 (1230 A.D.), of a king to whom the epithet Candrabhānu is given [8]. There is no doubt, as M. Coedés has shown [9], that Candrabhānu of the Jaiya inscription is the same as the Jāvaka king Candrabhānu who twice raided Ceylon in the reign of Parākramabāhu II. The date of the accession of Parā-

---

[1] Chap. lxxxiv, vv. 11–14. [2] *Cūḷavaṁsa*, text, part II, p. 606.

[3] The 34th chapter, edited by the Rev. Pandit Mābōpiṭiye Medhaṁkara, Colombo, 1932, p. 33.

[4] The Sinhalese *Attanagaluvaṁsa*, Colombo edition of 1925, p. 47; and *Daṁbadeṇi Asna*, Colombo edition of 1917, p. 3.

[5] English translation by James de Alwis, Colombo, 1866, p. 128

[6] *South Indian Inscriptions*, vol. ii, p. 109.

[7] *Ibid.*, vol. iii, Introduction, p. 21, and *Mv.* lxxvi. 63.

[8] *Bulletin de l'École française d'Extrême-Orient*, tome XVIII, pp. 15 ff.

[9] See Monsieur Coedés's paper 'A propos de la chute du royaume de Çrīvijaya' in *Bijdragen tot de Taal-Land-en Volkenkunde van Nederlandsch-Indie*, Deel 83, pp. 459-472.

kramabāhu II is 1234 A.D.[1], and he and Candrabhānu of the Jaiya inscription were therefore contemporaries. This epigraph tells us that Candrabhānu was the king of Śrī Dharmmarāja (Nagara Śrī Dharmmarāja, the modern Nakhon Si Thammarat or Ligor) and also gives him the epithet of Tāmbraliṅgeśvara (the lord of Tāmbraliṅga). It thus proves that *Tāmbraliṅga* (P. *Tambaliṅga*) was another name for Nagara Śri Dharmmarāja, the modern Ligor. And, as we have shown above that the names *Tambaraṭṭha* and *Tambaliṅga* in Pāli were applied to the same country, Tambaraṭṭha must be identified with Ligor.

Professor Sylvain Lévi, in his paper *Ptolémée, le Niddesa et la Bṛhatkathā*[2], has pointed out that Tamali, which occurs in a stereotyped list of geographical names in the *Mahāniddesa*, is the same as Tambaliṅga; and has identified it with Ligor. Nagara Śri Dharmmarāja, in the vernacular language of the country, is called Nakhon Si Thammarat; and it appears that *Tambaraṭṭha* of the *Mahāvaṁsa* is nothing but the vernacular form 'Thammarat' in a Pāli garb.

The country with which Tambaraṭṭha can thus be identified, namely, the modern Ligor or Nakhon Si Thammarat, and which was known in ancient days as Srī Dharmarāja Nagara, was a centre of Indian culture from the early centuries of the Christian era, and at the time of this record, Theravāda Buddhism was flourishing in that region. It was from this country that Rāma Khomhĕng, one of the earliest kings of Sukhodaya, invited a learned *mahathera* to organize the Buddhist religious institutions of the newly founded state of Siam[3]. Therefore it is not improbable that there were relations between the monks of Ceylon and those of Nakhon Si Thammarat[4]; and our inscription may well be taken as referring to that country when it mentions Tambaraṭṭha.

On the other hand, there is also evidence for the existence, in South India, of a region known as Tambaraṭṭha. Anuruddha, who was the author of three treatises on the Abhidhamma, and who is generally believed to have flourished at the beginning of the twelfth century, says, in the colophon of one of his works, the *Paramattha-vinicchaya*, that he, who was born at Kāvīra-nagara in the country round Kāñcīpura, composed that work while he was staying at the city

---

[1] *Ceylon Antiquary and Literary Register*, vol. i, p. 98.

[2] In *Études asiatiques*, published on the occasion of the 25th anniversary of *l'École française d'Extrême-Orient.*

[3] Fournerau, *Le Siam ancienne*, Paris, 1895, part I, p. 237.

[4] See my paper 'Religious Intercourse between Ceylon and Siam in the 13th–15th Centuries', in *J. R. A. S., C. B.*, vol xxxii, pp 190–213.

of Tañja (Tanjore) in Tambaraṭṭha[1]. This would show us that Tambaraṭṭha was that part of the Coḷa country in which Tanjore was situated, unless we assume that there was a town called Tañja in the Malay Peninsula as well. The coupling of Tambaraṭṭha, in our inscription, with the Coḷas would also lend weight to the argument that it was in South India. But in South Indian inscriptions and in Tamil literature, so far as I know, there is no territorial division of this or a similar name.

The evidence forthcoming in our inscription is not sufficient to attempt an identification of the *thera* Ānanda mentioned therein with one of the many *theras* of this name who are known to us from Pāli literature, and who can roughly be ascribed to the period of this record.

TEXT

1 ස්වස්ති ශ්‍රී [।*]
ආනන්දනාමවිදිතො ජයති(ද්ධි)පත්තො
ලංකාතලුස්සිතධජො
2 පවරො යති[සො] [।*]
යො තම්බරට්ඨයති – ∩ ∩ ථෙරනුතො
චොලෙසු සාසන ∩ – ∩ ∩ කාසි ථ[illegible]රො [॥*][2]
3 සිරිවත් අපිරියන්ලොවුතුරුන්ගුණ්මුළින්නුතුරන් මුවදඹදි
4 වනි අන්තැගුලු පාමිලි කළ ඔකාවස්රජපරපුරෙන් බට ලො
5 ශාශාසමෙනෙකාචරණවැ දශරාජධම්ම් නොකොපා මුළුලක්දිව එක්ස
6 ත් කැර් රජ කළ සිරිසඟබො විජයබාහුදෙවියන් උරෙහිද
7 ම්ත්‍රාලොකාසුදෙවියන්ට අගමෙහෙසුන් වූ රවිකුලකොත් සුන්දරමහාදේ
8 (වින්) .. ..

TRANSCRIPT.

1 Svasti Śrī[।*]
Ānanda-nāma-vidito jayat=i(ddhi)-patto
Laṁkātal=ussita-dhajo

[1] *Seṭṭhe Kañci-pure raṭṭhe Kāvīra-nagare vare*
Kule sañjāta-bhūtena bahussutena ñāṇinā
Anuruddhena therena anuruddha-yasassinā
Tambaraṭṭhe vasantena nagare Tañja nāmake.

[2] වසන්තතිලකා වෘත්තයයි.

2 pavaro yatī[so] [।*]
Yo **Tamba-raṭṭha**-yati – ⏑ ⏑ thera-bhūto
Coḷesu sāsana ⏑ – ⏑ ⏑ kāsi dhīro[॥*][1]

3 Sirivat apiriyat-lo-ikut-guṇa-muḷin=uturat muḷu-Dambadi-

4 -vahi an-kät-kula pāmili kaḷa Okāvas-raja-parapuren baṭa lo-

5 -ka-śāsan=aika-śaraṇa-vä daśa-rāja-dharmma no-kopā muḷu-Lakdiva ek-sa-

6 -t kärä raja kaḷa **Sirisaṅgabo Vijayabāhu**-devayan urehidā

7 **Vikramabāhu**-devayanṭa aga-mehesun vū rivi-kula-kot **Sundara-mahāde-**

8 -(**vīn**) .. ..

TRANSLATION.

Hail! Prosperity! May that noble chief of monks, known by the name of **Ānanda**, be victorious—[he] who has attained psychic power, who is like unto a banner raised aloft in the land of Laṁkā, who is a *thera* . . . . . the monks of the **Tamba** country and who, the Wise One, has effected . . . . . . of the religious discipline among the **Coḷas**.

Sundaramahādevī, the pinnacle of the Solar dynasty, the chief queen of His Majesty **Vikramabāhu**, who is the son of His Majesty **Sirisaṅgabo Vijayabāhu**, who was descended from the royal line of the Okkāka[2] dynasty which, abounding in an assemblage of illustrious, boundless and transcendental virtues, has made the other *kṣatriya* dynasties of Jambudvīpa its vassals[3], and who reigned, after having made the island of Laṁkā [subject to the authority] of one umbrella, being the only refuge of the world and the religion of Buddha, and without violating the ten principles of royal conduct[4] . . . . . .

---

[1] Metre *Vasantatilakā*.

[2] Skt. *Ikṣvāku*.

[3] Lines 3–4 of this record contain the stereotyped phrases occurring in many inscriptions of the tenth and twelfth centuries, see *E. Z.*, Vol. I, p. 234, Vol. II, p. 213, and Vol. III, p. 321.

[4] The *daśa-rājadharmma* are, charity, piety, liberality, rectitude, gentleness, religious austerity, freedom from wrath, humanity, forbearance, and absence of malice. They are given in the following mnemonic verse in Pāli:—

Dānaṁ sīlaṁ pariccāgaṁ ajjavaṁ maddavaṁ tapaṁ
Akkodho avihiṁsā ca khantī ca avirodhatā.

No. 10. BATALAGOḌA-VÄVA SLAB-INSCRIPTION.

By S. Paranavitana.

Batalagoḍa-väva is an ancient irrigation reservoir situated about eight miles from Kuruṇägala on the road to Daṁbulla. It was restored by the Ceylon Government about forty years ago, and is now irrigating many thousands of acres of rice fields. Mr. H. Parker, who was in charge of the work of restoration, has, in his well-known work *Ancient Ceylon* (pp. 252 and 397–400), given a detailed account of the reservoir. Close to the Batalagoḍa-väva, there is the site of an ancient town, now known as 'Paraṇa-nuvara', which has also been dealt with by Mr. Parker. This site, which has been identified beyond doubt with Badalatthalī of the *Mahāvaṁsa* [1], has now passed into private ownership and is covered with coco-nut plantations.

The slab-inscription discovered near this reservoir, which forms the subject of the present paper, seems to be the same as No. 166 of Müller's *Ancient Inscriptions in Ceylon*, referred to by the name Batalagoda-luva [2]. Dr. Müller gives neither a reading nor a translation of the inscription and incorrectly ascribes it to the fifteenth century [3].

Mr. Parker has the following reference to this inscription in his account of the adjoining ancient site:—'The last reference to the place (Paraṇa-nuvara) is contained in an inscription which was left on a large slab on the embankment of the reservoir, by Queen Kalyāṇavatī (1202–1208 A.D.), the widow of King Niśśamka-Malla, in the third year of her reign, that is 1204 or 1205. In it she recorded her restoration of the tank at "Batalagoḍa at Mahalapura", the old town, and her reconstruction of a wihāra—now termed Koṭā-wēriya [*sic* ?], from its "short" dagaba, the Koṭa Waehaera—at an adjoining village, Pannala, as related in the Mahāvansa (II. p. 268) [4].' In his account of the tank, Mr. Parker says:—'There is a worn inscription in characters of the tenth century on a pillar at the embankment, which indicates that it was then restored, or was in working order [5], and a longer one on a large slab left there by Queen Kalyāṇawatī (1202–

---

[1] See Parker, *Ancient Ceylon*, p. 253 and Codrington, in *J. R. A. S., C. B.*, vol. xxix, p. 66.

[2] Probably a misprint for 'Batalagoḍa-väva'.

[3] *A. I. C.* p. 71.

[4] *Ancient Ceylon*, p. 254.

[5] This inscribed pillar is not to be seen at the place now. When I visited Batalagoḍa in 1931, I was told that it is in the bed of the reservoir, and can only be seen when the water level is low.

1208 A.D.) and cut in the third year of her reign, in which she relates that she had examined the sites of "the known sluices" and had rebuilt one of them; besides causing three breaches to be filled up'[1]. Again, he says, 'A tradition, to which the inscription of Kalyāṇawatī appears to contain a reference, states that the reservoir once possessed seven sluices; it seems to have been without any foundation'[2].

Mr. Parker has given neither the text nor a translation of the record; and he also seems to have misunderstood certain parts of it. He gives the date incorrectly as the third year of Kalyāṇavatī; and the presumption that the modern name, 'Paraṇavuvara', of the ancient site near by, goes back to a considerable antiquity, had led him to read the alternative name of Badalagoḍa as 'Mahalapura'. As will be seen from the translation given below, Mr. Parker's statements that it was Queen Kalyāṇavatī herself who was responsible for the repairs to the reservoir and religious benefactions mentioned in the document, and that the record seems to support the modern tradition of the reservoir having had seven sluices, are not supported by the inscription.

The text and translation of this epigraph were first published by Mr. H. C. P. Bell[3] to whom we are indebted for bringing to light many Sinhalese records of historical value. Mr. Bell corrected Mr. Parker's error of attributing the record to the third year of Kalyāṇavatī; and his translation also pointed out the inaccuracy of some of Mr. Parker's statements regarding the history of the reservoir. But he retains Mr. Parker's wrong reading 'Mahalapura'; and there are also several other points in the text as read by him, which admit of improvement. Mr. Bell himself admits that his text and translation are only tentative; hence, a new edition of this interesting document may be found useful.

The slab on which this inscription is engraved measures 4 ft. 6 in. by 2 ft. 10 in. It has been broken into several fragments, some of which are missing. The preserved pieces have been joined, and the gaps filled with cement, by some one, presumably by Mr. Parker when he was in charge of the restoration of the reservoir. The slab thus restored has been built to the parapet of the culvert over the sluice. The restorer's zeal for the preservation of this inscription has led him to overdo the work; for he was not content with merely putting together what was left of the record, but has also tried to restore, conjecturally,

---

[1] *Ancient Ceylon*, p. 299.
[2] *Ibid.*, p. 400.
[3] *Ceylon Antiquary and Literary Register*, vol. iv, pp. 29–31.

the lacunae in the text, and had these inscribed on the cement, in characters resembling those of the period to which the inscription belongs. The conjectural restorations thus made are generally unacceptable, except in the case of the most obvious ones, and they have, for the most part, been ignored in the text given below.

The record now consists of seventeen lines; but, as the end of the last line does not bring the sentence to a close, a few more letters must have formed an eighteenth line of which no traces are now visible. The **letters** are, on an average, $1\frac{1}{2}$ inches in size. The **script** agrees in detail with that of the numerous inscriptions of Niśśaṁka Malla and his successors, and calls for no remarks.

As regards **orthography**, the following points are noteworthy:—In line 1, *ek-sät* is used for the usual *ek-sat*; the Sanskrit *tatsama* form *pureśvara* is written in line 4 as *puresvara*; the ligature *tvā* is found in the Sinhalese word *pavatva* in line 6; and *partya* in line 12 stands for *pratya*. *Lakvijaya Saṁ Siṅgu* in line 9 is perhaps a clerical error for *Lakvijaya Siṅgu*; but there is also the possibility that it is a name distinct from that occurring in line 3. As regards **grammar**, the only point worth mentioning is the active verbal form *kaḍā* in line 5 which seems to have been used here in a passive sense. The **style** is that of other documents of the period. Unusual words occurring in the record are *alpasa* (line 11), *pän-päl* (line 12), *kasu-dagaba* (line 11), and *kävuṇuvä* (line 16) which will be dealt with in the notes attached to the translation.

The record is **dated** in the fifth year of **Queen Kalyāṇavatī** who ascended the throne in 1202 A.D. The object of the inscription was to record the repairs effected to **the Batalagoḍa-väva**, and the benefactions made to a neighbouring shrine, by an officer (*adhikāri*) named **Cūḍāmaṇi.** That part of the record containing the titles of this dignitary is mutilated; and we are, therefore, deprived of the means by which we could have ascertained what the position he held was. There is also no other mention of this officer, so far as I know, in the records of the period.

The general **Lakvijaya Ābo Siṅgu Senevinā** is also mentioned; but in what connexion, it is not clear, as that part of the record in which his name occurs is very fragmentary. It may, however, be surmised that it was at his command that Cūḍāmaṇi carried out the works at Batalagoḍa. This general is obviously the same as Lakvijaya Siṅgu Senevi Ābonā, who placed Sāhasamalla on the throne[1], and Lakvijaya Siṅgu Senevi Tāvurunā who is mentioned in

[1] See *E. Z.*, Vol. II, p. 220.

Niśśaṁka Malla's inscriptions as the general who led that monarch's expedition to South India and to whom was entrusted the work of building the Vaṭadāgē at Poḷonnaruva [1]. In the Sanskrit portion of the inscription of Sāhasamalla at Poḷonnaruva, this general is referred to by the name 'Āyuṣmat' [2]; and therefore it is reasonable to believe that he is the same as the general, called Āyasmanta [3] in the *Mahāvaṁsa*, who placed Kalyānavatī on the throne and administered the kingdom in her name, and who, together with the infant ruler Dhammāsoka, was put to death by Aṇikaṅga, an adventurer from South India [4]. As the title 'Tāvurunā' is given to this general in the epigraphical records, he was possibly the same as Tāvuru Senevirat who, according to the *Pūjāvalī*, murdered Vīrabāhu, the son and successor of Niśśaṁka Malla [5]. But the *Pūjāvalī* refers to the general who maintained Kalyāṇavatī on the throne, by the title 'Elalu Ābō Senevirat' [6]; hence this last identification is not beyond question.

Dr. Wickremasinghe [7] has also suggested the identification, with the same general, of Lakvijaya Siṅgu Kit Senevi who, according to the Abhayaväva pillar inscription, was the prime minister of Līlāvatī and is called Kitti in the *Mahavaṁsa*. But the reasons given by him for this identification are not conclusive. However that may be, this general seems to have been the most important figure in Ceylon during the first decade of the thirteenth century—a veritable king-maker who held the reins of government in his own hands whilst maintaining puppet sovereigns on the throne.

It is not certain whether the general named Lakvijaya Saṁ Siṅgu, mentioned in line 9, was the same as Lakvijaya Ābo Siṅgu mentioned earlier in the record. If we take the syllable *Saṁ* to be a clerical error, we may consider the two names as identical; but, on the other hand, *Saṁ* can easily stand for *Saṅgha*, a personal name common enough in mediaeval times. It is stated that Cūḍāmani repaired a monastery, at Batalagoḍa, founded by this general, but which was, in the reign of Kalyāṇavatī, dilapidated and abandoned. It is difficult to believe that an edifice built by Lakvijaya Ābo Siṅgu would have been of so ephemeral a character as to require extensive repairs during his own lifetime. I am therefore inclined to take these two names as those of two different personages.

---

[1] *E. Z.*, Vol. II., pp. 167 and 176.

[2] *Ibid.*, p. 221.

[3] *Āyasmanta* is the Pāli form of the Sanskrit *Āyuṣmat.*

[4] *Mahāvaṁsa*, chap. lxxx, vv. 33–34 and 43–44.

[5] *Pūjāvali*, chap. xxxiv, ed. B. Gunasekara (Colombo, 1893), p. 31.

[6] *Ibid.*, p 31.

[7] *E. Z.*, Vol. II, p. 191.

The record, so far as it is preserved, does not contain anything to show that Queen Kalyāṇavatī herself was concerned with the works of repair to the Batalagoḍa-väva and the religious foundations at the place. But she is said, in the *Mahāvaṁsa*, to have founded a *vihāra* at the village named Paṇṇasāla which has been identified with the modern Pannala near Batalagoḍa.

Touching the **geographical names** occurring in this record, Badalagoḍa (now Batalagoḍa) has been identified by Messrs. Parker and Codrington with the Badalatthalī of the *Mahāvaṁsa*. This place seems to have been of considerable importance in the eleventh and twelfth centuries. It was one of the strongholds captured by the general of Vijayabāhu I in his campaign against the Coḷas in the Dakkhiṇadesa[1]. The town was the head-quarters of Saṅkha-senāpati, a trusted general of Kittisirimegha; and it was here that the ceremony of investing with the sacred thread was performed on the young prince Parākramabāhu[2]. It was also here that Parākramabāhu, in order to escape from the guardianship of his uncle, Kittisirimegha, caused the murder of Saṅkha-senāpati, whilst he was enjoying the hospitality of that general[3]. The place also figures in the story of the reconciliation of Parākramabāhu to his uncle after his escapade in the Rājaraṭṭha[4]. The longer version of the 34th chapter of the *Pūjāvalī*[5] states that in the reign of Parākramabāhu II, the king's eldest son Vijayabāhu, after fortifying Kuruṇāgala and establishing monasteries there, appointed the people of Badalagoḍanuvara to guard that fortress. The Laṅkātilaka inscription of the reign of Bhuvanaikabāhu IV records the grant, to that temple, of lands in Paraṇa (old) Badalagoḍa and Alut (new) Badalagoḍa[6]. This town is said, in the present record, to have been in the Māyā kingdom, which is as one would expect; but it is not clear in what connexion the territorial division Madhyadeśa occurs. A district of this name, in ancient Ceylon, has not been met with elsewhere. At the time of this inscription, Badalagoḍa had also the appellation 'Maṅgalapura' (the auspicious city). Parker has read this name as 'Mahalapura' and equates it with the name 'Paraṇa-nuvara' by which the ancient site at the place is now known. Sotemuṇa, the land granted to the *vihāra* at Badalagoḍa, does not admit of identification.

---

[1] *Mahāvaṁsa*, chap. lviii, v. 43.
[2] *Ibid.*, chap. lxiv, vv. 6–17.
[3] *Ibid.*, chap. lxv.
[4] *Ibid.*, chap. lxvii, vv. 81–82.
[5] Edited by the Rev. Paṇḍit Mābōpiṭiye Medhaṅkara Thera (Colombo, 1932), p. 46.
[6] *J.R.A.S., C.B.*, vol. x, p. 91.

TEXT.

1 .. .. [ත්‍රි]සිංහලයෙහි එක්සැත්‍රජසිරි පැ(මිණි] .. .. [අගා ස

2 ලමෙ]වන් කල්‍යාණවතී පස්වන්නෙහි රාජශාසන .. .. ශාසන(ය) .. .. ..

3 .. .. ශිත ලක්විජය අංබො සිඟු සෙනෙවිනාවන් වැ .. .. මායාරාජ්‍ය .. .. ..

4 .. .. ැ මධ්‍යදෙශ ස .. .. ය බදලගොඩ නැමැති මහලපුරෙසර .. .. ාධිකාරි මන .. .. ..

5 චූඩාමණි තෙමැ මෙ .. .. වැව තුන්කඩෙකින් කඩා හැලිසොරො සුන් [බූන්]වැ නොපවත්[වැ]

6 තුබූ කල්හි මෙ බ .. .. හැලිසොරො ලවා පවත්වා පෙරැමැ දෙවැනි සො රොවක් නැති හෙයින්

7 බොහො කෙත්[වත් නො]පවත් සෙ දැකැ සවබුධීන් [සොරො]කිම් බලා සුදුසු කිමක් දැකැ එතැ

8 න්හි තමන් නමින් අධිකාරසොරොවයැ යන සොරොවක් ලවා යැපි මියරින් කණව .. .. ..

9 පි නැජවැ හස්වදනා කොටැ මෙමැ නුවරැ ලක්විජය සං සිඟු සෙනෙවි නාවන් කැරැවූ [සෙ]

10 නෙවිරන්පිරිවෙනයැ [යන] විහාරය ජීර්ණවැ අනාවාසවැ තුබූවා දැකැ පිළිමගෙය

11 කරවා දාගබ කසුදාගබ කොටැ බඳුවා මෙහිමැ ජීර්ණවූ සංඝාරාමය ද අත්පස

12 පැන්පැල් සහිත කොටැ කරවා මහසංඝයා වඩා හිඳුවා චතුබ්බිධපත්‍ය යෙන්[1] උප

13 සථාන කෙරෙමින් මෙසෙ [ලො]සසුන්වැඩ කරන්නාහු තමන් වැවට ගත් දූත් අනිශයෙ[න්]

14 සාඝික කරනු කැමැතිවැ තමන් නමින් ලැවූ සොකෙමුණන් කණුමුල් උදුරා විසල බහා තැනු

15 බිජුවට සත[රඅමුණක් විහා]රයට කුසලාත් කරනු කැමැතිවැ පෙරැ කුසලාත්හස්නම

[1] 'ප්‍රත්‍යයෙන්' යි කියවනු.

Poḷonnaruva: Fragmentary Slab-Inscription of Sundara-mahādevi

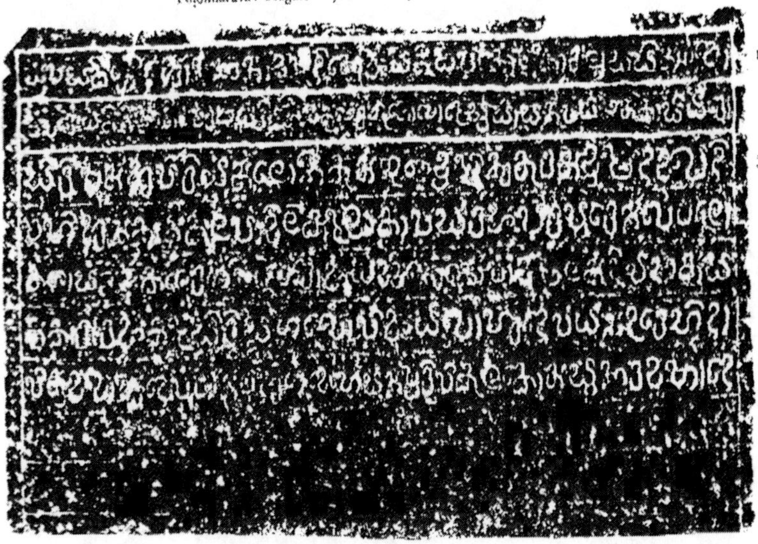

Scale 3½ inches to 1 foot

Batalagoḍa-väva Slab-Inscription of Kalyāṇavatī

Scale about 1½ inches to 1 foot

16 .. .. [මෙ] කුසලානට උධරණයක් කළ එකෙක් ඇත් නම් කා වුණුවෑ ලූ බත් කෑ සේය බලූකවූ

17 (වූ වූයේයෑ අටමම)හනරකයෙහි පැසුණේයෑ [||*] මෙ අප කළ කුසල මතු වැන්නවුන් තමන් කළ සෙ අ .. [1]

TRANSCRIPT.

1 .. ..[2] [Tri]-Siṁhaḷayehi ek-sät-raja-[3] siri pä(miṇi) .. .. [**Abhā Sa-**

2 **-lame**]van **Kalyāṇavatī** pas-vannehi rāja-śāsana .. .. śāsana(ya) .. .. ..

3 .. .. ṣita **Lakvijaya**[4] **Ābo Siṅgu Senevinā**van vä .. ..[5] Māyā-rājya .. .. ..

4 .. .. ä Madhyadeśa sa .. .. ya **Badalagoḍa** nämäti **Maṅgala**[6]**-puresvara** .. .. **ādhikāri**[7] **Man** .. .. ..[8]

5 **Cūḍāmaṇi**[9] temä me .. ..[10] väva tun-kaḍekin kaḍā häli[11]-soro sun-[bun]-vä no-pavat-vä

6 [12]tubū kalhi me b .. .. häli-soro lavā pavatvā perä-mä deväni sorovak näti heyin

7 boho ket-[vat no]-pavat se däkä sva-buddhīn[13] [soro]-bim balā sudusu bimak däkä e-tä-[14]

8 -nhi taman namin Adhikāra-sorova-yä yana sorovak lavā yäṭi-[15]miyarin kaṇäva[16] .. .. ..

9 -ṭi näti-vä has-[17]vadanā koṭā memä nuvara[18] **Lakvijaya Saṁ**[19] **Siṅgu senevi-nā**van kärävū[20] [**Se**]-

---

[1] 'ආරක්‍ෂාකළයුතු' නියා වාක්‍යය සම්පූර්ණ කරගත හැකිපි

[2] The two syllables missing might have been *Svasti*. Mr. Parker's restoration has *śrīḥ*.

[3] Bt. *rāja*.

[4] Bt. (*Lolupāla*) *kulaku Vijaya*.

[5] Bt. *vädu*. Mr. Parker has restored as *vädärumen*. *Vädārumen* may be a likelier restoration.

[6] Bt. *Mahala*.

[7] Mr. Bell reads (*Laṅkā A*)*dhikāri* which is a possible restoration.

[8] Bt. *Man*(*da-nāvan*).

[9] Mr. Bell, leaves the letters after *Cūḍā* unread, but the above reading is supported by what is left on the stone, ignoring Mr. Parker's restorations.

[10] Mr. Parker restores as *maha-väva*.

[11] Bt. *gälā*.

[12] The sixth line up to the 18th *akṣara* has been read by Mr. Bell as *tu* . . *Kaligimbe Alisorolivā Vijambe* which gives no sense.

[13] Bt. *Sedu Käsba Budim*.

[14] Bt. *bim madak e*(*ta*).

[15] Bt. *Lacha dheṭi*.

[16] Bt. *kaṇävā*.

[17] Bt. (*vehasa*).

[18] Bt. *Mänyavarä*.

[19] Bt. *yaṇ*.

[20] Bt. *kaḷa*.

10 **-nevirat-pirivena**-yä [yana][1] vihāraya jīrṇṇa-vä anāvāsa vä[2] tubuvā dākä piḷima-geya

11 karavā[3] dāgaba[4] kasu-dāgaba[5] koṭä bandavā[6] mehi-mȧ[7] jīrṇṇa- vū saṁghārāmaya[8] da atpasa

12 pän-päl sahita koṭä karavā maha-saṁghayā vaḍā hinduvā[9] caturbbidha-partyayen[10] upa-[11]

13 sthāna keremin mese [lo]-sasun-väḍa karannāhu taman vävaṭa gat duk[12] atiśaye[n[13]]

14 sārtthaka[14] karanu kämäti-vȧ taman namin lävū **Sotemuṇin**[15] kaṇu-mul udurā viyala bahā tänu ..[16]

15 bijuvaṭa sata[ra-amuṇak vih]ārayaṭa kusalān karanu kämäti-vä perä kusalān-hasna-ma[17]

16 .. .. [me] kuṡalānaṭa uddharaṇayak[18] kaḷa ekek ät nam kāvuṇuvä lū[19] bat kā sēya[20] balu-kavu-

17 -(ḍu vūyē-yä aṭa-ma)ha-narakayehi[21] päsuṇe-yä[22] [II*] Me apa kaḷa kusala matu vannavun taman kaḷa se a ..[23]

TRANSLATION.

[Lines 1–6] . . . . . . In the fifth year of **Abhā Salamevan Kalyāṇavatī**,[24] . . . . . . who has attained[25] the supreme regal splendour in the three Siṁhaḷas[26] . . . . . . royal decree . . . . . . decree . . . . . . (? by the order) of the generalissimo **Lakvijaya Ābo Siṅgu**, the *adhikāri* **Man . . . Cūḍāmaṇi**, lord of **Maṅgalapura**

---

[1] Bt. *se* (. . *na*). [2] Bt. *an vadava.*
[3] Bt. *dükävä vimasā Yatalavā.* [4] Bt. *Dägaba.* [5] Bt. *Kaḍu Däga*(*ba*).
[6] Bt. (*kara*)*vā.* [7] Bt. *mo.* [8] Bt. *pusphārāmaya.*
[9] Bt. *väḍä hindavä.* [10] Read *pratyayen* which is Mr. Bell's reading. [11] Bt. (*dasa*).
[12] Bt. *du* . . . [13] Bt. *atiśayin.* [14] Bt. .. .. *ka.*
[15] Bt. *Lävu-Sotemumijni.* [16] *Viyala bahā tänu* is wanting in Mr. Bell's text.
[17] Bt. *gastra*(*ra*). [18] Bt. *hasaranayak.* [19] Bt. *kävuḍu bälu.*
[20] Bt. *käyok.* [21] Bt. *narakayedī duk.* [22] Bt. *pasuṇoya.*
[23] Perhaps the missing portion is to be restored as *ārakṣā kaḷa yutu*. Mr. Bell has *kaḷā sē veyi.*
[24] The *viruda* title Abhā Salamevan is given to this queen in other records also, see *E. Z.*, Vol. II, p. 191 and *J. R. A. S., C. B.*, vol. vii, p. 181.
[25] According to the reading *pämiṇi*. If the reading *pämiṇä* be preferred, the translation should be altered to 'who, having attained'.
[26] The three kingdoms into which Ceylon was divided in ancient times, viz., Ruhuṇu, Māyā, and Pihiti.

alias **Badalagoḍa** . . . Madhyadeśa in the kingdom of Māyā [1], at the time this . . . reservoir was lying unused,[2] [its embankment] being breached in three places [3] [and its] canals and sluice being destroyed . . . . . . repaired the canals and the sluice and made them to be of use.

[Lines 6–13] Having seen that not many fields and gardens were flourishing, as there was no second sluice even in former times, he, by his own judgement, examined sites [fit] for sluices, and having found a suitable site [for a sluice], he constructed there a sluice called, after his own name, the Adhikāra-sluice and brought under cultivation . . . .[4] from the lower embankment [5]. Having seen that the monastery called **Senevirat-pirivena**, established in this town by the generalissimo **Lakvijaya Saṁ Siṅgu**, remained dilapidated and uninhabited, he repaired the image-house, rebuilt the *dāgaba* making it a mantle-*dāgaba* [6], repaired also the dilapidated residences of the monks in the same place, including the latrine [7] and the water-closet [8], invited the members of the great community of monks, made them reside therein and attended on them with the four requisites [9].

[Lines 13–15] Performing, in this wise, service to the world and to the religion, and being desirous of making the pains that he had taken on account of this reservoir exceedingly fruitful, and also being desirous of making a religious endowment [10], to the *vihāra*, of the sowing extent of four *āmuṇas* [11] of

---

[1] See *E. Z.*, Vol. II, p. 330, n. 4. [2] *Nopavat* = Skt. *apravṛtta*.

[3] *Tun-kaḍekin*. *Kaḍa* may mean 'breach' (Skt. *khaṇḍa*) or 'place' (cf. T. *kaḍai*).

[4] The fragmentary nature of the record does not permit us to guess the meaning of the word *kaṇāva*, which does not occur elsewhere, from the context.

[5] *Yäṭi-miyarin* may also be rendered as 'from below the embankment'. This might be more appropriate as there is no evidence of the reservoir having had two embankments.

[6] *Kasu-dāgaba* is taken as equivalent to P. *kañcuka-dhātugabbha*. Cf. the word *kañcuka-cetiya* occurring in the *Mahāvaṁsa* (chap. i, v. 42) and in the Pāli *Thūpavaṁsa* (Colombo edition of 1896, pp. 46 and 47). The Sinhalese *Thūpavaṁsa*, in the printed editions, has *kasuk-dāgaba* and *kasun-dāgäba* in the corresponding passages. Probably these readings are due to clerical errors and the correct reading ought to be, as in the present epigraph, *kasu-dāgaba*.

[7] The word *atpasa* occurs with the same meaning in the *Heraṇasika*, Colombo edition of 1911, p. 24.

[8] *Pänpäla* occurs in the *Pūjāvalī* (34th chapter, *op. cit.* p. 29) with the same meaning.

[9] The four requisites of the Buddhist monks (P. *catupaccaya*) are:—robes, food, residences, and medicaments.

[10] *Kusalān*:—See *E. Z.* Vol. III, p. 95, for the meaning of this word.

[11] See *E. Z.*, Vol. III, p. 325, n. 7.

seed paddy[1] from **Sotemuṇa**, which was made suitable for sowing[2] by having the stumps of trees[3] and roots removed, and which was granted in his own name . . . . the former endowment-decree itself.

[Lines 16-17] Should there be any one who has caused harm to this religious endowment, he is as if he has eaten the rice put in the *kävuṇuva*[4]; he also will become a crow or a dog and will be boiled in the eight great hells. This merit that we have performed (should be protected) by those of the future as if it has been performed by their own selves.

No. 11. TWO ROCK-INSCRIPTIONS AT KOṬṬANGĒ.

By S. PARANAVITANA.

THE two inscriptions[5] dealt with in this paper were copied by the Archaeological Department, in 1931, from the village called Koṭṭangē in the Mādurē Kōraḷē of the Vāuḍavili Hatpattu in the Kuruṇāgala District. The first inscription (Reg. No. 689) is engraved on the top of a boulder in a land, belonging to the villagers, and known as Puvak-araṁba or Koṭṭangē-araṁba. The second inscription (Reg. No. 690), though engraved on a flat rock not more than twenty feet from the first, is within the boundaries of a coco-nut plantation, called the Ōgoḍapola Estate, in the Delviṭa Group. The soil washed down from the hill-side had completely buried this rock; and its existence was altogether

---

[1] Fields were measured in mediaeval Ceylon, as they are in the villages to-day, according to their capacity of being sown with seed paddy.

[2] *Viyaḷa bahā tänu* :—The word *viyaḷa* is current in the modern colloquial language to mean 'a heap of mud', for example in *mati-viyaḷa*. In inscriptions of the tenth and twelfth centuries, it seems to denote the fields prepared for sowing paddy by making them muddy. In the slab-inscription of Mahinda IV near the Stone Canoe in the Citadel of Anurādhapura, we find the expressions *viyaḷ nerut, viyaḷ no nernā, viyal neḷ tanhi* (*E.Z.*, Vol. I, p. 117). In an unpublished slab-inscription found near the Malvatu Oya, and now in the Anurādhapura Museum, belonging to the reign of Parākramabāhu I, we have the phrase *däturē tänū viyaḷa*.

[3] *Kaṇu* = P. *khāṇu*, for which see P.T.S. *Pāli Dictionary, s.v.*

[4] *Kävuṇuvä lū bat kā seya* :—Similar imprecations occur in other records of the period. In the Galapāta Vihāra rock-inscription we have *kävaṇuyehi lū bat kävun samānayo yä* Mr. Bell explains *kävaṇuva* as 'the bowl or other utensil in which rice is received for eating by Roḍiyas and beggars or sherds for feeding crows and other birds' (*J. R. A. S., C. B., Notes and Queries*, April, 1914, p. xxiv).

[5] A preliminary account of these epigraphs will be found in the *A. S. C. A. R.* for 1930-31, p. 6, and in *C. J. Sc. (G.)*, vol. ii, pp. 187-188 and 217.

unsuspected till a villager, who had seen it many years ago, informed the writer about it when he visited the site to copy the first inscription. It was necessary to remove the earth to a depth of about two feet before the inscription was exposed. The existence of an inscription at this place is mentioned in the *Return of the Architectural and Archaeological and other Antiquities existing in Ceylon*, published by the Ceylon Government in 1890; but the records do not seem to have been studied by any one before they were copied by the Archaeological Department. No other antiquities of any description are to be seen in the vicinity of these rock-inscriptions.

I.

The first epigraph is incised in two panels separated from each other by a natural transversal crevice at the middle of the rock surface, which has been avoided by the engraver. The panel on the left-hand side measures 3 ft. $9\frac{1}{2}$ in. by 2 ft. $0\frac{1}{2}$ in. and is enclosed in a rectangular framing. Parallel horizontal lines, drawn at distances varying from $3\frac{1}{2}$ to $2\frac{1}{2}$ inches from one another, divide this area into eight unequal spaces in which the letters are engraved. The last letters of all the lines, excepting the fourth and the eighth, are written partly outside the framing on the right-hand side. Above the inscribed area are engraved the figures of the sun and the crescent moon; and to the left of it is the figure of a crow, facing the inscription. The right-hand side panel measures 4 ft. $0\frac{1}{2}$ in. by 1 ft. 3 in. and is also enclosed in a rectangular linear framing; and the whole area is divided into five spaces by horizontal parallel lines drawn at a distance varying from $3\frac{1}{4}$ in. to $2\frac{3}{4}$ in. from one another. To the right of this panel is engraved the figure of a dog, facing the inscription.

The **letters**, engraved fairly deep, vary in size from 2 to $1\frac{1}{2}$ inches. The execution of the record, on the whole, has been done with some care; but in line 3, the syllable *se* has been left out by mistake and added later, below the line. The document is in a fairly good state of preservation; and it is only in lines 4 and 10, that some letters—three in each—are too weathered for a reading which is beyond doubt.

The **script**, on the whole, resembles that of the inscriptions of Niśśaṁka Malla and other monarchs of the later Poḷonnaruva period; but, in certain particulars, it has points in common with the script of about a century later. For instance, the medial vowel sign for *ä*, occurring in this record, differs markedly from that of the inscriptions of Niśśaṁka Malla. This symbol, in the script of that king's records, consists of a vertical stroke slightly curved towards the left, detached, and written to the right of the consonantal symbol; but, in the present record, it comprises an almost semicircular stroke joined to the consonantal symbol by means of another short vertical stroke, and on a much higher level. The letters, in general, assume more rounded forms than in the script of Niśśaṁka Malla's reign. This difference in script seems to be due more to the individual idiosyncracies of the scribe rather than to natural development caused by the passage of time, for in the particulars noted above, the script of the Daṁbadeṇiya period, which is about half a century later than the date of this record, seems to agree with that of Niśśaṁka Malla's inscriptions.

There is nothing noteworthy about the **orthography** of the document; and, as for **grammar**, the use of the verbal form *siṭi* in connexion with inanimate objects may be worth mentioning. In the modern language, as well as in the classical literature, *pihiṭi* would have been used instead. The **language** and **style** are in keeping with those of other documents of the period to which this inscription belongs.

The record is of considerable historical interest. Its **object** was to register the grant of a village named **Kaḷama** to the general **Loke Arakmenā**, by king **Lokeśvara-bāhu Cakravartti**, in recognition of the former's services in defeating the Coḷas. The name Lokeśvara-bāhu in this record obviously stands for Lokissara or Lokeśvara of the chronicles. Two rulers of this name are mentioned in the historical writings of Ceylon; and both of them occupied the throne for short periods in troubled times and were not distinguished for any remarkable achievements. The first of these was the general, named Loka and Lokanātha in the *Mahavaṁsa*[1], and Lokeśvara in the *Pūjāvalī* and other Sinhalese writings[2], who, when the Coḷas were dominating the greater part of Ceylon, wielded some authority over the Rohaṇa country for six years, having Kataragama as his head-quarters, and was in the end vanquished by Kitti, the prince who later repelled the Coḷas and ascended the throne of Poḷonnaruva as Vijayabāhu I[3]. The second Lokeśvara reigned for seven months at Poḷonnaruva in 1210 and was preceded and also followed on the throne by Līlāvatī[4]. On palaeographical grounds, the record ought to be ascribed to Lokeśvara II, of whom this is the only document so far brought to light.

---

[1] *Mv.* lvii. 1–2.

[2] *A Contribution to the History of Ceylon, translated from 'Pūjāvaliya'*, by B. Gunasekara (Colombo, 1895), p. 33, and *Rājāvaliya*, B. Gunasekara's translation (Colombo, 1900), p. 59.

[3] *Mv.* lvii. 64.

[4] *Ibid.*, lxxx. 46–50.

The chronicles say nothing more about Lokeśvara beyond the fact that he had been wounded in the shoulder by a spear and that he, after possessing himself of the throne with the help of a great Tamil army from the opposite shore, ruled for seven months till he was ousted by a general named Parakkama[1]. The authorities are silent about his lineage; and Dr. Wickremasinghe considers him to have been a usurper[2]. The present record informs us that he had the throne name Sirisaṅgabo and belonged to the Kāliṅga dynasty. The last piece of information shows us that he must have been related somehow to Niśśaṁka Malla and Sāhasamalla, both of whom were members of the Kāliṅga dynasty; but neither this inscription nor any other record helps us to determine what the relationship was. At any rate, he must have had as good a title to the throne as any of the ephemeral kings and queens who followed one another in quick succession in the period between the death of Niśśaṁka Malla and the invasion of the island by Māgha.

The encounter, referred to in this record, between the Colas and the Sinhalese, in which the latter were victorious, is not mentioned in the chronicles. Nothing is said as to whether the struggle took place in Ceylon or abroad; but we can be quite certain that, in the confused times in which Lokeśvara reigned, he could not have fitted out and sent an expedition to give battle to the Coḷas in their own territories. The fight, therefore, must have been with an army sent by the Coḷa king to this island. The Coḷa monarch at this time was Kulottuṅga III, whose reign began in 1178 A.D. and lasted till 1216[3]. Kulottuṅga, in his inscriptions dated the 9th and 21st years of his reign, boasts of victories he gained over the Sinhalese[4]; but these cannot refer to the encounter in the reign of Lokeśvara, as they occurred before the latter's accession. I have elsewhere shown that these expeditions must have occurred sometime between 1190 and 1200 A.D.[5] This particular invasion which was repelled by Loke Arakmenā does not seem to have been mentioned in the South Indian inscriptions, which is quite natural as the Coḷas were not successful in their attempt.

The general Loke Arakmenā also figures in the Ruvanvälisāya slab inscription of Niśśaṁka Malla. He is said there to have been entrusted with the care of the Ruvanvälisāya after the great offerings made to that shrine by the king[6]. 'Arakmenā' is a title which was given to the officials who guarded the Bō-tree

[1] *Ibid.*, lxxx. 47-48.

[2] *E. Z.*, Vol. III, p. 24.

[3] *South Indian Inscriptions*, vol. iii, pp. 204 and 43.

[4] *Ibid.*, p. 206.

[5] *J. R. A. S., C. B.*, vol. xxxi, pp. 384-386.

[6] *E. Z.*, Vol. II, p. 83

at Anurādhapura; and the first to hold this office was Jutindhara, one of the Maurya princes who are said to have accompanied the sacred tree to Ceylon in the time of Aśoka[1].

The land granted, it is stated, was to be enjoyed in the **Māpaṇḍi** family, having had any disputes concerning it settled by the senior *thera* of the Vapasinā-āyatan of the **Vilgammuḷa** fraternity. 'Māpaṇḍi' is obviously the same as 'Mahāpaṇḍi', the name of the family to which the author of the *Pūjavalī* belonged, as stated in the 34th chapter of that work[2]. This family is said therein to have been a branch of the Gaṇaväsi clan which traced its origin to the Maurya princes. The *Saddharmmaratnākara*[3] states that Gaṇaväsi is another name for the Lämäni family to which belonged most of the kings of mediaeval Ceylon. Loke Arakmenā was, in all probability, a scion of the Lämäni or Gaṇaväsi stock, a supposition strengthened by what we learn from the other inscription[4] at the site and also by the title Arakmenā which he bore.

The fraternity of monks known as **Vilgammuḷa** (P. *Sarogamamūla*), so far as I know, figures in history for the first time in the Poḷonnaruva period. Moggallāna Thera, the author of the Pāli lexicon *Abhidhānappadīpikā*, and who lived in the Jetavana-vihāra built by Parākramabāhu I at Poḷonnaruva, was a member of this fraternity[5]. The authors of several well-known Sinhalese and Pāli works produced in the fourteenth century were of this fraternity of monks[6]. Vapasinā Āyatan which seems to have belonged to this college of monks, is not known from other sources.

As regards the **geographical names** occurring in the record, **Kaḷama** is obviously the old name of the land in which the inscription is found. Its boundaries, which are given, cannot now be identified, as most of them, for instance, 'the silk-cotton tree standing by the side of the high road' and 'the

---

[1] *Siṁhala Bodhivaṁśa* (Colombo edition of 1928), p. 220. The Pāli word translated by *arakmenā* is *ārakkha-pāricariya* (see *Mahābodhivaṁsa*, P.T.S. edition, p. 166).

[2] *Ubhaya-kula-pariśuddhava pāväti Gaṇaväsi-kulehi avinaṣṭa-vū Mahāpaṇḍi-vaṁśa äti* . . . . *Mayūrapāda-pariveṇādhipati Buddhaputra-sthavirayan.*
(The 34th chapter of the *Pūjāvalī*, edited by Rev. Pandit Mābōpiṭiye Medhaṅkara Thera, Colombo, 1932, p. 50.)

[3] Colombo edition of 1923, p. 296.

[4] See below, pp. 88–90.

[5] See *Abhidhānappadīpikā*, Colombo, 1883, p. 313.

[6] Wickremasinghe, *Catalogue of Sinhalese Manuscripts in the British Museum*, p. xviii, and Malalasekara, *The Pāli Literature of Ceylon*, pp. 253–254.

Koṭṭangē Rock-Inscription, No. 1, of Lokeśvarabāhu

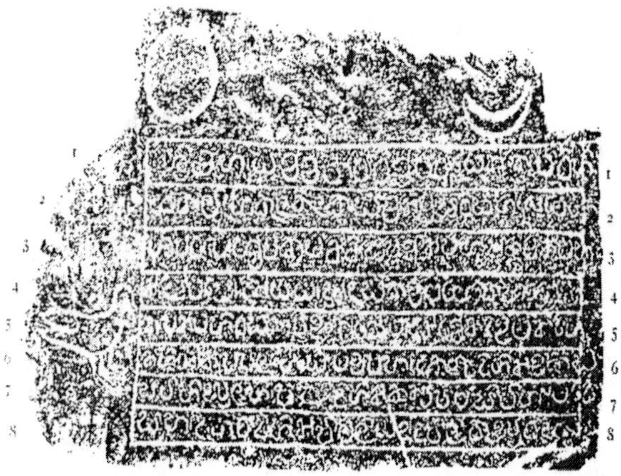

Scale 1 3/4 inches to 1 foot

Koṭṭangē Rock-Inscription, No. 2

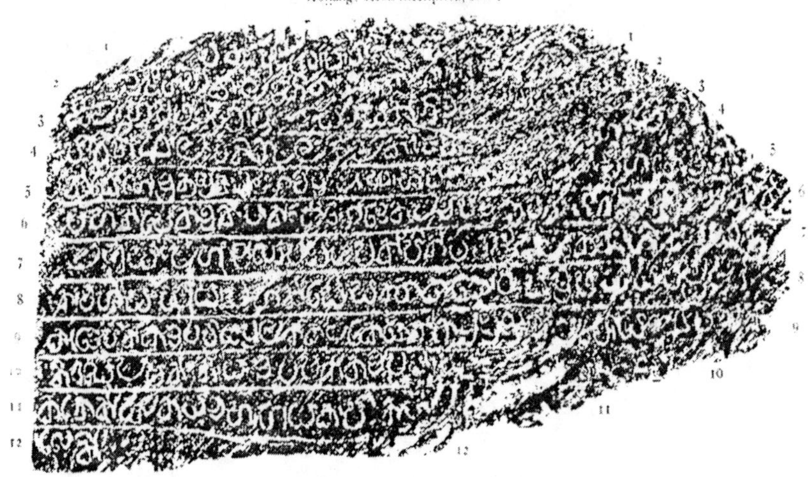

Scale 1 3/16 inches to 1 foot

gäṭa-kos tree standing on the side of the hill', are not permanent landmarks. I was, however, told by the villagers that a field called Pilikumbura still exists. 'Villiya', too, still exists in the names of the villages 'Uḍavili' and 'Yaṭivili' and possibly has given its name to the Villi- or Väuḍavilli-Hatpattu.

TEXT.

1 ශ්‍රීමහාසම්මතපරම්පරායෙන් නොපිරිහී
2 ආ කාලිඟකුලතිලකායමානවූ **සිරිසඟබො ලෙ[ා]කෙ**
3 **ශ්වරබාහු චක්‍රවර්ත්ති**ස්වාමින්වහන්සෙ තමන්වහ
4 න්සෙට සොළීන් සාධා දුන් දස්කමට **ලොකෙ අ[රක්මෙ]**
5 **නාවන්ට** හිරසඳපමුණු කොටැ දුන් මෙ **කළමට** නැගෙ
6 නහිරින් කප්පලගොඩ ටඹ හා දකුණුදිගින් මංකඩ
7 සිටි හිඹුල හා පැළදිගින් කඳුපිට සිටි ගැටකො
8 ස හා උතුරුදිගින් විල්ලිය මැද පිලිකුඹුර ඈ
9 තුළු කොට කඳුරෙ සිටි ඈටඹය හා මෙ පමු
10 ණුවට සතරදිගැ හිමි [॥*] මෙ (හිමැ වූ) .. .. .. **විල්ගම්**
11 **මුළ** වපසිනැආයතන්නායක මලුවරුන්වාන්
12 සෙගෙන් කන්ලැවූ පසිඳුවා **මාපඬිවං**
13 සයෙ ඈත්තවුන් වළඳනු සිරිති [॥*]

TRANSCRIPT.

1 Śrī-Mahāsammata-paramparāyen no-pirihī
2 ā Kāliṅga-kula-tilakāyamāna-vū **Sirisaṅgabo L[o]ke-**
3 **-śvara-bāhu cakravartti**-svāmīn-vahanse[1] taman-vaha-
4 -nse-ṭa Soḷin sādhā dun das-kamaṭa **Loke A[rakme]-**
5 **nāvan-ṭa** hira-sanda-pamuṇu koṭā dun me **Kaḷama-ṭa** näge-
6 -nahirin Kappalagoḍa ṭamba hā dakuṇu-digin maṁ-kaḍa
7 siṭi himbula hā päḷa-digin kandu-piṭa siṭi gäṭa-ko-
8 -sa hā uturu-digin Villiya mäda Pilikumbura ä-
9 -tuḷu koṭa kandure siṭi äṭambaya hā me pamu-
10 -ṇuvaṭa satara-digä himi [॥*] Me (himä vū) .. .. .. **Vilgam-**
11 **muḷa** Vapasinä-āyatan-nāyaka maluvarun-vān-
12 -segen kanlävu pasinduvā **Māpaṇḍi-vaṁ-**
13 -saye ättavun vaḷandanu siriti [॥*].

---

[1] Written below the line.

TRANSLATION.

[Lines 1–10] To this [village of] **Kaḷama**, granted, as a *pamuṇu*[1] [to exist till] the Sun and Moon endure, by His Majesty, the Emperor **Sirisaṅgabo Lokeśvara-bāhu**, who is descended in unbroken succession from the lineage of the illustrious Mahāsammata and who is like unto an adornment of the Kāliṅga dynasty, to **Loke Arakmenā**, for the valour shown[2] in disposing[3] of the Coḷas for His Majesty—to this *pamuṇu* [village]—the boundaries on the four directions are:—on the east, the pillar at Kappalagoḍa, on the south, the silk-cotton tree standing by the side of the high-road, on the west, the *gäṭa-kos*[4] tree standing on the side of the hill, on the north, the *äṭamba*[5] tree standing near the mountain stream, thus including, [within its limits], the field called Pilikumbura in the middle of Villi.

[Lines 10–13] It shall be customary for the land within these boundaries to be enjoyed by those of the **Māpaṇḍi** family, getting any complaints[6] [regarding it] settled by His Worship the prior[7] who is the head of the Vapasinä Āyatan of **Vilgammuḷa**.

II.

The second inscription at the site, as has already been mentioned, is engraved on a rock very close to the first. It covers an irregular rock-surface measuring, approximately, 7 ft. 4 in. by 3 ft. 2 in. The rock has not been dressed before the writing was executed and, in avoiding the uneven areas at the right-hand side, the lines have become of unequal length. The letters have been engraved between parallel lines which are, on an average, $3\frac{1}{2}$ inches from one another. The average height of the letters is about $2\frac{1}{4}$ inches. The record has suffered badly from the action of the weather, particularly the right half of it, and about a third of the document is completely illegible.

---

[1] See *E. Z.*, Vol. II, p. 117, n. 5.

[2] The above rendering is by taking *das* as equivalent to Skt. *dakṣa*. It may also stand for Skt. *dāsya*, in which case 'services rendered' may be substituted for 'valour shown'.

[3] The root *sadh*, from which the gerund *sādhā* comes, has the primary meaning of 'to make', 'to prepare', &c.; but it is capable of assuming various shades of secondary meaning. This verb is used with the same meaning as in this record, in the following passage from the *Nikāya Saṅgraha* (Colombo edition of 1890, p. 20):—*Mahalu Vijayabāhu nam maharajāṇō sayāsū havuruddak muḷullē Lakdiva gam niyamgam rājadhāni purā un Demaḷa-mahasenaga sādhā Sirilaka eksat koḷa.*

[4] A species of jack.

[5] A species of mango.

[6] The word rendered by 'complaints' is *kanlävu*. I have taken it to be a variant form of *kannalavu*, occurring with this meaning in literature.

[7] *Maluvarun*, a contraction of *mahaluvarun*. The form *maluvarun* also occurs in the Laṅkātilaka rock-inscription, l. 10. (See *J. R. A. S., C. B.*, vol. x pp. 87 and 95).

The **script** shows more developed forms than in that of the first inscription and it may therefore be inferred that this record belongs to a somewhat later date—a conclusion which is also supported by a study of its contents. No date is given in the document. It opens with a Sanskrit verse of which not a single line is completely preserved. The rest of the document, which is in Sinhalese, tells us that a *mahāthera* of the **Vilgammuḷa** fraternity, whose name is obliterated, granted to the *saṅgha* the *pamuṇu* village of **Kaḷama**, and some other lands belonging to him. This *mahathera* is said to have been the grandson of a personage who belonged to the Lämäni family; but, unfortunately, the name of the latter is also not preserved. We may presume that the *mahāthera* was a grandson of Loke Arakmenā, to whom the village was originally granted by Lokeśvara, as recorded in the first inscription. This supposition gains further strength from the fact that, as shown by the title 'Arakmenā', general Loke belonged to the Lämäni stock. His connexion with the Vilgammuḷa fraternity is also shown by the stipulation in the first inscription that any disputes concerning the lands in question were to be settled by a *mahathera* of that religious institution.

TEXT.

1 .. .. චතුද්දිශායාත .. ..
2 .. .. මෙ දීර්ඝකාලම්හිතාය .. නා .. ..
3 ශිලා (භවථ) .. මො ප්‍ර .. [||*] ස්වස්ති ශ්‍රීමත් .. .. [නො]
4 පිරිහී ආ ලැමැනිකුලතිලකායමාන .. .. වහ
5 න්සේගේ මුනුබුරු **විල්ගම්මුළැ අභය** .. .. මහතෙරුන්
6 වහන්සෙ තමන්වහන්සෙගෙ මෙ **කළම්** පමුණුවත් .. .. වින්
7 උඩුසැළ ගම්බාවසටවන් පින් පිණ්ස සතරදිගින් වඩ
8 න මහසංඝයාවහන්සේ සනාතක තොට සිවුපසයට ලූසේ
9 කැ[||*]මෙ පින්කම්ට වියවුලක් කළ කෙනෙක් කවුඩු බලු වූවොය අටමහ
10 නිරයෙ උපන්නොය මට පින්කම්ට .. ..
11 කෙනෙක් ඇත සමභාගයක පින් ලැ
12 බෙත් [||*]

TRANSCRIPT.

1 .. .. caturddiśāyāta .. ..
2 .. .. me dīrggha-kālam-hitāya .. na .. ..
3 śilā (bhavatha) .. mo pra .. [||*]Svasti śrīmat .. [no]-
4 pirihī ā Lämäni-kula-tilakāyamāna .. .. vaha-

5 -nsēgē munuburu **Vilgam-muḷä Abhaya** .. .. mahaterun-
6 vahanse taman-vahansege me **Kaḷam-**pamuṇuvat .. .. vat
7 Uḍusäḷa Gambāvasaṭavat pin piṇisa satara-digin vaḍa-
8 -na maha-saṁghayā-vahansē santaka koṭa sivu-pasayaṭa lū-sē-
9 -kä[॥*]Me pin-kamaṭa viyavulak kaḷa kenek kavuḍu balu vūvoya aṭa-maha-
10 niraye upannoya maṭa pin-kamaṭa .. ..
11 kenek äta sama-bhāgayakā pin lä-
12 -bet[॥*]

TRANSLATION.

. . . . . . come from the four directions . . . . . . for my benefit for a long time . . . . . . Hail! His Worship, the great *thera* **Abhaya** . . . . . . of **Vilgammuḷa**, the grandson of His Holiness . . . . who was like unto an adornment to the Lämäni family, and who was descended in unbroken succession from the illustrious . . . . . . for gaining merit, made this *pamuṇu*[1] [village called] **Kaḷama** and . . . . . . **Uḍusäla** and **Gambāvasaṭava**[2], belonging to His Holiness, the property of the *saṁgha* coming from the four directions, and gave them for the four requisites.

Any persons who shall cause hindrance to this act of charity will be [born as] crows and dogs and will [also] be born in the eight great hells. If there be any persons who (would support) me in this act of charity they would receive the merit of an equal share.[3]

No. 12. GAḌALĀDEṆIYA ROCK-INSCRIPTION OF DHARMMAKĪRTTI STHAVIRA.

By S. PARANAVITANA.

AT Gaḍalādeṇiya, a village in the Uḍunuvara division of the Kandy District, there is, on a wide stretch of flat rock, a Buddhist shrine of the fourteenth century. This temple, which was originally built entirely of stone, is remarkable

[1] See *E. Z.*, Vol. III, p. 267, n. 3.

[2] Though the letters of this name are quite clear, it does not look like an ordinary place name in Ceylon.

[3] *I.e.* half of the merit.

for the fact that, though it was intended for purposes of Buddhist religious worship, it resembles, in its architectural features, the contemporary Hindu shrines of South India in the early Vijayanagara style. A roof in the later Kandyan style, constructed of timber, on brick piers, covers the *vimāna*; and thus the original architectural design is much obscured at present[1].

The ascent to the rock on which the shrine is built was, in olden days, on the north-eastern side; and, to the right of the rock-cut steps, as one ascends, a large area of rock-surface, measuring, roughly, 24 ft. by 13 ft., is covered with inscriptions contiguous to one another, all more or less damaged. The record which occupies the top-most position of this inscribed area is a short and much weathered one of four lines, datable in the fifteenth century, of a king styled Sirisaṅgabo Śrī Parākramabāhu Vikramabāhu. Below this is another record of five lines, also very fragmentary, and of the same period, dated in the third year of a Sirisaṅgabo Śrī Parākramabāhu. The record dealt with in the present paper is incised immediately below this, and occupies more than half of the inscribed rock-surface at this place. Immediately below this epigraph is the inscription of Senāsammata Vikramabāhu, edited by Mr. H. W. Codrington (see *ante*, pp. 8–15), which is followed by a much weathered record dated 2054 of the Buddhist era. On the rock near the Bo-tree, there are two other inscriptions which are almost totally obliterated; and a slab-pillar, now standing near the entrance to the shrine, bears inscriptions which have also been dealt with by Mr. Codrington (*ante*, pp. 16–27)[2].

The inscription now dealt with, which is the earliest in date of all the records found at this site, is also the longest; and covers a rock-surface measuring, approximately, 14 ft. by 13 ft. 6 in. It consists of 45 lines of which the last three are almost totally effaced. The first line extends about a foot more to the right than the other lines; possibly it has been done so in order to finish the opening Sanskrit stanza in this line alone. The letters, which are, on an average, 3 in. in size, have been boldly incised to a considerable depth and, in the preserved portions of the record, are clearly legible. Large patches of the inscribed rock-surface have peeled off, thereby causing many lacunae in the text. The incumbent priest told me that this damage has been wantonly caused by the

[1] For a description of Gaḍalādeṇiya, see H. W. Cave, *The Book of Ceylon*, New edition, pp. 341 ff.

[2] For a preliminary account of the inscriptions at Gaḍalādeṇiya, see *C.J. Sc., G.*, vol. ii, pp. 109 and 205–206.

villagers at the instance of a certain chief who lived about a century ago, with the intention of depriving the temple of the lands mentioned in the record as having been dedicated to it. Whether this story is true or not, the peeling off of the rock-surface seems to have been due to the kindling of fire on it.

The **script** is Sinhalese of the fourteenth century. As this is the first example of an inscription of this period to be reproduced in facsimile in the *Epigraphia Zeylanica*, a few remarks about the script may not be out of place here. Between the script of the fourteenth century and that of the Poḷonnaruva period, of which numerous examples have been reproduced in this journal, there is not much of a divergence. The letters which have undergone considerable change during the one and a half centuries which divide these two periods are *ṇa*, *na*, *ma*, *ra*, *va*, *sa*, and *ḷa*, as may be seen from the symbols for these syllables in the two periods shown side by side:—

ṇa *na* *ma* *ra* *va* *sa* *ḷa*

Twelfth century

Fourteenth century

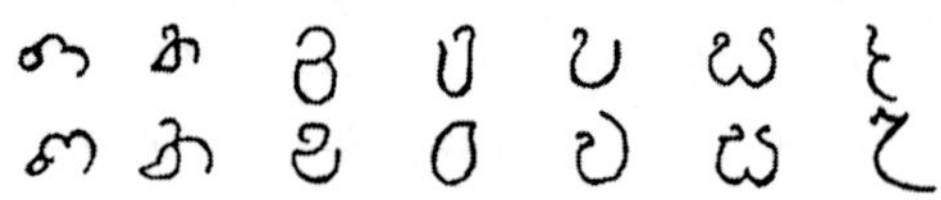

The general tendency of the script during this period is to emphasize, much more than in the preceding one, the sinuous curves which are characteristic of the modern Sinhalese alphabet. The script of the fourteenth century differs but little from the modern; and any one familiar with the Sinhalese writing of to-day will find no difficulty in recognizing the letters in an inscription of the Gampoḷa period, except the symbols for *i*, *ja*, *ṇa*, *ma*, *ra*, and *ḷa*. Even in the case of these letters, the relation of the modern symbols to their prototypes of the fourteenth century requires very little explanation to be understood. Within this inscription itself, there are certain letters which are not uniform in type. For example, we find the letter *ma*, almost identical with the Poḷonnaruva form, side by side with the more developed form shown above; compare the 17th letter of line 31 with the 15th of line 14. Other letters of which we find slightly differing types are *na*, *ja*, *ra*, and *ḷa*.

This want of uniformity is a characteristic feature of the script of the Gampoḷa period in general. The Laṅkātilaka rock-inscription[1], dated in the same year as this record, contains forms which are closer to the Poḷonnaruva

---

[1] See *J. R. A. S., C. B.*, vol. xxii, plate C facing p. 360, which gives only a section of this record.

script; for example the letter *ra* ර. The Hapugastänna[1] and the Vigulavatta[2] inscriptions, which are, respectively, only fifteen and sixteen years later than the present document, have forms of *ra*, *ḷa*, *ṇa*, and *na* differing widely from the corresponding letters in this epigraph. Nevertheless, the script of all these records shows, even without the aid of the dates given therein, that they belong to the same period.

After the auspicious words at the beginning, the first line contains a Sanskrit *śloka* in the *Indravajrā* metre; and the rest of the record is in Sinhalese. The document belongs to the period which has produced the best Sinhalese prose writings; hence, as may be expected, the language, reminiscent of that of these works, is correct and grammatical. Many Sanskrit *tatsamas* have been introduced into the document, as is also the case with the literary Sinhalese prose of the period. In the fourth line of the Sanskrit verse, however, the rules of prosody have been infringed by making the seventh syllable a long one. This is perhaps due to having overlooked the fact that a short vowel followed by a combination of consonants is counted as long. The following orthographical peculiarities may also be noted:—*Maddhaye* (l. 12), *Mayitrī* (l. 13), and *Niś-śaṁkha* (l. 29), should correctly have been *madhyaye*, *Maitrī*, and *Niśśaṁka* respectively. As in the South-Indian Grantha documents, the medial sign for the vowel *ṛ* is the same as the symbol for the consonant *ra* occurring as the last member of a ligature. Hence the words *vṛkṣa* (ll. 15–16) and *mātṛ* (l. 16) can also be read as *vrakṣa* and *mātra*. The form *narendraya-haṭa* occurring in l. 3, might be a variant form of, or a clerical error for, *narendrayā-haṭa*. The words *kumāra* (l. 31) and *gamin* (l. 32) have been repeated owing to an inadvertence of the engraver. *Kaḍavara* in the compound *gam-kaḍavara* (l. 35), does not occur in any other document of the period; and the Sanskrit word *sthapati* 'sculptor' (l. 11) has not been found in any other Sinhalese writing, literary or epigraphical, except in this and the Laṅkātilaka inscriptions.

The record is **dated** in the third year of **Bhuvanaikabāhu (the Fourth)** and also mentions the Śaka year 1266, expired. That part of the sentence which contains the date has been interpreted to mean that the Śaka year given is the same as the year of accession of Bhuvanaikabāhu[3], but a proper analysis of the sentence is against such an interpretation and would show that the Śaka year mentioned in the epigraph is equivalent to the third year of the king. According

---

[1] *Ibid.*, plate D facing p. 362.

[2] *Ibid.*, plate E facing p. 362

[3] Bell, *Report on the Kägalla District*, p. 92, n. 1, and Codrington, *Short History of Ceylon*, p. 88.

to the context, it is rather difficult to take *Śrī Śaka-varṣayen . . . . . piruṇu sanda* as an adverbial clause modifying *raja pämiṇi*. The occurrence of the word *mekal* between the two is against such an analysis of the sentence; and hence, the Śaka date cannot, in my opinion, be taken as that of Bhuvanaikabāhu's accession. On the other hand, the more reasonable way of analysing this sentence would be to take the two clauses *Śrī Śaka-varṣayen . . . . . piruṇu sanda* and *mekal raja pämini . . . . . tunvanne* as independent of each other and both qualifying that part of the sentence in which details regarding the month and day of the date are given. If the sentence be thus analysed, the Śaka year has to be taken, not as the date of Bhuvanaikabāhu's accession, but as equivalent to his third regnal year. The passage giving the date in the Laṅkātilaka rock-inscription [1] is almost in the very words of the corresponding passage in our inscription; hence, the above remarks apply to it as well.

The Śaka year mentioned in this inscription as well as in the Laṅkātilaka record has already been correctly read by Mr. Bell as 1266 [2]; the text of the Laṅkātilaka inscription published by Mudaliyar B. Gunasekara also gives the same year as the date of that document [3]. Mr. Codrington, in his *Short History of Ceylon* (p. 88) has similarly given the Śaka year mentioned in both these records. Dr. Wickremasinghe, however, on the authority of a manuscript copy of the Laṅkātilaka inscription, found in the British Museum, has taken Śaka 1264 as the date given in that record [4], and Professor Geiger [5] also follows Dr. Wickremasinghe in this respect. In both these inscriptions, the reading *sasäḷa* is quite clear on the rocks and the date in the British Museum copy of the Laṅkātilaka record can easily be taken as a clerical error (*susäḷa* for *sasäḷa*).

Messrs. Bell and Codrington, who take the Śaka year given in this epigraph as that of Bhuvanaikabāhu's accession, come to the conclusion that this monarch's initial regnal year was 1344-5 A.D. Dr. Wickremasinghe, who interprets the

---

[1] See *J. R. A. S., C. B.*, vol. x, p. 83.

[2] See *Report on the Kegalla District*, p. 92, n. 1, and *A. S. C. Annual Report* for 1911-12, p. 120.

[3] The text of the Laṅkātilaka inscription published in the *J. R. A. S., C. B.*, vol. x, pp. 83-86, by Mudaliyar Gunasekara, towards the end, differs widely from what is on the rock. Perhaps this text is based not on the rock-inscription but on some other version of the same document written on copper-plates or palm-leaves.

[4] *E. Z.*, Vol. III, p. 29.

[5] *Cūḷavaṁsa*, English translation, Part II, p. xxii. Professor Geiger in n. 1 at p. 211 of the same work takes the date as Śaka 1266.

sentence similarly, but reads the date differently, has given 1342 A.D. as the first year of Bhuvanaikabāhu IV. Professor Geiger, however, places more reliance on a statement in the *Nikāya Saṅgraha*, which will be noticed in the sequel, than on contemporary documents engraved on stone, and comes to the conclusion that this king's reign began in 1350–51 A.D.

If, on the other hand, the passages which contain the date in these two inscriptions be interpreted in the manner I have suggested above, the Śaka year 1266 has to be taken not as the date of Bhuvanaikabāhu's accession but as equivalent to his third regnal year. The exact date of the present record is the full-moon day of the month of Vesaga (Skt. *Vaiśākha*) in Śaka 1266, which is equivalent to Wednesday, April 28, 1344 A.D.[1]; and as the third regnal year was current at this date his reign must have commenced in 1341–2 A.D.

As has already been referred to, the *Nikāya Saṅgraha*[2], and, following it, the *Saddharmmaratnākara*[3], and the *Mahāvaṁsa*[4], equate the fourth year of this king with 1894 A.B., which makes his first year 1350–1 A.D., as has been taken by Professor Geiger. Between this and the date arrived at by us, there is a discrepancy of nine years. Dr. Wickremasinghe and Professor Geiger try to explain this discrepancy between the authorities by assuming that the earlier date was the one on which Bhuvanaikabāhu became the *āpā* (heir-apparent) of his predecessor and the later one, 1347 A.D., was that of his accession to the throne[5]. But this hypothesis becomes untenable when we consider the fact that in this inscription, which is dated 1344 A.D., Bhuvanaikabāhu is referred to by epithets which are applicable to a reigning king only, and not to an *āpā*. We should, I think, place more reliance on the statements found in contemporary stone inscriptions than on those in literary works, the earliest of which was written about half a century after the accession of Bhuvanaikabāhu IV. Mr. Codrington has shown that the *Nikāya Saṅgraha* is definitely wrong in two other dates given therein[6].

About this monarch himself, our record does not help us to learn anything new. He was the first Sinhalese king to rule from Gampoḷa, and in the chronicles there is nothing to show why he left the earlier capital. He is rather a vague personage and, in the writings of the period, his figure is overshadowed by that of his powerful minister, Senā Laṁkādhikāra.

---

[1] According to Dewan Bahadur Swamikannu Pillai's *Indian Ephemeris*.

[2] Colombo edition of 1890, p. 25. [3] *Ibid.*, 1923, p. 293. [4] Chap. xc, v. 108.

[5] *E. Z.*, Vol. III, pp. 29–30 and *Cūḷavaṁsa*, translation, pp. xxii–xxiii.

[6] *Ceylon Antiquary*, vol. ix, p. 186.

The **contents** tell us about the foundation of a shrine of Buddha at **Gaḍalādeṇiya** by the great *sthavira* **Dharmmakīrtti** who came of the Gaṇavāsi stock. The account of the building of the temple, which comprises more than one-third of the record, is followed by a long list of lands dedicated to it by various personages. The Gaṇavāsi family is said to have come to Ceylon bringing the Sacred Bo-tree. The origin of this family, which produced some of the greatest figures in the history of Ceylon during the fourteenth century, is similarly given in the Sagama inscription of the reign of Bhuvanaikabāhu V [1]. According to the *Saddharmaratnākara* [2], *Gaṇavāsi* is another name for the Lämäni family which had, as its progenitors, the Śākya princes Sumitra and Bodhigupta who were sent to Ceylon by Aśoka to accompany the branch of the sacred Bodhi tree. The name *Gaṇavāsi* is said to have attached itself to this family because its members, in course of time, became numerous and constituted themselves into a corporate body (*gaṇa*) [3].

The hierarch Dharmmakīrtti of this record was one of the greatest figures of the Buddhist Church in Ceylon in the middle of the fourteenth century. He belonged to the sect of forest-dwelling monks, which had its head-quarters at the hermitage founded at Paḷābatgala (P. *Puṭabhattasela*) near Adam's Peak, in the reign of Parākramabāhu II [4]. Laudatory accounts of this hierarch, from which we can also gather a few biographical facts about him, are given in the *Nikāya Saṅgraha* [5] and the colophon of the *Saddharmmālaṅkāra* [6], both of which are works of his pupil and namesake, Dharmmakīrtti, and in the *Saddharmaratnākara* [7], a work of Vimalakīrtti who was a pupil of the second Dharmmakīrtti. These accounts not only confirm what we learn about him from the inscription, but add that he was the author of several Pāli works among which were included

---

[1] *J. R. A. S., C. B.*, vol. xxii, pp. 364–365.

[2] *Op. cit.*, p. 296.

[3] *Kramayen samūhava gaṇivū heyin Gaṇavāsivaṁśaya yi kiyā da.* There is no doubt that this is a popular etymology of the word *Gaṇavāsi.* It can be interpreted to mean 'monastery official'. *Gaṇa* means 'the Buddhist congregation' and later acquired the secondary meaning of 'monastery'; and *vasi* is found in the tenth century inscriptions with the meaning 'employee' or 'official' (see *E. Z.*, Vol. III, p. 113). The family probably had its origin in some temple officials who acquired power and influence. This derivation of the word does not preclude the possibility of the family having been descended from the princes who accompanied the Bo-tree in the third century B.C. The officials entrusted with the administration of the vast estates of the mediaeval monasteries were often of noble birth.

[4] See *Pūjāvali*, Colombo, 1922, p. 694 and *Mv.* lxxxiv. 24.

[5] *Op. cit.*, pp. 28 and 32.

[6] Colombo edition of 1924, pp. 764–765.

[7] *Op. cit.*, p. 490.

Pāramīsataka and *Janānurāgacarita*[1]; that he, in addition to the Gaḍalādeṇiya-vihāra, also built a *vihāra* adorned with stone-work at Alavatura (in the Kāgalla District). He was also responsible for the purification of the *saṅgha* and the unification of the sects carried out during the administration of the great Alakeś-vara, and is said to have lived up to the age of 110.

Our record also tells us that Dharmmakīrtti, before he started the building of the Gaḍalādeṇiya temple, constructed, or rather repaired, a two-storied image-house at **Śrī Dhānyakaṭaka** (i.e. Amarāvatī) in India[2]. This statement is also confirmed by the *Saddharmaratnākara* which gives a more detailed account of Dharmmakīrtti's works of religious devotion at Amarāvatī. The passage in question in the *Saddharmaratnākara*, which is also interesting to show how the images were worshipped in the Buddhist shrines of the fourteenth century, is translated below:—

'Abroad, he (Dharmmakīrtti) also restored a stone-built *vihāra* named Śrī Dhānyakaṭaka making it, in workmanship, as it originally was. The marble image of the Lord, in sitting posture, eighteen cubits in height, which was in that stone shrine, and which was daily being anointed with water, he besmeared with scented paste to a thickness of two inches and offered to it *sevuvandi* flowers, affixed thereon so that the stalk of one flower touched that of the other. In the morning of the second day, he anointed the stone image, which appeared like an image of flowers, (firstly) with scented water, secondly with pots of sesamum oil, thirdly with milk, and fourthly with pure water, after the image was rubbed with scented powder; and was thus made exceedingly clean. He next offered to the image five thousand balls of rice, fifty at a time, in addition to dishes filled with milk-rice and bowls of rice and curries. Moreover, in one day alone, he lighted nine thousand lamps with sesamum oil and offered twenty *koṭis* of *idda* flowers and seventy-five lakhs of jasmine flowers. Thus he made different kinds of offerings to that image of the Lord.'

The references to Amarāvatī in our inscription and in the *Saddharmaratnākara* contain, I think, the last recorded events in the history of that great monument of the Āndhra country before it was discovered in modern times; and it is rather a pity that the author of the *Saddharmaratnākara* has not given a fuller

---

[1] For *Pāramīsataka*, see Malalasekara's *Pāli Literature of Ceylon* (London, 1928), p. 242. Manuscripts of the *Janānurāgacarita* have not been heard of.

[2] For the identification of Dhānyakaṭaka with the modern Amarāvatī, see Burgess, *Amarāvatī and Jaggayyapeṭa Stūpas*, p. 13.

account of the place as it then existed. The work of Dharmakīrtti at Amarāvatī is not the only instance of the Ceylon Buddhists of the fourteenth century striving to revive the dying flame of South Indian Buddhism. The great minister Senā Laṁkādhikāra, who was a contemporary of Dharmakīrtti, is said to have dispatched men and money to Kāñci and established a Buddhist shrine in that city[1].

The inscription also gives certain details about the architectural features of the shrine and the images and paintings with which it was adorned. The shrine is said to have been of three storeys which seem to have been calculated by taking the terraced roof of the *ardha-maṇḍapa* and *antarāla* as the second storey and a cell in the *vimāna*, on a higher level, as the topmost storey, in addition to the ground floor. As stated in the inscription, there are three images on the ground floor—a seated Buddha attended by two standing figures. On the *makara-toraṇa* behind the Buddha are figures of deities. No trace can be seen, however, of the representation of a Bodhi-tree under which the Buddha figure is said in the record to have been shown seated. We cannot be certain whether the paintings to be seen in the cella, which are only decorative designs, are the ones mentioned in the inscription. Inside the cell of the *vimāna*, the inscription says, there was originally an image depicting the Buddha preaching the Abhidhamma to the gods. This image has now disappeared; and on the walls are to be seen some scenes from the Vessantara Jātaka painted during Kandyan times. We cannot expect anything of the original paintings of this shrine to be preserved till now as it is stated that Parākramabāhu VI (1412–1467) renewed the plaster work[2]. The name of the architect who designed the building is given as **Gaṇeśvarācāri**. His name indicates, as we can also guess from the style of architecture, that he was a South Indian.

Among the persons who granted lands to the shrine, after it was completed, are a number of the great dignitaries of the time—princes, feudal lords, generals, bankers, and so forth. The majority of these personages are not known from other sources, while a few are mentioned in the other epigraphical records of the time as well as in literature. The most important among these is **Senā Laṁkādhikāra** who has already been referred to. It was this minister who built the other great architectural monument of the Gampola period, the Laṅkātilaka-

[1] See *Nikāya Saṅgraha*, English translation, p. 24.

[2] See *Saddharmaratnākara*, *op. cit.*, p. 298.

vihāra, about three miles from Gaḍalādeṇiya. The two long inscriptions at Laṅkātilaka, one in Sinhalese and the other in Tamil, and the rock inscription at Alavaḷa in the Kuruṇāgala District[1], give an account of the building of that shrine and the lands dedicated to it by this minister as well as by others. Senā Laṁkādhikāra is also one of the signatories in the Vigulavatta (Gampola) inscription[2] and he is mentioned in the *Nikāya Saṅgraha*[3], *Saddharmaratnākara*[4] and other Sinhalese writings. **Vīrasiṁha Patirāja** was also one of the signatories in the Vigulavatta inscription. Prince **Vīrasundara** is mentioned in an inscription of about the fourteenth century, discovered at the village called Malvattegala in Hēvāgam Kōraḷē[5], as the founder of a *vihāra* at that place. There is not sufficient ground to take, as Mr. Bell has done[6], that **Niśśaṁka Patirāja** of this inscription is the same as the great warrior and statesman, Niśśaṁka Alakeśvara, who was the most important figure in Ceylon a decade or two after the date of this inscription.

As regards the **geographical names** mentioned in the record, Dhānyakaṭaka has already been dealt with. Siṅguruvāṇa (also spelt Siṅduruvāṇa) was the name of this part of the country in mediaeval times ; and the two *nuvaras* (cities) of Siṅguruvāṇa are now preserved in the two territorial divisions 'Uḍu-Nuvara' and 'Yaṭi-Nuvara'. Our inscription shows that, in the fourteenth century, the site of the Gaḍalādeṇiya temple was at the boundary of these two districts. Among the names of villages in which lands were dedicated to the shrine, I have not been able to find Ilupändeṇiya, Māyatgamu, Nāraṁ-riyana, Miṅginiyāpotta, and Uṇapatäṅge, in the official village lists or in the maps of the topographical survey. The majority of the others are still known by the same names as are given in the inscription; and are situated, as may be expected, not very far from the shrine. Gaḍalādeṇiya, Pamuṇuva, Rangama, Dälivela, Kirivavula, and Piligama are in Mädapaḷāta Kōraḷē of the Uḍunuvara Division. Ambäkka and Sāpāṇa are the modern Ämbäkka and Häpāṇa of the same Kōraḷē. Sandessa is the modern Handessa in Gaṅgapaḷāta Kōraḷē in Uḍunuvara. Piḷimatalavuva is in Mädapaḷāta Kōraḷē of the Yaṭinuvara Division and Ämbulmīgama is most probably the modern Äṁbilimīgama in the same Kōraḷē. Gannoruva and

[1] The Sinhalese inscription at the place has already been noted. The Tamil inscription is yet unpublished. For the Alavaḷa record, see *C. J. Sc.* (*G.*), vol. ii, p. 188.

[2] *J. R. A. S., C. B.*, vol. xxii, p. 363.

[3] *Op. cit*, p. 25.

[4] *Op. cit.*, pp. 293–294.

[5] *C. J. Sc.*, *G.*, vol. ii, p. 200.

[6] *Ceylon Antiquary and Literary Register*, vol. ii, p. 184.

Maṅgalagama are in Gaṅgapaḷāta Kōraḷē in the Yaṭinuvara Division. Uḍuvela is in Gandahē Kōraḷē of the Pāta Hēvāhäṭa Division and Aludeṇiya in Uḍapaḷāta Kōraḷē of Tumpanē. All the above-mentioned villages are in the Kandy District. Bisōvaḷa is a village in Kaňdupiṭa North, Beligal Kōraḷē, and Iddavela in Tunpaḷāta West, Paraṇakūru Kōraḷē, both in the Kāgalla District. Uturālla may be the same as Uturala in Egoḍapota Kōraḷē, Kāgalla District. In that case Eḷirata, in which Uturālla is said to have been included, must have been a territorial division of the fourteenth century which comprised that part of the modern Kāgalla District. I have not come across an old territorial division of this name in the *Kaḍaimpot* which deals with the geography of late mediaeval Ceylon.

TEXT.

1 ස්වස්ති ශුභමස්තු [।*]
ශ්‍රීධර්මකීර්ත්තිස්ථවිරාධි(කාරෛ) ∩ ∩ – ∩ ∩ –
ර්ජනාඤ්ජි ∩ ∩ [।*]
∩ ∩ – තු[ං] පුණ්‍යමනෙකරූපං කාරාපයන් ශ්‍රීඝනශ්‍රීවිහාරං [॥*]

2 ශ්‍රීශකවර්ෂයෙන් එක්වා[දහස්] දෙසිය සසැට අවුරු[ද්දක් පි]රුණු [ස]ඳ
[මෙ]කල් රජපැමිණි ත්‍රිසිංහ

3 ළාධිශ්වර භුවනෛකබා[හු න]රෙන්‍ද්‍රයහට තුන්වනු (වෙසග) [පුර] පසළො
ස්වක ශ්‍රීමහාබොධි වඩා

4 ශ්‍රීලංකාද්වීපයට පැමිණි [ගණ]වැ[සි]වංශාභිජාත ධර්මකීර්ත්තිස්ථවිරපාදයන්
වහන්සෙ ද

5 ඹබදිවැන් ශ්‍රීධාන්‍යකමයෙ[1] (දෙමා)ල් පිළිමගෙයක් .. .. බොහො
[ර]න්[රුවන්] .. .. .. [ලං]කාද්වීප

6 යෙහිත් [බොහො]කාලයක් පවත්නා ලෙසැ සි[ලාමය පිළි]මගෙයක් කර
වනු කැමැතිවැ රජ හුව

7 රජ අ[ධිකාර සෙ]නෙවිරත් (අතම්)නාය[ක] .. .. .. නායක .. .. .. නායක
.. .. ලිය

8 න්නත් ආ[දිවූ පෘ]පුවීශ්වරයන්[2] ද .. .. .. න් ද (ක්ෂත්‍රිය) බ්‍රා(හ්මණ වෛ)
ශ්‍ය ශූද්‍රාදි [උත්තම]මා

9 ධම ජනයන් ද සිංහළ දෙමළ ආදිවූ .. .. .. සෙනා කෙ .. .. තන .. ..
කරවා පණමින් ල[ක්]

10 ෂයක් විවරත් වී තුන්සියක් යාළ විවරත් [දී] වාස්තුශාස්ත්‍රප්‍රතිමාශ[ාස්ත්‍රාදි]
යෙහි වි .. ..

---

[1] 'ධාන්‍යකටකයෙ' සි කියවනු. [2] 'පෘථිවීශ්වරයන්' සි කියවනු.

11 සඵපතිගණාධිපති ග[ණෙ]ශ්වරාචාරීන් ප්‍රධාන කොට ඇති ආචාරිවරුන් ලවා සි[ඟුරු]වාණිදෙ

12 නුවර මධයෙ[1] දික්ගලඅතලෙ නුන්මාල් පිළිමගෙය[2] කරවනසෙක් පල්ලෙ මාලෙ ශක්‍ර බ්‍රහ්ම

13 සුයාම සන්තුෂිත නාථ මයිත්‍රී[3] ආදි දෙවියන් විසින් පිරිවරනලද වජ්‍රාසනාරූඪවූ බොධිත්වහ

14 න්සෙට පිට ලා වැඩැ හුන් සධාතුක මහපිළිමසාමි[නුන්] අනුපිළිම දෙදෙනාවහන්සෙන් [නො]

15 යෙක් චිත්‍රකර්ම්මාන්තයෙන් විචිත්‍ර කොට කරවා මුදුන්මාලෙ චෛත්‍යගර්භයෙහි පා[රිජාත]වෘ

16 ක්‍ෂමූලයෙහි පාණ්ඩුකම්බලා[සනාරූ]ඪවූ මාතෘදෙවපුත්‍රප්‍රමුඛ ශක්‍රබ්‍රහ්මාදි දෙ[වියන් පි]රි .

17 වරා විජම්දෙශනාවට වැඩ හුන් [බුධ]රූපය කරවා වි[හාර]යට ආරක්‍ෂාවකුත් උව මැනැවැ යි .. .. දෙ

18 විරජගෙයකුත් කරවා බොධි චෛත්‍ය පුෂ්පාරාම ඵලාරාමා[දීන්] සරහා තමන්වහන්සෙ .. .. ය

19 න් කරවනලද .. .. ධර්ම්මකීර්ති නම් මෙවිහා[රය දූකැ] සමාධිවැ .. .. දෙණි .. .. ඉ

20 හියා ෙ .. .. [කර්ම්මා]න්තයට පණම් නුන්දූසක් වි[චරන්] .. .. .. ගෙවළ ද(වෙල් වහ)ල්

21 සරක් ස .. .. .. නරබත්ගමින් පිදූ කිඳු .. .. සෙ[නෙවි] රදු

22 න් හා විරසිංහ පතිරාජයන් (හා) දෙන්නා ෙ .. .. ඉලුපැ(න්දෙණියෙ)න් පිදූ මුල්කිඳු

23 සාමුණෙක් සෙනා ලංකාධිකාරයන් තම(න්ට අ)වෙලට සිටි සං[දෙස්සෙ]න් පිදූ කුඹුරු කි

24 ඳු එක්යාළ දසාමුණෙක් කෙසව වණ්ණක්කයන් හා දන්(ගමු) .. .. මන් හා දෙන්නා

25 සතු ස .. (ගඩ)ලාදෙණිගම් දෙභාගයෙන් මුල්කිඳු .. .. මුණක් මුලාර ළිහ[යෙහි පි]

26 දූය ෙ(දු)වගිරි පතිරාජ[යන්] තමන්ට අවෙලට සිටි .. .. ල්පිටිගමින් කිඳු සාමුණක්

27 පුදූ .. .. සරක්රූ දසයෙක් බිසොවල දෙ පතිරාජයන් එළිරට උතුරාලි

---

[1] 'මධ්‍යයෙ' යි කියවනු. [2] ගෙයක්? [3] 'මෛත්‍රී' යි කියවනු.

28 ලත්[1] [පිදූ කුඹු]රු බිජු යාළෙක් **කළු සිවාණන්** මායන්ගමු බත්ගමින් පිදූ කු

29 ඹුරු [බිජු] .. .. .. ක් හා ගෙවත්තෙන් **නිශංඛ පතිරාජයන්** පවුළුවෙන්

30 පිදූ බි[ජු අමුණෙ]ක් **විජයා පතිරාජයන්** රත්ගමින් පිදූ කුඹුරු බිජු දෑමුණක් හා

31 වගල්රු තුණෙක් **වීරසුන්දර** (කුමාර)[2] **කුමාරයන්**ගෙ නාරංරිය[නින්] පිදූ කුඹුරු බිජු

32 අමුණෙක් **අනුරා අග්නරුන්** ගත්නොරුගමින් (ගමින්)[2] අය ඔතු දී බත්[බුත්තු]න්

33 ප්‍රයොජන විඳිනා ලෙසට පිදූ කුඹුරු බිජු පසමුණෙක් (දෙසිම දෙකෙක්) **ජීවසිං[හ] කුමාරයන්**

34 මිගිනියාපොත්තෙන් පිදූ කුඹුරු බිජු දසාමුණෙක් **යුව කුමාරයන්** සං දෙස්[සෙන් පිදූ] කුඹුරු

35 බිජු .. .. .. මූණක් හා ගම්කඩවර එකෙක් **යුව[පතිරා]ජයන්** උඩුවෙලින් පිදූ ගම්කඩවරක් හා කු

36 ඹුරු [බිජු අ]මු[ණෙ]ක් මෙසෙම දූලිවෙලි[න් කුඹුරු] බිජු දෑමුණෙක් අළුදෙණියෙ ගත්තරදී

37 වෙලින් අමුණෙක් පිළිමතලවුවෙ[න් අමුණෙක්] කිරිවවුලෙන් අමුණෙක් සෑපාණීන් අ

38 මුණෙක් ඉද්දවෙලින් අමුණෙක් අ .. .. න් අමුණෙක් ඇඹුල්ඹිගමින් තුන්පැළෙ

39 **ක් උණ්**පතාගෙන් තුන්පැළෙක් මංගලගමින් තුන්පැළෙක් පිලිගමින් දෙපැළෙක් **දීගි**

40 **ළි සෙනානායකයන්** අම්බැක්කෙ බොකේකුඹුරෙන් පිදූ බිජු දෑමුණෙක්

41 **මින් දහම්සසන්නාවන්** කිරිවවුලෙන් පිදූ බිජු [අමුණෙක්] .. .. දෙපැළෙ

42 ක් වටනාපස දෙපැළෙක් යටිවිගොත් දෙරුවෙ[ක්*] කුඹු[රු බිජු] .. .. ක්

43 (සෙට්ටි) .. .. ක් (බෙ)රෙගමින් පණම .. .. .. ක් දී ග[ත්] .. .. .. ක්

---

[1] 'උතුරාල්ලෙන්' සී කියවනු.

[2] මේ අක්ෂර තුණ වැරදීමකින් දෙවරක් ලියවී තිබේ.

Gaḍalādeṇiya Rock-Inscription of Dharmmakirtti

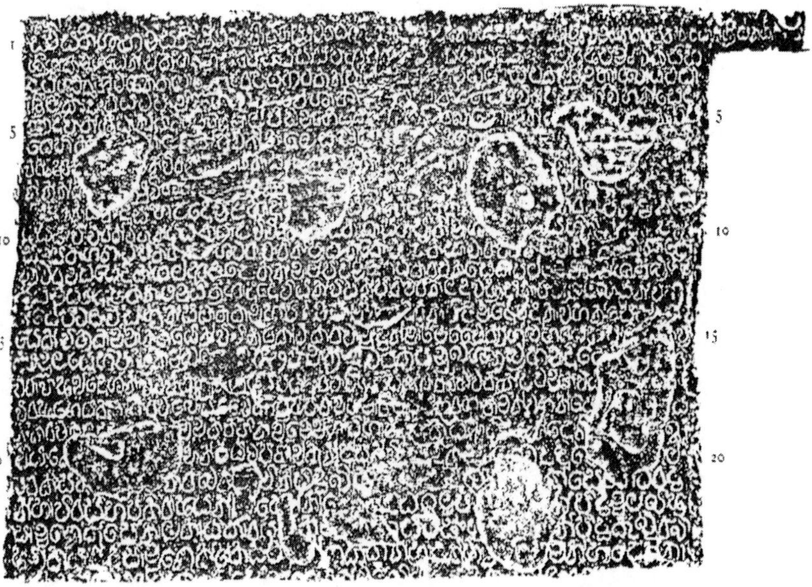

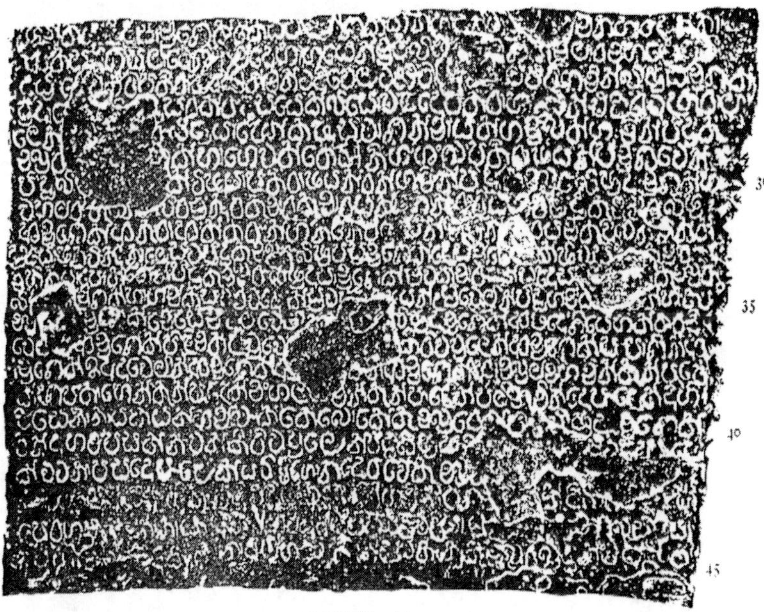

Scale ½ inch to 1 foot

44 පෙරගම [සෙ]නානාය[කයන්] අ .. .. (පිළියාය) .. ..
.. .. ..

45 .. .. කොට නාර .. .. න් උඩ තැනූ කුඹුරු කිජු
නව .. .. ..

TRANSLITERATION.

1 Svasti śubham=astu[1*]
Śrī-Dharmmakīrtti-sthavirādhi(kārai) ⏑ ⏑ – ⏑ ⏑ –
janān=vi ⏑ ⏑ [1*]
⏑⏑–tu[ṁ] puṇyam=anaika-rūpaṁ kārāpayan Śrīghana-śrī-vihāraṁ[‖*]

2 Śrī-Śaka-varṣayen ek-vā-[dahas] de-siya sa-säṭa avuru-[ddak pi]ruṇu [sa]nda [me]-kal raja-pämiṇi Tri-Siṁha-

3 ḷādhīśvara **Bhuvanaikabā[hu** na] rendraya-haṭa tun-vanu (Vesaga)[pura] pasaḷosvaka śrī-mahā-bodhi vaḍā

4 Śrī-Laṁkadvīpaya-ṭa pämiṇi [Gaṇa]vä[si]-vaṁśābhijāta **Dharmmakīrtti**-sthavira-pādayan-vahanse Da-

5 -mbadivät **Śrī-Dhānyakaṭaye**[1] (demā)l piḷima-geyak .. .. boho [ra]n-[ruvan .. .. .. [Laṁ]kā-dvīpa-

6 yehit [boho]-kālayak pavatnā lesä si[lāmaya piḷi]ma-ge(yak karavanu kämätivä raja) yuva-

7 raja a[dhikāra se]nevirat (arttha)nāya[ka] .. .. .. nāyaka .. .. .. nāyaka .. .. liya-

8 -nnan ā[di-vū pṛ]thuvīśvarayan[2] da .. .. .. n da (kṣatriya) brā(hmaṇa vai)śya śūdr=ādi [utta]m=ā-

9 -dhama janayan da Siṁhaḷa Demaḷa ādi-vū .. .. .. senā ke .. ṭta .. .. karavā paṇamin la[k]-

10 -ṣayak vicarat vī tun-siyak yāḷa vicarat [dī] vāstu-śāstra-pratimā-ś[āstr=ādi]yehi vi .. ..

11 sthapati-gaṇādhipati **Ga[ṇe]śvarācārīn** pradhāna koṭa äti ācārivarun lavā **Si[ṅguru]vāṇā**-de-

12 nuvara maddhaye[3] Dikgala-ataḷe tun-māl piḷima-geya[4] karavanasek palle māle Śakra Brahma

13 Suyāma Santuṣita Nātha Mayitrī[5] ādi deviyan visin pirivarana-lada vajrāsan=ārūḍha-vä Bodhīn-vaha-

---

[1] Read *Dhānyakaṭakaye*.
[2] Read *pṛthivīśvarayan*.
[3] Read *madhyaye*.
[4] Perhaps to be read as *geyak*.
[5] Read *Maitrī*.

14 -nse-ṭa piṭa lā väḍä hun sadhātuka maha-piḷima-sāmī[nut] anu-piḷima de-denā-vahanset [no]-

15 -yek citra-karmmāntayen vicitra koṭa karavā mudun-māle caitya-garbbha-yehi pā[rijāta] -vṛ-

16 -kṣa-mūlayehi pāṇḍu-kambalā[san=ārū]ḍha-vä Mātṛ-devaputra-pramukha Śakra-Brahm=ādi de[viyan pi]ri-

17 -varā vijam-deśanāva-ṭa väḍa hun [Buddha]-rūpaya karavā vi[hāra]ya-ṭa ārakṣāvak-ut uva mänävä yi .. .. de-

18 -viraja-geyak-ut karavā bodhi caitya puṣpārāma phalārām=ā[dīn] sarahā taman-vahanse .. .. ya-

19 -n karavana-lada .. .. **Dharmmakīrtti** nam me-vihā[raya däkä] samādhi-vä .. .. deṇi .. .. i-

20 -miyā e .. .. [karm]māntaya-ṭa paṇam tun-dāsak vi[carat] .. .. gevaḷa di(vel vaha)l

21 sarak sa .. .. .. nara-batgamin pidū biju .. .. **se[nevi]-radu-**

22 **-n** hā **Vīrasiṁha Patirājayan** (hā) dennā . e .. .. Ilupä(ndeṇiye)n pidū mul-biju

23 sāmuṇek **Senā Laṁkādhikārayan** tama (n-ṭa) (divelaṭa) siṭi Saṁ[desse]n pidū kuburu bi-

24 -ju ek-yāḷa dasāmuṇek **Kesava Vaṇṇakkan** hā **Dan(gamu)** .. .. **man** hā dennā

25 satu sa .. (Gaḍi)lādeṇi-gam de-bhāgayen mul-biju .. .. muṇak mūlā-rambha[yehi pi]-

26 -dūya **(D)evagiri Patirāja[yan]** taman-ṭa divelaṭa siṭi .. .. Ipiṭi-gamin biju sāmuṇak

27 pudā .. .. sarak-rū dasayek **Bisovaḷa De Patirājayan** Eḷiraṭa Uturāli-

28 -len[1] [pidū kumbu]ru biju yāḷek **Kaḷu Siṭāṇan** Māyatgamu batgamin pidū ku-

29 -mburu [biju] .. .. .. k hā ge-vattek **Niśśaṁkha**[2] **Patirājayan** Pamu-ṇuven

30 pidū bi[ju amuṇe]k **Vijayā Patirājayan** Rangamin pidū kumburu biju dāmuṇak hā

31 vahal-rū tuṇek **Vīrasundara** (kumāra)[3] **Kumārayan**ge Nāraṁriya[nin] pidū kumburu biju

---

[1] Read *Uturāllen*.

[2] Read *Niśśaṁka*.

[3] Three *akṣaras* have been repeated here by mistake.

32 amuṇek **Anurā Attarun** Gannoru-gamin (gamin)[1] aya otu dī ban[dhūnu]t

33 prayojana vindinā lesaṭa pidū kumburu biju pas⸗amuṇek (desima deke)k **Jīvasiṁ[ha] Kumārayan**

34 Miṅginiyāpotten pidū kumburu biju das⸗āmuṇek **Suva Kumārayan** Saṁdes[sen pidū] kumburu

35 biju .. .. .. munak hā gam-kaḍavara ekek **Suva [Patirā]jayan** Uḍuvelin pidū gam-kaḍavarak hā ku-

36 -mburu [biju a]mu[ṇe]k mese-ma Däliveli[n kumburu] biju dāmuṇek Aḷudeṇiye Gattara-di-

37 -velin amuṇek Piḷimatalavuve[n amuṇek] Kirivavulen amuṇek Sāpāṇin a-

38 -muṇek Iddavelin amuṇek A .. .. n amuṇek Ämbulmigamin tun-päḷe-

39 -k Uṇapatāṅgen tun-päḷek Maṅgala[ga]min tun-päḷek Piligamin de-päḷek **Digi-**

40 **-ḷi Senānāyakayan** Ambäkke Bokē-kumburen pidū biju dāmuṇek

41 **Min Dahampasak-nāvan** Kirivavulen pidū biju [amuṇek] .. .. de-päḷe-

42 -k vaṭanā-pasa de-päḷek yaṭi-mīgon de-ruve[k*] kumbu[ru biju] .. .. k

43 (Seṭṭi) .. .. k (Be)regamin paṇam .. .. .. k dī ga[t] .. .. .. k

44 **Peragama [Se]nānāya[kayan]** a .. .. (viḷi-yāya) .. ..

45 .. .. koṭa Nāra .. .. n uḍa tänu kumburu biju na[va] .. .. ..

TRANSLATION.

[Line 1] Hail! Let there be Happiness! By the exertion of **Śrī Dharmma-kīrtti-sthavira**, ... people . . . . . merit of diverse kinds, in causing a *vihāra* for Buddha[2] to be constructed.

---

[1] Three *akṣaras* have been repeated here by mistake.

[2] The word *vihāra*, which originally meant a monastery, is here applied, as it is also in modern Sinhalese, to an image-house, on the ground that it is the abode of Buddha (i.e. the image of Buddha).

[Lines 2–3] When One Thousand Two Hundred and Sixty Six years had been completed from the year of the illustrious Śaka, and in the third year unto King **Bhuvanaikabāhu**, the overlord of the three Siṁhaḷas[1], who has attained sovereignty at the present time—on the fifteenth day of the waxing moon in Vesaga.

[Lines 3–5] His Holiness **Dharmmakīrtti-sthavira,** born in the family of Gaṇaväsi which has come to the island of Śrī Laṁkā bringing the holy Mahābodhi (tree), (restored) a two-storied image-house at **Śrī Dhānyakaṭaka** in Dambadiva[2], too, [by spending] much gold and jewels.

[Lines 5–12] He, being desirous of causing an image-house of stone to be founded in the island of Laṁkā, so that it may last a long time, ... lords of the earth such as kings, sub-kings, officers of state, commanders of the army, judges[3], ... chiefs ..... chiefs, scribes, high and low folk such as *kṣatriyas*, *brāhmaṇas*, *vaiśyas*, and *śūdras*, ... army, such as Sinhalese, Tamils .... being made ....[4] and having given about a hundred thousand in *fanams*[5] and three thousand *yāḷas*[6] of paddy, he caused to be built, on the expanse of flat rock called Dikgala, between the two towns of **Siṅguruvāṇā**, a three-storied image-house, by engaging master-artisans, at whose head was **Gaṇeśvarācāri**, the chief of the guild of sculptors, who was (well versed) in such arts as architecture and image-making.

[Lines 12–18] In the lowest storey [of that image-house, he] caused to be made, beautified by diverse paintings, the principal image, containing relics[7], which [depicted Buddha] seated on the *vajrāsana*[8], with his back to the Sacred Bodhi-tree and attended by gods such as Sakra, Brahma, Suyāma[9], Santuṣita[10],

---

[1] See *E. Z.*, Vol. III, p. 330, n. 2, for the three kingdoms into which Ceylon was theoretically divided.

[2] Skt. *Jambudvīpa*, i.e. India.

[3] *Arthanāyaka*.

[4] The purport of this part of the sentence, which is fragmentary, seems to be to state that Dharmmakīrtti secured the co-operation of various dignitaries of state, as well as ordinary men, in the work of building the shrine.

[5] For this coin, see Codrington, *Ceylon Coins and Currency*, pp. 80–81.

[6] See *E. Z.*, Vol. III, p. 183.

[7] The practice of depositing relics inside images is first mentioned in this period.

[8] Buddha was seated on a *vajrāsana*, under the Bodhi-tree, when he attained omniscience. For the *vajrāsana* in Buddhist iconography, see B. Bhattacarya, *Buddhist Iconography*, p. 11.

[9] The king of the heaven called Yāma, the third from below according to Buddhist cosmology.

[10] The king of the heaven called Tuṣita, the one above Yāma.

Nātha[1], and Mayitrī[2]; and two attendant images. In the cell of the *caitya*[3] on the top-most storey, he caused to be made an image of Buddha [depicting him seated], for delivering the discourse on the Abhidharmma[4], on the throne Paṇḍu-kambala[5] under the Pārijāta[6] tree, and attended by the gods Śakra, Brahma, and others, led by Mātṛ-devaputra[7]. [Thinking] that there should also be a protection for this *vihāra*, he caused a shrine of . . . . . , the king of gods, too, to be built[8].

[Lines 18–45] Pleased at seeing this great *vihāra*, named **Dharmmakīrtti**[9], caused to be established by . . . . . . His Holiness, and which was provided with Bodhi-trees, *caityas*, flower gardens, &c.[10] . . . . . Deṇi . . . imiyā . . . . . about three thousand *fanams* for the work, ...[11] maintenance lands[12], slaves, cattle . . . . . . and [the sowing extent of] . . . . seed from the *batgama*[13] . . . . nara; the sowing extent of six *amuṇas*[14] of sprouted seed[15] paddy from Ilupä(ndeniya),

---

[1] *Nātha* is the shortened form of *Lokeśvara Nātha*, the name by which the Mahāyāna Bodhisattva Avalokiteśvara is known in Ceylon (see *C. J. Sc.*, (*G.*), vol. ii, pp. 52 ff.).

[2] *Maitreya*, the Buddha-to-be, is believed to exist, at present, as a god in the Tuṣita heaven.

[3] What is referred to as a *caitya* here is the dome-shaped *vimāna* of the shrine.

[4] The third section of the Pāli Tipiṭaka (in Sinhalese *Vijam*), which deals with psychological matters, is said to have been first delivered by Buddha to the gods.

[5] The stone seat of Śakra, king of the gods.

[6] A celestial tree in the Nandana park in Śakra's heaven.

[7] Queen Māyā, the mother of Buddha, who died a week after his birth, is said to have been born in the Tuṣita heaven and is known as Mātṛ-devaputra.

[8] The shrines of Hindu gods now attached to almost every Buddhist temple in Ceylon, seem first to have been introduced in order to install these deities as guardians. The title *dev-raja* 'king of gods' being applicable to more than one god, we are not in a position to say what particular deity was originally installed at Gaḍalādeṇiya.

[9] According to the *Saddharmmaratnākara* (*op. cit.*, p. 490), the *vihāra* at Gaḍalādeṇiya was known as Saddharmmatilaka.

[10] The record being fragmentary here, the connexion of this clause to those which follow is not clear. The missing words probably expressed the idea that the personages, whose names follow, granted lands, &c., to the shrine for its maintenance.

[11] The fragmentary nature of the text here does not permit us to conjecture what *gevaḷa* stands for.

[12] *Divel*, see *E. Z.*, Vol. III, p. 191, foot-note 9.

[13] A *batgama*, in Kandyan times, was a royal village tenanted by people of the Padu caste, see Codrington, *Glossary of Native, Foreign, and Anglicised Words, s.v.*

[14] See *E.Z.*, Vol. III, p. 184.

[15] *Mul-biju* :—Paddy, before being sown, is kept in water till roots sprout forth. In the fourteenth century, as it is still in Sinhalese villages, fields were measured according to the quantity of paddy with which they were capable of being sown.

granted by the two,...... **Senevirad** and **Vīrasiṁha Patirāja** [1]; fields [of the sowing extent of] one *yāḷa* and ten *amuṇas* of seed from Saṁdessa, which has been held as maintenance lands of his, granted by **Senā Laṁkādhikāra**; [the sowing extent of]..... *amuṇas* of sprouted seed [paddy] from the two shares of the (Gaḍi)lādeṇi village, belonging to the two, **Kesava Vaṇṇakka** [2] and **Dan(gamu)**...... **man**, were granted at the beginning of the work; [the sowing extent of] ten *amuṇas* of seed from..... piṭigama, which is a maintenance land of his,.... and ten head of cattle granted by **(D)evagiri Patirāja**; fields [of the sowing extent of] a *yāḷa* of seed from Uturālla in Eḷiraṭa granted by **De Patirāja** [3] of Bisovaḷa; fields [of the sowing extent of].... seed, and one house and garden from the *batgama* Māyatgamu, granted by **Kaḷu Siṭāṇa** [4]; [the sowing extent of] an *amuṇa* of seed from Pamuṇuva, granted by

---

[1] *Patirāja*, occurring in this as well as in several other names of persons figuring in this record, is obviously a title. Persons bearing this title also figure in other contemporary records (see *J. R. A. S., C. B.*, vol x, p. 91 and vol. xxii, p. 363) and in literary works of the period such as the *Pūjāvalī* (*op. cit.* p. 698) and the *Attanagalu-vaṁsa* (Colombo edition of 1925, p. 48). In the printed editions of these works, the word, however, is given as *pratirāja*; and Sinhalese pandits take it as a compound of Skt. *prati* and *rājan*, and interpret in some way to mean 'viceroy'. But the Sanskrit compound *pratirāja* means 'enemy king' and is altogether inappropriate for the title of a state official or courtier. Our inscription mentions a number of *patirājas* who flourished in the reign of Bhuvanaika bāhu IV, and probably there were others who had this title at that time. All of those could not have been 'viceroys'. Moreover, the inscriptions invariably use the form *patirāja*, and as it is reasonable to assume that the contemporary documents used the correct form, we may take *pratirāja* as due either to the ignorance of copyists, or to the pedantry of the modern editors, of the literary works. We may therefore take this word as a compound of Skt. *pati* and *rājan*. The material part of the compound is *pati* 'lord' and *rāja* is most probably suffixed as an honorific, precisely as it occurs in the Sinhalese word *senevirada* (Skt. *senāpatirāja*). The *Nikāya Saṅgraha* (*op. cit.* p. 27), in order to justify the title of *prabhurāja* borne by Alakeśvara, says that there were five catagories of persons to whom the title *rāja* can be applied, namely, supreme ruler of the island (*dipādhirāja*), ruler of a district (*maṇḍalika-rāja*), ruler of a province (*pradeśa-rāja*), feudatory nobles (*antarabhogika-rāja*) and counsellors (*anuśāsaka-rāja*). *Pati* and *prabhu* being synonymous, the titles *patirāja* and *prabhurāja* might have had the same significance and were possibly adopted by the feudatory nobles who, in mediaeval Ceylon, wielded a good deal of influence, like the feudal barons of contemporary Europe. The title *patirāja* first occurs in the thirteenth century and continued in use till about the end of the fifteenth.

[2] *Vaṇṇakka* means 'appraiser'. In Kandyan times, there was an official called 'Vaṇṇaku Nilame' (see D'Oyly, *Constitution of the Kandyan Kingdom*, Colombo, 1929, p. 137).

[3] The expression *Bisovaḷa de patirājayan* can also be translated as 'the two *patirājas* of Bisovaḷa'. I have taken *De* as a personal name equivalent to *Deva*.

[4] *Siṭāṇa* is the Sinhalese form of Skt. *śreṣṭhin*, P. *seṭṭhi* 'a banker'. Compare 'Joti Siṭāṇa' in the Maḍavala rock inscription (*E. Z.* Vol. III, p. 239).

Niśśaṁka Patirāja; fields [of the sowing extent of] two *amuṇas* of seed from Rangama and three head of slaves [1] granted by **Vijayā Patirāja**; fields [of the sowing extent of] an *amuṇa* of seed from Nāraṁriyana, granted by **Prince Vīrasundara**; fields [of the sowing extent of] five *amuṇas* of seed, from the village of Gannoru, and two *desima* [2], granted by **Anurā Attara** [3], reserving the right for his relations to enjoy [them] paying [the usual] dues and tithes [4]; fields [of the sowing extent of] ten *amuṇas* of seed from Miṅginiyāpotta, granted by **Prince Jīvasiṁha**; fields [of the sowing extent of] . . . . . *amuṇas* of seed and one *gam-kaḍavara* [5] from Saṁdessa, granted by **Prince Suva**; one *gam-kaḍavara* and fields [of the sowing extent of] one *amuṇa* of seed from Uḍuvela granted by **Suva Patirāja**; likewise [granted by the same person], fields [of the sowing extent of] two *amuṇas* of seed from Dälivela, an *amuṇa* from Piḷimatalavuva, an *amuṇa* from Kirivavula, an *amuṇa* from Sāpāṇa, an *amuṇa* from Iddavela, an *amuṇa* from A . . . . . three *päḷas* [6] from Ämbulmigama, three *päḷas* from Uṇapatāṅga, three *päḷas* from Maṅgalagama, two *päḷas* from Piligama; [the sowing extent of] two *amuṇas* of seed from Bokē-kumbura in Ambäkka, granted by **Digiḷi Senānāyaka** [7]; [the sowing extent of] an *amuṇa* of seed from Kirivavula granted by **Min Dahampasaknā** [8]; two *päḷas* . . . . two *päḷas* for requisites [9] for the

---

[1] *Vahal-rū*, literally 'bodies of slaves'. The same expression is used in connexion with cattle in line 27, *sarak-rū dasayek*.

[2] The reading of this word is doubtful and its meaning is altogether obscure.

[3] *Attara* occurring in this name appears to be a title, the significance of which is not known. It also occurs in an earlier form in the names Parākrama Atvara, and Mīnd Atvara in the Nākolaganē inscription, see *E. Z.*, Vol. III, p. 70. It is also preserved in the place-name *Attaragama*.

[4] *Otu*:—For details regarding the levying of this due in Kandyan times, see D'Oyly, *Constitution of the Kandyan Kingdom*, *op. cit.*, p. 55, and Codrington, *Glossary of Native, Foreign, and Anglicised Words*, *op. cit.*, *s.v*

[5] The term *gam-kaḍavara*, so far as I know, occurs only in this document. *Gam* means 'village' or 'estate'. *Kaḍavara* may be the same as *kaḍavar* occurring in the expression *kämbur-kaḍavar* in the Poḷonnaruva Council Chamber pillar-inscription, which, I have conjectured, may mean 'share' (see above, p. 44, n. 3).

[6] For *päla*, see *E. Z.*, Vol. III, p. 184.

[7] 'Digiḷiya' was the name by which Haṅguranketa was known in the time of Rājasiṁha II (see Robert Knox, *An Historical Relation of Ceylon*, Glasgow, 1911, p. 9). 'Senānāyaka' means 'commander of the army'.

[8] *Daham-pasak-nā* is an official title. A dignitary having this title was one of the chief state officials in the system of administration established by Parākramabāhu I (*Nikāya Saṅgraha*, *op. cit.*, p. 21); but it is not known what the precise duties of this functionary were.

[9] The expression *vaḷanā pasa* occurs in the Nākolaganē rock-inscription, *Nāgalaḷa vaḷanā-pasayaḷa pidū Muṅgayiṅayi* (*E. Z.*, Vol. III, p. 70); and not infrequently in Sinhalese literary works

maintenance [of the monks], two head of buffaloes[1], fields [of the sowing extent of] . . . . . . seed . . . . . (Seṭṭi) . . . . . . from Beragama which was bought by paying . . . . . . *fanams* . . . . . **Peragama Senānāyaka** . . . . . the stretch of fields, field [of the sowing extent of] nine . . . . . prepared above Nara . . . . having made.

POSTCRIPT.

Since going to press, I have been supplied, through the kindness of the Rev. Välivịṭa Saranaṅkara Thera of Malvatte Vihāra, Kandy, with four manuscript copies of this inscription written on palm-leaves. It is not known by whom or when these copies were made; but, from a comparison of the variant readings found in them, it becomes apparent that the four copies contain two different attempts made in deciphering this inscription. The lacunae in the text seem to have been very much the same as they are now when these copies were made; and attempts have been made, in many places, to restore the missing words and phrases, particularly in the Sanskrit stanza in l. 1. As may be expected, these attempts at restoration are altogether arbitrary and sometimes go very wide of the mark. Some of the words, which are even to-day legible on the stone, have been left out in these copies, for instance *sthapati* in l. 11. On the other hand, there are certain readings which might have been due to the preservation, at that time, of letters which are now worn. But one cannot be certain on this point, as these might very well be only lucky guesses. However, I have adopted the following readings on the authority of these manuscript copies: (*Kesaga*) in l. 3, *si*(*lamaya*) and (*karavanu kämäti-vä*) in l. 6, *Dan*(*gamu*) in l. 24 and (*D*)*evagiri* in l. 26. On the whole, these copies do not help us in arriving at a better and more complete text of this epigraph.

---

of the thirteenth and fourteenth centuries, for example, in the *Nikāya Saṅgraha* (*op. cit.*), p. 29. *Pasa* is derived from P. *paccaya* and means 'the requisites of the Buddhist monks'. *Vaṭanā* may be equivalent to P. *vaṭṭa* (as in *dāna-vaṭṭam*), and Skt. *vṛtti* or *vartlana* and may mean 'maintenance'. The compound therefore may be rendered as 'requisites necessary for the maintenance (of monks in a *vihāra*)'. In a secondary meaning the word is used, as it is here, to denote lands dedicated for the above purpose.

[1] *Yaṭi-mīgon*:—What the word *yaṭi* means in this expression is not clear. *Mīgon* means 'buffalo' and *yaṭi* (Skt. *yaṣṭi*) ordinarily means 'staff'. Perhaps *yaṭi-mīgon* meant buffaloes trained to be yoked to wagons.

No. 13. ANURĀDHAPURA: SLAB-INSCRIPTION OF KHUDDA-PĀRINDA.

By S. Paranavitana.

THIS inscribed slab, which is now preserved in the Archaeological Museum at Anurādhapura, is said to have been discovered in the area of the Abhayagiri (mis-called the Jetavana) Vihāra at that ancient city. It is included in *A. S. C., A.R.* for 1911–12, p. 73, as No. 16 in the list of lithic inscriptions from Nuvara-kalāviya exhibited at Anurādhapura; but I have not been able to find out any other reference to it giving further details about its provenance.

The slab, excluding its base which is now buried below ground, measures 5 ft. 2 in. by 11½ in. by 5 in. It is inscribed not only on its face (A) but also on one of the sides formed by its thickness (B), and on the back (C) which has not been dressed. The lines of writing run vertically, there being three on side A and one line each on B and C. The line on side C consists of only a few letters. Side A is well preserved, but for two letters at the beginning of line 3, which are totally illegible. Side B is considerably weathered, many letters both at the beginning and the end of the line on this side being completely effaced, and side C is also partly effaced. The letters, which are well formed and boldly engraved, measure two to three inches in size.

The **script** of this record is somewhat archaic for its date which, as will be seen, is the last quarter of the fifth century. The alphabet of the Tissamahārāma slab-inscription of Mahānāma (*A.I.C.* No. 67), which is somewhat earlier in date than this epigraph, is distinctly of a more developed type. Similarly, the Nāgirikanda rock-inscription of Kumāradāsa[1], which is only about three-quarters of a century later, is written in a script considerably more developed than that of this epigraph. The changes which one notices between the scripts of the two epigraphs would have justified the assumption, if both of them had been undatable, that the period which separated them from each other was much greater than it actually is. Of the individual letters in the present epigraph, *ṭa* is of a form hardly distinguishable from the *ḍa* occurring in other inscriptions of a slightly earlier date and *a*, , helps us to understand how the second-century form of this letter, , came to assume the form which it had in the eighth and ninth centuries,

[1] See below, pp. 115–128.

. Two types of *ma* occur in the epigraph; compare, for instance, the letter occurring as the third in line 1 with that which is the third from the end of line 3. The *na* occurring in this inscription is also of a form worth noticing. The horizontal bar at the base of the second-century form of this letter has, in this record, lost that part which extended to the left of the vertical stroke and the right half of this stroke is diagonal instead of being horizontal.

As regards **orthography,** it is worthy of note that the medial *e*-sign is not marked in places where it should occur. For instance, the first five letters legible of line 4 read *ma da-kariha*, whereas, on the analogy of other inscriptions of the period, it should be *me de-kariha*. This peculiarity is also noticed in some words in the Nāgirikanda inscription and the Vessagiriya epigraphs of the sixth century dealt with below. It is, therefore, justifiable to treat this as a peculiar orthographical feature of the period rather than as a clerical error. As regards **grammar,** the forms *mapurumu* and *biseva* show phonetic decay of a degree which we should not have suspected that the fifth-century language had reached. The first of these two forms is equivalent to Skt. **mahāpramukha*; and occurs in an inscription of the reign of Buddhadāsa [1], less than a century earlier than this record, in the form of *mapurumaka*, showing that this interval of time was sufficient for the complete loss of the last syllable and the change of *a* in the preceding one to *u*. Thus the word had already, in the fifth century, assumed a form almost identical with *mapurum*, which was current in the tenth century [2]. *Biseva* is equivalent to Skt. *abhiṣiktā* and is almost identical with its tenth-century form *bisev* [3]. In the modern language it occurs as *bisō*. The word *tiri* (l. 2) is evidently the same as Skt. *śrī* (P. *siri*) and may be compared with Tamil *tiru*. Another word which shows Tamil influence is *ḷa* in the name 'Ḷapaṙideva', which will be discussed in the sequel. These Tamil influences are not surprising, for they occur in the names of a Tamil king and his consort. The form *vahira* (l. 4) for the earlier *vihara* (P. *vihāra*) is also noteworthy.

Mr. Bell, in the list of inscriptions already referred to, has given the name of the king occurring in this epigraph as Buddhadāsa Dāpura. No king of such a name is known in the period to which this record belongs palaeographically. What Mr. Bell has read as *Dāpura* is, in fact, *Ḷapari-* and the full name of the king, as appearing in the record, is *Budadasa Ḷa-Parideva*. *Parideva* may be taken as a clerical error for, or a variant form of, *Paridadeva* [4], particularly in

[1] *E. Z.*, Vol. III, p. 122. [2] *E. Z.*, Vol. I, pp. 25 and 46. [3] *Ibid.*, pp. 46 and 91.

[4] As the syllable *da* occurs immediately before *de* in this word, the former might very well have been slurred over in pronunciation and thus given rise to the form *Parideva*.

view of the fact that the latter name occurs in an inscription found at Aragama in the Kuruṇāgala District[1]. *Parida* is obviously the same as *Pārinda*, the name given in the chronicle to one of the six Tamil rulers who occupied the throne of Anurādhapura before the accession of Dhātusena. *Deva* can be added to the name of any royal personage and there should be no objection to the assumption that *Paridadeva* and *Pārinda* refer to the same person. *Ḷa* in Sinhalese means 'tender' or 'young' and is etymologically connected with Tamil *iḷai* of the same meaning[2]. *Ḷa-Pari(da)deva* would therefore mean 'Pārindadeva the Younger' and is equivalent to *Khudda*[3] *Pārinda* (the lesser Pārinda), the name given in the chronicle to Pārinda's younger brother and successor. We can, therefore, assign this record without any doubt to **Khudda Pārinda**, the Tamil king who reigned, according to Wickremasinghe, from 498 to 513. According to the chronological tables of Wijesinha and Geiger, Khuddha Pārinda's date was about half a century earlier.

The **object** of the epigraph was to register some donations made to a Buddhist monastery by the queen of Khudda Pārinda. Neither the name of the queen nor that of the monastery which benefited by her munificence is, however, preserved in full. The name of the monastery ended in *la* and, therefore, it was not the Abhayagiri Vihāra, in the precincts of which the inscription was found. It is therefore reasonable to assume that this inscribed stone had been removed from its original position to the Abhayagiri Vihāra, probably for some architectural purpose.

The queen of Khudda Pārinda figures in this record as the benefactress of a Buddhist monastery. Khudda Pārinda himself is given the epithet of Budadasa 'the servant of Buddha'. Pārinda also, in his inscription found at Aragama, has recorded his donations to a Buddhist monastery. I have elsewhere[4] given plausible reasons for the identification of Mahadaḷi Mahana (P. Mahādāṭhika Mahānāga) and his father Sarataraya (P. Sirīdhara), mentioned in an inscription

---

[1] See *C.J. Sc., G*, vol. ii, p. 181.

[2] The Tamil *iḷai* becomes *iḷa* in compounds. Compare *iḷaṅkō* and *iḷavarasaṉ*, corresponding to Skt. *yuvarāja*. *Iḷa-* in *Iḷanāga*, the name of a first-century king of Ceylon, is also probably connected with T. *iḷai*.

[3] P. *Khudda* and Sin. *kuḍā*, though literally meaning 'small', are found prefixed to the names of kings to distinguish them from their earlier namesakes. Thus, in the *Pūjāvali*, Aggabodhi II is called Kuḍā Agbō to distinguish him from his uncle and predecessor Aggabodhi I. Compare also *Mahāvaṁsa*, chapter 42, v. 40.

[4] *C.J. Sc., G*, vol. ii, pp. 181–182.

at Kataragama[1], with Dāṭhika and Tirītara, who belonged to the same Tamil dynasty as Pārinda and Ḳhudda Pārinda. Mahadaḷi Mahana is represented in that inscription as making gifts to the Buddhist shrine at Kataragama. It appears, therefore, that the Tamil princes who ruled at Anurādhapura for twenty-seven years towards the end of the fifth century were Buddhist by faith. Owing to its fragmentary nature, it is not possible to say what exactly were the gifts recorded in this epigraph; they, however, included fields to the extent of two *karīsas*.

TEXT.

1 Siddham Mapurumu **Budadasa Ḷa-Parideva**[2] ma-
2 -haraja-apayah-aṭa biseva-r(e) jana[3] **Tiri-maha**
3 .. **..saba** rej(e)na[4] Acabalaṇa Valakaya Kadaba-namabara[5]
4 .. .. m(e) d(e)-kariha kubura nava thama[6] ca (dukula dasa ca) .. .. va ..
5 .. .. la-vahiraṭa dina

TRANSLATION.

Hail! Queen **Tiri Maha** .. **..saba**, queen of His Majesty[7] the great king **Budadasa**[8] **Ḷaparideva**[9] **Apaya**[10], gave Acabalaṇa, Valakaya, Kadaba-nama-

---

[1] *E.Z.*, Vol. III, pp. 216–219.

[2] Perhaps to be corrected to *Ḷa-Paridadeva*, see above, p. 113.

[3] The *e*-sign of *re* is not clear. There are two strokes visible, attached to the *na*, which, if they are not due to the weathering of the stone, would justify the reading of this syllable as *no*.

[4] The short vertical stroke attached to *ja* is unlike the sign for the medial vowel *i*. It has been conjecturally read as the sign for the medial vowel *e*.

[5] The *akṣaras* occurring in line 3 after the word *rej(e)na*, are meant to indicate some place-names and it may be possible to separate them into words somewhat differently from the way in which it has been done above.

[6] May be read as *ṭhama* also. The only difference between *ṭha* and *tha* is the dot in the centre of the circle. What appears as a dot in the estampage may be due to the weathering of the stone.

[7] What has been translated by 'His Majesty' is the word *mapurumu*, for which, see above, p. 112.

[8] P. *Buddhadāsa.*

[9] *Ḷa-Parideva* = P. *Khudda-Pārinda*, see above, p. 113. The word *Pārinda* seems to be a hybrid compound of T. *pār* 'earth' and P. *inda* 'lord'. The name therefore means 'lord of the earth'.

[10] The word *Apaya* (P. *Abhaya*) occurs after *maharaja* and is used as a title, rather than as a part of the personal name, of the king. See *E. Z.*, Vol. III, p. 124.

Anurādhapura : Slab-Inscription of Khudda Pārinda

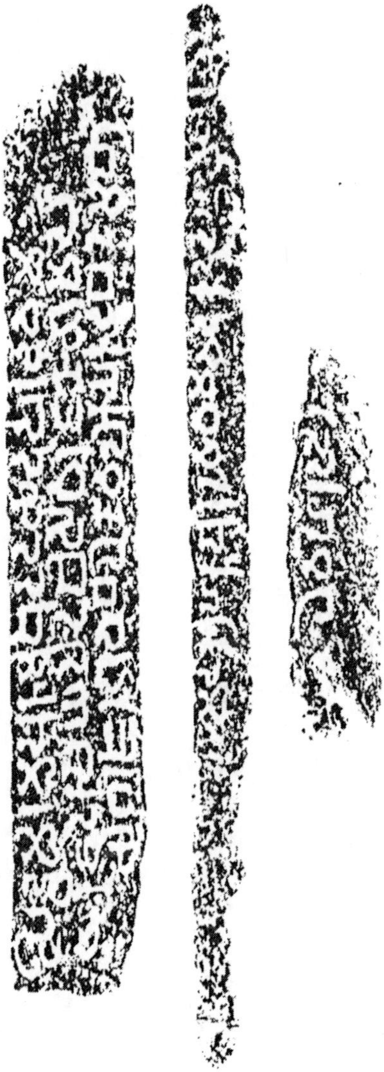

Scale 1 1/8 inches to 1 foot

Nāgirikanda Rock-Inscription of Kumāradāsa

Scale 1 inch to 1 foot

bara[1] . . . . these two *karīsas*[2] of fields, nine pillars[3], (ten silk cloths[4]) . . . . . to the monastery of . . . . la.

No. 14. NĀGIRIKANDA ROCK-INSCRIPTION OF KUMĀRADĀSA.

By S. Paranavitana.

Nāgirikanda[5], situated in the Kadavat Kōraḷē of the North-Central Province, about half a mile to the east of the fourth mile-post on the road from Mädavacciya to Käppiṭigollāva, is the site of an ancient Buddhist monastery which was re-occupied in the Kandyan period, after having been abandoned for centuries. The modern shrine is in an old cave and contains images and paintings of the usual Kandyan style. Very few vestiges are to be seen of the ancient monastery which, as we know from the evidence of inscriptions found at the site, existed there in the early centuries of the present era. Two inscriptions, both on rocks, have been discovered at the place. The earlier one is a short record of three lines and, from the script, can be assigned to about the fourth century; the later and longer one is the record dealt with in the present paper.

The two inscriptions at Nāgirikanda are included as No. 97 in Müller's *A. I. C.* Müller's texts of both inscriptions contain numerous errors, as was natural at a time when the study of Ceylon epigraphy was in its infancy, and his translations are consequently not accurate. The inscriptions are also included in the list appearing on p. 9 of the *Annual Report of the Archaeological Survey of Ceylon* for 1890; and eye-copies of them, prepared in 1894 under the direction of Mr. Bell, are preserved in the library of the Archaeological Department. The inscription now edited was re-copied by me in 1928, has been numbered *A.S.I.* 445, and a short notice of it has been included in the 'Epigraphical Summary' published in the *C.J. Sc. G.*, vol. ii, part 2 (p. 103).

---

[1] See above, p. 114, footnote 5.

[2] For *karihi* (P. *karīsa*, mediaeval Sin. *kiri*), see *E. Z.*, Vol. III, pp. 189–190.

[3] *Thama* is taken as equivalent to P. *thambha*, Skt. *stambha*, Sin. *ṭäm*. Even if the alternative reading *ṭhama* be adopted, there would be no change in the meaning as it could be of the same origin. Compare *thabhe* (*thabha*) in the Paḍeria Edict of Aśoka (*Ep. Ind.*, vol. v, p. 4).

[4] The reading *dukuḷa dasa ca*, which has been tentatively translated as 'ten silk cloths', is very doubtful. Even if the reading be correct, there is some difficulty in equating *dukuḷa* with Skt. *dukūla* (woven silk) in order to get the above meaning, for, in Skt., the word is spelt with a dental *l*.

[5] A brief notice of Nāgirikanda is found in *A. S. C. Annual Report* for 1890, p. 8.

The inscription covers a rock surface of $7\frac{1}{2}$ ft. by 2 ft. and contains seven lines of writing. The first line is rather badly damaged, five letters being completely obliterated and the upper portions of another five being partly broken away. The other four lines are in a fairly good state of preservation. The average size of the letters is 2 inches.

This epigraph is written in a script which represents the transitional stage between the Brāhmī and the mediaeval Sinhalese. Till about the third or fourth century, the Brāhmī script in Ceylon was practically the same as that which was in vogue in India; but, by about the fifth century, the development of the alphabet in Ceylon took a distinctive turn and by the eighth century was evolved an alphabet which can definitely be called Sinhalese, as it differed, in the shape of its letters, from the many alphabets that were then prevailing in India. Our inscription comes midway between these two dates and is, therefore, of considerable value for an understanding of the evolution of the Sinhalese script. This period is the most obscure in the epigraphical history of the island, for it has left very few inscriptions which contain the name of the reigning king and can, therefore, be dated. The present record is one of the only two inscriptions, known so far, belonging to the sixth and seventh centuries, which can be assigned without any doubt to particular reigns[1]. No inscription of this period has yet been published in the *Epigraphia Zeylanica* and some detailed remarks about the script may not therefore be out of place.

Comparing the script of this record with that of the Tōṇigala inscription of the reign of Śrīmeghavarṇṇa[2], which also we have examined in some detail, we find that, in the period of about one and a half centuries which intervened between the dates of these two epigraphs, the script has undergone a considerable degree of development. The letters in which much change is noticed are *a*, *ca*, *ja*, *ḍa*, *ta*, *cha*, *ma*, *ya*, and *sa*, as may be seen from the symbols for those syllables from the two epigraphs shown in the chart reproduced on Plate 15. The letters *ka*, *ga*, *ḷa*, *ṇa*, *na*, *pa*, *ba*, *ra*, *va*, and *ha*, show very little or no change. In the case of *ja*, *ta*, and *ya*, though the forms appearing here differ considerably from those of the Tōṇigala inscription, there were forms closely resembling them in records contemporary with, or even somewhat earlier than, that epigraph.

The *ja* occurring as the twelfth letter in l. 5 is of archaic type and differs from the symbol for that *akṣara* occurring elsewhere in the record. The letter

[1] The other is an inscription, recently discovered at Nilagama in the Mātaḷē District, dated in the reign of Daḷa-Mugalana (Mogallāna II, *circa* 542–561).

[2] See *E.Z.*, Vol. III, pp. 172–188.

ḍa, too, shows variant forms, the form occurring in l. 1 being markedly different from that in l. 3, the former being distinctly cursive in type. It is also noteworthy that the auspicious word *siddham*, with which the record begins, is written in letters which are different in form from those used in the rest of the document, and nearly identical in type with the corresponding symbols of the second century. This practice of writing a word, considered to be of auspicious significance or of special importance, in archaic letters, is met with in other records. For instance, in some records of the first or second century, the word *śagaśa* is written in the earliest form of the Brāhmī script which, for ordinary writing, had gone out of use at that time. In the matter of attaching signs for the medial vowels, the script does not show any departure from the methods which were prevalent in the fourth century.

In comparing this script with that of the succeeding period, i.e., the eighth to the tenth centuries, we find that certain letters like *ka*, *ja*, *pa*, *ma*, *ya*, *ra*, and *sa* are very similar in both; and, in the case of those letters, the forms appearing in this and other contemporary records can be regarded as the prototypes of the corresponding symbols of the eighth century. But in certain other *akṣaras* like *a*, *ca*, *ṇa*, *na*, *ba*, &c., it is difficult to see the connexion between the forms of the two periods. When we compare the writing of the sixth century with that of the eighth and ninth centuries, one fact which strikes us is that there must have been, in the intervening period, some influence at work which accelerated the change in the form of the letters; and that this has worked in a direction somewhat different from that in which the evolution of the script during the first five centuries of the Christian era seemed to be tending. Up to about the sixth or seventh century, the script favoured horizontal lines and angular forms; but after this period, they are, as far as possible, avoided, curved lines and circular forms coming into favour. It is precisely in such letters as do not contain horizontal lines and angular forms, that there is the least change between the two periods. It is true that there are certain documents, dating from about the fourth century, which show a preference for curvilinear forms of writing and, as I have already suggested [1], many of the eighth- and ninth-century forms can be traced to symbols appearing in those. But such documents are not very common and we might, therefore, inquire as to why the Sinhalese script assumed curved and rounded forms in the eighth century or thereabouts. The Pallava Grantha script may have had some influence in this sudden change; but, in my opinion,

---

[1] See *E.Z.*, Vol. III, pp. 120–121 and 173–174.

the most important factor seems to have been a change in the material used for writing.

In Ceylon, the material used for writing before the introduction of paper by Europeans, consisted of palm-leaves, on which the letters were incised with a sharp-pointed stylus. As the palm-leaves contain longitudinal fibre, they tend to split if straight horizontal strokes are incised and the studious avoidance of such strokes may be due to the adoption, at this period, of palm-leaves as the common writing material. Curved and rounded forms of writing have been developed in all parts of India and the neighbouring countries which have adopted palm-leaves as material for writing upon. In North India, where they are not so commonly used for the purpose, the development of the script has been in a different direction[1].

If we accept this hypothesis, it naturally follows that, before the Sinhalese alphabet assumed distinctly round and curved forms, and when horizontal strokes were not avoided as such, the common material used for writing must have been something other than palm-leaves. The commentator of the *Mahāvaṁsa*, in his remarks on chap. xi, v. 13, of that chronicle, mentions bamboo boards of books, suggesting that they were used as writing material[2]. The word meaning 'a missive' in classical Sinhalese is *käṭa-pat* which, being a compound of two words derived from Skt. *kāṣṭha* and *patra*, would etymologically mean 'wooden board'. The use of such a word points to a time when documents were written on wooden tablets with a paint brush as was the custom among the Indianized people of Central Asia[3].

The **language**, which is old Sinhalese, shows, in some particulars, considerable development from the stage reached in the fourth century as exemplified by the Tōṇigala inscription. The change of intervocalic *da* to *ta* is seen in *Kumaratasa* for *Kumāradāsa*; the similar change of *b* to *p* is noticed in earlier records[4]. Other phonetic changes, affecting consonants, which are found in this record, are also noticed in the language of the period between the second and fourth centuries. The vowel changes noticed in the words *vahera* for P. *vihāra*

---

[1] For the influence of writing material on the shapes of letters, see John Beames, *A Comparative Grammar of the Modern Aryan Languages of India*, vol. i, pp. 64–65.

[2] See *Mahāvaṁsa-ṭīkā*, Colombo edition of 1894, p. 210: *Potthakavaṁsaphalake vaṇṇādikammāni viya.*

[3] Hundreds of examples of such documents written on wooden tablets have been found by Sir Aurel Stein in his excavations in the sand-buried cities of Central Asia (see Sir Aurel Stein, *On Central Asian Tracks*, London 1933, pp. 75 ff.).

[4] See *E.Z.*, Vol. III, p. 121 and p. 172, n. 2.

and *peta* for *pati* (P. *patti*) are also found in earlier records [1]. The change of *o* to *e* is seen in *beja-* (or *beji-*) *pati* which represents *boji-pati* of the second century inscriptions [2]. The phonetic changes undergone by the word *vavi*, occurring in the second-century inscriptions, in assuming the form *veva*, found in this record, are the same as those of the change of *pati* to *peta*; but the word *veva* has not been found in any earlier record. By the change of *e* to *ä*, this word has assumed the form which has been in use from the eighth century up to the present day. In the conjunction *ce* (Skt. & P. *ca*), the vowel *a* has changed to *e*. This conjunction is found in the earliest Sinhalese documents as *ca* and later as *ica*, and *īca* [3]. The dropping of an intervocalic consonant (possibly *k*) is found in the words *Tavaa* and *Gajaa*, the result being that the vowel *a* is immediately followed by another. This is the only document in which this phenomenon has been noticed in the Sinhalese language, though it is the rule in most Prakrit dialects, particularly in Mahārāṣṭrī [4]. In Sinhalese, the place of the intervocalic *k*, *g*, *t*, and *d* are very often taken by *y*; and arguing from evidence in the present document it may be permissible to hold that this *y* is no other than the weakly articulated *y* (*laghu-prayatnatara-ya-kāra*) which was pronounced in the Prakrits in place of the omitted consonant. This *y* was never graphically represented in the Prakrits, except in manuscripts written by the Jainas [5]. The *y* in such Sinhalese words as *paya* (P. *pāda*) *diya* (P. *udaka*), &c., which takes the place of intervocalic consonants dropped in most Prakrits, is articulated very weakly when compared with initial *y* occurring in words such as *yatura* (Skt. *yantra*), *yakā* (P. *yakkha*), &c. The dropping out of a whole syllable (*ta*) is found in *cara* (P. *cattāri*), if this is not taken as a clerical error. But as the form *catara* occurs in the same line, we are, I think, justified in regarding it as a clerical error and not as a variant form. If it is taken as a variant form, it is possible to treat it as the prototype of the forms *sār* and *sāra* occurring in the later language. The length of the vowel in this form would, however, point to an earlier form **cayara* and not *cara*.

As regards inflexions, the genitive singular (used in an instrumental sense) terminating in *-ha*, the use of the stem form to denote the nominative and accusative singular of neuter nouns, and the nominative singular in *-e*, are features common enough in earlier records and they are also found in the later

---

[1] *Ibid.*, pp. 121 and 175.

[2] *Ibid.*, p. 117. The word also occurs in the variant forms *bojaka-pati* and *bojiya-pati*.

[3] *Ibid.*, pp. 116 and 176.

[4] See Pischel, *Grammatik der Prakrit Sprachen*, para. 186.

[5] Pischel, *op. cit.*, para. 187, and A. C. Woolner, *Introduction to Prakrit*, p. 12.

stages of the language. Three forms of the dative are found in this record, namely, in the words *vaheraṭaya* (l. 1) *bikusagahaṭa* and *pacayaṭa* (l. 4). The last form has the modern termination for this case [1]. The locative singular terminates in *-e*, e.g., *vahere* in l. 3. This termination has not been found in earlier records, in which the locative ends in *-śi* or *-hi*. The earliest form is *-śi* which, if we recollect that the palatal *ś* is almost universal in the Brāhmī script of Ceylon, would seem to be the same as the locative termination in the Khālsī and Dhauli edicts of Aśoka [2]. With the change of *sa* to *ha*, this termination became *-hi*. It is difficult to imagine how the termination *-e* could have been derived from the earlier *-hi*; and one has to come to the conclusion that its origin lies in the termination of *a*-bases in Sanskrit, Pāli, and Prakrit. The form *vahere* occurring in this record would thus be equivalent to Skt. P. and Pkt. *vihāre*; and in the later stages of the Sinhalese language it assumed the form *veherä*. We should not be justified in assuming, on account of the fact that it has not been found in any earlier document, that this termination came into the Sinhalese language in the fifth or sixth century. It was probably existing side by side with the termination *-hi*, though not preferred by the writers of inscriptions, and came to be regarded as a good literary form about this period. This termination changed to *-ä* in the eighth century or so; and, in classical Sinhalese, it existed side by side with *-hi* and its variants. The change undergone by this case-ending is additional evidence for the conjecture that the vowel *ä* in the Sinhalese language is a modification of *e* [3]. In the nominative and accusative cases of words denoting inanimate objects, there is no termination by which the plural can be distinguished from the singular. For instance, the word *veva* in the phrases *mevataka veva* and *me catara veva* seems, from the context, to be in the plural, while the same word, occurring elsewhere in the record, must be in the singular. In the modern language the plural of neuter *a*-stems is formed by the elision of the final vowel, while the stem form itself indicates the singular. In the script of this period, the use of the *virāma* sign to indicate that a consonant is not vocalized has not come into vogue and it is therefore possible that, though the singular and plural forms are graphically represented alike, there was some difference in pronunciation. Possibly, the retention, in the later language, of the vowel in the last syllable of forms in the singular number, was due to the fact that this was accented. In *atano*, we seem to have the Pāli and Prakrit genitive single termination of *n*-stems.

---

[1] For this termination, see Müller, *A. I. C.*, p. 10.

[2] See *E. Z.*, Vol. I, p. 58.

[3] See *E. Z.*, Vol. III, p. 121.

As regards verbal forms, we have only examples of the past passive participle (*dine*) and the gerund (*koṭu*) with its causative form (*keṇavi*). These do not show any development from the earlier stage of the language, except in the case of the last in which the earlier termination *-vaya* has contracted to *vi*.

The object of the record was to register the gift of some tanks and paddy fields to the ancient monastery on the site, which was called Bamaṇagiriya (P. Brāhmaṇagiri), by king **Maha-Kumaratasa.** The king's name is unfortunately not preserved intact and Dr. Müller, in the text of this record given in *A. I. C.*, has read it quite differently and has not even recognized a proper name. However not even one of the seven letters comprising the king's name has been entirely obliterated and the lower portions, which are still preserved, of the damaged letters, leave us in no doubt as to what they are. The first letter *ma* is quite intact and of the next one, *ha,* only a small portion, at the end of the right-hand stroke, is missing. The only other letter which can be mistaken for it is *pa*; but comparison with other *pa*'s and *ha*'s occurring in the record makes it reasonable to take this *akṣara* as a *ha.* Of the third letter, the short cross-bar in the centre, of which the left half is clearly, and the right half faintly, visible, makes it impossible to mistake it for *ru*, the only other *akṣara* which has a resemblance to it. The lower half, which is preserved, of the next letter, makes it certain that it is a *ma* and the letter which follows is almost intact and can be read as *ra* only. The next two letters are quite clear and are *ta* and *sa.* Thus the whole name reads *Maha-Kumaratasa.* This stands etymologically for Skt. *Mahā-Kumāradāsa.* The shortening of long vowels is a rule in early Sinhalese and the change of intervocalic *d* to *t* is noticed in other records of the period, Skt. *pāda*, for instance, becoming *pata*[1]. The word *maha* 'great' can be ignored, as this is often found prefixed to the names of kings who in no sense can be called great; and the part of the name which matters is Kumāradāsa.

No Sinhalese king of this name occurs in the *Mahāvaṁsa*; but the ruler who is called **Kumāra-Dhātusena** in that chronicle, is referred to, in all Sinhalese historical writings from the *Pujāvalī* (thirteenth century) downwards, as **Kumāradāsa** (Sin. Kumaradas)[2]. This inscription proves that there was

---

[1] This word occurs in the Diyagama inscription of about the fifth century. See Müller, *A. I. C.*, p. 77, where the word has, however, been wrongly read as *pita.* Compare also *patagaḍa* in the Kataragama inscription (*E. Z.*, Vol. III, pp. 215–216).

[2] See *Pūjāvalī* (37th chapter) translated by B. Gunasekara (Colombo, 1895), p. 27; *Nik.* C. M. Fernando's translation (Colombo, 1908), pp. 16 and 18; and *R.*, B. Gunasekara's translation (Colombo, 1900), p. 55.

actually a king called Kumāradāsa sometime in the sixth century and in view of the fact that there was only one king of Ceylon, known from any sources, who bore this name, and the similarity of the names 'Kumāra-Dhātusena' and 'Kumāradāsa', we may be certain that the present record is of that monarch. Our inscription does not contain any historical information concerning this king, and the *Mahāvaṁsa* also dismisses him with the statement that he was a son of Moggallāna I, that he caused a revision to be made of the sacred texts and that he died in the ninth year of his reign, beside a few conventional words of praise about his prowess and liberality towards the religion. Later legends, alluded to in the *Pūjāvalī*, have, however, been busy with his name and have identified him with his namesake, the author of the Sanskrit poem *Jānakīharaṇa*. They also make him a contemporary of the great Indian poet Kālidāsa who is said to have come to Kumāradāsa's court and both are said, in a popular story, to have lost their lives through their common attachment to a courtesan, the king sacrificing his own life in his grief at the death of his friend the poet. The incident is said to have taken place at Mātara in the south of the island; and the very spot where the king was cremated is still pointed out to visitors by the inhabitants of the place. These stories, however, are not taken seriously by sober students of history; and Sanskrit scholars do not admit the alleged contemporaneity of the author of the *Jānakīharaṇa* with Kālidāsa. Nor do they admit that that poem was the work of a Ceylon king[1]. The date of Kumāradāsa cannot be exactly determined. According to Wijesinghe, his initial regnal year was 515 A.D., and Codrington has adopted this merely for the sake of convenience. According to the systems of Ceylon chronology evolved independently by Geiger and Wickremasinghe, this date has been given respectively as 513 and 570.

The record enables us to learn that the ancient name of the monastery which existed at Nāgirikanda was **Bamaṇagiri** (P. Brāhmaṇagiri). No *vihāra* of this name finds mention in the chronicles.

---

[1] See A. B. Keith, *History of Sanskrit Literature*, p. 80. Prof. Keith and other scholars also doubt the tradition that the author of the *Jānakīharaṇa* was a native of Ceylon. But the verses appearing at the end of the last canto, in a manuscript of the poem recently found in Malabar, definitely state that the author of the poem was a member of the royal family of Ceylon. These verses also give some biographical details of Kumāradāsa the poet, which do not fit in with what we know of Kumāradāsa the king. It is therefore evident that though the king and the poet were two distinct personages, the latter was also a scion of the Sinhalese royal family. For the subject, see Mr. M. Doraswamayya in *Tirumalai Śrī Veṅkaṭeśvara*, vol. i, pp. 203-212.

TEXT[1].

1 Siddham **Maha-Kumaratasa**-raja-Apaya[ha **Bamaṇaga]riya**-vaher≠ aṭaya keṇavi caḍa[2] koṭu

2 dinaka Mahagariya veva-sara c[e] Cugariya veva-sara c[e] Kabube veva-sara c[e] Kaṭacanaka-pula sara ce

3 v[e]va c[e] ma catara veva-sara daka-peta kaḍaya beji-peta **Bamaṇa-gariya**-vahere bika-sagah≠aṭa cara[3]

4 pacayaṭa dine[4] saga-begi- kereyani ma atano sime[5] Tavaa-veva ce Nilasa-veva ce Gajaa-veva ce Paḍa-veva ce ma

5 vataka veva daka-p[e]ta ce beja-peta ce **Bamaṇagariya**-vahere bika-sagah≠aṭa de-peta-kara-kaḍaka saga-sari.

TRANSLATION[6].

Hail! By king **Maha-Kumaratasa Apaya** were caused to be purchased and granted as donations to the **Bamaṇagariya** monastery, the tank [and] wet lands of Mahagariya, the tank [and] wet lands of Cugariya, the tank [and] wet lands of Kabuba [and] the wet lands [and] the tank of Kaṭacanakapula. Of these four tanks [and] the wet lands, the water-share has been remitted and the proprietor's share granted to the *bhikkhu* community at the **Bamaṇagariya** monastery, for their four requisites. These have been made possessions of the community [of monks]. Of the following tanks which belong to himself, namely, Tavaa

---

[1] Müller's text runs as follows :—. . . . . . ta . . . mama parumaka sakaṭa puta ha Bamanogiriya vehera ḍayo kino wenadaka dawaka maha-bariye (2) wawisara kanugariya wawisara kabuba (?) wawisara kaṭinaka-pulasara (3) wawa sama satara wawisara dakapati kaṇaya badipita Bamanogiriya wihara bikasagahaṭa caka (4) paca yaṭa dine saga baga kariya kama atanā samita wa awiwa nila sawiwa . . gata awiwa kahawaṇa (5) wataka wawi daka pata . . bojapata . . Bamanogiriya wihara bikasaga dina pita karakaṭaka saga sari.

[2] This reading is not quite certain. The symbol read as *da* differs from that letter occurring elsewhere in the record.

[3] Possibly to be read as *catara*.

[4] The sign for the medial vowel in *di* is not clear and the word might also be read as *dene*.

[5] The stroke read as the sign for *i* is not so extended as the *i*-sign in other *akṣaras* of this record. But this may be due to the fact that the *pa* of the line above does not permit of its being further extended. May be also read as *seme*.

[6] Müller's translation runs :—. . . . . I the parumaka and his (?) son the Bamanogiriya temple . . . . the tank of the great queen and the Kanugariya tank and the Kabuba tank and the Kaṭinaka tank, altogether four tanks, having seen the embankments to the priesthood of the Bamanogiriya wihara six and five (?) he gave . . . . the karshāpaṇas at the Wataka tank, having seen . . . . . after having assigned he gave the Bamanogiriya wihāra to the priesthood. . . . . . .

tank, Nilasa tank, Gajaa tank, and Paḍa tank—of the above mentioned tanks—the water-share and the overlord's share (were given) to the *bhikkhu* community at the **Bamaṇagariya** monastery. These are the wet lands belonging to the community, of which the dues on account of the two shares have been remitted.

REMARKS.

[Line 1]. *Maha-Kumaratasa-raja-Apaya*: The word *raja* 'king' stands between *Apaya* (P. *Abhaya*) and the rest of the name. For this, see *E.Z.*, Vol. III, p. 124 and above, p. 114, n. 10.

[Line 1]. *Keṇa(vi) caḍa-koṭu*: The reading of this phrase is not beyond doubt. The vowel sign in *vi* is not quite clear and the symbol read as *ḍa* is unlike the *ḍa* occurring elsewhere in the record. It also cannot be read definitely as any other *akṣara*; and possibly we have here a blunder of the engraver. A similar phrase occurs in an unpublished inscription at Burutankanda[1] in Māgam Pattu. In that epigraph, too, the reading is not quite certain, as the vowel signs are not well preserved. But, *caya* occurs there instead of *caḍa* in our inscription and I, therefore, propose to correct this phrase to *keṇavi caya-koṭu*. Even then, the sense of the words is not quite obvious, the rendering given above being purely conjectural and put forward with considerable diffidence. *Keṇavi* is taken as the causative form of the old Sinhalese gerund corresponding to Pāli *kiṇitvā*. Cf. *kiṇiya* in the Vihāregoḍa inscription of Saba[2]. In later Sinhalese, this verbal form occurs only with the prefix *vi* added, when it means 'selling' and not 'buying'. *Caya* is taken as equivalent to P. *cāga*, the change of *g* to *y* in the word being analogous to that of *t* to *y* in *paya* for *pāda*.

[Line 2]. *Veva-sara* is an expression which occurs several times in this inscription. It is obviously an earlier form of *vāsar* or *vāsara* which occurs in tenth-century records[3]. Dr. Müller takes it as a composition analogous to *candra-māsa*[4], i.e., he thinks that *veva* and *sara* both have the same meaning. Such compounds are, of course, not rare in the Sinhalese language; but the occurrence of the phrase *sara ca veva ca* (*sara* and tank) in one place, instead of *veva-sara*, indicates that *veva* and *sara* are used with two distinct meanings. *Veva*, of course, is from Skt. *vāpī* and means 'tank'; and the most obvious course is to take *sara* as equivalent to Skt. *saras* 'lake'. But this meaning does not suit the context. As the Sanskrit word *vāpī*, from which *veva* is derived,

---

[1] Referred to in *E. Z.*, Vol. III, p. 183.

[2] *E. Z.*, Vol. III, p. 168.

[3] *Ibid.*, Vol. I, pp. 49 and 93.

[4] *A. I. C.*, p. 51.

comes from the root *vap* 'to sow', there is room for the conjecture that *veva* actually denotes the area below a tank which is sown with paddy, i.e., the field, and that *sara* is used for the sheet of water in the tank. In translating thus, however, we are attaching to the word *veva* a sense which is not found in Sanskrit or Pāli for *vāpī*, though it is etymologically possible. We have also no other instance of the use of *vapi*, *vavi*, *veva* or *väva* with this meaning in Sinhalese epigraphy or literature.

If we knew exactly what *vāsar* connoted in the tenth century, we could have guessed the meaning of *sara* in this record; but, unfortunately, we do not. The word occurs in the phrase *Ät-vehera bad-tuvät(k) gam-bimin tumanaṭ dun dasakärä-mut vāsar-pät pamuṇu no gannā isā* in the Anurādhapura slab-inscription of Kassapa V [1]. Dr. Wickremasinghe has translated *vāsar-pät* as 'land on the tank-side'. The word also occurs in the tablets of Mahinda IV at Mihintaḷē, in the phrases *Maṇu-vāsara isā*, *Ḷahiniya-pavuychi uḍäsi yaṭäsi de vāsara isā* [2]. The word *vāsara*, in this place, has been translated by Dr. Wickremasinghe as 'tank'. It is clear that Dr. Wickremasinghe's renderings, varying as they do in different places, are pure guesses and do not bring out the exact meaning of the word. The contexts in which the word occurs do not suggest its exact meaning beyond making it likely that it meant some sort of agricultural land.

In the second of the two Sanskrit *ślokas* at the beginning of the Päpiliyāna inscription of Parākramabāhu VI [3] occurs the compound *vāpyāśraya*. No such compound is met with in Sanskrit literature and it is obvious that it is a term coined as a Sanskrit equivalent to Sinhalese *vāsara*. If we knew that the author of the Päpiliyāna inscription was certain of the etymology of *vāsara* when he coined this term, we could then take *-sara* in *veva-sara* and *vāsara* as equivalent to Skt. *āśraya*. Whether his etymology was right or wrong, we can at least assume that the Sanskrit word coined must have expressed, in a general way, what *vāsara* signified in his time. Therefore, even if *vāpyāśraya* is merely a pedantic restoration, into Sanskrit, of *vāsara*, we can rest assured that this word meant the lands which were dependent upon a tank for irrigation.

But, unlike *vāsara* in the language of the tenth century and later, *veva* and *sara* in our record seem to denote two different things. And as there is no doubt regarding the connotation of *veva*, *sara* should be taken as applying to the irrigated lands below a tank. It is not impossible that it is derived from Skt.

---

[1] *E.Z.*, Vol. I, p. 49. [2] *Ibid*, Vol. I, p. 93.

[3] Müller, *A. I. C.*, p. 106, and Sir D. B. Jayatilaka, *Katikāvat Saṅgarā*, Colombo, 1922, p. 43.

āśraya 'dependent upon' and meant 'the lands which were dependent upon a tank for irrigation'. It is, however, more likely that *sara* is from Skt. *saras* and was applied to marshy lands capable of being sown with paddy. In support of this suggestion it may be stated that the Sinhalese word *vil* which, in literature, means 'lake' and is a synonym of *sara*, is used in common parlance for a marshy land which, in the rainy season, is converted into a sheet of water and is capable of being formed into paddy fields. In the Päpiliyāna inscription (*op. cit.*) the word *vila* is used for a stretch of paddy fields. Compare, for instance, the phrases *Kehelsēṇā-vilin yāḷaka vapa hā*, *Bollatā-vilin yāḷaka vapa hā*, *Bōṁbuvala-vilin mul-bijuvaṭa de-yāḷak hā* occurring in that record. If the word *vila* which means 'lake' was used for a paddy field in the fifteenth century, it is conceivable that *sara*, the root meaning of which is also lake or marsh, was so used in the fifth century. I have therefore translated the word *sara* as 'wet lands', taking it as equivalent in meaning to *maḍabim* of modern usage.

The word *sara* occurs also in the following extract from the Habarana inscription: *eta eta gama-sara ataḍi koṭu me Agivaḍamana-vaviya mula-sara ca pacavaḍita sara ca do-karihi-sahasa ca eka-catalisa karihi ca*[1]. The suggested interpretation of *sara* seems to fit in well with this passage, for it appears to be mentioned therein that the Agivaḍamana tank had two *saras*, the original one (*mula-sara*) and another which had been added later (*pacavaḍita-sara*), of which the areas are given as 2,000 *karīsas* and 41 *karīsas* respectively. The fact that the areas of *saras* were given in *karīsas* seems to imply that they were fields.

[Line 3]. *Daka-peta* = P. *daka-patti*. See *E.Z.*, Vol. I, pp. 71-73. In dealing with the Thūpārāma slab-inscription of Gajubāhu I[2], I have suggested that *pati*, occurring in this compound as well as in *bojaka-pati*, should mean 'share' and not 'revenue' as suggested by Dr. Wickremasinghe. This supposition is confirmed by the occurrence of the form *daka-baka* (P. **daka-bhāga*) instead of *dakapati* in an inscription, of about the fourth century, found at Pīligama[3].

[Line 3]. *Kaḍaya* is taken as equivalent to P. *khaṇḍayitvā*, 'having broken', used in a secondary sense meaning 'having remitted'.

[Line 3]. *Beji-peta*, occurs in earlier records as *bojika-pati*, for the interpretation of which see *E.Z.*, Vol. III, p. 117.

---

[1] *A.I.C.*, No. 61. Müller's reading is somewhat different from that given above.

[2] *E.Z.*, Vol. III, p. 118.

[3] Müller, *A.I.C.*, No. 77. In the text of this inscription published by Müller, the word in question has been left undeciphered, though the letters are quite clear on the stone.

[Line 4]. *Saga-begi kereyani ma*: The meaning of this phrase is not quite clear and the rendering given above is only tentative. *Saga-begi* is doubtless equivalent to P. *saṅgha-bhogika* 'belonging to the *saṅgha*'; and the difficulty of interpretation lies in *kereyani ma*. It is not quite certain whether the division into words of the five syllables read as *kereyani ma* is the correct one, there being the possibility of dividing these as *kereya nima* also. *Kereyani* is taken, in the interpretation adopted by me, as equivalent to P. *kāritāni*, from which it can be derived by well-known rules of Sinhalese phonology. The only difficulty which presents itself is the neutral plural termination *-ni* which, though occurring in old Sinhalese inscriptions of about the second century B.C., has not been found in the language of the intervening period. *Ma* is taken as equivalent to *me* (P. *imaṁ*) and occurs in two other places in this epigraph, to wit, *ma catara* (l. 3) and *ma vataka* (ll. 4–5). If we read the phrase as *saga-begi kereya nima*, we may translate it as 'lands, held on *nima* tenure, belonging to the *saṅgha*'. *Nima* can be the same as *nimi* which occurs, as a word denoting a system of land-tenure, in the 'Jetavanārāma' slab-inscription, No. 2, of Mahinda IV[1]. Dr. Wickremasinghe conjectures that the word indicates 'a form of land tenure under which the grantee has the exclusive possession of the land[2].

[Line 4]. *Atano sime*: This is another of the phrases, occurring in the inscription, of which the exact meaning is doubtful and the translation given is tentative. *Atano* is taken as equivalent to *P. attano.* Genitive forms ending in *-no* are found in the early Brāhmī inscriptions of Ceylon, e.g. *batuno* (P. *bhātuno*) in an unpublished cave-inscription at Pilikuṭṭuva in the Colombo District[3], but have not been met with in any other record later than the first century. *Sime* is equated with Skt. *svāmya* and considered to be the earlier form of *himi* occurring in classical and modern Sinhalese. *Atano sime* would thus be the same as *taman himi* 'belonging to one's self' in the modern Sinhalese idiom. Similar phrases are found in Brāhmī inscriptions of the second to fifth centuries. An unpublished inscription of a king named Mahānāga, from Vessagiriya in Anurādhapura, has *atini samiya Ayibaravika vaviya bojaka pati.* The Situlpavuva inscription of Kaṇiṭṭha Tissa[4] contains *Citalapavata atini simaya Dakiṇi-tisa Aviya vavi.* Dr. Müller, whose reading of this passage is somewhat different, leaves these two words untranslated. An inscription of about the third century

---

[1] *E.Z.*, Vol. I, p. 236.
[2] *Ibid.*, p. 240, n. 2.
[3] Referred to in *A.S.C.*, *A.R.* for 1931–2, p. 9.
[4] Müller, *A.I.C.*, No. 16.

A.D. from Mōlahitiyavelēgala near Dimbulāgala[1] has *ati simiya gaṇavaya*, which Mr. Bell has translated as 'after having taken count of the boundaries belonging to'. The Piligama inscription, already referred to, has *atani simaṭa*; and an unpublished record of about the fourth century, found at Kaṭugampolagama[2], has *ata-samini*. If all these variant forms are of the same meaning as *atano sime* of this record, it is remarkable that the form *atano* is found only in this, the latest document, the others having *atani*, which should be taken as the locative singular (P. *attani*, in one's self), and *ata* or *ati* which might be regarded as the stem (P. *atta*), forming a compound with the word which follows.

[Lines 4–5]. *Me vataka*. For this word, see *E. Z.*, Vol. III, p. 186.

[Line 5]. *De-peta-kara*. The two shares are evidently the water-share (*daka-peta*) and the proprietor's share (*beja-peta*) mentioned earlier in the record. *Kara* is taken as the Sanskrit *kara* meaning 'tax', 'impost', &c.

No. 15. FOUR ROCK-INSCRIPTIONS FROM VESSAGIRIYA AT ANURĀDHAPURA.

By S. PARANAVITANA.

THE subjoined inscriptions are engraved on the eastern face of Rock B on the site of an ancient monastery now called Vessagiriya[3] in Anurādhapura, to the south of the rock-cut flight of steps between caves numbered 9 and 10 at that place[4]. Inscription No. 1 of this paper is at a distance of 80 ft. from the centre of the above mentioned flight of steps. Nos. 2 and 3 are engraved, one below the other, at a distance of 8½ ft. to the north of No. 1. No. 4 is 9 ft. to the north of Nos. 2 and 3.

Dr. Wickremasinghe, in his paper dealing with some of the inscriptions at Vessagiriya[5], seems to refer to Nos. 1 to 3 of these records in the following passages: 'The second rock inscription is on the vertical wall, facing south-

[1] Published by Mr. H. C. P. Bell in *Ceylon Antiquary and Literary Register*, vol. iii, p. 77.

[2] *A. S. I.*, No. 440, see *C. J. Sc.*, *G*, vol. ii, p. 110.

[3] For a brief description of this site, see *E. Z.*, Vol. I, pp. 10–12; and for its identification with the ancient Issarasamaṇa monastery, see *C. J. Sc.*, *G*, vol. ii, p. 182.

[4] See Plan reproduced at Plate 2 of *E. Z.*, Vol. I, and photograph reproduced at Plate 3.

[5] *E. Z.*, Vol. I, p. 22.

east, to the right of cave No. 12. It contains nine lines of writing, imperfect and too shallowly incised to admit of an estampage being taken.

'The letters are smaller than those of No. 1, and probably belong to the period (fourth to ninth centuries) of which records on stone are comparatively few and the script strangely irregular. It is possible that the nine broken lines cover two inscriptions.'

Inscription No. 1 (*A. S. I.* No. 606) covers an area of 3 ft. 7 in. by 1 ft. 3 in. and contains four lines of writing. The letters, on an average, are 2 in. in size. Nos. 2 and 3 (*A. S. I.* Nos. 607–608) together cover an area of 4 ft. 9 in. by 1 ft. 7 in. Each of these two records consists of three lines, the third line of No. 3 containing only four letters. The size of the letters in these two records is about the same as that of No. 1. No. 4 (*A.S.I.* No. 609) measures 4 ft. 5 in. by 1 ft. 11 in. and contains four lines of writing. The letters of this record are somewhat larger than those of the other three epigraphs, being on an average 3 in. in size.

The **script,** generally speaking, is of the same type as that of the Nāgirikanda inscription [1], the points of difference in some of the individual letters of the two records being such as would result through the individuality of the different scribes who drafted them. The letters in which this difference is more marked are *a*, *ca*, *ḍa*, *ta*, *da*, *na*, *ma*, *ya*, and *ha*, as can be noticed in comparing the *akṣaras* of these inscriptions given in the table on Plate 15. In inscription No. 1 occurs the symbol for *o* which is rarely found in the records of this period and is interesting in that it shows us the intermediate stage of development between the forms of this *akṣara* in the second and ninth centuries. This and the *u* found in No. 2 (l. 1) are not present in the Nāgirikanda record. The script of No. 4 differs slightly from that of the others and favours more angular forms. The *a* occurring in that record is distinctly of a more archaic type than the symbol for that letter found in the other three epigraphs and if we can rely on palaeography we may assign No. 4 to a date slightly earlier than Nos. 1 to 3. The symbols for *a*, *ca*, *ma*, *na*, and *ha* of these records show an earlier stage of evolution than the corresponding forms in the Nāgirikanda inscription; but the *akṣaras* *ḍa*, *da*, and *ya* appearing in the latter seem to be more archaic. Types belonging to two near stages of evolution are often found together in the same document and some epigraphs contain archaic forms of writing not generally found in other documents of the period to which they belong; but on the whole

---

[1] See above, pp. 115–122.

these inscriptions may, from considerations of palaeography, be slightly earlier in date than the Nāgirikanda epigraph.

As regards **orthography** and **grammar**, these records contain some interesting forms. In No. 1, l. 1, we have *opula* for P. *uppala*, showing an early stage in the development of the modern Sinhalese *ōlu*. The change of *u* to *o* is further instanced by the occurrence of *oluvadu* in No. 1, in place of *uluvadu* in No. 2. In *ma* (No. 1, l. 4) and *maha* (No. 4, l. 4), which stand for *me* (P. *imaṁ*) and *mehi* (P. *imasmiṁ*) of the earlier, as well as the later, language, we see that the vowels *e* and *i* have been changed to *a*. The same feature has also been noticed in the Nāgirikanda inscription. Vowel assimilation is noticed in *rici* (No. 2, l. 3) for P. *ruci*. On the whole, when studying these and other records of the period, it appears as if the vocal system of the language was then in a state of flux, there being no fixed usage as to what vowel was the correct form in a particular syllable of a word. For instance, compare the forms *vaharala, veherala, veharala* and *vaharila*, which are apparently variant forms of the same word occurring in the four inscriptions respectively. In *Opulavana* (P. *Uppalavaṇṇa*), we have the dental *n* in place of Skt. *rṇṇ*. In the earlier stage of the language, the cerebral *ṇ* invariably occurs in such places; compare *mekavaṇa* in the Tonigala inscription[1]. This change to the dental *n*, which seems to have developed about the fifth or sixth century, has remained the rule ever since[2]. In *sayaka* (P. *sataka*) and *Daḷameya* (P. *Dāṭhāmegha*), intervocalic surds and sonants have both been changed to *y*. The general tendency in the early Sinhalese language was to change the intervocalic sonant to a surd, for instance, the change of Skt. *Nāga*, *Abhaya*, and *pada* to *Naka*, *Apaya* and *pata*, respectively. In inscription No. 4, we have an instance of the opposite tendency in the word *Kasaba* (P. *Kassapa*) which occurs as *Kasub* and *Kasba* in the ninth century and later. No. 1, however, has *Kasapi*.

As regards nominal forms, inflexions are rather rare in these inscriptions, the crude form being used instead in many places. *Vahere* in No. 1, l. 3, has the locative singular in *-e*, *satanaṭa* in No. 1, l. 4, the dative in *-aṭa* and *daruyana* in No. 2, l. 2, the accusative plural or genitive plural in *-ana*. The suffix for the first person singular is attached to nouns, as in *Puyagonulami* (No 1, l. 1)—a practice which is frequently met with in the Sinhalese language of the ninth

[1] See *E. Z.* Vol. III, p. 177.

[2] See the pamphlet 'The use of *n* and *ṇ* and *l* and *ḷ* in the Sinhalese Language' by Julius de Lanerolle, Colombo 1934, p. 6.

and tenth centuries and is also common in Tamil [1]. Coming to verbal forms, *cidavi* (No. 1, l. 4; No. 2, l. 2; and No. 3, l. 2), if the interpretation of it adopted by me is correct, furnishes us with an example of a finite verb which is rarely, if at all, met with in the early inscriptions of Ceylon, the past participle passive being used with the force of a finite verb in most inscriptions. *Cidavi* is taken as the causative third person singular form in the past tense and indicative mood of the root derived from Skt. *chid.* It is equivalent to P. *chindāpayi* and modern Sinhalese *siňdavi.* The plural form of the same verb is found in No. 4, ll. 3 and 4, as *cidavayaha.* Another point which might be worthy of note is that, though the first personal termination *mi* is found in the subject in records 1-3, the predicate is in the third person. This is in contrast with the usage of the ninth and tenth centuries when the verb used as the predicate always ended in *mi*, if this suffix was attached to the subject. Compare, for instance, the passage *Simi mamad me-karaṇayehi givisä batak dinmi*' in the Kaludiyapokuṇa inscription [2]. The gerund *di* occurring in No. 4, l. 3, is almost the same as the corresponding modern form. The optative form *vayavaya* or *veyavaya* occurs in Nos. 2 (l. 3) and 3 (l. 3). This is the prototype of the modern *vēvā* and its plural occurs in the language of about the eighth century as *velvay* [3]. As Professor Geiger has already pointed out, this mode is formed by the addition of the optative form of the root *vū* (Skt. *bhū*) to the present indicative verbal forms [4]. The form *veya* or *vaya* has then to be taken as the present indicative singular form, in the sixth century, of the Sinhalese verb derived from the Skt. root *bhū.* This occurs in the classical and the modern dialects as *vē* and *veyi.* The optative form *vaya* itself has preserved the *y* of the old Indian termination *-yāt*, unlike the Prakrits in which this *y* has been changed to *j.*

These records are **not dated**; but two of them contain data which would help us in determining the upper limit of their date. Nos. 1 and 4 give the name of the monastery, at which the inscriptions are found, as **Boya-Opulavana-Kasapi-gari** (P. Bodhi-Uppalavaṇṇa-Kassapagiri) and **Kasaba-giriye** (P. Kassapagiri), respectively, which are alternative names of the Issarasamaṇa-vihāra. I have elsewhere [5] pointed out that, on the evidence of inscriptions found at the site, the modern Vessagiriya is really the ancient Issarasamaṇa-vihāra. This monastery was enlarged and richly endowed by the parricide king **Kassapa I** who renamed it after himself and his two daughters, **Bodhi** and **Uppalavaṇṇā** [6].

---

[1] *E. Z.* Vol., Vol. III, p. 255.

[2] *E. Z.*, Vol. III, p. 258.

[3] *Ibid.*, p. 198.

[4] See Geiger, *L. S. S.*, p. 79.

[5] *C. J. Sc.*, *G*, Vol. II, p. 182.

[6] *Mahāvaṁsa*, chap. xxxix, vv. 10-11.

As the monastery could not have been referred to by the name of Bodhi-Uppalavaṇṇa-Kassapagiri before the reign of Kassapa I (*circa* 526–552), these records must be later than the accession of that monarch. We have no means of deciding definitely the lower limit of their date. However, as I have pointed out in discussing the script of the records, they appear palaeographically to be earlier than the Nāgirikanda inscription and therefore we may assign them to the period between Kassapa and Kumāradāsa.

In their **contents,** the four epigraphs are all similar. They record the obtaining of freedom from slavery, of themselves or of their relatives, by various individuals who are named. The two individuals mentioned in Inscription No. 4 obtained their manumission by paying 100 *kahāpaṇas* to the Issarasamaṇa monastery which is also mentioned in this connexion in Inscription No. 1. This and the fact that the records of the manumission are engraved within the precincts of the monastery show that the slaves set free belonged to that religious establishment. We have epigraphical evidence to prove that slaves were owned by Buddhist monasteries of Ceylon in the second century A.D. and also in later times[1], though the practice does not seem to be in keeping with the spirit of Buddhism. From other Buddhist countries like Burma and Cambodia, too, we have evidence to show that Buddhist monastic institutions owned numerous slaves[2]. It must, however, be mentioned that the remarks about the contents of the inscriptions depend on the interpretation of the words *vaharala cidavi* and their variants which will be discussed in the sequel.

TEXT.

I.

1 Latakatala(hi) oluvaḍu Puyagonu-
2 -lami **B(o)ya-Opulavana-Kasapi-ga-**
3 **-ri**-raja-maha-vahere siya-agana vahara-
4 -la cidavi ma-pala sava-satanaṭa

II.

1 Si Durusava vasana uluvaḍu Boya-gonulami
2 daruyana cidavi veherala pala
3 sava-satanaṭa vayavaya rici Budu-bava vayavaya

[1] See below, the remarks on the word *vaharala* and the Galapāta Vihāra inscription in *J. R. A. S., C. B., Notes and Queries*, July, 1914, pp. lxxii–lxxiv.

[2] G. E. Harvey, *History of Burma*, p. 268, and Sir Chas. Eliot, *Hinduism and Buddhism*, vol. iii, p. 120 and footnote 6.

I

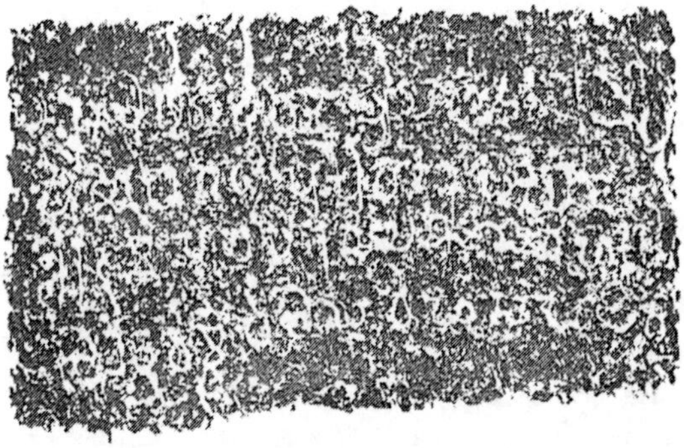

II and III

II

III

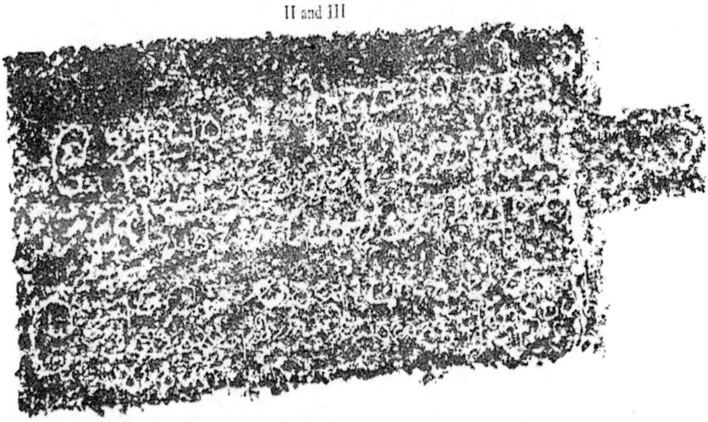

IV

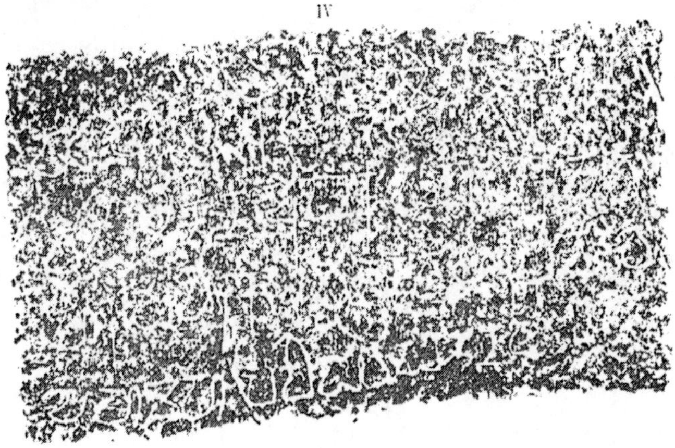

Scale about $1\frac{1}{8}$ inches to 1 foot

III.

1 Si Abagamayahi vasana Patisalalami daru-
2 -ya cidavi veharala pala sava-satanaṭa rici Budu-bava
3 veyavaya

IV.

1 Sahasavarala Daḷameya Sakaṇakana
2 Vesimiṇiya Aba **Kasaba-giriye** va-
3 -hara sayaka kahavaṇa di vaharila cidava-
4 -yaha maha pala sava-satanaṭa.

TRANSLATION.

I.

I, Puyagonula, the brick-layer of Latakatala, caused my wife to be freed from slavery in the royal monastery of **Boya-Opulavana-Kasapi-gari.** [May] the fruit of this [action be] for the benefit of all beings.

II.

Hail! I, Boyagonula, the brick-layer residing in Durusava, caused [my] children to be freed from slavery. May the fruit [of this action] be for the benefit of all beings. May there be Buddhahood as desired.

III.

Hail! I, Patisalala, residing at Abagamaya, caused [my] child to be freed from slavery. [May] the fruit [of this action be] for the benefit of all beings. May there be Buddhahood as desired.

IV.

Sahasavarala Daḷameya and Sakaṇakana Vesimiṇiya Aba gave a hundred *kahāpaṇas* to the **Kasabagiriye** monastery and freed [themselves] from slavery. May the fruit of this [action] be for the benefit of all beings.

REMARKS.

[I, l. 1]. *Oluvaḍu* is taken to be a variant form of *uluvaḍu* which occurs in inscription No. 2. The word *uluvaḍu*, in literary Sinhalese, means 'a mason'. *Vaḍu* is from Skt. *vardhakin*. *Ulu* is usually taken by Sinhalese scholars as derived from Skt. *iṣṭaka* (P. *iṭṭhaka*), but the occurrence of the dental, instead of the cerebral, *l* in the word militates against this view.

[I, l. 3]. *Siya-agana* : *Siya* is equivalent to Skt. *svaka* and occurs in literary Sinhalese in the same form. It is also found in the Tōnigala inscription where, however, it has the same meaning as Skt. *svayaṁ*, P. *sayam* [1], and has to be treated as an indeclinable. *Siya*, meaning 'one's own', has, in fact, no distinction of number and person; but I have translated it as 'my', as the subject of the sentence, to which the word refers, is in the first person. *Agana* is taken as derived from Skt. *aṅganā*, and to be the same as the classical Sinhalese *aṅgana*. It, therefore, means 'woman'; but may have been used in ordinary speech to mean 'wife'. In modern colloquial Sinhalese, a wife is often referred to as *gǟni* 'woman'.

[I, ll. 3–4]. *Vaharala cidavi*: The word *vaharala* and its variant forms *veherala*, *veharala*, and *vaharila* occur in all these four inscriptions either followed, or preceded, by the verb *cidavi* or *cidavayaha*. These words are found in the great majority of inscriptions of this period, very often with the verb *cidavi* and its variant forms. Some of these records are very brief ones and contain merely the name of an individual followed by *vaharala*. Sometimes the name of a monastery also occurs after the name of the individual. There have also been found a few records of this type which date from about the eighth century, when the script and the language had both changed from what they were in the sixth. For instance, a short record at Mädagama in the Kuruṇāgala District reads *Mihidala Simi dariyana sidăva veheraleya* [2]. The phrase *sidăva veheraleya* in this is obviously the same as *cidavi veherala* of Inscription No. 2. Another short record found at the same place reads *Kaḍa maḍabiyana veherala* [3]. The word *vaharala* also occurs in different contexts in other records. For instance, some records of about the sixth century from Rājaṅgaṇē in the Kuruṇāgala District [4] contain the phrases *sayamala va(harala)* and *alamala vaharala*, where the meaning of the words *sayamala* and *alamala* is not clear. In the inscriptions on the steps of a shrine near the so-called 'Burrows' Pavilion' at Anurādhapura, occurs the phrase *vaharala vaṭa kaṭa* (see below, p. 139). In other inscriptions at the same place we find *vahala* and *varala* as variant forms of *vaharala*. The expression *vaṭa koṭu* occurs in phrases like *ariyavasa vaṭa koṭu* and means 'for the maintenance of', *vaṭa* being equivalent to Skt. *vṛtti* and P. *vaṭṭa*. It, therefore, appears that *vaharala* and its variants must have meant

---

[1] *E.Z.*, Vol. II, pp. 177 and 181.

[2] *A.S.I.*, No. 722. See *J.R.A.S., G*, vol. ii, p. 222. See below, p. 144.

[3] *A.S.I.*, No. 723. See *C.J.Sc., G*, vol. ii, p. 222. The remarks made there regarding this and the preceding epigraph require modification. See below, p. 144.

[4] Müller, *A.I.C.*, No. 65.

something which was necessary for a monastic establishment and for the maintenance of which provision was made and the fact recorded in those inscriptions. In the epigraphs now under discussion, the verb *cidavi* occurs in connexion with *vaharala*. *Cidavi* means literally 'caused to be broken', but it may also be used with the secondary meaning 'discontinued' 'ceased to be', &c. In the records before us, certain individuals are stated to have caused the cessation of certain things at a monastery; but at the same time these individuals seem to have considered that they had done a meritorious thing, for they give the merit of the action to all beings. In other records, other individuals are represented as earning and distributing merit by providing for the same. *Vaharala*, therefore, must mean something paradoxical, of which it can be said that one can gain merit by providing it for a monastery as well as by removing it. The fact that the word follows the name of an individual shows that it must have been applied to a person. We may now consider whether the word *vaharala* can be interpreted in such a way as to suit all these contexts. One of the variant forms of the word noted above is *vahala* which is almost identical with *vahal* used in modern Sinhalese to mean 'slave'. This meaning, it would seem, suits all the contexts in which the word has so far been found. One, of course, gains merit by providing money for the maintenance of slaves at a monastery and, at the same time, one would equally gain merit by obtaining the freedom of these slaves which also would have to be done by paying money. Even if one obtains one's own freedom from slavery, as, it seems, is recorded in Inscription No. 4, there would yet be merit for the money paid to the monastery. Such records in which the word merely occurs after the name of an individual ought to be taken as registering the fact that the individual in question was a slave of the monastery in which the record is found.

The word has not so far been met with in any document earlier than the sixth century, the word *dasa* (Skt. *däsa*) being used for slaves in records of the second century[1]. Professor Geiger derives *vahal* from Skt. *vṛṣala* (P. *vasala*); and it is not impossible that *vṛṣala* took the form *vaharala* in the sixth century through the intermediate forms **varasala* and **varahala*. The context shows that, in some places where it occurs, *vaharala* ought to mean 'slavery', in which case, it may be taken as going back to a *taddhita* form of *vṛṣala*.

[I, l. 4]. *Pala sava-satanaṭa*: For this phrase, see *E. Z.*, Vol. III, pp. 125–126.

[1] For instance, an unpublished second-century inscription (No. 101 of *A. S. C.*, *A. R.* for 1892) from Ilukväva in the Anurādhapura District contains the phrases, *dasi Anula dini, dasa Kaḷa ca.*

[II, l. 2]. *Daruyana* is taken as the accusative singular of *daruya* (see Inscription No. 3, ll. 1-2) which is equivalent to P. *dāraka*. In modern Sinhalese these two forms are found as *daruvan* and *daruvā* respectively.

[II, l. 3]. *Rici Budu-bava vayavaya*: In modern Sinhalese this phrase would read *risi Budubava vēvā*. The words *rici* and *vayavaya* have been dealt with above; *Budu-bava* is equivalent to Skt. *Buddha-bhāva*. What is meant by Buddhahood here is evidently the attainment of Nirvāṇa or Bodhi which can be accomplished in any one of three ways, namely, by being the disciple of a Buddha (*śrāvaka-bodhi*), a private Buddha (*pratyeka-bodhi*), or a supremely enlightened Buddha (*samyak-sambodhi*). These are the three vehicles (*yānas*) of the Mahāyānists and are also recognized by the Theravādins of Ceylon. The usual benediction of the Buddhist monk in Ceylon ends with the wish that the devotee may attain Nirvāṇa through the medium of any that is desired among the three *bodhis* (*tuntarā bōdhiyen patannāvū ektarā bōdhiyakin*).

[IV, ll. 1-2]. *Sahasavarala Daḷameya Sakaṇakana Vesimiṇiya Aba*. In these two personal names, *Sahasavarala* and *Sakaṇakana* are evidently names of villages in which the individuals mentioned resided. We seem to have here the beginnings of the practice of using a place name as part of the personal name, which is frequently met with in the records of the ninth and tenth centuries and is also very common among the Sinhalese to-day[1].

[IV, l. 3]. *Sayaka kahavaṇa di*: The sum paid for the manumission of two slaves was 100 *kahāpaṇas*. It appears, therefore, that the average price of a slave was 50 *kahāpaṇas*.

No. 16. INSCRIPTIONS ON THE STEPS NEAR 'BURROWS' PAVILION' AT ANURĀDHAPURA.

By S. PARANAVITANA.

THE eight short records included in this paper are incised on steps leading to a ruined shrine near the reconstructed porch now known as 'the Stone Canopy' or 'Burrows' Pavilion'[2] in the area of the Abhayagiri (popularly known as the Jetavana) Vihāra at Anurādhapura. The three slab-inscriptions edited in

---

[1] See *E. Z.*, Vol. III, p. 105, n. 1.

[2] For this porch and its reconstruction by Mr. (later Sir) S. M. Burrows, see *A. S. C. Annual Report* for 1911-12, p. 33

the articles numbered 4, 19, and 20 of Vol. I of this Journal have also been found in the same vicinity. The flight of steps is 15 ft. in breadth and consisted of six treads, each of two pieces of stone. Inscriptions numbered 1 to 3 are incised on the second (right) piece of the first tread from the bottom. No. 1, consisting of six lines of unequal length, occupies the left-hand side of this stone and extends to a length of 1 ft. 6 in. No. 2 is inscribed to the right of No. 1 and No. 3 is below No. 2. No space has been left between the ends of the lines of No. 1 and the beginnings of those of Nos. 2 and 3; and at first sight it appears as if the writing on this stone comprised one inscription. No. 4 is on the first stone of the second tread and occupies a space of 2 ft. 8 in. by 7 in. Nos. 5 and 6, written one below the other, occupy a space of 3 ft. 4 in. by 8¾ in. on the first stone of the fourth tread, and No. 7, to the right of these two, covers an area of 1 ft. 6¼ in. by 6 in. On the extreme right end of this stone is another short record which is badly preserved and is not decipherable in full; it has not, therefore, been included in this paper. No. 8 is on the second stone of the fourth tread and measures 2 ft. 6½ in. by 5½ in. On this stone, as well as on some other treads, there are traces of inscriptions of which no intelligible text can be made out.

Like most of the records dating from the period between the sixth and the ninth centuries, these epigraphs have been carelessly executed. The letters are not incised to any considerable depth; and owing to this reason as well as to the fact that the writing is on steps which must have been continuously trodden upon for several centuries, the epigraphs are not in a good state of preservation. The letters vary in size from ¾ in. to 1¾ in.

The records are all written in a form of the ancient Sinhalese script which is definitely of a later stage of evolution than that of the Nāgirikanda inscription dealt with above. The letters are of a highly cursive type and it is somewhat difficult to distinguish between some letters like *na* and *ta* which are almost identical in form. The looped form of *ta* found in the Nāgirikanda inscription does not occur in these epigraphs which contain a form of that letter close to the one appearing in the Vessagiriya inscriptions [1]. Variant forms of the same letter are found in these epigraphs, sometimes in the same document. The signs for the medial vowels *i*, *o*, and *e* are rarely marked. As regards the individual letters, the table given in Plate 15 will enable the reader to compare them with the corresponding letters occurring in other records of somewhat

---

[1] See above, p. 129.

earlier and later dates. The degree of development shown in the script would justify us in concluding that these epigraphs date from the second half of the sixth, or the first half of the seventh, century.

As regards **orthography,** we notice, in the records, a tendency to substitute *a* for the medial vowels *i*, *u*, *e*, and *o*. Compare, for example, *-gara* in *Apahaya-gara* (I, ll. 3-4), *ulavaḍha* (I, l. 2), *kaṭa* (I, l. 4), and *vaharaṭa* (II, l. 2), which occur in earlier inscriptions as *giri*[1], *uluvaḍu*[2], *koṭu*[3], and *vaheraṭaya*[4]. In the later language, however, these words are found as *giri*, *uluvaḍu*, *koṭa*, and *veheraṭa*. It is, therefore, not certain whether the change of nearly all the other medial vowels to *a* was a peculiarity of the language of this period or whether the forms appearing in these inscriptions are due to the careless system of writing which was prevalent at the time. Words which show noteworthy **phonetic changes** in consonants are *Apahaya*, *jahasa* (III, l. 2), and *huna-kavaṇa* (IV, l. 2). In *Apahaya* (Skt. *Abhaya*) a vowel has been introduced between the aspirate and the *b*, the latter changing to *p*. In the tenth century, this word occurs in the form *Abahay*[5], thereby indicating that the change of the sonant to the corresponding surd, effected before the seventh century, did not persist in the next stage of the language. As regards the treatment of the aspirate in this word, comparison may be made with words like *daham*, *rajadahan*, and *dähän*, which stand for Skt. *dharma*, *rājadhāni*, and *dhyāna*[6]. *Jahasa* (mod. Sinh. *dahasa*), if it is taken as derived from Skt. *sahassa* shows the change of *s* to *j*[7]. No such phonetic change has been met with previously in the Sinhalese language. *Huna* is equivalent to Skt. *suvarṇṇa* and the dental *n* in place of *rṇṇ* is noteworthy[8]. In *kavaṇa* for the earlier *kahavaṇa* (Skt. *karṣāpaṇa*, P. *kahāpaṇa*), the syllable *ha* has been completely dropped out. It is, however, possible that this may be due to a clerical error. The verbal forms *daya* (II, l. 3) and *da* (III, l. 2) occurring in these records have not been met with elsewhere. The contexts in which they occur show that they are equivalent in meaning to *dine* (P. *dinna*) and its variant forms occurring in inscriptions from the third century B.C. to about the fifth century A.D. We may, therefore, conjecture that while *dine* is derived from P. or Pkt. *dinna*, *daya* and *da* go back to Skt. *datta* through the intermediate form *data*, which occurs in the name *Bamadata* (Skt. *Brahmadatta*) in a pre-

---

[1] See *E.Z.*, Vol. III, p. 116.
[2] See above, p. 132.
[3] See *E.Z.*, Vol. III, p. 116.
[4] See above, p. 123.
[5] See *E.Z.*, Vol. I, pp. 46 and 85.
[6] Compare Geiger, *L. S. S.*, ii, 18. 2.
[7] Geiger derives *dahasa* from Skt. *sahasra*, see *E. S.*, *s.v.*
[8] See above, p. 130.

Christian inscription from Riṭigala[1]. As regards **syntax,** we find that, in these records, the predicate does not agree with the subject, not only in person as in the Vessagiriya epigraphs[2], but in number as well. For instance, in No. 5, the subject is *Deva Kaḷa Sivayama,* the names of three individuals, to the last of which has been added the first personal suffix *-ma*, probably in the plural number; but we cannot recognize any termination indicating the first person or the plural number in the verbal form *de* used as the predicate.

The **contents** of the records are of no historical interest. They merely register grants of money by various obscure individuals to the **Abhayagiri-vihāra,** for the maintenance of slaves[3]. They are interesting only as examples of the script and language of about the seventh century, of which period no documents have yet been published in this journal.

TEXT.

I.

1 Marayu[4]vahahapa-gamayaha va-
2 -sana ulavaḍha Sadeva Gaṇayama ca
3 Apa .. va .. .. Apama ca **Apahaya-**
4 **gara-**vaha[ra] vaharala va[ṭa] kaṭa eka-
5 sayaka kahava[ṇa] da pa-
6 -la sava-satanaṭa

II.

1 Guta-kadaraha vasana Pa(lama) dama Apama **A-**
2 **-pahaya-gara-**vaharaṭa vaharala vaṭa kaṭa e-
3 -ka-sayaka kahavaṇa daya pala sava-(satanaṭa)

III.

1 Maha-daragalaha vasana Pajana Adasana Vasa-davayama **Apa-**
2 **-haya-gara-**vaharaṭa vahala vaṭa kaṭa dajahasa kahavaṇa da pala
3 sava-sa(tanaṭa)

---

[1] *E. Z.*, Vol. I, p. 150.
[2] See above, p. 131.
[3] This statement depends on the accuracy of the interpretation of the word *vaharala*, see above, pp. 134–35.
[4] The letter which has been read as *yu* can also be read as *pu* or as *a*.

IV.

1 Madararayana Gana[1] Apama **Apayagara**-vahara-
2 -ṭa vaharala vaṭa kaṭa eka saya huna-kavaṇa
3 da pala sava-satanaṭa

V.

1 Erayaha vasana (Da)va Kaḷa Savayama **Apahayagara**-va-
2 -haraṭa eka-sa[ya*] kahavana da pala sava-sata[naṭa]

VI.

1 .. .. marayu[2] - mahapa - gamayaha vasana Panapalata
2 .. .. daya-gamaya **A[pa*]ya-gara**-vaharaṭa ekajahasaka ka-
3 -havaṇa da maha pāla sava-satanaṭa

VII.

1 Lava-arana Gana Apama **Apaha-**
2 **-ya-gara**-vaharaṭa vaharala va-
3 -ṭa kaṭa eka-sayaka kavahaṇa da
4 pala sava-satanaṭa

VIII.

1 Nadanagumu Paya-vāpara Vahana Adasana Va-
2 -rayana Ganayama **Apahagara**-vaharaṭa varala va-
3 -ṭa kaṭa eka-sayaka kahavaṇa da maha pa[la*]sava-satanaṭa

TRANSLATION.

I.

I, Sadeva Ganaya[3], the brick-layer, residing in the village of Marayuvahahapa and I, Apa[4] .. va .. .. Apa, gave one hundred *kahavaṇas*[5] for maintaining slaves[6] at the **Apahayagara**[7] monastery. The merit [is given] to all beings[8].

---

[1] The letter *na* is written below the line.

[2] This syllable can also be read as *pu* or as *a*.

[3] This and some of the other names of persons and places occurring in these records appear rather outlandish. The fact that hardly any other vowels than *a* occur in these names makes it somewhat difficult to ascertain what their Sanskrit or Pāli equivalents were, if they had any.

[4] *Apa* = Skt. and P. *Abhaya*.

[5] Skt. *karṣāpaṇa*, P. *kahāpaṇa*. For the coin, see Codrington, *Ceylon Coins and Currency*, p. 2.

[6] *Vaharala vaṭa kaṭa*: for this phrase, see above, pp. 134–135.

[7] Skt. and Pāli *Abhayagiri*.

[8] See *E. Z.*, Vol. III, pp. 125–126.

Inscriptions on the Steps near Burrows' Pavilion

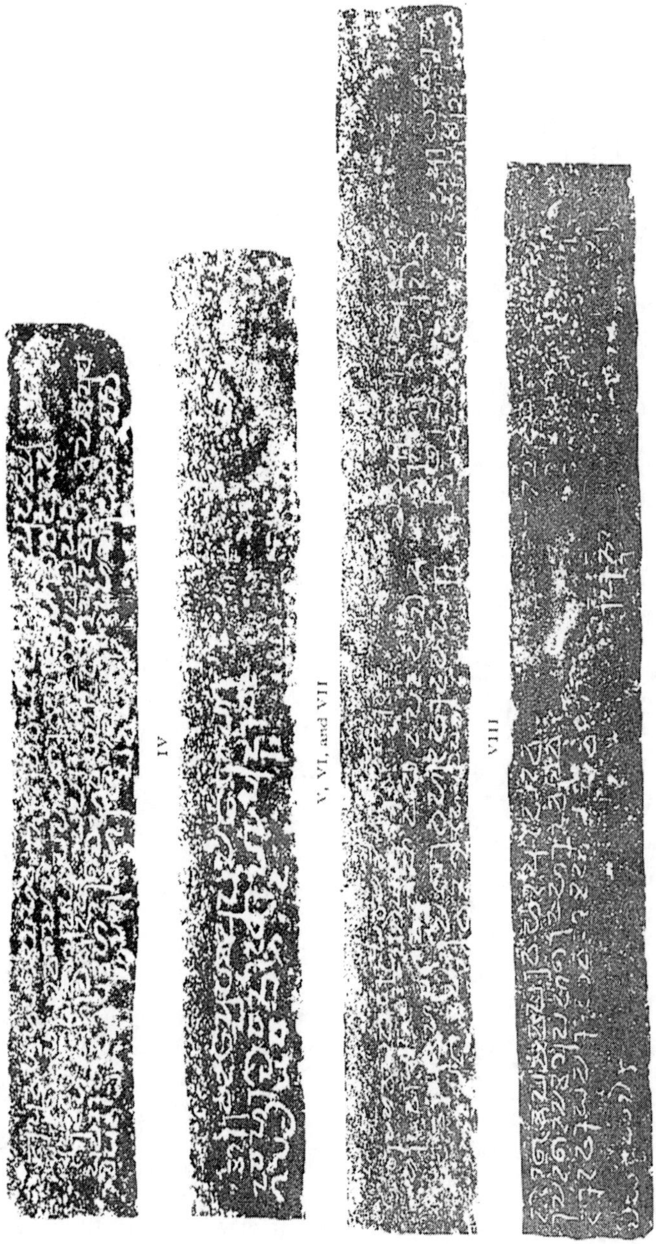

I, II, and III — IV — V, VI, and VII — VIII

Scale about 1½ inches to 1 foot

II.

I, Pa(lama)dama Apa, residing at Gutakadara[1], gave one hundred *kahavaṇas* to the **Apahayagara** monastery for the maintenance of slaves. The merit [is given] to all beings.

III.

We, Pajana, Adasana, and Vasadevaya[2], residing in Mahadaragala[3], gave two thousand *kahavaṇas* to the **Apahayagara** monastery for the maintenance of slaves. The merit [is given] to all [beings].

IV.

I, Gana Apa of Madararayana, gave one hundred *huna-kahavaṇas*[4] to the **Apayagara**[5] monastery for the maintenance of slaves. The merit [is given] to all beings.

V.

We, Deva, Kala, and Savaya[6], residing at Eraya, gave one hundred *kahavaṇas* to the **Apahayagara** monastery. The merit [is given] to all beings.

VI.

Panapalata .. .. daya-gamaya, residing in the village of .. .. marayu-mahapa, gave one thousand *kahavaṇas* to the **Apayagara** monastery, The merit of this [action is given] to all beings.

VII.

I, Gana Apa of Lava-arana[7], gave one hundred *kahavaṇas* to the **Apahayagara** monastery for the maintenance of slaves. The merit [is given] to all beings.

VIII.

We, Paya-vāpara[8], Vahana, Adasana, Varayana, and Ganaya of Nadanagumu[9] gave one hundred *kahavaṇas* to the **Apahagara** monastery for the maintenance of slaves. The merit of this [action is given] to all beings.

---

[1] P. *Gutta-kandara.*

[2] Skt. and P. *Vāsudeva.* The first personal suffix *ma* is attached only to the last of the three names. It has evidently to be understood as referring to the two preceding names as well.

[3] P. *Mahādāragiri.* A village of this name occurs in the *Mv*, chap. xliv, v. 96.

[4] For *huna*, see above, pp. 47–48.

[5] A variant form of *Apahayagara* (P. *Abhayagiri*).

[6] P. *Deva*, *Kāla*, and *Sīvaka.* The personal suffix *ma* is attached to the last name here also.

[7] *Arana* in this name is probably the same as Skt. *araṇya*, P. *arañña.*

[8] *Vāpara* is probably equivalent to Skt. *vyāpārin* 'trader'.

[9] P. *Nandanagāma.*

No. 17. SEVEN SINHALESE INSCRIPTIONS OF THE SEVENTH AND EIGHTH CENTURIES.

By S. Paranavitana.

In this paper I have made a study of seven short records, from various places far removed from one another, which can be assigned on palaeographical grounds to the seventh and eighth centuries. They are of little or no historical interest and have been published solely for the purpose of giving the reader some idea—very imperfect, though it is—of the development of the Sinhalese language and script during these centuries. The table on Plate 15 will enable the reader to compare the scripts of these records with one another as well as with those of the records of a somewhat earlier period dealt with in the four preceding papers, scripts, namely, which belong to the fourth and ninth centuries.

I.

The oldest of these epigraphs is engraved on a rock near the ruined *stūpa* at a place called Veherakema, in the heart of a dense forest, about six miles to the south-east of Lahugala in the Pānama Pattu of the Batticaloa District [1]. It covers an area of 6 ft. 6 in. by 1 ft. 9 in. and contains three lines of writing, of which the last comprises only six or seven letters, too weathered to be deciphered. The letters, which are boldly engraved, are, on an average, 5 in. in size. The first two lines of the record are in a good state of preservation. The **script** shows a later stage of development than that of any of the inscriptions dealt with in the four previous articles. The **letters**, on the whole, have a tendency to curvilinear forms. The *virāma* and the sign for the medial vowel *ä* are absent. This fact would justify us in giving an earlier **date** to this record than to the Gäraṅḍigala rock-inscription, in which both the *virāma* and the *ä*-sign occur and which I have ascribed to the reign of Kassapa III (*circa* 710–717) [2]. The unpublished record of Daḷa Mugalana (Moggallāna II, *circa* 542–561), already referred to, is in a script less developed than that of the present epigraph; and we may, therefore, conclude that this document belongs to a date between these two reigns. It is possible, however, that it is closer in date to the earlier reign than to the later one. The **language** shows no development from that which prevailed in the fifth and sixth centuries; but, as the record is a very

---

[1] *A.S.I.*, No. 594. See *C.J. Sc., G*, vol. ii, pp. 182 and 198.

[2] See *E.Z.*, Vol. III, pp. 195–199.

brief one of only a few words, we cannot speak with confidence in this matter. We can, however, be certain on one point; i.e., that the Sinhalese language, when this inscription was written, had not yet developed the characteristic of changing the original *c* to *s*, which is almost universal from about the eighth century onwards. The form *vaharaya*, presumably in the locative singular, is noteworthy and may be compared with the locative form *sē-sateyi* occurring in v. 47 of the *Haṁsa Sandesa*. *Kriya*, obviously intended for *kiriya* (P. *karīsa*) occurring in earlier records, is an interesting orthographical peculiarity. In *cata* for P. *cetiya* (*ceta* in earlier inscriptions), the vowel *e* has been changed to *a*.

The record tells us that a ruler named **Vahaka Maharaja** caused a *caitya* to be built at the **Macaḷa-vehera,** presumably the ancient monastery of which the ruins are to be seen on the site, and that he made certain donations to it. The title *maharaja* adopted by Vahaka shows that he was an independent ruler; but there is no name having even a remote resemblance to Vahaka in the lists of kings given in the chronicles. Vahaka was perhaps a prince who, in the unsettled political conditions which prevailed at Anurādhapura during the greater part of the seventh century, set himself up as an independent sovereign of Rohaṇa, within which principality the site of the record lies[1]. No monastery which can be reasonably identified with the Macaḷa-vehera of this record has been mentioned in the chronicles.

TEXT.

1 **Vahaka**-maharaja **Macaḷa-vaharaya**

2 cata karavaya[2] catara kriya kubura laba ..

3 .. .. (dina)

TRANSLATION.

The great king **Vahaka**[3], having caused the *caitya* at **Macaḷa-vahara**[3] to be constructed, (gave) .. .. .. received [from] four *karīsas* of fields.

II and III.

Inscriptions numbered II and III in this paper (*A. S. I.*, Nos. 722 and 723) have already been quoted in discussing the word *vaharala* occurring in the

[1] Verses 38 ff. of chap. 45 of the *Mv.* show that there were independent princes in Rohaṇa during the seventh century.

[2] There is a stroke attached to this letter, which, if it is not due to the weathering of the stone, can be taken as a *virāma* sign; but as this sign does not occur elsewhere in this record, I have hesitated to treat it as such.

[3] It is not certain what the Skt. or P. equivalent of this name is.

Vessagiriya inscriptions [1]. They are incised on a rock situated to the west of the ruined *stupa* at Mädagama Vihāra in the Tisāva Kōraḷē of the Kuruṇāgala District and consist of one line each. No. II is 3 ft. 1 in., and No. III 2 ft. 4 in., in length; the letters are from 1½ to 2 in. in size. The **script** of both is almost identical and is much more rounded in form than that of the preceding epigraph. The *virāma* sign does not occur in either, and this feature may indicate that these records are earlier in **date** than the Gäraṅḍigala inscription of Kassapa III [2]. Above the syllable *da*, occurring as the twelfth *akṣara* of No. II, is a curved stroke which also occurs in No. V below and which will be discussed in dealing with that inscription. As regards the **language**, the only important point worth noting is that in No. II we meet with an instance of the change of *c* to *s*. We may, therefore, infer that this phonetic change developed in the Sinhalese language for the first time in or about the eighth century. In **contents the two** records resemble the Vessagiriya inscriptions dealt with above.

TEXT.

II. **Mihidala Simi** dariyana sidăva [3] veheraleya

III. **Kaḍa Maḍabiyana** veherala [4]. . . . . .

TRANSLATION.

II. I, **Mihidala Si** [5], caused my daughters [6] to be freed from slavery [7].

III. The slave of **Kaḍa Maḍabi** [8] .. ..

IV.

The next inscription is engraved on a stone which seems to have been used as a tread in a flight of steps and is now preserved in the Archaeological Museum at Anurādhapura. Its original provenance is not known, it being only recorded that the stone was removed to the Museum from the Government Agent's premises at Anurādhapura. The record consists of two lines of writing,

---

[1] See above, p. 134.

[2] See *E. Z.*, Vol. III, pp. 196–197.

[3] For the diacritical mark in the second syllable of this word, see below, p. 146.

[4] This record seems to be incomplete.

[5] P. *Mahinda Siha.* In *Mihidala* we meet with the suffix *la* which in the form of *l* was, in the ninth and tenth centuries, often attached to personal names, probably as an honorific. See *E. Z.*, Vol. III, p. 276, n.

[6] *Dariyana* is taken as the accusative plural of *dariya* from P. *dārikā*. Compare *daruyana* in the Vessagiriya inscription, above p. 136.

[7] *Sidăva veheraleya* is obviously the same as *cidavi veherala* for which, see above, pp. 134–135.

[8] *Māḍabi* is a title, for which see *E. Z.*, Vol. III, pp. 256–257.

Seven Sinhalese Inscriptions of the seventh and eighth centuries

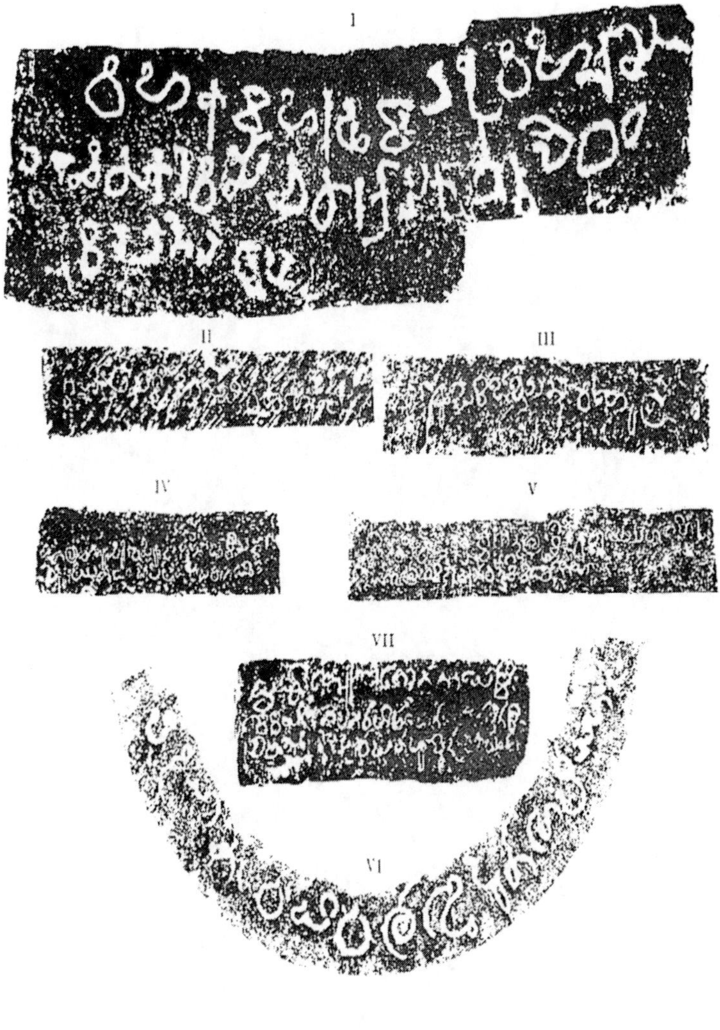

Scale about 1 inch to 1 foot

each 2 ft. $2\frac{1}{2}$ in. long; and is in a fairly good state of preservation. The **letters** are 1 to $1\frac{1}{2}$ inches in size and the **script** is of a somewhat florid character. The *virāma* sign does not occur; but the sign for the medial vowel *ä* is found. The latter, however, is not written in a line with the consonant, as is the rule in the Sinhalese script from the ninth century till modern times, but diagonally above the letter to its right. See, for example, *gä* in l. 2. This mode of writing the *ä*-sign is met with in a number of graffiti, datable in the eighth century, found on the gallery wall at Sīgiriya. In *ra* occurring in line 1, however, the mode of attaching the *ä*-sign is the same as in the script of the ninth century. Palaeographically, this record also seems to be earlier in date than the Gäraṇḍigala inscription; and it may therefore be assigned to about the end of the seventh century. The language differs from that of the ninth century in that it has not yet developed the characteristic of dropping the short vowel *a* at the end, or in an unaccented syllable in the middle, of a word: for instance, the phrase *sava-satanata*, occurring in this record, would have been *sav-satnaṭ* in the ninth century. The verbal form *demi* (l. 2), with the first person singular termination, is still current in literary Sinhalese. The forms *hāmi* and *karu*, for *himi* and *kāru* (P. *sāmi* and *kārita*) of the ninth century, are noteworthy if the readings are free from doubt. The former occurs in the same form in the modern colloquial language and the latter may be compared with *kāru* of the Kivulēkaḍa inscription of Sena I (*E.Z.*, Vol. III, p. 290). The purport of the record was to state that the step on which it was written was the gift of an individual, presumably a monk, named Daḷanā (P. Dāṭhānāga).

TEXT.

1 Gala-veherä **Pirivesikuṭa Daḷanā**-hāmiyana [1]

2 karu [2] piya-gäṭa mehi pala sava-satanaṭa demi

TRANSLATION.

The step [3] caused to be made by **Pirivesikuṭa Daḷanā**-hāmi [residing] in Gala-vehera [4]. I give the merit of this to all beings.

---

[1] The vowel sign attached to *hā* differs from the *i*-sign occurring in this record. It also differs from the *ā*-sign in the *nā* of *Daḷanā* in being more florid. The reading given above is, therefore, not free from doubt.

[2] The first letter of this word is not very well preserved and the reading, therefore, is open to correction.

[3] *Piya-gäṭa* = P. *pada-gaṇṭhi*. See *E.Z.*, Vol. III, p. 216.

[4] *Pirivesikuṭa* is presumably a place-name. *Daḷanā-hāmi* is equivalent to P. *Dāṭhānāga-sāmi*. The honorific *hāmi* attached to his name and the fact that he is said to have resided in a *vihāra* make it fairly certain that Daḷanā was a monk.

V.

This inscription (*A. S. I.*, No. 976) is inscribed on a flagstone on the pavement of the Ambasthala Cetiya at Mihintaḷē. It comprises two lines, the first 3 ft. 6 in., and the second 2 ft. 1 in., in length. The letters range in size from $1\frac{1}{4}$ to $2\frac{1}{2}$ inches. The record is either unfinished or some letters have been effaced at the end of the second line. The first half of the first line appears to be in a hand different from that of the rest of the document. The **letters** are well formed; and this and other documents of about the same period show that the art of the calligraphist which, judging from specimens of writing on stone, was neglected in the fifth to seventh centuries, received considerable attention in the eighth. The **script** is approaching the standard of the ninth century; but certain letters like *ṭa*, *ya*, and *va* are archaic in form.

The curved stroke which we noticed in No. II occurs seven times in this record; to wit, above the third, fourth, sixth, seventh, and nineteenth *akṣaras* of the first line and the seventh and fourteenth of the second. It also occurs in a number of graffiti, assignable on palaeographical grounds to the same age as this epigraph, on the gallery wall at Sīgiriya. We are not certain about the phonetic value which was intended to be conveyed by this symbol; but there are two possible conjectures. (1) It may be treated as an early method of writing the *ä*-sign. There is room for the supposition that the method of writing the *ä*-sign, noticed in No. IV, was a development from the way in which this symbol has been written in the present document; and in some of the graffiti at Sīgiriya the syllables above which this stroke has been added are those which contain an *ä* in the later stage of the language. For example, the symbol occurs above the initial *a* in the word *aya* meaning 'her' and this word assumes the form *äya* in the later language. But the symbol in question is also used in connexion with syllables where etymologically no *ä* is required. Moreover, it occurs in the same document with the type of *ä*-sign noticed in No. IV and is also used in syllables containing the vowel *u*. It is therefore doubtful whether it was the prototype of the *ä*-sign of the ninth century. (2) The symbol would read as the *anunāsika* if a dot were added. We may therefore conjecture that it indicates the half-nasal which is a peculiar feature of the Sinhalese language. In the record under review, the symbol is placed over the ligature *mba*; and *b* is one of the letters before which the half-nasal is pronounced in the modern language, the other letters having this peculiarity being *g*, *ḍ*, and *d*. But the symbol is also used in connexion with syllables containing the consonants *t*, *k*, *ḷ*, *h*, and *y* and in the Sīgiriya graffiti it is placed over the vowel *a*. It is therefore not possible to take this symbol as the half-nasal unless we assume that letters other than *g*, *ḍ*, *d*, and *b*, were also nasalized in the eighth century. We have, therefore, to leave the value of this symbol undecided for the present; but in the romanized text of the inscription I have placed a curved stroke, similar to the one appearing on the stone, above the vowel of the syllables in connexion with which the symbol occurs. Whatever the phonetic value of this symbol was, it was used in the Sinhalese script for but a short period in the eighth century, for it is not found in documents of the ninth century.

In the ligature *nd* occurring in this record, the forms of both the consonants are discernible, the *d* not being reduced, as it is in the ninth-century script, to an unrecognizable form. The *virāma* is marked throughout where it is necessary. This reflects a development in the language of the period, namely, the almost universal dropping out of the vowel *a* at the end of a word, and sometimes also when it occurs as a medial.

The other points in grammar and orthography to which attention may be drawn are the honorific suffix *l* in the name *Mihindal* and the forms *payha* and *daruyun*. Noteworthy also is the occurrence of the Skt. *svasti* as an auspicious word at the beginning of the record. From the earliest times up to about the sixth century, the auspicious word used when one was thought to be necessary at the beginning of a document was the Skt. *siddham* [1] or words derived from it, such as *sidha* [2] or *sidhaṁ* [3]. Sometimes it was abbreviated to *si* [4]. In early Prakrit records of India, too, the auspicious word used was *sidha* [5] or *sidhaṁ* [6]. This went out of use sometime about the seventh century and *svasti* took its place and has remained in favour ever since. After the ninth century, *sid̐dhi* was sometimes used at the end of a document [7] and has been found, but only in one epigraph, in association with *ārogya*, as an auspicious word at the beginning [8].

As stated above, the record is incomplete, and we do not know what its object was. In the preserved portion an individual named Mihindal (Mahinda) states that he salutes the officers in the palace of his king—with what object in view it is now impossible to discover.

---

[1] *E. Z.*, Vol. I, p. 69.
[2] *Ibid.*, p. 254.
[3] *Ibid.*, p. 61.
[4] *E. Z.*, Vol. III, p. 162.
[5] *Ep. Ind.*, vol. viii, p. 73.
[6] *Ibid.*, pp. 78 ff., and vol. xx, pp. 16 ff.
[7] *E. Z.*, Vol. II, p. 4.
[8] In an unpublished inscription from Ranava in the Anurādhapura District.

TEXT.

1 Svasti Tămbăṭikāḷá **Mihindal**mi apa raj-payhă gehi ra-

2 -jol-sam-daruyŭn vandmi (ma ṭabă no go) .. ..

TRANSLATION.

Hail! I, **Mihindal**[1] of Tămbăṭikāḷă, salute their lordships[2] the officials[3] in the palace of our noble king[4]. . . . . .

VI.

This inscription is engraved round the edge of a moonstone placed at the bottom of a flight of steps leading to the *dagăba* at an old *vihāra* called Tammannāgala in the Nāgampaha Kōraḷē of the Anurādhapura District[5]. It consists of only one line, 6 ft. 4 in. long, and the letters are from 3 to 6 in. in size. The language hardly differs from that of the ninth century and Mr. Bell has assigned the record to about that period. But it can be inferred from the **script** in which the record is written that it must belong to an earlier **date** than the ninth century; the forms of *ḷa* and *va* and the method of writing the signs for the medial vowels *a*, *i*, and *e*, attached to the consonants[6], are decisive on this point. The record may therefore belong to the period between Kassapa III and Sena I.

As regards **grammar**, the form *jeṭunge*, in which we find the honorific plural and the genitive suffix *ge*, is noteworthy. The **object** of the record is to state that the moonstone on which it is engraved was a gift of a person named **Valjeṭu** of Piḷiyāna. The record is interesting archaeologically as it informs us that the word *piya-găṭ*, used for a 'moonstone' in mediaeval times, is the same as that applied to an ordinary tread in a flight of steps. In this connexion, it is interesting to note that the expression *sōpanante pāṭikaṁ* (the step at the end of the stair-case), occurring in chap. xxxi, v. 61 of the *Mahāvaṁsa*, is explained by the commentator as *aḍḍhacandaka-padagaṇṭhikaṁ* 'a step of the shape of a half-moon'[7].

---

[1] See above, p. 147.

[2] *Sam-daruyun* is an earlier form of *sam-daruvan*, occurring in the inscriptions of the ninth and tenth centuries. For the meaning of the word, see *E. Z.*, Vol. III, p. 88.

[3] *Rajol* is equivalent to *rad-kol* and *radol* of later inscriptions. See *E. Z.*, Vol. I, p. 189, n. 9.

[4] *Raj-payha*, Skt. *rāja-pādasya*. *Pāda* is added to names in Sanskrit and Pāli as an honorific and forms derived from it are so used in Sinhalese.

[5] *A. S. C. Annual Report* for 1895, p. 7, No. 14.

[6] See *E. Z.*, Vol. III, p. 291.

[7] See *Mahāvaṁsa-ṭīkā*, Colombo edition of 1894, p. 415.

TEXT.

Piḷiyānä väsi **Val-jeṭunge**[1] piya-gäṭ

TRANSLATION.

The step of **Val-jeṭu,** residing at Piḷiyāna.

VII.

The last of the seven inscriptions included in this paper is engraved on the smaller of the two stone canoes found in the vicinity of the 'Stone Canopy', in the area of the Abhayagiri Vihāra at Anurādhapura. The record consists of three lines, the first and third being each 2 ft. 7 in. long and the second 2 ft. 9 in. The size of the letters varies from 1 to $2\frac{1}{4}$ inches. The **script** shows considerable development from that of the Gäraṇḍigala inscription; but contains forms of certain letters less evolved than those found in the inscriptions of Sena I[2]. We may therefore assign this record to the latter half of the eighth, or the beginning of the ninth, century. The influence of the Sanskrit (or the Pāli) on the Sinhalese language of the time is seen in the *tatsama* word *phala* for the *tad-bhava* form *pala* which we have come across already in a number of records of earlier date. *Vetvay* is the prototype of the classical form *vetvā*, the optative plural of the root *vū* (Skt. *bhū*). This may be compared with *vayavaya* and *veyavaya* occurring in the Vessagiriya inscriptions. *May*, occurring in l. 2, should be, from the context, the instrumental singular of the pronoun of the first person. On the analogy of *vetvay* becoming *vetvā*, *may* can be taken as the earlier form of *mā*, the instrumental singular of this pronoun in the classical language. As the long vowels were shortened in the early stage of the Sinhalese language and the final vowel was dropped in the mediaeval stage, we can be confident that *may* is derived from Skt. *mayā*. The object of the record is to state that the stone canoe was the gift of a novice (*sāmaṇera*) named Gonnā.

TEXT.

1 Svasti Heraṇ **Gonnāyemi**

2 me may lu gal-nävhi phala sav-satnaṭ dinmi

3 e phala [gen]ä sav-sat-hu bud vetvay

---

[1] This can also be read as *Piḷiyānavä Sivaljeṭunge*, in which case the translation should be Sivaljeṭu of Piḷiyānava. *Sival* may be a name equivalent to P. *Siva.*

[2] See *E. Z.*, Vol. III, pp. 289–294 and Plate 34.

TRANSLATION.

Hail! I, Gonnā the novice, give to all beings the merit of this stone boat granted by me. May all beings, having taken that merit, become enlightened[1].

* * *

From a study of the above inscriptions we find that there were, during the seventh and eighth centuries, some important developments in the evolution both of the Sinhalese script and of the language. A new vowel sound, *ä*, was evolved in the speech and a method of representing this graphically in the script was also invented. The final, and sometimes the medial, vowel *a* was dropped and this phonetic change was expressed by the *virāma* sign. It appears that the use of the *virama* was adopted later than was that of the *ä*-sign, for, in No. IV, the latter occurs while the former is absent. Another important phonetic feature which was introduced during this period was the change of *c* to *s*. This seems to have been evolved before either of the two innovations mentioned above, for it is found in No. II, in which neither the *virāma* nor the *ä*-sign is met with. We cannot, in the present state of our knowledge, say precisely at what date these changes occurred; we can only be certain that one particular innovation was relatively earlier than another.

In order that the reader may gain some idea of the evolution of the Sinhalese script from the fifth to the ninth centuries, I have given, on Plate 15, a table showing the *akṣaras* found in the inscriptions discussed in the above five articles. In this table I have also included the *akṣaras* found in another dated inscription, yet unpublished, of the same period, namely, the Nilagama rock-inscription of Daḷa Mugalana (Moggallāna II). The forms occurring in the Tōnigala inscription of Śrī Meghavarṇṇa and the Mannar Kacceri Pillar Inscription of Sena II or Kassapa IV, have also been included, so that the symbols of this period may be compared with those of the periods which preceded and followed it.

---

[1] Or, 'become Buddhas'.

Evolution of the Sinhalese Script between the fourth and ninth centuries

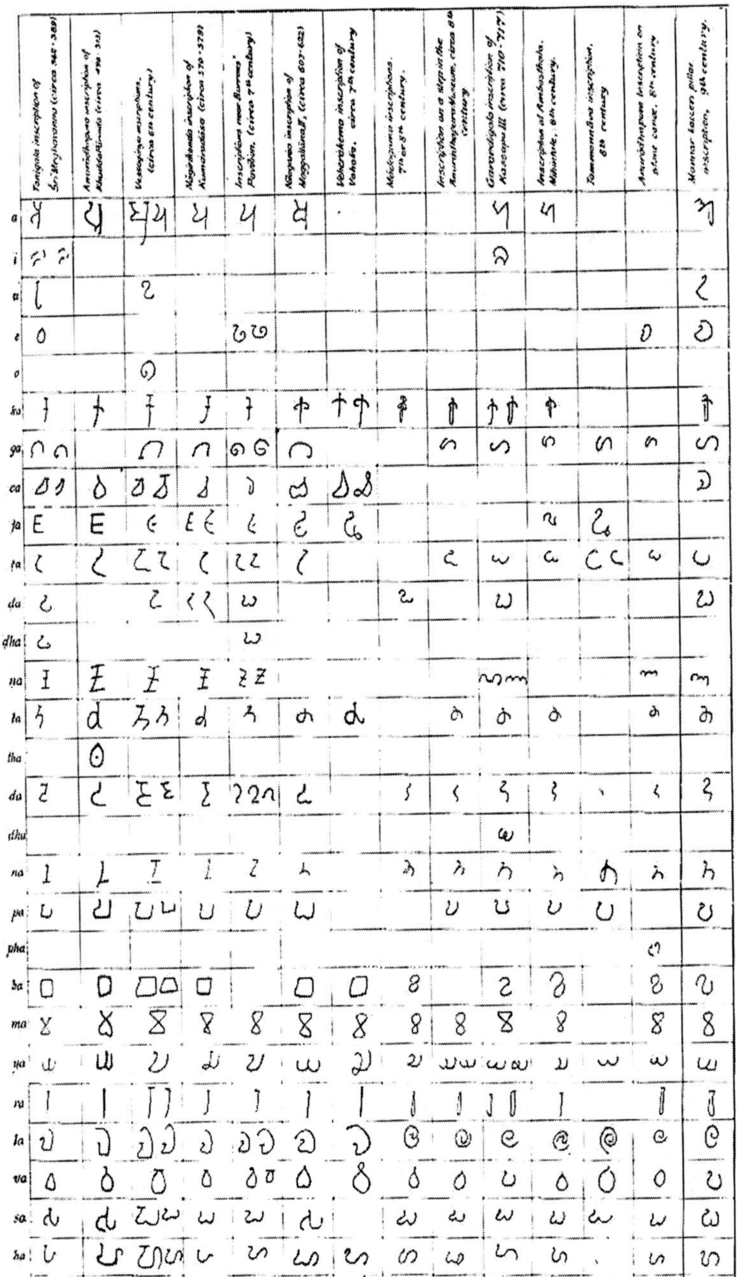

No. 18. TIRIYĀY ROCK-INSCRIPTION.

By S. Paranavitana.

TIRIYĀY is a Tamil village situated near the sea-coast about twenty-nine miles to the north of Trincomalee in the Eastern Province. About a mile to the west of this village, there is a hill, rising 210 ft. above sea-level and known by the Tamil name of Kandasāmimalai (the Hill of the Lord Skanda), on the summit and the slopes of which are the ruins of an ancient Buddhist monastery now called Nītupatpāṇa [1]. The summit is occupied by an interesting *vaṭadāgē* [2] containing a small *stūpa* in the centre, round which are concentric circles of graceful stone pillars, of the type seen at the Thūpārāma and the Laṅkārāma *dāgäbas* at Anurādhapura. The circular platform of the *vaṭadāgē* has a moulded stone revetment; and four flights of steps with guardstones and balustrades of the usual Sinhalese type lead to it from the four cardinal points. On terraces lower down the hill are vestiges of monastic structures, and the remains of a flight of steps, which ascended the hillside up to the *vaṭadāgē*, are also to be seen. At the foot of the hill there are two ponds (*pokuṇas*) with their sides faced with rubble, between which the path to the monastic buildings ran; and not far from these *pokuṇas* are the remains of an ancient stone bridge, indicating that a highway passed this place in ancient times. On the slopes of the hill are some rock caves, two of which bear Brāhmī inscriptions [3], one in the pre-Christian form of that script and the other dating from about the first century. The epigraph which is the subject of the present paper is engraved on a rock at a distance of about 200 ft. to the south of the *vaṭadāgē*.

The inscription covers an area of the rock-surface measuring 20 ft. by 5 ft. and contains eleven lines of writing. Owing to the weathering of the stone, the record is in a bad state of preservation. Lines 1 to 4 are totally illegible at the beginning for a distance of nearly three feet and the ends of lines 4 to 10 are much damaged. There are many other places where the letters are not preserved

---

[1] Nītupatpāṇa is mentioned in the list of Buddhist shrines, called the *Nampota*, which dates from about the eighteenth century. A tank called Nītupatpāṇa is mentioned in the *Pūjāvalī* as a work of Vasabha (*circa* 126–170). It is, however, doubtful whether the site was known by this name at any time in the past; for, in the inscription, it is called Girikaṇḍi-caitya.

[2] *Vaṭadāgē* (Circular Relic-House) is the name given in Sinhalese to a circular shrine enclosing a *stūpa*. Examples of *vaṭadāgēs*, besides those of Thūpārāma and Laṅkārāma, are found at Mihintale, Poḷonnaruva, Mädirigiriya, and Attanagalla.

[3] *A. S. I.*, Nos. 479–480. For their texts, see *C. J. Sc.*, *G*, vol. ii, p. 117.

well enough for decipherment; and therefore the text of the inscription given below contains many lacunae and doubtful readings. The size of the individual letters, without taking into consideration the long tails of such letters as *a*, *k*, &c., and the sign for the medial vowel *u*, varies from $1\frac{1}{2}$ to 2 inches.

The script of this record is one of its main features of interest. It resembles the Pallava Grantha of about the seventh century and in it have been written the few Sanskrit inscriptions of this period found in Ceylon. Dated Sinhalese epigraphs of this period are extremely rare; but a few Sinhalese stone inscriptions in a script resembling this have also been found. Among the graffiti on the gallery wall at Sīgiriya are a short record of a single Sanskrit verse and several verses in Sinhalese written in a similar script. The Sinhalese records naturally do not contain conjoint letters and the general appearance of the script, at first sight, is therefore somewhat different from that of records in Sanskrit. But when the individual letters are taken into consideration, the resemblance between the script of the Sinhalese and Sanskrit records mentioned above becomes quite evident. The inscription which is written in a script most closely resembling the one under discussion is a long but very fragmentary record on a rock near the Ambasthala Cetiya at Mihintaḷē, towards the end of which occurs the *Trikāyastotra*, a Sanskrit hymn praising the three bodies of the Buddha [1]. The Sanskrit inscription at Kuccavēli [2], only six miles to the south of Tiriyāy, is written in a script somewhat earlier than that of this epigraph, as may be seen by comparing the letters *ka*, *ra*, *ṇa*, *ya*, and *ḷa* of one document with the corresponding symbols of the other.

In South Indian epigraphy, so far as is known to me, the script which has the closest resemblance to the one under discussion is that of the Kuram plates of the Pallava king Parameśvaravarmman I (*circa* 660–680). The symbols for the *akṣaras*, *ka*, *ga*, *gha*, *ta*, *pa*, *ya*, *ra*, and *va*, occurring in the two records, are almost identical in form; but, on the other hand, the letters *kha*, *ja*, *ṇa*, *ba*, *ha*, and *sa* of our epigraph differ slightly from the corresponding symbols of the Kuram plates [3]. These differences, however, are of a type which may easily be due

---

[1] Müller, *A. I. C.*, p. 52, *A. S. C. Annual Report* for 1911–12, p. 93 and *C. J. Sc.*, *G*, vol. ii, pp. 42–43. I am indebted to Professor Sylvain Lévi for the information that the verses referred to in pp. 42–43 of the *C. J. Sc.*, *G*, vol. ii, form the *Trikāyastotra*, for which see *Revue de l'Histoire des Religions*, tome xxxiv, Paris 1896, pp. 17–21, and *Bulletin de l'Académie Impériale des Sciences de St Petersbourg*, 1911, pp. 837–845.

[2] *E. Z.*, Vol. II, pp. 158–161.

[3] Compare plate xvi and column 24 in Tafel vii of Bühler's *Indische Paläographie*.

merely to the individuality of the different scribes and the difference in the material on which the records are engraved. It must, nevertheless, be emphasized that the script of this record is not quite identical with any found in South India.

The script which was prevalent in Ceylon during the fifth and sixth centuries favoured, on the whole, straight lines and angular forms; and if the tendencies which were noticeable in the development of the Ceylon script during the first five centuries of the Christian era had full play, it would be difficult to imagine the formation in the seventh century of such a rounded script as is noticed in this document. On the other hand, there are documents such as the Ruvanvälisāya pillar-inscription of Buddhadāsa[1], in which a script favouring rounded forms is met with; and it is quite possible for the script in this record to have been evolved from such forms. Nevertheless, the resemblance to the Pallava Grantha in the script of this and other records from Ceylon noted above is striking; and a certain foreign influence—probably Pallava—in the development of the alphabet in Ceylon during the sixth and seventh centuries seems very likely. The political history of the island in the seventh century was profoundly influenced by the Pallavas, as is seen from the account of Mānavamma (*circa* 668–703) given in the *Mahāvaṁsa* (chap. xlvii); and undoubtedly there was cultural intercourse between the two countries, though of this we have no recorded details. It is also noteworthy that most of the Ceylon inscriptions which are written in a script resembling the Pallava Grantha are in the Sanskrit language and of Mahāyānistic character. The appearance of the Mahāyāna in Ceylon was always due to Indian influences, and the native tradition, originating from the cultural contact of Ceylon with India in the time of Aśoka, and embodied in the orthodox community of the Mahāvihāra, strenuously opposed these influences whenever they gained strength; but they were, it seems, strong enough to have left enduring traces in popular religion as well as in the domain of letters.

Considering the resemblance of the script to that of South India in the period of Parameśvaravarmman I, who flourished in the latter half of the seventh century, and comparing it with the degree of development of the alphabet noticed in Ceylon records dating from the eighth and ninth centuries, we may be justified in assigning this epigraph to the closing decades of the seventh century or the first half of the eighth. The record furnishes us with no other data which would enable us to fix its probable date.

The **language** of the inscription, as has already been stated, is Sanskrit

---

[1] *E. Z.*, Vol. III, pp. 120–126.

and is in prose. As is usual in Sanskrit prose writings with any pretence to elegance, the style affects long compounds. There are no grammatical errors of any note and the author of the document seems to have had considerable proficiency in the Sanskrit language. As regards **orthography**, however, it should be noted that the cerebral *ḷ* occurs in such words as *sulaḷita* and *siṁghaḷendra*. The *gha* in place of *ha* in the latter word is also noteworthy. Both these orthographical peculiarities, particularly the latter, may be due to the influence of the vernacular language of the author.

The record begins with an account of a company of sea-faring merchants. The major part of the document is occupied by a long eulogy of a shrine named **Girikaṇḍi-** (or **°kaṇḍika-**) **caitya,** in which the author of the document speaks in the first person, but his name is not found in the preserved portion of the record. The eulogy is followed by the pious wish of the author that, by the merit he has gained by praising the shrine, the world may be freed from the miseries of existence. After this occurs the statement that Girikaṇḍi-caitya was founded by the guilds of merchants named **Trapussaka** and **Vallika.** The record ends with the Buddhist formula about the transitoriness of things mundane.

The merchants mentioned in the beginning of the document are described as 'skilful in navigating the sea, engaged in buying and selling and who possessed a display of goods laden in sailing vessels of divers sorts', but the fragmentary nature of the text does not enable us to know in what connexion they have been introduced. It is, however, justifiable to conjecture, from the history of the Girikaṇḍi-caitya which will be discussed in the sequel, that they are identical with the merchants Trapussaka and Vallika mentioned towards the close of the record as the founders of the *caitya*. *Trapussaka* and *Vallika* seem to be corruptions of *Trapuṣa* (*Tapussa* and *Tapassu* in Pāli) and *Bhallika* (*Bhalluka* in the *Nidānakathā*), the names of the two merchants who offered food to the Buddha immediately after his enlightenment[1]. They are counted as the first among the Buddha's lay disciples and were the recipients of some hair-relics of the Master.

The view that the merchants are introduced, towards the beginning of the document, in order to make it clear that they were the founders of the *caitya*, seems to gain support from the reference to a friendly deity of theirs. In the

---

[1] See *Mahāvagga* (*Vinaya Piṭaka*, edited by H. Oldenberg, vol. i), pp. 3–4, *Nidānakathā* (*Jātaka*, edited by Fausböll, vol. i), pp. 80–81, and *Lalitavistara*, Lefman's edition, vol. i, pp. 381 ff.

Mahāvagga as well as in the *Nidānakathā*, it is stated that the merchants Tapassu and Bhalluka were led to the Buddha by a *deva* who had been a blood relation of theirs in a previous existence. It thus becomes fairly certain that, according to this inscription, the *caitya* at Tiriyāy was founded by these merchants to enshrine the hair-relics given to them by the Buddha.

The *Mahāvagga*, the *Nidānakathā* and the *Lalitavistara* state that the two merchants came from a country called Ukkala (Skt. Utkala) in North India, and that the *stūpa* built by them to enshrine the hair-relics was in their native country. The Chinese pilgrim Hieun Tsang, on his journey from Balkh to Bamian in Gandhāra, noticed the remains of two *stūpas* built over these relics [1]. But it seems that other Buddhist countries were not prepared to concede to Gandhāra the honour of possessing this particularly holy shrine, built in the life-time of the Buddha himself. The Burmese Buddhists firmly believe that the two merchants enshrined these precious relics in their own Shwe Dagon at Rangoon [2].

In the Sinhalese religious work named *Pūjāvalī*, written in the thirteenth century, it is definitely stated that the merchants Tapassu and Bhalluka built a *stūpa*, enshrining the hair-relics, in Ceylon; and, moreover, the name of the place where, according to that work, this shrine was built, is almost the same as the appellation of the *stūpa* at Tiriyāy, which occurs in this inscription. The *Pūjāvalī*, in its account of the legend of Tapassu and Bhalluka, agrees, in the main, with the *Nidānakathā*; but at the end the following additional information is given: 'They received those hair-relics in a jewelled casket and took them to their own town where they worshipped them. In course of time they went on a sea-voyage and came to the island of Śrī Laṅkā; and, going in search of firewood and water, they came to the place named Girihaṇḍu. They placed the casket of relics on the summit of the rock; and when they returned after having cooked and eaten their meals they were unable to move the relic-casket from the place where it was. They then knew that this was a holy place and, having honoured it, covered (the casket) with a heap of stones, offered flowers and went their way. In later times, there was a *vihāra* named Girihaṇḍu at that place [3].' The Sinhalese name *Girihaṇḍu* in the *Pūjāvalī* and the Sanskrit form *Girikaṇḍika* occurring in the inscription are doubtless identical, the change of *k* to *h* occurring not infrequently in Sinha-

[1] Watter's *Yuan Chwang*, vol. i, pp. 111–113.

[2] Bigandet, *The Legend of Gaudama*, vol. i, p. 110, footnote.

[3] See *Pūjāvalī*, Colombo edition of 1922, p. 184.

lese. The form *Girikaṇḍika*, on the other hand, might well be taken as a Sanskritized form of the vernacular name which, in the seventh or eighth century, must have approximated more to the Sanskrit than in the thirteenth century.

The identity of *Girikaṇḍi* with *Girihaṇḍu* is proved beyond doubt by the fact that, in the Sinhalese paraphrase (*sanne*), by Parākramabāhu II, of the Visuddhimagga, the word *Girikaṇḍa-mahāvihāra* occurring in the Pāli text (see below) is paraphrased as *Girihaṇḍu-vehera*[1]. Therefore we may be quite certain that, at the time when this inscription was written, there was a local legend connecting Tapassu and Bhalluka with the ancient *stūpa* at Tiriyāy and that it was believed that this *stūpa* contained the hair-relics said to have been presented by the Buddha to these merchants. This tradition seems to have persisted down to the thirteenth century and was known to the author of the *Pūjāvalī*, who added this additional information to the legend of Tapassu and Bhalluka given in the *Nidānakathā*.

Just as there were several Buddhist countries competing for the honour of possessing this first relic of the Buddha, so it appears that there were, in ancient Ceylon, more shrines than one which claimed to have been founded by the merchants Tapassu and Bhalluka. For there is at present a *stūpa* called Girihaṇḍu (Girikaṇḍa) at Ambalantoṭa on the southern coast of Ceylon, near the mouth of the Valave Gaṅga. Local tradition asserts that the hair-relics of the Buddha given to these two merchants are now in the *stūpa* at this place. But the *Pūjāvalī* account agrees with the topography of Tiriyāy rather than with that of the shrine at Ambalantoṭa. For it is said that the merchants placed the relic-casket on the top of a rock whence, being restrained by superhuman power, it could not be removed; and the *stūpa* was erected over it. The *stūpa* at Tiriyāy is on the top of a rock while that at Ambalantoṭa is not so. The site now called Girihaṇḍu Vehera at Ambalantoṭa, however, is of great antiquity, for a marble slab containing a sculpture, in the Amarāvatī style, depicting the Buddha's renunciation, has recently been discovered there[2]. But there is no definite proof to show that its old name was really Girihaṇḍu Vehera.

Archaeologically, the record is important in that it enables us to learn that the ancient name of the *stūpa* at Tiriyāy was Girikaṇḍika-caitya. The purpose of the epigraph was to sing the praises of this shrine and the name occurs

---

[1] See *Visuddhimārga-sannaya*, edited by M. Dharmaratna, p. 510.

[2] See *C. J. Sc., G*, vol. ii, plate L.

several times in it. It is unreasonable to assume that such an epigraph would have been indited at a site other than the one referred to therein. *Girikaṇḍika* is obviously identical with *Girikaṇḍaka*, a monastery of which name occurs in the *Mahāvaṁsa* (chap. lx, v. 60) in a list of *vihāras* repaired by Vijayabāhu I. But there is nothing to decide the question whether it was the ancient monastery at Tiriyāy or a monastery of a similar name situated elsewhere. A district and a mountain named Girikaṇḍa are mentioned in the tenth chapter of the chronicle, in connexion with the legends of Paṇḍukābhaya. This prince, when he first raised the standard of revolt against his uncles, set up his first encampment at Girikaṇḍa-pabbata, after gaining 700 followers at the town called Paṇa near Kāsapabbata. One of his uncles was called Girikaṇḍa Sīva, as he was the ruler of that district; and the romantic episode, in which Paṇḍukābhaya won his uncle's daughter as his future queen, also has this district as its scene. But the *Mahavaṁsa* does not give any topographical details that would enable us to decide whether Girikaṇḍa-pabbata was on the north-eastern coast of Ceylon. A Girikaṇḍaka-vihāra and the *caitya* at that place are mentioned by Buddhaghosa in the *Visuddhimagga*[1] in a story narrated in order to illustrate how the state of exhilaration of mind caused by rapturous delight (*ubbega-pīti*) is powerful enough to transport a person through the air.

Of particular interest is the statement, in line 5 of the inscription, that Girikaṇḍaka-caitya was an abode of **Avalokiteśvara.** As I have pointed out elsewhere[2], the worship of this Mahāyāna Bodhisattva was widespread in ancient Ceylon and is still prevalent. But, both in the literature as well as in the epigraphs of the island hitherto discovered, he is referred to as Lokeśvara, Lokeśvara Nātha, or Nātha, the last of which is the name by which he is now known. This is the first time that the best known appellation of the Bodhisattva has been met with in a Ceylon document. The statement also proves—what can also be inferred from the fact that the document is written in Sanskrit—that the ancient monastery at Tiriyāy was, in the seventh or eighth century, inclined towards Mahāyānism, if not avowedly Mahāyānistic. The author of the document was undoubtedly a Mahāyānist, as is shown by the wish expressed that the merit gained by him should be for the salvation of the whole world. Mahāyānists seem to have been influential on the eastern coast of Ceylon at this period, for the inscription at Kuccavēli, referred to above, is also Mahāyānistic. This also explains why the Girikaṇḍika-caitya which, from this inscription,

---

[1] P. T. S. edition, pp. 143-144.

[2] *C. J. Sc., G*, vol. ii, pp. 52-64.

appears to have enjoyed a great reputation for sanctity, hardly finds mention in the chronicles written by the Theravādins. Nor does the claim of the votaries of this monastery that their *stūpa* contained the hair-relics of the Buddha seem to have found recognition by the Mahāvihāra fraternity, for the *Nidāna-katha* knows nothing of the episode which brings the two merchants to Ceylon.

TEXT.

1 .. .. (a)virata-bhakti-yukta-hṛdayair⸗avadāta-guṇaiḥ prathamatara-pradāna-guṇa .. .. bhir⸗eka-gurau Bhagavati Śākya-rāja-tilake Sugate sutarām⸗adhigata-dhātu-ga .. .. ti-sammukham⸗evam⸗a

2 .. .. [sa]lilanidhi-prayāṇa-caturaiḥ kraya-vikrayibhiḥ[1] ı bahuvidha-yānapātra-paripūrita-bhāṇḍa-(ta)taiḥ[1] ı kuśala-vaśāt sahāya-nija-devatayā .. .. .. (bhavati) [bha]viṣyad⸗alpa .. .. kam⸗ ity⸗udite

3 .. .. (sali)lanidhi .. (sta ha) samavatīryya sameta-guṇair⸗upagata-nagara-ja[na*]- sahitair⸗upaśāntataraiḥ (sarvvaiṛ)⸗ vaṇig-gaṇaiḥ kṛtavad⸗apravihata-mudā vara-**Girika(ṇḍika-cait-yam⸗i)**ti yat⸗prathitam⸗bhuvane

4 .. .. ma .. .. ha .. .. kara-kṛtopahāra-ruc-ir-āṅgaṇa-bhūmi-tala[ṁ] satatam⸗abhiprasanna-nara-maṇḍala-bhakti-nata-vara-**Girikaṇḍi[ka-cai]tya[m⸗a]**bhinamya .. .. ..

5 ma .. .. (kata)-sphuṭa-mahā-munirb⸗Buddhāṁkuro nivasati yatra sadā sura-kinnara-pūjyatam[o] gurur⸗**Avalokiteśvara** iti prathito Bhagavān .. .. taṁ **Girikaṇḍika-caityam**⸗ahaṁ⸗a(pi) .. ..

6 munir⸗api mañju-vāg⸗mano-doṣa-viṣa-dahara .. .. .. kanaka-vibhūṣaṇ-ojvala-vicitrita-gātra-rucin⸗niyatam-upaiti yatra sukumāra-tanur⸗ Bhagavān tad⸗aham⸗api praṇaumi **Girikaṇḍika-caitya**-varaṁ .. ..

7 Ṣura-sarid-abja-parṇṇa-puṭa-pūrita-gandha-jala .. .. kara-bhṛta-puṣpa-dhūpa-maṇi-dīpa-(ni)vedya-dharāḥ s(u)laḷitam[2]⸗aṁgaṇā(s)⸗ sura-purād⸗avatīryya mudā vidadhati pūjāni Bhagavato **Girikaṇḍi** .. ..

8 sura-patir⸗apy⸗aneka-parivāra-surā-nugataḥ sulaḷita[3]-divya-śaṁkha-paṭaha

---

[1] The *daṇḍa* is clear on the stone; but a punctuation mark is not necessary here.

[2] Read *sulalitam*.

[3] Read *sulalita*.

Tiriyāy R

Scale abou

Tiriyāy Rock-Inscription

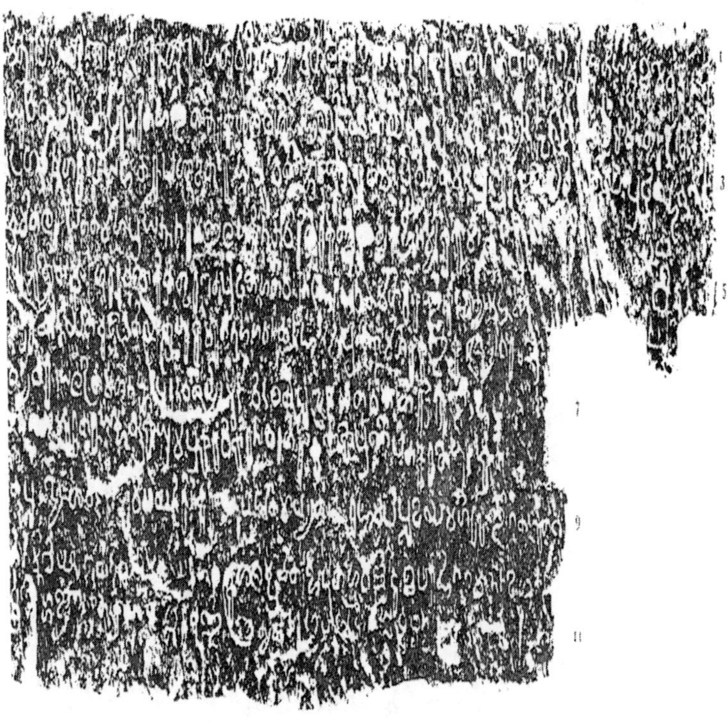

Scale about ¼ inch to 1 foot

(praṇi) .. .. sura-taru-sambhav-ārdra-kusuma-prakaraṁ vikiran vara-**Girikaṇḍike** praṇipātaṁ kurute .. .. kata .. ..

9 pratidinam=arccamāna[ṁ] mahā-girau .. .. (a)viraḷa-[1] **Siṁghaḷendra-**[2] jana-kalpita-pūjya-śata .. .. .. viṣaya[ṁ] nirīti-karaṇa[m]= upāsitam=āryya-(gaṇai)r=aham=api pūjayāmi **Girikaṇḍi**-gata-sugata .. ..

10 sakala-tamo 'paham=Bhagavato da .. .. (vara)-**Girikaṇḍi-caitya**-nilaye pratinimna-dhiyā .. .. yad .. .. kuśalam= pracitam=bhavatu bhav-ābdhi-duḥkha-parihīṇam anena jagataḥ . . . .

11 kṛta-prati .. .. yane **Trapussakairv= Vallikairv**=vaṇig-gaṇaiḥ kṛta .. .. g=**Girikaṇḍi-caityam**[॥*] abhāva-svabhāvās=sarvva-dharmmāḥ [॥*]

TRANSLATION.[3]

. . . . . . by [those] who were having hearts of unceasing devotion, of pure virtue, who desired the merit of being the very first to give[4]. . . . . . . in the Blessed One, the incomparable teacher, the ornament of Śakya kings, the Sugata . . . . . . who had excellently obtained relics[5] . . . . . . in the presence of . . . . . . by the companies of merchants who were skilful in navigating the sea, engaged in buying and selling and who [possessed] a display of goods laden in sailing vessels of divers sorts, owing to the influence of merit, by a friendly *devatā* who was of their own [kin][6] . . . . to come . . . . . . having crossed the ocean, ... as performed by all the companies of merchants who were very tranquil, who possessed [various] virtues united together [in them], including the inhabitants of the city who had come [there][7], with unabated pleasure . . . . . . that which is known in the world as the excellent **Girikaṇḍika-caitya** . . . . where offer-

---

[1] Read *avirala*.

[2] Read *Siṁhalendra*.

[3] Owing to the fragmentary nature of the text, the connexion to each other of the various phrases occurring in ll. 1–3 is not quite clear. In the translation, therefore, I have given the English rendering of what is preserved, in the same order as the phrases occur in the original, without attempting to arrange them according to the syntax.

[4] Assuming that these phrases are eulogies of the merchants led by Tapassu and Bhalluka, we may take this as a reference to the fact that they were the first to make any gifts to the Buddha.

[5] Perhaps we have here a reference to the obtaining of hair relics of the Buddha by the merchants.

[6] See above, p. 155.

[7] It is not clear to what city and to what incident the allusion is here.

ings have been made, which contains charming grounds of courtyards, which is frequently worshipped with devotion by multitudes of pious men, having worshipped that excellent **Girikaṇḍika-caitya** . . . . the Great Sage, who is manifested . . . . . . where dwells always the Bodhisattva [1], the teacher, known as **Avalokiteśvara,** who is worthy to be honoured by gods and *kinnaras*, ... the Blessed One . . . . that **Girikaṇḍika-caitya,** I, too, ... the Sage, too, of sweet speech, the burning poison of mental transgression [2] . . . . where the Blessed One, of very delicate body, attains indeed a corporeal splendour beautified by the brightness of golden ornaments [3], that excellent **Girikaṇḍa-caitya,** I, too, do worship . . . . **Girikaṇḍi[ka-caitya]**, to which divine nymphs, [bearing] scented water in receptacles made of lotus leaves from the celestial river, and carrying, held in their hands, flowers, incense, jewel-lamps, and oblations, descend gracefully from the heavenly city, and perform, with delight, the worship, of the Blessed One. . . . . the king of gods, too, followed by numerous attendant gods, does obeisance at the excellent **Girikaṇḍika,** [sounding] very lovely celestial chanks, drums . . . . . and scattering heaps of fresh flowers produced in the celestial trees . . . . worshipped daily, on the great rock . . . . . [at which are] hundreds of . . . ., worthy to be honoured, prepared by the **lord of the Siṁhalas** and [his] people . . . . . . which causes freedom from affliction . . . . I, too, worship the [relic] of the Buddha deposited in **Girikaṇḍi** which is adored by multitudes of noble ones . . . . of the Blessed One, which dispels all darkness, ... with mind bent on the shrine of the **Girikaṇḍi-caitya** . . . . . . whatever merit has been caused, by that let the miseries of existence of the world be reduced . . . . . . the **Girikaṇḍi-caitya** founded by the companies of merchants [named] **Trapussaka** and **Vallika** [4]. All phenomena are transitory.

[1] *Buddhāṁkura*, a Buddha in embryo.

[2] *Mano-doṣa-viṣa-dahara*: None of the meanings usually attached to *dahara* (see M. W. Dict.) seems to be applicable here. It is translated above as being an error for *dahra*.

[3] This is perhaps an allusion to a Buddha image decked with ornaments. Such images were in use among the Mahāyānists.

[4] According to the *Nidānakathā* (*op. cit.*, p. 80), Tapassu and Bhalluka were the leaders of a caravan of 500 waggons. Hence the word *vaṇigganaiḥ* would be applicable to them and to the merchants who accompanied them.

No. 19. TWO INSCRIPTIONS OF VIHĀRA-MAHĀ-DEVĪ FROM MAGUL-MAHA-VIHĀRA.

By S. PARANAVITANA.

THE two inscriptions dealt with in this paper have been found among the ruins of an ancient monastery, now known as Magul-maha-vihāra, situated in the Pānama Pattu of the Batticaloa District, about a mile to the south of the eighth mile-stone on the road from Potuvil to Vällavāya. The site is still occupied, at least periodically, by a Buddhist monk and is occasionally visited by pilgrims; but the ancient *stūpa* and the monastic structures are all in ruins and buried in the forest which extends for miles on all sides of the place. References to the interesting architectural and archaeological features of the site will be found in the *Ceylon Journal of Science, Section G*, vol. ii, pp. 76–77, under its ancient name of Rūṇu-maha-vehera or -vihāra; photographs of some remains at the place are reproduced on Plates XXXIX–XLII and XLV–XLVI, and a plan of the site on Plate XLIII, of the same journal. Some short donative records of the ninth century are found on the coping-stones of the retaining wall of the platform on which the *stūpa* is built and on a stone used in the pavement. A fragment of a much weathered tenth-century pillar-inscription is built into the retaining wall of the platform, and a ninth-century inscription is found on a stone slab belonging to the outer *prākāra* which encloses the whole group of buildings at the site[1]. Of the two epigraphs now edited, the slab-inscription (*A. S. I.*, No. 453) is found to the left of the flight of steps at the entrance to the ruined structure marked on the plan referred to above as 'Building A'; and the fragmentary pillar-inscription (*A. S. I.*, No. 454) is also found near the same building.

The first of these two records (referred to below as I) is written as a palimpsest over a long tenth-century inscription which has thus been obliterated, but for thirteen lines at the end. The slab measures 6 ft. $7\frac{1}{2}$ in. in height by 2 ft. 4 in. in breadth; but the area occupied by the epigraph under discussion is 4 ft. 2 in. by 2 ft. $2\frac{1}{2}$ in. The document comprises twenty lines of writing and is engraved shallowly and rather carelessly in a somewhat sprawling hand. The letters, which are not uniform in size, vary from 1 to 2 inches in height. The epigraph has suffered much from the weather and some letters in ll. 1, 2, 7, 12–13,

[1] For some of these inscriptions, see *C. J. Sc.*, *G*, vol. ii, p. 113.

and 15–18 are either totally illegible or can be read only conjecturally. The second inscription (II) is engraved on three sides of a pillar, of which the upper half is broken away and missing. The preserved fragment measures 10 in. square by 2 ft. 9 in. in height. Side A has four lines of writing preserved on it, in addition to some engraving, the exact nature of which cannot be made out; side B has twelve lines and side C thirteen. The execution of this record is much better than that of the slab-inscription. The letters are, on an average, 2 in. in size on side B and $1\frac{1}{4}$ in. on sides A and C. The remaining portions of sides A and B are in a good state of preservation; but side C is somewhat weatherworn.

The **script** of the records is definitely later than the Poḷonnaruva period and agrees, in many particulars, with that of the inscriptions of the Gampoḷa period. A comparison of *na, ma, ra, sa,* and *ḷa* of these records with the same letters of the Gaḍalādeṇiya inscription of Dharmmakīrtti [1], dated in the third year of Bhuvanaikabāhu IV (1341–2 A.D.), will make this fact clear. Some letters, e.g., *va*, are, however, less developed than the corresponding ones in the Gaḍalādeṇiya inscription, and the present epigraphs also contain a form of *ra* identical with the symbol for that letter in the Poḷonnaruva period side by side with the more developed form which was common in the Gampoḷa period. Palaeographically, these records seem, therefore, to be slightly earlier than the Gaḍalādeṇiya inscription and may be assigned to the first quarter of the fourteenth century.

The **language** resembles that of the classical Sinhalese prose works which date from the thirteenth to the fifteenth century. The last syllable of *tubūva* (I, l. 5) and the first syllable of *vera* (I, l. 19) have short vowels, against standard usage according to which they should have been long. Active and passive constructions are mixed up together in the same sentence in inscription No. 1. A construction like *mā visin . . . . karavā* (I, ll. 10–11) would not be accepted as correct by grammarians.

The records tell us that **Rūṇu-maha-vehera**, the ancient monastery at the site, which was then an abandoned ruin in the wilderness, was completely renovated by **Vihāra-mahā-devī**, the consort of the two brother kings named **Pärakumbā** or **Parākramabāhu**, and that she endowed it with lands, &c., for its maintenance. From Inscription I we learn that these two brother kings had vanquished the Coḷa army and were ruling the Rohaṇa principality. It also appears

---

[1] See above, pp. 92–93 and Plate 10.

that both brothers had the name of Parākramabāhu and that Vihāra-mahā-devī was their common spouse. The pillar-inscription appears to have contained a more detailed account of the Coḷa invasion which was repelled by these rulers; but, unfortunately, the record is mutilated just at the point where the reference to this historical event begins. This record also appears to have been set up after the demise of the brother kings, for Vihāra-mahā-devī is referred to therein as 'who *was* the chief consort of the two brother kings'.

In the tentative account of these records, which was based on defective estampages supplied to me in 1929, given by me in the 'Epigraphical Summary' included in the *C.J.Sc.G*, vol. ii, part II (p. 106), I have suggested the identification of the Parākramabāhu of this inscription with Parākramabāhu V and of his brother with Bhuvanaikabāhu IV. From the inscriptions it becomes evident that the reigns of Parākramabāhu V and Bhuvanaikabāhu IV ran concurrently, and Mr. Codrington has also surmised that these two monarchs were brothers [1]. Palaeographically, these inscriptions can belong to the time of Parākramabāhu V; but, after further study of the inscriptions with the help of better estampages prepared under my direction, I am now of opinion that my first identification is untenable.

In inscription I, wherein the portion containing the royal names is fairly well preserved, the name of Bhuvanaikabāhu does not occur at all, and the context does not leave us in any doubt as to the fact that both the brothers were known as Parākramabāhu. Moreover, the two brothers are described in the epigraph as ruling over Rohaṇa, whereas Bhuvanaikabāhu IV and Parākramabāhu V had their respective capitals in the Māyā kingdom and claimed suzerainty over the whole of Ceylon, though their actual authority did not probably extend to some parts of the island. If her husbands had claimed the dominion of the whole island, Vihāra-mahā-devī would not have been content with referring to them merely as rulers of Rohaṇa. It is, therefore, reasonable to assume that the princes mentioned in these epigraphs are not identical with any of the monarchs figuring in the lists of paramount rulers of the island; but that they were petty kings who wielded independent authority in Rohaṇa while the northern part of the island was in a state of confusion owing to an invasion from South India. So far as my knowledge goes, these princes have not been mentioned in any of the available sources for the history of the period; but the

---

[1] *A Short History of Ceylon*, London, 1926, pp. 83 and 88–89.

events which occurred between the reign of Parākramabāhu IV of Kuruṇāgala and Bhuvanaikabāhu IV of Gampoḷa have been very imperfectly recorded in the chronicles and our knowledge of the history of this period contains many wide gaps.

No information is available from other sources about the **Coḷa invasion** which these two rulers are said to have repelled. It is noteworthy that, in the period to which these records have to be assigned on palaeographical grounds, the Coḷas who had, from the ninth to the beginning of the thirteenth century, played such a decisive part in the history of South India and Ceylon, had ceased to be of any importance; and it is doubtful whether they were at that time powerful enough to have dispatched an expedition to Ceylon. Perhaps the Coḷas who invaded Ceylon on this occasion did so on behalf of the Pāṇḍyas or the Vijayanagara kings of whom they were then the feudatories [1]. It is also possible that as the South Indians who had been invading Ceylon for several centuries past were the Coḷas, any invaders from the Tamil country were referred to by that name. But against such a supposition is the fact that in the *Mahāvaṁsa* [2] the invaders from South India, who sacked Yāpahuva in the reign of Bhuvanaikabāhu I, are called Pāṇḍyans, as, in fact, they were.

The records also inform us that the ancient name of Magul-maha-vihāra was Rūṇu-maha-vehera (P. Rohaṇa-mahā-vihāra) and that it was originally founded by King **Dāsen-käli** (Dhātusena, *circa* 516–526) [3]. The chronicles do not credit Dhātusena with the establishment of this *vihāra* and, on the other hand, according to the *Mahāvaṁsa* [4] and the *Pūjāvalī* [5], a monastery named Ruhuṇu-vehera (P. Rohaṇa-vihāra) was founded by Dappula I, a ruler of Rohaṇa, who held the sceptre at Anurādhapura for a short period in or about 661 A.D. Rūṇu-maha-vehera of this record and Rūṇu-vehera (P. Rohaṇa-vihāra) of the chronicles are doubtless identical, and there is therefore a discrepancy between the epigraph and the chronicles. The inscription is about a century or so later in date than both the *Pūjāvalī* and that part of the *Mahāvaṁsa* in which the reference to the monastery occurs. More weight may

---

[1] The *Rājāvaliya* (Gunasekara's translation, p. 66) states that the Tamils who invaded the Sinhalese territories towards the close of the fourteenth century were from the Soḷī (Coḷa) country.

[2] Chap. xc, vv. 43–47.

[3] Dhātusena is referred to in Sinhalese historical writings like the *Pūjāvalī* (*op. cit.*, p. 27) and *Nikāya Saṅgraha* (*op. cit.*, p. 16) as Dāsen-käli or -käliya.

[4] Chap. xlv, v. 54.

[5] *Op. cit.*, p. 27.

therefore be attached, in this particular, to the chronicles than to the present epigraph; but, as both refer to an event which took place about 600 years or more anterior to their times, there is not much choice between the two. Dappula I is called 'Dāpulusen' in Sinhalese writings; and the similarity of this name to 'Dāsen-käli' may have resulted in the confusion of one with the other. In what is preserved of the tenth-century record, over which the first inscription of Vihāra-mahā-devī has been indited, the name Ruhuṇ-maha-vehera occurs, thus showing that this monastery had that appellation in the tenth century.

TEXT.

I

1 (සවසත්) [ශ්‍රී සි]රිලක්හි රජ
2 ක[ළ] **දසෙන්කැලි** රජද
3 රුවන්දු කැරැවූ මෙ **රු**
4 **හුණුමහවෙර** මහවල්
5 ව නුබූව දැකැ සොළිසෙ
6 නාව මැඩැ රුහුණුරටැ රජ ක
7 (රඃන) **පැරකුම්බා** දෙබෑරජදරු
8 වන් දෙදෙනාට අගමෙහෙ
9 සුන් වූ **විහාරමහදෙවි** නා
10 ම් මඃ විසින් මුල් පිසැ ක
11 රවා දරුගම් වටනාපස පරිවා
12 ර සහිත වැ .. .. (බද
13 වස්) කොටැ මා [විසින්] කරවනල
14 ද මෙ සියලු පිඃන්කම් මිනු ව
15 න රජ යුවරජ .. ..
16 ආදීනුන් අනු .. ..
17 පැවැත්විය යුතු බැවි
18 න් මා නමින් කළ (**විහාර**)**දෙ**
19 **විපිරිවෙන** මෙ වෙර බ
20 ද බව දත යුතු

II.

A.		B.		C.	
+ 1	ත් ලංකාව	+ 1	[ප]රාක්‍රම	+ 1	.. ..
+ 2	ට සොළීත්	+ 2	බාහු නම්	+ 2	.. .. (ද ද)
+ 3	බැසැ ලො	+ 3	දෙබෑ රජ	+ 3	(ඩූන් කප්රැ
+ 4	සසුන්	+ 4	දෙදෙනාට	+ 4	න් නම් වූ)
	* * * * * *	+ 5	අගමෙහෙ	+ 5	මෙ තිසූවට
		+ 6	ෂුන් වූ සි	+ 6	.. ..
		+ 7	ට විහාර	+ 7	ධම්මරත්න
		+ 8	මහාදෙවි	+ 8	යට පිදූ(ව
		+ 9	න් හිමි පි	+ 9	ට) මනු පත්
		+ 10	සැ කැරැවූ	+ 10	වන පිනැනි
		+ 11	රුණුමහ	+ 11	යනුත් මෙ පි
		+ 12	වෙහෙර පි	+ 12	න් පුරා පැවැ
				+ 13	ත්වය යුතු

TRANSCRIPT.

I.

1 (Svasti) [śrī Si]ri-Lak-hi raja
2 ka[ḷa] **Dāsen-käli** raja-da-
3 -ruvan-dä kärävū me **Rū-**
4 **-ṇu-maha-vera** maha-val
5 va tubūva däkä Soḷī-se-
6 -näva mäḍä Rūṇu-raṭä raja ka-
7 -(rana) **Pärakumbā** de-bā-raja-daru-
8 -van de-denāṭa aga-mehe-
9 -sun vū **Vihāra-maha-devī** na-
10 -m mā visin mul pisā ka-
11 -ravā daru-gam vaṭanā-pasa parivā-
12 -ra sahita vä .. .. (bada-
13 vas) koṭä mā [visin] karavanala-
14 -da me siyalu pin-kam matu va-
15 -na raja yuva-raja [1] .. ..

---

[1] The traces of the damaged letters to be seen on the stone do not warrant us in filling the lacuna by supplying such words as are usually found after *raja yuvaraja* in other documents.

Two Inscriptions of Vihāra Mahā Devī from Māgul Mahā-Vihāra

II

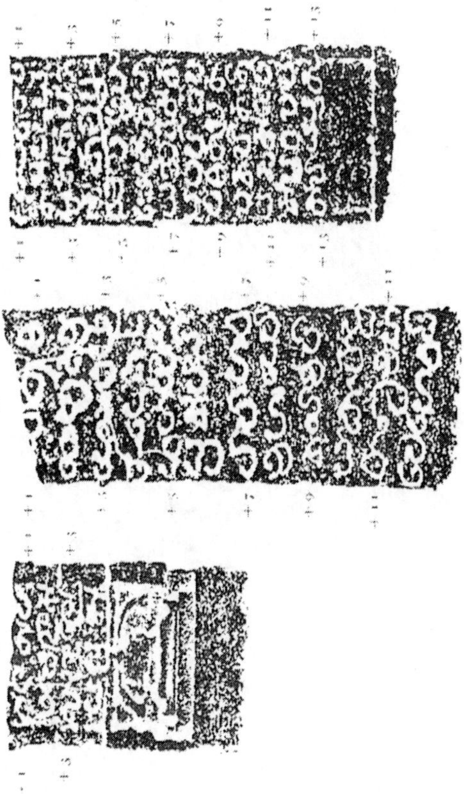

I

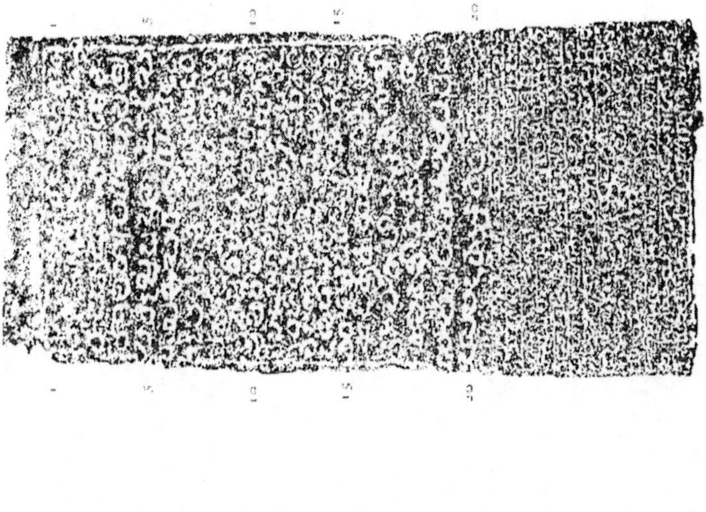

16 ādinut anu [1] .. ..
17 pävätviya yutu bävi-
18 -n mā namin kaḷa (**Vihāra**) [2]**-de-**
19 **-vi-pirivena** me vera ba-
20 -da bava data yutu

II.

A.		B.		C.	
+ 1	-n Laṁkāva-	+ 1	[P]**arākrama-**	+ 1	.. ..
+ 2	-ṭa Soḷīn	+ 2	**bāhu** nam	+ 2	.. .. (da da)
+ 3	bäsä lo-	+ 3	de-bā raja	+ 3	(vun kap-ru-
+ 4	sasun	+ 4	de-denā-ṭa	+ 4	-k nam vū)
	* * * * * *	+ 5	aga-mehe-	+ 5	me bijuvaṭa
		+ 6	-sun va si-	+ 6	.. ..
		+ 7	-ṭi **Vihāra-**	+ 7	dharmma-ratna-
		+ 8	**mahā-devi-**	+ 8	-yaṭa pidū(va-
		+ 9	**-n** bim pi-	+ 9	-ṭa) matu pat
		+ 10	-sä kärävū	+ 10	vana pināti-
		+ 11	**Rūṇu-maha**	+ 11	-yanut me pi-
		+ 12	**vehera** yi	+ 12	-n purā pävä-
				+ 13	-tviya yutu

TRANSLATION.

I.

Hail! Prosperity! Having seen that this **Rūṇu-maha-vera** [3], founded by His Majesty King **Dāsen-käli** [4] who reigned in prosperous Laṅkā, had become a great wilderness, by me, named **Vihāra-maha-devī**, the chief consort of the

---

[1] The context would justify the restoration of this part of the line as *anumōdan vā*; and there is just sufficient space on the stone for the four syllables required for the suggested reading. But such traces of the effaced letters as can still be seen are against this restoration.

[2] About three letters are completely obliterated here. As it is said that the *pirivena* was named after Vihāra-mahā-devī, the missing letters might have read *vihāra*, as conjectured, or possibly *mahā*.

[3] P. *Rohaṇa-mahā-vihāra*.

[4] *Dāsen-käli raja-daruvan-dā*: *Dāsen* is equivalent phonetically to P. *Dhātusena*. What *käli* stands for is not clear. *Dā* or *dā* is found in the classical Sinhalese language suffixed to nouns to denote respect or affection. In the modern language, too, it is so used; but not so much to denote respect as affection and familiarity.

two brother kings named **Pärakumbā**[1] who vanquished the Soḷī[2] host and are reigning in the Rūṇu[3] country, it was restored from its very foundations[4]. . . . . . . including *darugam*[5] [the lands supplying] the requisites for the maintenance [of the *saṅgha*[6]], and the attendants . . . . . having made it to be resided in continuously[7] . . . . . As all these acts of merit performed by me should be maintained . . . . . . by kings, sub-kings . . . . . . and others who will flourish in the future, it should be known that the **(Vihāra)-devī-pirivena** founded in my name is attached to this monastery.

II.

. . . . . . the Soḷī, having descended upon Laṁkā . . . . the state and the church[8], ... the **Rūṇu-maha-vehera**, caused to be entirely rebuilt[9] by

---

[1] Skt. *Parākramabāhu*, P. *Parakkamabāhu*.

[2] Skt. *Coḷa* or *Coḍa*, T. *Coḷa*. [3] P. *Rohaṇa*.

[4] *Mul pisä karavā*: This expression literally means 'having swept away the roots and caused to be made'. It seems to have been an idiomatic way of expressing the idea of completely renovating a building after having removed the decayed structures. It occurs in Sinhalese literature; for example, in the 37th chapter of the *Pūjāvalī* (edited by Mudaliyar B. Gunasekara, Colombo, 1893, p. 33), where we read: *Käḷaṇi-vehera Demaḷun visin naḷa maha-säya baňdavā kot palaňdavā ehi pūrvva väsala mul pisä karavā*. The expression *bim pisä karavā*, which also appears to be of the same meaning, occurring in Inscription II, may also be compared.

[5] *Darugam* occurs in the *Nikāya Saṅgraha* (Colombo edition of 1922, p. 26), as it does in this record, in association with *vaḷanā-pasa*. The translator of that text has rendered the word into English by 'wooded villages'. This interpretation, which is due to the uncritical assumption that *daru* is equivalent to Skt. *dāru*, does not suit the context in which the word occurs. The word appears to signify some kind of village dedicated to the *saṅgha*. As such, it would be equivalent to *daru-kusalān* occurring in the Galpota inscription of Niśśaṁka Malla (*E. Z.*, Vol. II, p. 111). It is very unlikely that *daru* in either of these words is equivalent to P. *dāraka* and means 'child'. In the Galpota inscription, the word *daru-kusalān* is followed by *maha-kusalān* (wrongly read by Dr. Wickremasinghe as *maňga-kusalān*) and Mr. Bell (*Ca*, vol. x, p 6) conjectures that *daru* means the opposite of *maha*, i.e., small, and quotes the expression *daru geḍi maha geḍi* 'small fruits and big fruits' used in the colloquial language, to support his interpretation. If this view is adopted, *darugam* would mean 'small village' which does not quite suit the context.

[6] *Vaḷanā-pasa*, see above, p. 109, n. 9.

[7] This interpretation is based on the reading *bada-vas* (Skt. *baddha-vāsa*) which is not free from doubt.

[8] *Lo-sasun*:—See *E. Z.*, Vol. III, p. 324, n. 7.

[9] *Bim pisä karavā*:—See above, n. 4. This expression also occurs in the *Pūjāvalī* (*op. cit.*) p. 30, where we read *Anurādhapurayehi bohō vihāra bim pisä karavā*; and on p. 41, the phrase *ē geya bim pisä karavā* occurs. *Bim pisä* means literally 'having swept the ground' and the expression seems to be used with the same meaning as *mul pisä karavā*.

Vihāra-mahā-devī, who was the chief consort of the two brother kings named **Parākramabāhu.** . . . . . . (called a wish-conferring tree [1]), this field of the sowing extent of . . . . seed was dedicated to the *dharmma-ratna* [2]. Meritorious people coming in the future should enjoy the merit in full and maintain it.

No. 20. THREE ROCK-INSCRIPTIONS AT RĀSSAHELA [3].

By S. Paranavitana.

THE three short records dealt with in this paper are engraved on the side of a boulder, under which is a cave (numbered 20), at a rocky hill called Rājagala or Rāssahela in the Vävugam Pattu of the Batticaloa District. There are, at this site, the remains of an extensive ancient monastery; and no less than twenty-two Brāhmī inscriptions have been found incised under the drip-ledges of the numerous caves to be seen at the place. Among these are five records containing the names of an early king of the island, two of his sons, and their wives. These important records will be dealt with elsewhere. Particular interest is attached to the inscriptions now published, for one of them is the only record, so far discovered, which can be definitely dated in the period of over a century between the reigns of Kassapa III and Sena I; and, on palaeographical grounds, the other two records must also be assigned to about the same period. On the same boulder has also been found a fragment of an inscription of a slightly later date. As it contains nothing more than the stereotyped phrases found in mediaeval Sinhalese grants of immunities, it has not been included in the present paper. I edit the inscriptions from estampages prepared by Mr. W. E. Fernando, the Draughtsman of the Archaeological Department, who was sent by me to the site, for that purpose, in 1935.

The inscription referred to as No. I in this article (*A.S.I.*, No. 1564) consists of nine lines and occupies an area of 3 ft. 6 in. by 3 ft. 7 in. No. II (*A.S.I.*, No. 1565), immediately to the left of No. I but somewhat lower down

---

[1] *Kap-ruk nam vū*: This reading is doubtful. If it is correct, it is perhaps an allusion to the fact that a gift to the religion is like a celestial tree in that it bestows the desired objects.

[2] The second of the three jewels (*tri-ratna*) of Buddhism. By a gift of the *dhamma* is generally meant a donation to meet the expenses of copying of the scriptures or the delivering of religious discourses by monks.

[3] For a brief account of the inscriptions at Rāssahela, see *A. S. C. A. R.* for 1935, p. 9.

the rock, also comprises nine lines and the rock surface covered by it measures 3 ft. square. No. III (*A.S.I.*, No. 1566), engraved about 10 ft. to the north of the other two, measures 3 ft. 11 in. laterally and is $4\frac{1}{2}$ ft. in depth. The size of the individual **letters** varies from 2 to $5\frac{1}{2}$ inches. A few letters in l. 2 of No. I are somewhat obscured by chisel marks which seem to have been on the rock before the inscription was engraved. Likewise, some letters of line 6 of the same record have become indistinct owing to a linear engraving. But for these, inscriptions numbered I and II are in a good state of preservation. No. III, however, has weathered considerably; but the whole record can be deciphered with certainty.

The **script** of all the three records is definitely earlier than that of the inscriptions of Sena I and II [1]. The letters *ja*, *ṭa* and *ḷa* of these records, for example, show a distinctly earlier stage of evolution when compared with the corresponding *akṣaras* of the inscriptions of Sena I. At the time when the epigraphs under discussion were indited, the *virama* and the *ä*-sign had already been introduced to the Sinhalese script [2]. In comparing the three records with one another, we find that the scripts of Nos. I and III are almost identical, while No. II shows a more cursive type of writing. This difference in the form of writing cannot be taken as an indication of a considerable difference in date, for, as will be seen below, inscriptions I and II cannot be separated from each other by more than a decade or two. The *ḷa* occurring as the tenth *akṣara* in the fifth line of No. I is of peculiar form, which seems due to the regular form of this letter being reversed and written upside down. It is perhaps the result of the blunder of an illiterate stone-mason. Above the *ga* forming the sixth *akṣara* of II, l. 7, is to be seen the stroke, resembling an *anunāsika*, which we have noticed in an inscription on the pavement of the Ambasthala Cetiya at Mihintaḷē [3].

The **language** differs very little from the standard of the ninth century. The use of *j* in words like *vajanin*, *janavu*, *vaḷaj*, and *vajāḷamha* (normally found in the documents of the ninth and tenth centuries as *vadanin*, *danavu*, *vaḷand*, and *vadaḷamha*) shows an earlier stage in the evolution of the Sinhalese language than that met with in records of the ninth century, for the *j* in these words is either the same as in their Sanskrit or Pāli prototypes, or stands for an

---

[1] For inscriptions of Sena I, see *E. Z.*, Vol. III, plate 34, II and III. Plate 18 of this volume illustrates an inscription of Sena II.

[2] See above, p. 150.

[3] See above, p. 146.

original *c*. Similar forms are, however, sometimes found as late as the tenth century[1]. *Yisā* (I, l. 7) for *isā* is also noteworthy. The introduction of the semi-vowel *y* before an initial *i*, which we notice in this word, has not been met with elsewhere in the Sinhalese language, and reminds us of certain Tamil forms, such as *yiṭṭu* for *iṭṭu*, occurring in epigraphy[2]. The expression *himi-ge ek-tän koṭ*, occurring in No. II, has not been met with elsewhere and seems to throw some light on the term *ek-tän-samiya* so often found in Sinhalese inscriptions of the ninth and tenth centuries. It will be discussed in connexion with the somewhat similar expression *hat-pasä sam-jarvan ek-tän koṭ* occurring in the Viyaulpata pillar-inscription dealt with below[3]. *Väyutu* does not occur in other records. The forms *a*, *siṭ*, and *äpäy* correspond to *ā*, *siṭä*, and *āpā* of the inscriptions of the ninth and tenth centuries[4].

The three documents are all concerned with grants of lands, by local rulers of Rohaṇa, to a monastery called **Arittārā-vehera**, of which religious establishment the ruins now seen at Rāssahela are doubtless the remains. Of the personages who figure in these records as the donors, only one, **Äpāy Daḷsiva,** can be recognized in the *Mahāvaṁsa*. 'Äpāy Daḷsiva' would be 'Ādipāda Dāṭhāsiva' in Pāli; and a Rohaṇa prince of this name figures in the reign of Udaya I[5]. The chronicle says of this prince: 'At that time there lived in the province of Rohaṇa a nobleman Mahinda by name, a son of the Ādipāda Dāṭhāsiva who administered the revenues of the country. He fell out with his father and betook himself to the King. When the King beheld him, he was much pleased and showed him grace according to his deserts. To strengthen the friendship with him, he gave him his daughter, by name Devā, and sent troops to Rohaṇa. Mahinda set out, laid Rohaṇa waste with the help of the royal army, drove out his father to Jambudīpā and took possession of Rohaṇa[6]'.

There can be no reasonable doubt as regards the identification of Äpāy Daḷsiva of this record with Ādipāda Dāṭhāsiva of the chronicle. The inscription, it is true, does not expressly state that Daḷsiva was a ruler of Rohaṇa, but the title *äpāy* (*ādipāda*), the term *vat-himi* used in the record in referring to him, and the fact that he issued the order embodied in the document without any reference

---

[1] See *E. Z.*, Vol. I, p. 77.

[2] See *E. Z.*, Vol. III, p. 311.

[3] See below, pp. 178–9.

[4] See *E. Z.*, Vol. III, Index, *s.v.*

[5] This monarch is referred to as Dappula II, in the lists of Wijesinha, Codrington, and Wickremasinghe. For the mistake regarding his name, see Geiger's note in the *Cūḷavaṁsa*, translation, part II, p. 126.

[6] *Cūḷavaṁsa*, Geiger's translation, part II, p. 128.

to a higher authority, make it reasonably certain that he was the ruler of the ancient principality in which the inscription is found, i.e., Rohaṇa.

From the extract from the *Mahāvaṁsa*, quoted above, it will be seen that Dāṭhāsiva was driven away from his principality during the reign of Udaya I, which lasted for only five years from about 787 A.D. It is therefore quite possible that the inscription in which he is the donor dates from the reign of Udaya I's predecessor, Mahinda II (*circa* 767–787). At any rate, we can be certain that this record belongs to the second half of the eighth century.

The order of Dāṭhāsiva, granting lands to the monastery, has been engraved by an officer named **Day,** who seems to have been the administrative head of the district called **Lam-janavu,** presumably the territorial division in which the monastery and the lands dedicated to it were situated. Similarly, in No. I, the order was delivered by **Sen**; and its publication, by having it engraved on stone, was effected by **Vīrāṁkurā** of Lam-janavu. We may therefore conclude that Sen, too, was a dignitary of a status equal to that of Dāṭhāsiva, i.e., that he was a ruler of Rohaṇa, though the title *äpāy* (*āpä*. P. *āpipāda*) which was borne by princes who ruled over this principality, is not applied to him in the record. Inscription No. II is a grant of Vīrāṁkurā, the executor in No. I. Neither Sen nor Vīrāṁkurā can be identified with any personage mentioned in the chronicles. A monastic building named Vīrāṁkurā is referred to in the *Nikāya-saṅgraha*[1] and in a tenth-century inscription from Vessagiriya in Anurādhapura[2]. But there is no ground for assuming that it was named after the Vīrāṁkurā of these inscriptions. We are also unable to decide whether inscriptions I and II, which must be contemporaneous with each other, as Vīrāṁkurā figures in both of them, are earlier or later than III which can be approximately dated. But from palaeographical considerations, we can conclude that these two cannot be far removed in date from the record of Dāṭhāsiva.

Of the **geographical names** occurring in these records, Arittārā-vehera and Lam-janavu have already been referred to. Neither of these two names is forthcoming elsewhere. The river named **Gaḷ-hoy,** on the right bank of which some of the lands granted to the monastery were situated, is still known by the same name[3], and is, as the crow flies, sixteen miles to the south of Rāssahela. The other places cannot now be identified.

---

[1] C. M. Fernando's translation, Colombo, 1908, p. 18. [2] See *E. Z.*, Vol. I, p. 28.

[3] The aspirate, however, is dropped in the modern form of this name and the vowel *a* has been added to the last consonant.

TEXT.

I.

1 සවසති සෙන්හු වජනින් අ[භින්නා]රා
2 වෙහෙර වැසි වත්හිමියනව් සතර්
3 පස වැදූනු කරන කොට් ගල්හො
4 ය් දකුණ් තෙර්හි පිනිපි දිගැ(පිඩු)
5 ල්ලෙ අ සොරුවුර් පයල සි
6 සා ලම්ජනවූ .. .. යට්වැග
7 කලල්වැලි සතර්පයල් පිසා
8 වජාලෙසින් ලම්ජනවූ විරාංකුරාමි
9 සිට් ලියැවීමි ස්වසති සිධි

II.

1 සවසති විරා[ං]කුරා වජ
2 නින් අභින්නාරා
3 වෙහෙර වසන
4 වත්හිමිසරන
5 ට් සතර්පස වැදූ
6 නු කරනූ කොට් සරට්වැ
7 ගහි මහාවැග්ණෑ
8 සතර්පයල් හිමිගෙ
9 එක්තැන් කොට් දින්මි

III.

1 ඇපාය් දල්සිවය්හු වජනින් අප
2 අභින්නාරාවෙහෙර වැසි වත්
3 හිමියනට් මාළත්තෙ
4 ගුළවැල්ලෑ මිවත්ගමූ
5 සතර්පයල් දිහි තෙල් කි
6 ර් මිසෑ අත් වළජ් නොකර
7 න කොට් වජාළම්හ ව
8 ත් හිමියන් වජාලෙසි
9 න් ලම්ජනවූ දස්මි සි
10 ට් ලියැවීමි

TRANSCRIPT.

I.

1 Svasti **Senhu** vajanin **A[rittā]rā-**
2 **veherä** väsi vat-himiyanaṭ satar-
3 pasa väyutu karana koṭ **Gaḷ-ho-**
4 **-y** dakuṇ-terhi pihiṭi Digä(piḍu)-[1]
5 -lle a Soruyur payala yi-[2]
6 -sā Lam-janavu .. .. yaṭväga
7 Kalalväli satar-payal yisā
8 vajāḷeyin Lam-janavu **Vīrāṁkurāmi**
9 siṭ liyävịmi svasti siddhi

II.

1 Svasti **Vīrā[ṁ]kurā** vaja-
2 -nin **Arittārā-**
3 **-veherä** vasana
4 vat-himisarana-
5 -ṭ satar-pasa väyu-
6 -tu karanu koṭ Saraṭ-vä-
7 -gahi Mahāvăğaṇā
8 satar-payal himi-ge
9 ek-tän koṭ dinmi [3]

III.

1 **Äpäy Daḷsivayhu** vajanin apa
2 **Arittārā-veherä** väsi vat-
3 himiyanaṭ Māḷatte
4 Guḷavällä Mivangamu
5 satar-payal dihi tel ki-
6 -r misä an vaḷaj no-kara-
7 -na koṭ vajāḷamha va-

---

[1] It is tempting to read this name as *Digämaḍulle*. But the penultimate *akṣara* of line 4 is more like *pi*, than *ma*, occurring elsewhere in the record.

[2] The two short vertical strokes to be seen at the end of this line do not evidently form part of the inscription.

[3] It is also possible to read this word as *jinmi*.

Rock-Inscriptions at Rässahela

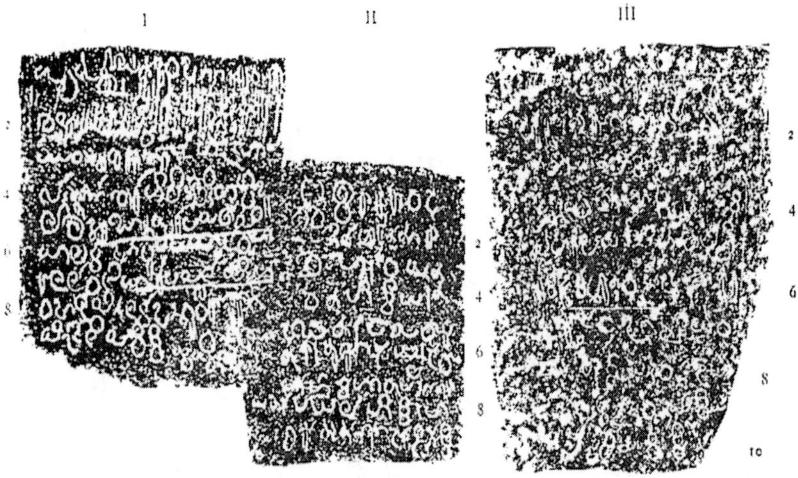

Scale ⅛ inch to 1 feet

Viyaulpata Pillar-Inscription

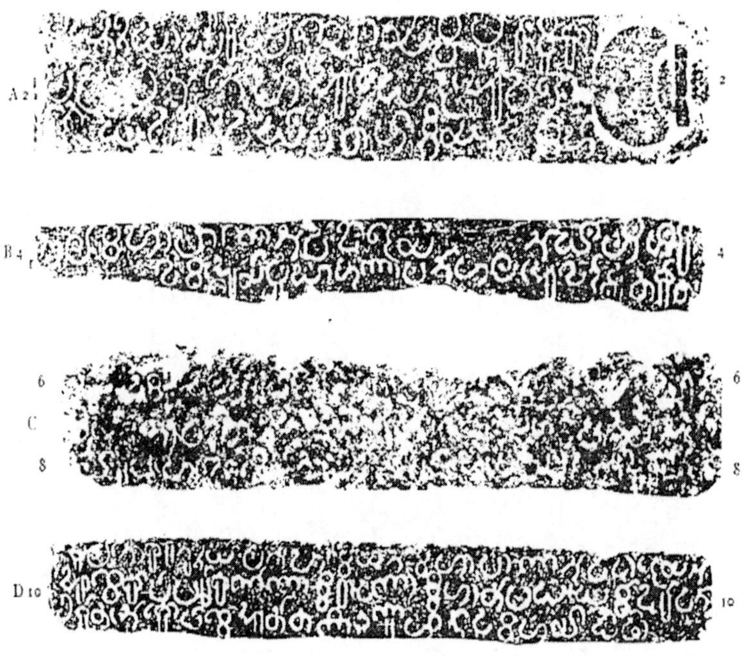

Scale about 1¾ inches to 1 feet

8 -t- himiyan vajāḷeyi-
9 -n Lam-jaṇavu **Daymi** si-
10 -ṭ liyävīmi

TRANSLATION.

I.

Hail! By the order[1] of **Sen**[2]. In order to provide[3] the four requisites[4] for their lordships[5] residing in the **Arittārā Monastery,** [we grant] the *payala*[6] of Soruyur in Digä(piḍu)lla, which is situated on the right bank of the **Gaḷ-hoy,** and the four *payal* of Kalalväli in . . . . . yaṭaväga in the [district of] Lam-janavu. In accordance with the order, I, **Vīrāṁkurā** of Lam-janavu, stayed [here] and caused [this] to be written. Hail! Success.

II.

Hail! By the order of **Vīrāṁkurā.** In order to provide the four requisites for their lordships residing in the **Arittārā Monastery,** I have given, after assembling together [the chief men of the district] at the house of the lord[7], the four *payal* of Mahāvägaṇā in Saraṭväga.

III.

By the order of **Äpāy Daḷsiva.** We have ordered that the four *payal* of Māḷatta, Guḷavälla, and Mivangamu should be granted to their lordships residing

[1] *Vajanin* means literally 'by the word'. This formula is used when the actual order delivered by the king or some other dignitary is embodied in the inscription, as it is in these documents. Accordingly we find the termination of the first person with the honorific plural in the finite verb.

[2] *Sen* = P. and Skt. *Sena*.

[3] *Väyutu-karana koṭ*: Though the meaning of *väyutu* is fairly certain from the context, the etymology of the word is not clear.

[4] *Satar-pasa* = P. *catu-paccaya*, for which see *P. T. S. Dictionary*, *s.v.*

[5] *Vat-himi*, applied here to the monks, see *E. Z.*, Vol. III, pp. 85-86.

[6] *Payala* is obviously a term of land measurement. It is probably the same as *paya*, for which see *E. Z.*, Vol. III, p. 189. It is doubtful whether *payala* is, as Dr. Wickremasinghe assumes (*E. Z.*, I, p. 55, n. 3), the same as *pāḷa*, a measure of capacity, also used as a term for land measurement from the twelfth century onwards. There is no evidence to show that terms denoting measures of capacity were used in Ceylon, before the twelfth century, to indicate the areas of fields. Moreover, *pāḷa* is invariably spelt with a cerebral *ḷ*, whereas the *l* of *payala* is dental.

[7] *Himi-ge*: By *himi* is presumably meant the overlord of the territorial magnate Vīrāṁkurā who is the donor of this grant. The reference is probably to the prince of Rohaṇa.

in the **Arittārā Monastery,** on condition that nothing should be enjoyed [out of the income derived therefrom] but curd, oil, and milk [1]. As His Highness [2] has ordered [thus], I, **Day** [3] of Lam-janavu, stayed [here] and caused [this] to be written.

No. 21. VIYAULPATA PILLAR-INSCRIPTION.

By S. PARANAVITANA.

THIS inscription [4] is engraved on the four faces of a rough stone pillar which is now lying near the village called Viyaulpata in the Ināmaḷuva Kōraḷē of the Mātalē District. No other antiquarian remains are to be seen at the site. The pillar has not been dressed and its edges are therefore not straight. The lines of writing, which run vertically along the height of the pillar, are, consequently, irregular and not of equal length. On side B, there is a gap in line 1, due to a rough area of the pillar being left uninscribed. The second line of this side starts somewhat higher up than the first line, for the reason that the width of the lower portion on this side of the pillar does not provide room for two lines of writing. On the top of side A is a delineation of a pot filled with flowers (*pūrṇṇa-ghaṭa*). The inscribed area of the pillar measures 5 ft. 2 in. in length; the width of sides A and C is 10 inches each, while side B, at its broadest point, measures 6 inches, and D, 7 inches. Each of sides A, C, and D contains three lines of writing and B only two. The **letters,** which on side A range in size from $1\frac{1}{2}$ to $4\frac{1}{2}$ inches and on the other sides from $1\frac{1}{2}$ to $2\frac{1}{2}$ inches, have been boldly incised. The preservation of the record is excellent so far as sides A, B, and D are concerned; but on side C, the writing has been almost totally effaced.

The **script** is Sinhalese of the ninth century and is uniform with that of other contemporary records. Attention may, however, be drawn to the form of *ka* occurring in this inscription. The *ṇa*, ණ, of this record shows a later

---

[1] This unusual stipulation is evidently meant to prevent the misuse of the income derived from the lands which were granted to provide some particular needs of the monks.

[2] *Vat-himiyan* here refers to an *āpa* (prince). I have therefore adopted the above rendering in this place.

[3] The name *Day* may represent P. *dhātu* which, however, has not been found elsewhere as a proper name excepting in compounds like *Dhātusena.*

[4] *A. S. I.*, No. 476, noticed in *C. J. Sc. G*, vol. ii, p. 117.

stage of development when compared with a variant form of this letter, ග, occurring in other records of this period. As regards the **language**, the use of the conjunction *isa* (Skt. *ca*) after the auspicious word *svasti*, the forms *vajāḷeyin* and *sam-jarvan*, containing *j* in place of *d* in the later forms of these words, and *ayvū* and *tak*, corresponding to *āvū* and *tāk* of later documents, are points worthy of note. The auspicious word *siddhi* coming at the end of this document occurs in only a few records of the ninth and tenth centuries. In *mahāpāṇan*, the vowel of the second syllable is long; in most other documents where this word occurs, it has a short vowel in the corresponding place. On the other hand, we have in this inscription the form *attaṇi* in place of *attāṇi* occurring very often in mediaeval records.

The epigraph is **dated** in the first year of a king styled **Sirisaṁboy** (P. Siri-saṁghabodhi) and contains an edict issued by the heir-apparent (*mahāpā*) of the time, named **Mihindal (Mahinda),** granting certain immunities to a monastic dwelling called **Sāṅguṇā-panhala.** 'Sirisaṁbo' or 'Sirisaṁboy' is a *viruda* title and was borne by several kings of the ninth century, to which period this epigraph has to be assigned on palaeographical grounds. The only Sirisaṁbo of this century whose *mahāpā* had the name of Mahinda was **Sena II** (*circa* 846–880)[1] and we can confidently assign this inscription to the reign of that monarch.

The inscribed pillar was set up, and the edict engraved thereon thus proclaimed, by **two officers named Kaṇṇā (Kṛṣṇa) and Rāvaṇā,** members of the body-guard, presumably of the *mahāpā*. It is interesting to note that two minor officials of Ceylon in the ninth century were named after two of the most well-known figures in Hindu mythology, one a deified hero of the *Mahābhārata*, later identified with the Supreme Being, and the other the demon king of Laṁkā which, in popular belief, is the same as Ceylon. The two officials, before setting the pillar up, are said to have assembled together the notables in the vicinity, presumably of the monastic establishment in question. This was doubtless done to give publicity to the royal order, so that the privileges granted by it might be respected by those concerned. The expression used in this connexion, *hät-pasä sam-jarvan ek-tän koṭ*, considered together with the phrase *himi-ge ek-tän koṭ*, occurring in an inscription at Rässahela[2], seems to throw some light on the technical term *ek-tän samiyen* occurring so often in the inscriptions of the ninth and tenth centuries, and of which the real significance has so far remained

[1] See *Mahāvaṁsa*, chap. li, v. 7. Mahinda predeceased Sena II and Udaya, his younger brother, succeeded to the rank of *mahāpā*.

[2] See above, p. 174.

obscure[1]. From these two records we learn that, in one case when the edict was published and in the other when it was delivered, notables concerned were assembled together at the place affected by the royal order, or at the residence of the prince who issued the edict. An analogous procedure prevailed in South India, as we learn from the Tiruvālaṅgāḍu plates. The royal order granting privileges was entered in various registers by the secretaries, and officers were nominated to proceed to the village concerned and publish it with due ceremony. On the arrival of the royal officers, the chief men of the district came out, received the royal order, placed it on their heads and, accompanied by a female elephant, circumambulated the village[2].

With these instances to guide us, we may conjecture that when decrees granting immunities were delivered by the king, it was done in an assembly consisting of the various officials and chiefs. We learn from the expression *kariyaṭa niyukta äma-denā mända vadaḷa mehevarin* 'by the command delivered in the midst of all engaged in state affairs', occurring in the Uḍugampola copper-plate inscription[3], that it was so in the fifteenth century. *Ek-tän-samiya* may therefore be taken as equivalent to Skt. *eka-sthana-samūha* or *-samiti*, meaning 'assembled in one place'. It also seems that decrees delivered in such assemblies were themselves referred to as *ek-tän-samiya.*

Sāṅguṇā-panhala, the monastic residence which was the object of the immunities granted by the edict, is not mentioned elsewhere. It may, however, be presumed that this institution was situated not far from the place where the inscription was found, i.e., the modern village of Viyaulpata. It was included in the district of **Sihigiri** (P. *Sīhagiri* and modern Sinhalese **Sīgiri**). This famous rock fortress is, in a straight line, about six miles from Viyaulpata and the present inscription shows that it was an important place in the ninth century, as it had given its name to, and was therefore the headquarters of, a district of considerable size.

TEXT.

1 සවසනි ඉසා සිරිසංබොය් මපුර්මුකා
2 පළමුවන්නෙහි ඇසෙළැ අව දෙ
3 ළොස්වක් දවස් වත්ගිමියන් මියු
4 ළල් මහාසාමින් වදාළෙයින් සිහිගිරි
5 තිමැ අය්වූ සාඟුණාපන්හලැ අබද්වූ තන් තැ

---

[1] For the suggested interpretation of this term, see *E. Z.*, Vol. III, pp. 107–108.

[2] *S. I. I*, vol. iii, pp. 429–430.

[3] Müller, *A. I. C.*, p. 108.

6 (නට් දු)නුම(ඬු)ල්ලන් රට්ලදු .. ..
7 .. (යන් නොවද්නා ඉසා).. .. ..
8 .. .. (නොවද්නා ඉසා) .. .. අ
9 වුල් නොකරනු ඉසා වත්හිමියන් මහාපාණන් වජාළෙයින්
10 ආ මෙකාප්පර් කණ්ණාමි රාවණාමි හාත්පසැ සම්ජර්වන්
11 එක්තැන් කොට් මෙ අත්තණිකණු හින්ද්වූම්හයි සිඩි

TRANSCRIPT.

1 Svasti isā **Sirisaṁboy** mapurmukā
2 paḷamuvannehi Äseḷā ava do-
3 -ḷosvak davas vat-himiyan **Mihi-**
4 **-ndal Mahāpāṇan** vajāḷeyin **Sihigiri-**
5 bimä ayvū **Säṅguṇā-panhalä** abad-vū tak tä-
6 -(naṭ du)nu-ma(ṅḍu)llan raṭ-ladu .. ..
7 .. (yan no-vadnā isā) .. ..
8 .. .. (no-vadnā isā) .. .. a-
9 -vul no-karanu isā vat-himiyan mahāpāṇan vajāḷeyin
10 ā mekāppar **Kaṇṇāmi Rāvaṇāmi** hāt-pasä sam-jarvan
11 **ek-tän koṭ** me attaṇi-kaṇu hindvūmhay siddhi

TRANSLATION.

Hail![1] On the twelfth day of the waning moon in the month of Äseḷa[2] in the first year of His Majesty **Sirisaṁboy**[3]. Whereas it was so decreed by His Highness **Mihindal Mahāpā**[4], [it is ordered] that *dunumaṇḍullan*[5] and governors of districts[6] ...... shall not enter ...... shall not enter ...... shall not create disturbance to the lands belonging to **Säṅguṇā-panhala**[7] which is in the **Sihigiri** District. I, **Kaṇṇā** and I, **Rāvaṇā**, (both members of) the body-guard,

[1] The conjunction *isā*, which follows *svasti*, has been ignored in the translation. It has possibly an auspicious significance.

[2] Skt. *Āṣāḍha*, June–July.

[3] P. *Sirisaṁghabodhi*.

[4] *Mihindal* is equivalent to P. *Mahinda*. For the title *mahāpā* (*mahādipāda*), see *E. Z.*, Vol. III, p. 82.

[5] See *E. Z.*, Vol. III, p. 110.

[6] *Raṭ-ladu*, see *E. Z.*, Vol. III, p. 111.

[7] *Pan-hala* (P. *paṇṇa-sāla*) means 'leaf-hut'. In early days, the abodes of Buddhist monks, who were vowed to poverty, were huts made of sticks and leaves. The word (*pansala*) is used to-day in Ceylon for monasteries which are no longer formed of leaf-huts, but are very often palatial buildings, just as the term *bhikkhu* which originally meant 'beggar' or 'mendicant' is applied to Buddhist monks, some of whom are rich landlords.

who have come in accordance with the decree of His Highness, the *mahapā*, set up this *attaṇi*-pillar[1] having had the gentlemen[2] of the neighbourhood assembled together. [Let there be] Success.

No. 22. MALAGAṆĒ PILLAR-INSCRIPTION.

By S. PARANAVITANA.

THE pillar, on the four faces of which the subjoined inscription[3] is engraved, is now lying within the premises of the Buddhist temple at Malagaṇē in the Girātalān Kōraḷē of the Kuruṇāgala District. It is said to have been removed to its present position, some fifty years ago, from Nuvarakälē, an extensive ancient site about three miles to the north-east of Malagaṇē, and utilized in the construction of a shrine which is no longer standing. The sides of the pillar are 10 in. and $10\frac{1}{2}$ in. in breadth and the inscribed portion, which was above ground, is 6 ft. in height. The writing is engraved between parallel lines, $3\frac{5}{8}$ in. apart from each other on sides A and B, and 3 in. on sides C and D. There are eighteen lines of writing on each of sides A and B, twenty on C, and nine on D. The last side also contains drawings of a fan, a scythe, a crow, and a dog.

As will be seen from the facsimile reproduced on Plate 19, the inscription is in a rather bad state of preservation, the writing on sides C and D being considerably weathered. A portion of the pillar surface has been peeled away on all the four sides, probably when the pillar was transported from its original position, and thus two lines on sides A and B are partly, and three on side C altogether, lost. The **letters** on side A, averaging 2 in. in height, are larger than those of the other sides which are, on an average, $1\frac{1}{2}$ in. in height.

The **script,** which is Sinhalese and can be attributed, on grounds of palaeography, to the second half of the ninth century, calls for no remarks in particular. As regards **orthography,** attention may be drawn to the form *Lag-div* (A 7–8) which may be compared with *Lag-divu* occurring in the Devanagala inscription

---

[1] See above, p. 66, n. 3.

[2] *Sam-jarvan* is an earlier form of *sam-daruvan*, for which see *E. Z.*, Vol. III, p. 88.

[3] *A. S. I.*, No. 763. No. 105 of Appendix F of *A. S. C. A. R.* for 1910–11, p. 119.

of Parākramabāhu I[1]. *Dana-maḍulu* (A 16-17) is obviously a clerical error for *mala-maḍulu* or *-maṇḍulu* which occurs in other records of the period[2].

The epigraph is **dated** in the tenth year of a king styled **Abhā Maharad** and records immunities granted to a religious foundation called **Saṅgradūn Pirivena** in the monastery of **Mirisipiṭi** at **Muhunnaru**. King Abhā is described, in almost the same words as are found in the Tiṁbiriväva inscription[3] in connexion with Udaya II (I)[4], as one who had brought Rohaṇa and Malaya under his dominion. And, in the *Mahāvaṁsa*[5], Udaya II (I) is said to have quelled risings in Rohaṇa and Malaya and made his writ run in those parts of the island. The relationship of King Abhā to another, and presumably earlier monarch, named Abhā Sirisaṅgbo, had also been given in the epigraph; but the word which expresses the relationship is, unfortunately, not preserved now on the stone. In an eye-copy of the inscription, made under Mr. Bell's direction and preserved in the office of the Archaeological Survey, the missing word occurs as *daru* 'son'. From the Ällēväva pillar-inscription[6] we learn that 'Abhā Sirisaṅgbo' was a title of Sena II and, if we can rely on the eye-copy mentioned above, Abhā Maharad of this record may be identified with **Kassapa V** (*circa* 908-918) or **Dappula IV** (V) (*circa* 918-930), both of whom were sons of Sena II and had the *viruda* title of Abhā Salamevan[7]. The script in which the record is written does not militate against its being assigned to either of these two monarchs; but no particular mention has been made in the chronicles of their connexion with Rohaṇa and Malaya. If we take the missing word as *maḷu* 'younger brother', we may then identify Abhā with Udaya II (I) (*circa*, 880-891), who is referred to in inscriptions as Udā Abhā Salamevan or Udaya Abhaya[8], and whose subjugation of Rohaṇa and Malaya is referred to, as we have noted above, in the chronicles as well as in contemporary records. The script of our record, however, contains forms of certain letters which are younger than those corresponding to them found in inscriptions definitely dating from the reign of Udaya II (I).

The *pirivena* to which immunities were granted by this edict was obviously

---

1 *E.Z.*, Vol. III, p. 321.

2 *Ibid.*, Vol. II, p. 12 and Vol. III, p. 273.

3 *Ibid.*, Vol. II, pp. 9 ff.

4 For the number given in parenthesis in the names of this and other kings, see *Cūḷavaṁsa*, Geiger's translation, part I, p. 126, n. 1.

5 Chap. 51, vv. 94 *et seq.*

6 *A. S. C. Seventh Progress Report*, p. 45.

7 See *E. Z.*, Vol. III, p. 19.

8 See the Tiṁbiriväva pillar-inscription, *E. Z.*, Vol. II, p. 13 and the Colombo Museum Pillar-inscription of Kassapa IV, *E. Z.*, Vol. III, p. 275.

named after **Saṅghā**, the queen of Sena II. In the *Pūjāvalī*[1], she is referred to as Saṅgā-radū. *Muhunnaru* occurs in the *Mahāvaṁsa* as the name of a stronghold in the Dakkhiṇapassa captured by the general of Vijayabāhu I in his campaign against the Coḷas[2]. It is reasonable to suppose that this was the ancient name of the site where the pillar originally stood; and if we can be certain that it was removed to its present location from Nuvarakälē, we may then identify this site as the stronghold of Muhunnaru[3]. At Nuvarakälē can still be seen the remains of two fortresses with ramparts of earthwork and brick, which make the identification of the site with a military post of the eleventh century quite plausible. Remains of monastic buildings and shrines, some of which are much earlier in date than the eleventh century, are also to be seen at the place.

Another point to which attention may be drawn is the fact that, in this edict granting immunities to a place in Dakkhiṇapassa (Sin. *Dakuṇ-pasa*, 'the Southern Country'[4]), there is no mention of the *mahapā* to whose government this territory was usually subject in mediaeval times. In all other edicts of the ninth and tenth centuries, discovered at sites which were in the Dakkhiṇa-passā, the order is delivered by the *mahapā*.

TEXT.

A.

1 සවසති
2 සිරිබර්
3 කැතකුල
4 කොත් ඔකා
5 වස්රද්
6 පරපුරෙ
7 ත් බටි ල
8 ශ්දිවපො
9 ලොයොත් ප
10 රපුරෙන්
11 ගිමි වූ අ
12 හා සිරිස
13 [ග්බො මහ]
14 රද්නු .. ..
15 රුනු[ණු]දන
16 [වූ] දනමබූ
17 ලූ' තමගටි
18 එකආත්නැ

---

[1] *A Contribution to the History of Ceylon*, translated from *Pūjāvaliya*, by B. Gunasekara, Colombo, 1895, p. 32.

[2] *Mahāvaṁsa*, chap. lviii, v. 42.

[3] For the identification of Muhunnaru, compare also Mr. Codrington in *J. R. A. S., C. B.* vol. xxix, p. 64.

[4] For the 'Southern Country', see Mr. Codrington, *op. cit.*, p. 65.

මෙය 'මලමබුලු' යන්නට වැරදී ලියවිණැයි සිතිය හැක.

B.

1 සිරිභොග[1] ක
2 ළ අභාමහර
3 ද්ගු නුමා සඃන්
4 ලැඟු දසවන
5 ගඩ්රැදුයෙ
6 ඡී පොසොත්ම
7 ස්ගි පූර දස
8 වික් දවස් ද
9 කුණ්පස්ගි අ
10 වූ මගුන්නරැ
11 මිටිසිටිවිංව
12 හෙරඋ සග්රදු
13 න් පිරිවෙනම
14 වදළ එක්තැ
15 න්සමියෙන්
16 මෙකාප්පරවැ
17 දූරැම් ක .. ..
18 මගලරද් සෙ

C.

1 නු වරඋ වන ව
2 .. .. රා ගණයි
3 ම් ඉසා මණින
4 [ලා කි]ලිසිම් ඉ
5 [සා මහලෙ] ..
6 .. .. රග්සම
7 ණන වරඋ වන
8 කුඩසලා .. ..
9 .. .. ඉසා මෙනු
10 වාක් දෙනමො ව
11 දළ එක්තැන්
12 සමියෙන් මෙ අ
13 ත්තාණ්කණු පැ
14 රඋහැර් දෙනු ල
15 දි වැරි පෙරෙනාවි
16 [වියම්] .. .. ..
17 .. ..
18 .. ..
19 නා කොට් ඉසා ම
20 ගිව පෙගිව නො
21 වද්නා කොට් ඉ
22· සා රද්කොල්කැ

D.

1 මියත් නොවද්
2 නා කොට් ඉසා දෙ
3 රුවනැ දෙකම්තැ
4 ත් නොවද්නා කො
5 ට් ඉසා පියොවදු
6 රන්නත් නොවද්නා
7 කොට් ඉසා ගම්ගො
8 ත් කිර්ගෙරි නොගත්
9 නා කොට් ඉසා

A.

1 Svasti
2 Siri-bar
3 käta-kula
4 kot Okā-
5 -vas-rad-
6 parapure-
7 -n baṭ La-
8 -g-div-po-

---

[1] මෙය 'පිරිභොග' නොහොත් 'පරිභොග' වෙනුවට වැරදී ලියැවුණක් වියහැක.

9 -ḷo-yon pa-
10 -rapuren
11 himi vū **A-**
12 **-bhā Sirisa-**
13 **-ṅgbo** maha-
14 rad-hu .. ..
15 Ruhuṇ[u]-dana-
16 -v[u] Dana-maḍu-
17 -lu[1] tamahaṭ
18 ek-ānnä

B.

1 siri-bhoga[2] ka-
2 -ḷa **Abhā-maha-ra-**
3 **-d-hu** tumā sat
4 läṅgu dasa-vana
5 havuruduye-
6 -hi Poson-ma-
7 -s-hi pura dasa-
8 vak davas Da-
9 -kuṇ pas-hi a-
10 -vū **Muhunnaru**
11 **Mirisipiṭi-ve-**
12 **-herä Saṅg-radū-**
13 **-n pirivenaṭ**
14 vadāḷa **ek-tä-**
15 -n-samiyen
16 Mekāppar-vä-
17 -dārum ka .. ..
18 **Maṅgalarad Se-**

C.

1 **-nu** varä vana **Va-**
2 .. .. **rā Gaṇayi-**
3 **-m** isā **Manita-**
4 [-lā **Ki**]**liyim** i-
5 [-sā mahale] .. ..
6 .. .. **Rak-sama-**
7 **-ṇan** varä vana
8 **Kuḍasalā** .. ..
9 .. .. isā metu-
10 -vāk denamo va-
11 -dāḷa ek-tän-
12 samiyen me a-
13 -ttāṇi-kaṇu pä-
14 -rähär denu la-
15 -di väri perenāṭ-
16 -ṭiyam .. .. ..
17 .. ..
18 .. ..
19 nā koṭ isā ma-
20 -giva pegiva no-
21 vadnā koṭ i-
22 **-sā rad-kol-kä-**

D.

1 -miyan no-vad-
2 -nā koṭ isā de-
3 ruvanä dekam-tä-
4 -n no-vadnā ko-
5 -ṭ isā piyo-vadā-
6 -rannan no-vadnā
7 koṭ isā gam-go-
8 -n kir-geri no-gan-
9 -nā koṭ isā.

---

[1] Probably a clerical error for *mala-maḍulu*, see above, p. 181.

[2] *Siri-bhoga* is evidently written in error for *piribhoga* or *paribhoga*. In the corresponding passage of the Tiṁbirivāva pillar-inscription, occurs the word *piribo* (see *E. Z.*, Vol. II, p. 12) and the Colombo Museum Pillar-inscription of Kassapa IV has *piribhoga* (*E. Z.*, Vol. III, p. 273).

Malaganē Pillar-Inscription

Scale about 1½ inches to 1 foot

TRANSLATION.

Hail! On the tenth day of the waxing moon in the month of Poson [1] in the tenth year of the raising of the umbrella [of dominion] by the great king **Abhā** [2] who secured for himself the sole dominion over the Ruhuṇu [3] Province and Mala [4] District, and the enjoyment of the prosperity [5] [thereof], who is the .... of the great king **Abhā Sirisaṅgbo** [6], descended from the lineage of king Okāvas [7], the pinnacle of the very illustrious *kṣatriya* race, and who is, by right of descent, the lord of the young damsel, the land of Lakdiv [8].

In accordance with the decree delivered in assembly (*ek-tän-samiya*) [9] touching the **Saṅgradūn Pirivena** [10] of the **Mirisipiṭi** [11] monastery at **Muhunnaru,** included in the Southern Quarter, I **Va .. .. Gaṇaya** and I, **Manitalā Kili,** [both] in the service of **Maṅgalrad Senu** [12], the Commander of the Bodyguard, and I, **Kuḍasalā .. .. ..** in the service of .. .. .. **Raksamaṇa,** the Chief Secretary —we, the aforesaid persons—have granted the immunities [recorded on] this *attaṇi*-pillar [13], in accordance with the decree delivered in assembly (*ek-tän-samiya*).

---

[1] Skt. *Puṣya* or *Pauṣa*, May-June.

[2] P. and Skt. *Abhaya*.

[3] *Ruhuṇu* = P. and Skt. *Rohaṇa*. This was the name of the principality which comprised the southern and eastern parts of Ceylon.

[4] Malaya, the central mountain region of Ceylon, which was often under a separate ruler.

[5] The above translation is offered on the assumption that *siribhoga*, occurring in the text, is correct. If, however, it be taken as an error for *piribhoga*, the translation may be altered to 'who secured for himself the possession, under his sole dominion, of the Ruhuṇu Province and the Mala District'.

[6] P. *Abhaya Sirisaṅghabodhi*.

[7] P. *Okkāka*, Skt. *Ikṣvāku*.

[8] Skt. *Lāṅkā-dvīpa*.

[9] For Dr. Wickremasinghe's interpretation of the term *ek-tän-samiya* and its tentative rendering adopted hitherto by me, see *E. Z.*, Vol. III, pp. 107–108. But a consideration of the expressions *himi-ge ek-tän koṭ* occurring in an inscription at Rāssahela (see above, p. 171) and *hāt-pasä sam-jarvan ek-tän koṭ* in the Viyaulpata pillar-inscription (above, pp. 177–8) coupled with the analogy in the case of the procedure adopted in proclaiming royal orders granting privileges to religious institutions, afforded by South Indian records, which we have noted in discussing the second phrase quoted above, makes it necessary to modify the tentative rendering of 'decree of unanimous assent' previously adopted by me. *Ek-tän-samiya* doubtless signifies the assembling together of the dignitaries on the occasion of the delivering of an order by the king or heir-apparent. *Ek-tän* may therefore mean 'one place' and *samiya* be equivalent to Skt. *samūha* or *samiti*. The word is often used with a technical meaning to denote an order delivered in the midst of the assembled dignitaries. In those places where it has the force of an adverbial phrase, as in the expression *ek-tän-samiyen vadāḷen*, it may be rendered 'as commanded in the midst of [the dignitaries] assembled together'.

[10] *Saṅg* is equivalent to P. *Saṅghā* and *radū* to P. *rājadhītu*. *Pirivena* is P. *pariveṇa*.

[11] P. *Maricapiṭṭhi*. There was a Maricavaṭṭi *stūpa* and monastery at Anurādhapura.

[12] P. *Maṅgala-rāja Sena*.

[13] See above, p. 66, n. 3.

[It is enacted] that [this *pirivena*] is not to be entered by *väri*[1], *perenäṭṭiyam*[2], ... not to be entered by *magiva* and *pegiva*[3], not to be entered by the officers of the royal household, not to be entered by the functionaries of *deruvana* and *dekam-tän*[4], not to be entered by *piyo-vadäranunan*[5], and that village oxen and milk cows shall not be impressed [for service].

No. 23. INSCRIPTION ON A PILLAR FRAGMENT AT THE GONNĀVA DĒVĀLE.

By S. PARANAVITANA.

THE upper half of an inscribed pillar[6], said to have been found in a land named Malhēna or Polgasyāya, is now lying in the *maṇḍapa* of the modern *dēvāle* at Gonnāva in the Dēvamädi Kōraḷē of the Kuruṇägala District. The sides of the pillar measure 11 in. and $8\frac{1}{2}$ in. in width, and the height of the preserved fragment is 3 ft. 6 in. The letters, ranging in size from 1 to $1\frac{1}{2}$ in., are written, as usual in the mediaeval pillar-inscriptions of Ceylon, between horizontal lines which, in this case, are $2\frac{1}{2}$ in. apart from one another. Sixteen lines of writing are preserved on each of the sides A, B, and C. Side D has only two lines, but it also contains the engravings of various symbols, to wit, two concentric circles, the inner of which is divided into quadrants by straight lines at right angles to each other, a semicircle and the symbol usually described as representing a monk's fan. The writing on the remaining fragment of the pillar is in a good state of preservation, but for a few letters on side C which are somewhat indistinct.

The script is Sinhalese of the early part of the tenth century. A point worthy of note is the occurrence, in l. B 7, of the cerebral *ṣ*, which is rarely met with in mediaeval Sinhalese records. The form of *ka* found in this document is of an earlier type than that met with in other known inscriptions of either of the two kings to whom it can be assigned. The orthography and grammar call for no remarks; but it may be worth mentioning that the record contains

---

[1] See *E. Z.*, Vol. I, p. 53, n. 7.

[2] See *E. Z.*, Vol. III, p. 144.

[3] For these two words, see *E. Z.*, Vol. III, p. 146.

[4] For *deruvana* and *dekam-tän*, see *E. Z.*, Vol. III, p. 143.

[5] See *E. Z.*, Vol. III, p. 110.

[6] *A. S. I.*, No. 718. See *C. J. Sc.*, *G*, vol. ii, p. 221.

certain words and phrases not met with in other documents of the period. Attention may also be drawn to the form *mahāpāṇan* (A 5–6) which corresponds to *mahapāṇan* in other records of the period.

The epigraph is **dated** in the eighth year of a king referred to by his throne name of **Abhā Salamevan** and contains a decree of the heir-apparent **Udā** (Udaya) granting immunities to a *pamuṇu* land belonging to a person named **Agbo Mugayin Varadāṇa.** There were two Sinhalese kings of the tenth century who, according to the order of succession, were entitled to the throne name (*viruda*) of Abhā Salamevan and who also had princes named Udaya as heirs-apparent. These were **Dappula IV (V)** (*circa* 918–930) and **Sena III** (*circa* 933–942) both of whom enjoyed reigns exceeding eight years in duration [1]. There is no evidence by means of which we can decide which of these two sovereigns was the ruler in whose reign the edict was issued. As the two reigns were separated by an interval of only three years, palaeography is of no help in arriving at a decision on this point.

Varadaṇan, occurring in the name of the grantee, requires some comment. *Varada*, the basic form of the word, is the Sinhalese equivalent of Skt. and P. *yuvaraja*. It is therefore reasonable to conclude that the grantee was a prince who had the title of *yuvarāja*. He was the recipient of privileges in a decree issued by the *mahapā* (P. *mahādipāda*); hence, *mahapā* and *yuvarāja* were titles or offices which were distinct one from the other, the former being the higher of the two [2].

The land to which immunities were granted by this edict is said to have been included in a territorial division called **Maha-miṇilā-bim.** Assuming that the pillar was found at its original site, we may infer that the modern village of Gonnāva and the neighbouring tracts were in the ancient district of Maha-miṇilā. This geographical name has not been found elsewhere, and we are not in a position to determine how far the boundaries of the district extended. **Maha-vehera,** mentioned in this record, is obviously the same as the well-known **Mahā-vihāra,** which was the head-quarters of the orthodox Theravādins, at Anurādhapura.

---

[1] Dappula IV (V) is given this title in the Vessagiriya Slab Inscription No. 1 (*E. Z.*, Vol. I, p. 25). As the two titles Sirisaṅgbo and Abhā Salamevan were used alternately by the mediaeval kings of Ceylon (see *E. Z.*, Vol. II, p. 9), and as Sena III succeeded Udaya II who was a Sirisaṅgbo (*E. Z.*, Vol. III, p. 141), he was entitled to the *viruda* of Abhā Salamevan.

[2] For the titles *yuvarāja*, *uparāja* and *mahādipāda*, see Prof. Geiger in the *Journal of the Greater India Society*, vol. ii, pp. 103 ff.

TEXT

A.

1 අභා සලමෙව
2 ණ් මපුර්මූකා අ
3 ටවන්නෙ බැගෑ
4 පුර දසවක් දව
5 ස් ලද මහාසෑණ
6 ණ් වහන්සෙ ම
7 හවෙහෙර ඇත්
8 වෙහෙරට කැරෑ
9 ණු හසැ කිරිඅ
10 මුණොබා දී වළ
11 ඇනු කොට අ[ග්]
12 බො පුගයින් ව
13 රදුණන්ට ගෙ
14 විහයින් පම
15 ණු කොට වදළ
16 මහමිණ්ලැබි
17 (මිගි ආවු) .. .. ..

* * * * * *

B.

1 ල්නා බොසන්
2 දෙමුන් වර ව
3 න කිලිග් දෙව්
4 සල්දෙවිම් ඉ
5 සා මහාලෙ අ
6 ග්බොසා රජ්
7 සමණන් වර
8 වත ශුඩිස
9 ලා දෙමු ඇතු
10 ළු වැ මෙතුවාක්
11 දෙනමො එක්සෙ
12 වැ මෙකුළියැ
13 ආවු තාක් තැ
14 නට වැරි පෙරෙ
15 නාවටු නොව
16 දනා කොට ඉ
17 (සා) .. ..

* * * * * *

C.

1 සා පු(ද) සුත්වන්
2 සුවර් මහවර් නොන
3 න්නා කොට ඉසා තු
4 ඩියැ සොළියැ ග
5 සා නොවදනා කොට
6 ඉසා මිනී කොටා ව
7 න්නත් මෙගැමිනි ලා
8 නොගන්නා කොට ඉ
9 සා දෙරුවිනැ නොව
10 දනා කොට ඉසා බ
11 ලන් රහැණැ ගසා
12 නොවදනා කොට ඉ
13 සා කුඩසලා යහ
14 න්ගොඩුවන් නොවද
15 නා කොට ඉසා දෙලො
16 ස්මහවෑතැන් සු

* * * * * *

D.

1 කොට ඊය දෙ
2 නු ඉසා සි

Pālanoṭṭai Slab-Inscription

Scale about [illegible] inches to 1 foot

Gonnāva Dēvāle Pillar-Inscription

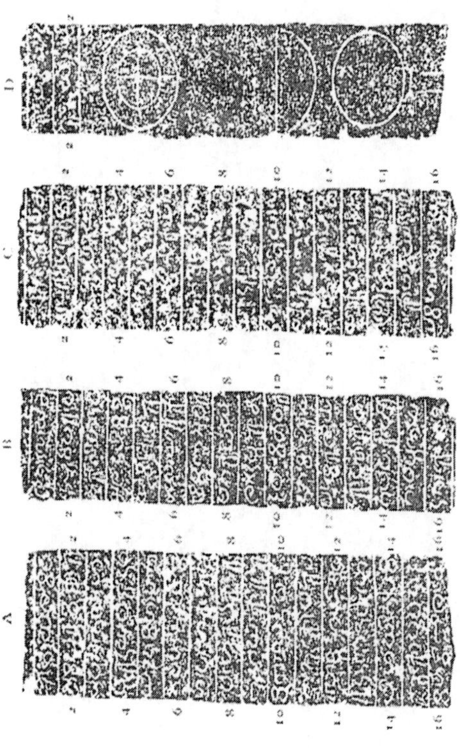

Scale about [illegible] inches to 1 foot

TRANSCRIPT.

A.

1 **Abhā Salameva-**
2 **-n** mapurmukā a-
3 -ṭ-vanne Bägä
4 pura dasavak dava-
5 -s **Udā Mahāpäṇa-**
6 **-n** vahanse **Ma-**
7 **-ha-veherä** ät-
8 veheraṭ käru-
9 -ṇu hasä kiri-a-
10 -muṇā-bā dī vaḷa-
11 -ndanu koṭa **A[g]-**
12 **-bo Mugayin Va-**
13 **-radāṇanṭa** ge-
14 -ṭi-hasin pama-
15 -ṇu koṭa vadāḷa
16 **Maha-miṇilā-bi-**
17 **(-mhi** ävū) .. .. ..

* * * * * *

B.

1 **-lnā Bosat-**
2 **deṭun** varä va-
3 -na **Kiliṅg Devi-**
4 **-yal-deṭim** i-
5 -sā mahāle **A-**
6 **-gboyā Rak-**
7 **-ṣamaṇan** varä
8 vana **Kuḍsa-**
9 **-lā Devu** ätu-
10 -ḷ vä me-tuvāk
11 denamo ek-se
12 vä me-kuliyä
13 āvū tāk tä-
14 -naṭa väri pere-
15 -nāṭṭu no-va-
16 -danā koṭ i-
17 -(sā) .. ..

* * * * * *

C.

1 -sā pu(da) sutvat
2 suvar mahavar no-ga-
3 -nnā koṭ isā tu-
4 -ḍiyä soḷiyä ga-
5 -sā no-vadanā koṭ
6 isā mini koṭā va-
7 -nnan me-gämhi lā
8 no-gannā koṭ i-
9 -sā deruvanä no-va-
10 -danā koṭ isā ba-
11 -lat rähäṇä gasā
12 no-vadanā koṭ i-
13 -sā kuḍasalā yaha-
14 -n-govuvan no-vada-
15 -nā koṭ isā doḷo-
16 -s-maha-vā-tan su-

* * * * *

D.

1 koṭ diya de-
2 -nu isā yi

TRANSLATION.

On the tenth day of the waxing moon in [the month of] Baga[1] in the eighth year of His Majesty **Abhā Salamevan** ...... in the **Maha-miṇilā District,** which was assigned, by means of the *geṭi* seal[2], by His Highness **Udā Mahapā,** as a *pamaṇu*[3] [land] to **Agbo Mugayin Varadāṇa,** so that it may be possessed on condition that a share [consisting] of one *amuṇa* [of paddy] for one *kiri* [of field][4] at each harvest gathered[5] be given to the Inner Monastery[6] of the **Mahā-vihāra**[7] ...... We, the aforesaid persons including **Kiliṅg Dēviyal-deṭu,** in the service of[8] .... **Inā Bosat-deṭu** and **Kuḍsalā**[9] **Devu,** in the service of **Agboyā Rakṣamaṇa,** the Chief Secretary, conjointly [order] that, regarding all lands included in this *kulíya*[10], they should not be entered by *väri*[11] and *perenäḷu*[12],

[1] March–April. Skt. *Caitra.*

[2] *Geṭi-hasin pamaṇu kaṭ*: The same expression occurs in the Nāgama Pillar-Inscription, ll. A 10–12 (*E. Z.*, II, p. 17), but has, however, been somewhat differently read by Dr. Wickremasinghe. It seems to state that the seal named *geṭi-hasa* was used in sealing the document granting the *pamaṇu* lands. *Hasa* means 'seal' and occurs frequently in epigraphy as well as in literature. There is no possibility of even a conjecture regarding the meaning of *geṭi*.

[3] For this word, see *E. Z.*, Vol. II, p. 19, n. 3.

[4] *Kiri-amuṇā-bā*: This expression which is also found in the Daḷadāgē inscription, l. 10 (*E. Z.*, Vol. I, p. 117), is etymologically the same as *karihaminiya-baka* which occurs in an inscription of about the second century at a place called Mōlāhiṭiyavelēgala near Diṁbulāgala in the Tamankaḍuva District. Mr. Bell, who has edited that record (*Ca*, vol. iii, pp. 77–78), reads the phrase somewhat differently and his interpretation of it, given only tentatively, does not bring out its sense accurately.

[5] *Käruṇu hasä*: *Käruṇu*, lit. means 'has been done'; *hasa* is taken as equivalent to P. *sassa.*

[6] *Ät-vehera* = P. *anto-vihāra.*

[7] The famous monastic establishment at Anurādhapura, the seat of the orthodox Theravādins.

[8] For this tentative rendering of *varä*, see *E. Z.*, Vol. II, pp. 108–110.

[9] *Kuḍasalā*, occurring in this as well as in many other names of *dūtakas* mentioned in the mediaeval Sinhalese records, is apparently the title of an office. The officers who had this title seem to have been placed under the orders of the Chief Secretary (*mahalē*) who had also the title of Raksamaṇa. In this inscription the *kuḍasalā* are included among the officers whose entry is forbidden to the land to which the immunities were granted. It is not possible to determine exactly what the duties of the *kuḍasalā* were, but it may be useful to note that the word occurs in the following passage of the *Butsaraṇa* (edited by the Rev. W. Sorata, Colombo, 1931, p. 292), which gives a list of the functionaries in a royal palace: *Kuḍasalā balatun hā arakkämiyan kiliṅgun visin vaṇana lada ... rāja-mandirayehi.* In this passage, as well as in the inscriptions, *kuḍasalā* and *balat* are mentioned together.

[10] *Kulíya* is presumably a variant form of *kuliya*, for which see *E. Z.*, Vol. II, p. 142.

[11] For this word, the meaning of which is obscure, see *E. Z.*, Vol. I, p. 53, n. 7.

[12] *Perenäḷu*, which is often found together with *väri*, still remains obscure in meaning.

. . . . . . that gifts, toll dues [1], *suvar* and *mahavar* [2] should not be levied, that one shall not enter [this land] sounding *tuḍi* and *soḷi* [3] [drums], that those who have come after committing murder should not be arrested in this village, that *deruvanä* [4] shall not enter, that royal messengers shall not enter cracking whips [5], that *kuḍasalā* [6] and officers in charge of royal conveyances shall not enter, that . . . . . in the localities of the twelve great reservoirs [7] . . . . . . and that water should be given so as . . . . . .

No. 24. A TAMIL SLAB-INSCRIPTION FROM PĀLAMŌṬṬAI.

By S. PARANAVITANA.

THE subjoined inscription, which was discovered by the present writer in 1933, is engraved on a slab, measuring 2 ft. 10 in. by 1 ft. 4 in., found among the ruins of a Śaiva *kōvil* at a place named Pālamōṭṭai near Kantaḷāy [8] in the Trincomalee District of the Eastern Province [9]. The site is now overgrown with jungle and the remains of the temple are buried in an accumulation of debris. The shrine seems to have been mainly of brick construction, stone

[1] *Sut-vat*, an earlier form of *sum-vat*, also occurs in the Badulla Pillar-Inscription. See *E. Z.*, Vol. III, p. 76.

[2] *Suvar* and *mahavar* occur in the Īripinniyāva Pillar-Inscription. Dr. Wickremasinghe (*E. Z.*, I, p. 171) translates the two words as 'goldsmiths' and 'chief artisans'. The context in which the two words occur in this record makes it clear that they must have been some kinds of imposts remitted in the case of the lands to which the immunities were granted. As it occurs in juxtaposition with *mahavar*, we may conjecture that *suvar* is a contraction of *suḷuvar*, *maha* meaning 'great' or 'principal' and *suḷu* 'small' or 'secondary'. *Var.* (Skt. *vāra*) means 'turn' and may denote, in a secondary sense, the forced labour which was exacted from the peasants, at regular intervals or turns, in Sinhalese times. With these may also be compared the technical terms *kiri-var* and *tel-var* (*E. Z.*, III, p. 112) which literally mean 'milk-turn' and 'oil-turn'; but in practice must have denoted the levy exacted from each of the peasants, in his turn, of milk and oil. *Mahavar* may therefore be rendered as the 'principal turn (of service)' and *suvar* 'the secondary turn (of service)'

[3] For the interpretation of the two words *tuḍi* and *soḷi*, see *E. Z.*, Vol. III, pp. 146–147.

[4] See *E. Z.*, Vol. III, pp. 143–144.

[5] *Rähän gasā*: See *E. Z.*, Vol. III, p. 148.

[6] See above, p. 190, note 9.

[7] The expression *doḷos-maha-vä-tän* occurs in one or two other unpublished records of the tenth century. From these, it becomes clear that twelve of the largest among the innumerable reservoirs in ancient Ceylon were considered to be of special importance and were possibly under the care of a separate department of the administration. We have no means of finding out what these 'great reservoirs' were.

[8] Usually spelt 'Kantalai' on maps and in official publications.

[9] See *A. S. C. Annual Report for* 1933, p. 14.

being used only for the basement and the pillars. The architectural style of this ruined temple enables us to assign it to the Poḷonnaruva period—a conclusion which is confirmed by what we learn from the inscription. Among the ruins is to be seen the upper half of a mutilated stone image of Pārvatī.

The record is considerably weatherworn and some of the letters of lines 1–4, being much damaged, can be read only conjecturally. A few letters at the end of line 14 are completely illegible. The slab contains twenty-five lines of writing, incised between parallel lines drawn about $1\frac{1}{4}$ in. apart from one another. The letters, excluding those containing long vertical strokes such as *a*, *ka*, &c., are, on an average, $\frac{1}{2}$ in. in height.

The script is Tamil, with a fair proportion of Grantha letters, particularly in the proper names and words of Sanskritic origin in the first nine lines. The language, too, is Tamil and contains certain forms of words and phrases such as *nandavāṉam* (l. 12) and *nilappoli-y-ūṭṭukku* (ll. 12–13) which are not found in the literary, or the modern colloquial, idioms of that language but are common enough in South Indian Tamil inscriptions. In palaeography as well as in style, the record is in agreement with Tamil inscriptions of the eleventh and twelfth centuries found in South India.

Owing to the very bad state of preservation of the first three lines, considerable doubt exists as to the name of the king in whose regnal years the record is dated. In the preliminary account of the discovery of this inscription, included in the *Annual Report of the Archaeological Survey of Ceylon for 1933*, p. 14, I have tentatively taken the king's name as Jayabāhu and the regnal year as the eighth. In so doing I was influenced by the occurrence in the record of the name of Vikramabāhu as Vikkirama Calāmega, the use of the throne name Calāmega (P. *Silāmegha* or *Abhaya Silamegha*) suggesting that that prince had already assumed ruling powers after the death of his father. The dating of records issued in the reign of Vikramabāhu in the regnal years of his predecessor Jayabāhu is known from several other epigraphs [1].

Mr. K. V. Subrahmanya Aiyer, however, the former Superintendent for Epigraphy in the Indian Archaeological Survey, whose knowledge of Tamil epigraphy is probably unrivalled and to whom I had the good fortune to show an estampage of this inscription, is of opinion that what is now left of lines 2 and 3 warrants the reading of the royal name as 'Vijayabāhu', rather than as 'Jayabāhu', and that the regnal year, given in figures, is undoubtedly 42.

---

[1] See *E. Z.*, Vol. II, pp. 200–202, Vol. III, p. 304.

The symbols for 42 are fairly clear on the estampage and if the regnal year be read as such, the epigraph should date from the reign of **Vijayabāhu I** (1058-1114). For this reason, and also because I am influenced by the regard which must naturally be paid to the opinion of Mr. Subrahmanya Aiyer, I have adopted his reading of the king's name and the regnal year. On the other hand, it must be pointed out that in the 42nd year of Vijayabāhu, Vikramabāhu had possibly not yet become the heir-presumptive; and in that case it would seem strange to find him referred to by the throne name Calāmega. No similar instance has yet been found elsewhere. If the record was dated in a regnal year of Jayabāhu, then Vikramabāhu was the actual ruler of the northern part of the island when this inscription was indited, and it would be perfectly natural for a regiment to be named after him, as it is in this record, and for his personal name to have the throne name appended to it.

The **object** of the record is to register donations to the god Śiva in the temple named **Teṉ-Kailāsam** (the Southern Kailāsam) at Kantaḷāy, by a Brahmin lady named **Nāgaiccāṉi**, in memory of her husband. The epigraph also informs us that the shrine had the surname of **Vijayarāja Īśvaram** and that Kantaḷāy was also called **Vijayarāja Caturvedimaṅgalam.** The term 'Caturvedimaṅgalam' is of frequent occurrence in South Indian inscriptions and is appended to the names of villages inhabited by Brahmins [1]. As it was called Vijayarāja Caturvedimaṅgalam, Kantaḷāy at that time must have had a colony of Brahmins who lived there under the protection of Vijayabāhu I. The place kept its character as a seat of Brahmins for at least a century longer, for we read in an inscription of Niśśaṁka Malla found there [2] that it was then named Caturveda-Brahmapura and that an alms-hall called Pārvatī-satra was maintained there by that monarch. Probably Kantaḷāy became a centre of Hindu influence during the period of Coḷa rule in the eleventh century; and the Sinhalese kings who succeeded the Coḷas maintained the Brahmins and patronized their shrines. The Śaiva shrine at Kantaḷāy, since it was called Vijayarāja Īśvaram, must have been founded by Vijayabāhu I, or at least under his patronage. The chronicles, and the inscriptions of Vijayabāhu so far brought to light, represent that monarch as a great patron of Buddhism, who exerted all his power to raise that religion from the degraded position to which it had sunk during the period of Coḷa dominance. But his zeal for Buddhism did not, as shown by this record,

---

[1] See K. A. Nilakanta Sastri, *Studies in Coḷa History and Administration*, p. 77.

[2] *E.Z.*, Vol. II, pp. 283-290.

prevent him from extending his patronage to such other faiths as were prevalent among his subjects.

In order to ensure the maintenance, without any hindrance, of the charitable endowment registered in this record, it was given the name of **Śrī Vikkirama-Calāmega-t-terinda Vaḷaṅgai Veḷaikkāraṉ**, i.e., the selected left-hand Veḷaikkāra regiment of Śrī Vikkirama Calāmega. In other words, the charity was placed under the protection of that regiment. The practice of placing a religious institution and its endowments under the protection of a regiment like the Veḷaikkāras is not unknown from epigraphic records found in South India as well as in Ceylon [1]. The long Tamil inscription on the Quadrangle (Daḷadā Maḷuva) at Poḷonnaruva [2], dating some time after the death of Vijayabāhu I, states that the Temple of the Tooth was placed under the protection of the Veḷaikkāras. That record also enables us to learn many interesting facts about the constitution of the Veḷaikkāra forces. In my edition of that inscription [3] I have collected together the information that can be gathered from the *Mahāvaṃsa*, the Tamil literature, and South Indian and Ceylon epigraphy, concerning those mercenaries. The present record does not add anything more to what we already know about this military corporation.

TEXT.

1 Svasti Śrī [॥*] Ko-(c-**Ciri-Caṅgabodi**)-
2 **-varm**[**mar**⸗āṉa] uḍaiyār **Śrī** (**Vijayabā**)-
3 **-hu- devaṟkku** [4] yā[ṇḍu] 42 [āvadu] (**Kantaḷā**)-
4 **-y**⸗āṉa **Vijayarāja-caturvvedi-maṅgalattu** (**Teṉ**)-
5 **kaiḷāsam Śrī-Vijayarāja-Īśvaram-uḍaiyārk-**
6 **-ku** .. .. [5] irukkum brāhmaṇaṉ **Kārāmbac-**
7 **-ceṭṭu Yajñiyakramavittaṉ** dharmma-patni-y-ā-
8 -na [6] **Nāgaiccāṉi** taṉ bharttā-v-āṉa Yajñiyakramavittaṉ [ma]-
9 -ritta piṉbu avaṉai nōkki-c-ceyda dharmmam⸗āva[du] [॥*]
10 Aṟu-kaḷañcu-poṉṉāl muḍiyum mu-k-kaḷañcu-
11 poṉṉāl mālaiyum sandhi-viḷakk⸗o[ṉṟukku]
12 iṭṭa kācu ı m tiru-nandavāṉañ⸗ceyvāṉuk[ku ni]-

---

[1] See *Travancore Archaeological Series*, vol. iii, p. 35 and *E. Z.*, Vol. II, p. 247.

[2] See *E. Z.*, Vol, II, pp. 242–255.

[3] *Ep. Ind.*, vol. xviii, pp. 330–338.

[4] Read *dēvarkku*.

[5] The two symbols which are not recognizable and therefore left unread may possibly stand for a place name.

[6] Read *āṉa*.

13 -lappoli-y-ūṭṭukku iṭṭa kācu 8 m idil po[ṉ]
14 aḻivu cōrvukku iṭṭa kācu 1 m .. ..
15 aḻivu cōrvukku iṭṭa kācu 2 m [tē]va[r-a]-
16 diyār=āga-p-peṇḍugaḷ eḻuvarai-t-ta[lai-i]-
17 -laiccinai-y-iṭṭu ivargaḷukku ni[lai]-
18 poli-y-ūṭṭu nibandham=āga iṭṭa kācu 23 ā-
19 -ga mudal niṟka-p-poli-y-ūṭṭināl nilai-niba-
20 -ndhañ=celvaṉa-v-āga iṭṭa kācu 35 po-
21 -ṉ onbadiṉ-kaḻañcu [‖*] Ippaḍi ceyyappaṭṭa
22 i-d-dharmmam aḻivu vārāmal nilai-niṟuttu-
23 vār=āga **Śrī-Vikkirama-Calāmega-t-terinda Va[ḷa-**
24 **-ṅgai] Veḷaikkāṟan**[1]=eṉṟu tiru-nāmañ=cāt
25 -[2] tiyadu [‖*] Śrī [‖*]

TRANSLATION.

[Lines 1-9] Hail! Prosperity! In the (42nd) year of King **(Ciri-Caṅgabodi)**[3]-**varman** *alias* **Śrī (Vijayabā)hu-devar.** [The following are] the religious donations made to [the god] **Śrī-Vijayarāja Īśvaram-uḍaiyār** at [the shrine called] **(Teṉ)-Kaiḷāsam** in **Kantaḷāy** *alias* **Vijayarāja-Caturvvedi-maṅgalam** by **Nāgaiccāni,** the wife of the Brāhmaṇa **Kārāmbacceṭṭu Yajñiyakrama-vittaṉ**[4], residing at . . . . ., after the death of her husband Yajñiyakramavittaṉ, and in his memory[5]:—

[Lines 9-21] A crown of six *kaḻañcus*[6] of gold; a necklace of three *kaḻañcus* of gold; 1 *kācu*[7] granted for one evening lamp; 8 *kācu* granted so that its interest may be secured permanently for the benefit of the person who maintains the sacred flower garden; 1 *kācu* granted for the purpose of making up any loss to this gold; 2 *kācu* granted for the purpose of making up any loss . . . . . . having placed fore-head marks on seven females (dedicating them) as dancing girls of the god, 23 *kācu* were deposited as an endowment, so that the interest

---

[1] Read °*kāraṉ*.

[2] A *Śrī* occurs here at the beginning of the line, possibly written to balance with *Śrī* at the end of the line.

[3] P. *Siri Saṅghabodhi*, the throne name adopted alternatively with *Silāmeghavaṇṇa* by the mediaeval kings of Ceylon. See *E. Z.*, Vol. II, p. 9.

[4] *Kārāmbacceṭṭu* is evidently a place name and is found prefixed to the names of Brāhmaṇas occurring in South Indian inscriptions. *Kramavittaṉ* is also a title often found in such names.

[5] *Avaṉai nōkki*: Literally, 'having considered him'.

[6] See *E. Z.*, Vol. III, p. 336, n. 6.

[7] *Ibid.*, p. 311, n. 3.

may be secured permanently for their benefit. Thus 35 *kācu* and nine *kaḻañcus* of gold have been granted so that the perpetual endowments may continue from what is accrued as interest, the capital remaining unspent.

[Lines 21–25] In order that this charity, performed in this manner, may continue without any loss, the glorious name of the **Veḷaikkāras** of the Left-hand, (composed of) the selected (troops) of Śrī Vikkirama-Calāmega [1], is given to it. Prosperity!

No. 25. GALAPĀTA VIHĀRA ROCK-INSCRIPTION.

By S. PARANAVITANA.

THIS inscription is engraved on a rock by the side of the flight of steps leading to the shrines and monastic buildings at the Galapāta Vihāra, situated about two miles south-west of the Rest House at Bentoṭa in the Valallāviṭi Kōraḷē of the Southern Province. As the inscription itself testifies, Galapāta Vihāra is a foundation of the twelfth century, or the thirteenth if the record be attributed to the reign of Parākramabāhu II and not to the first king of that name. This *vihāra*, along with other Buddhist shrines on the western sea-board, must have suffered from Portuguese vandalism. A modern *vihāra* has been founded on the site during the last century and very few remains of the mediaeval monastic establishment are to be seen there now. A carved door-frame preserved on the site has been removed, some time ago, from the ruins of a Hindu shrine in a neighbouring village [2].

The inscription covers a rock surface measuring 11 ft. 9 in. by 5 ft., and consists of twenty-eight lines of writing which are separated by parallel horizontal lines engraved two inches apart from one another. The average size of the **letters** is $1\frac{1}{2}$ in. The record has weathered considerably, particularly towards the end. There are consequently a number of lacunae in the text given below; but they occur, for the most part, in the long list of temple slaves, and in the portion of the document containing the names of witnesses; and do not, therefore, prevent us from getting a reasonably clear idea of the contents of the epigraph as a whole.

This inscription is No. 165 in Müller's *A. I. C.* Dr. Müller gives neither the

[1] P. *Silāmegha*, Sin. *Salamevan*, the throne name of Vikramabāhu I.

[2] For an account of the Galapāta Vihāra, see *Ceylon Antiquary and Literary Register*, vol. vi, pp. 40–43.

text nor the translation of the record but states that 'it gives an account of the repairs which King **Parākramabāhu of Daṁbadeṇiya** executed at this temple, having heard that the dāgoba attached to it contained a relic of Mahā Kassapa the first hierarch of Buddhism'[1]. What Dr. Müller says of the contents of the record is, as will be seen from the translation given below, not exactly correct. In fact, it does not seem as if he had personally studied the record with any care. He seems to have contented himself with reporting what he was told by the people of the place about the contents of the inscription. The Buddhist monks of the modern Galapāta Vihāra, most of whom are well versed in Pāli and Sinhalese, are able to read the opening lines of the record, wherein the name of a king Parākramabāhu occurs. From the *Mahavaṁsa* they are aware of the fact that Parākramabāhu II of Daṁbadeṇiya was responsible for some works of religious merit at a *vihāra* in Bentoṭa, and they have therefore assumed that the inscription records this event. I myself, when I went to the place to re-copy the inscription, was told the same story.

An article on this inscription giving its text and translation (excluding lines 15 to 22, which contain the names of slaves dedicated to the temple) has been published by Mr. H. C. P. Bell[2]. That distinguished archaeologist, too, has assumed that king Parākramabāhu of this inscription is the second of that name and moreover states, without giving any reason therefor, that **Demaḷa-adhikāra Kahambalkuḷu Mindal** (Mahendra) who, according to the record, was the founder and benefactor of the Galapāta Vihāra, is identical with **Deva Patirāja** of the Dunukēvatu family, who is stated in the chronicles to have planted an orchard and carried out other works of public utility and religious merit in and around Bentoṭa at the behest of his royal master, Parākramabāhu II. But neither Dr. Müller nor Mr. Bell has critically examined this record to ascertain the identity of the king mentioned therein. They, as well as the Sinhalese pandits, have proceeded on the mere assumption that an inscription of a Parākramabāhu found at Galapāta Vihāra must be of Parākramabāhu II, since that monarch's name is connected in the chronicles with a religious establishment at Bentoṭa. It is therefore necessary to examine such evidence as we can find in the inscription to decide which of the many kings named **Parākramabāhu** is the ruler in whose **thirtieth year** this record is **dated.**

There were only three Parākramabāhus who enjoyed reigns of thirty years or more. Of these, the sixth of that name is out of the question, since the record

---

[1] *A. I. C.*, p. 71.

[2] *Ceylon Notes and Queries, R. A. S., C. B.*, July 1914, pp. lxix–lxxvii.

is written in a script which is much earlier in form than that of the inscriptions of that monarch. The Parākramabāhu of this record must, therefore, be either the first or the second, both of whom reigned for more than thirty years.

Palaeography cannot settle this question decisively. The script of our record does not materially differ from that of the Gal-vihāra rock-inscription of Parākramabāhu I, as may be seen by comparing the letters on Plate 21 with those of Plate 37 of *E.Z.*, Vol. II. But the interval between the two reigns was only 72 years; and this is too short a period within which to decide a date by depending only on the development of the script. It is a well-known fact that records, even those dating from the same reign, are sometimes found to contain scripts of different stages of development. The difficulty is further aggravated by the fact that inscriptions which can definitely be dated in the reign of Parākramabāhu II are very few[1]. In fact, there are only two of them, namely, an epigraph found at Yāpahuva dated in his twenty-ninth year and mentioning the regent Vijayabāhu and the prince Bhuvanaikabāhu[2], and another found at Anurādhapura, recording a grant by the king's younger brother Bhuvanaikabāhu Mahapā[3]. Of these two, the script of the Yāpahuva inscription deviates very little, if at all, from that of the records of the Poḷonnaruva period; but the Anurādhapura epigraph contains forms more developed than those found in the inscription under discussion. Thus on purely palaeographical grounds the Galapāta Vihāra inscription may be dated from the reign of Parākramabāhu I.

We may now examine the **contents** of the inscription to ascertain whether they furnish us with evidence to settle the date of the record. It states that a dignitary named **Mindal** (Mahendra) who held the office of **Demaḷa-adhikāra** and was administering the **Pasyodun** District, founded the **Galapāta Vihāra,** with the royal assent and with the co-operation of his mother, his nephews **Kodānāvan** of Miyaṅguṇubim and **Vijayānāvan** of Degalaturubim, and his kinsman **Kaṭuvitnā Sätumba** or **Devu.** The record also gives a long list of the lands and serfs granted to the temple by its founders and ends with the signatures of the donors and of the witnesses to the document.

Now it is difficult to believe that the works of religious merit mentioned in this inscription are the same as those which, according to the chronicles, were effected at Bentoṭa in the reign of Parākramabāhu II. As we have already

---

[1] There are a few records of an unidentified Parākramabāhu, for instance the inscriptions at Vaharakgoḍa (Bell, *Report on the Kegalla District*, pp. 82–83) which may possibly date from the reign of Parākramabāhu II.

[2] *A. S. C., A. R.* for 1911–12, p. 63.

[3] *E. Z.*, Vol. III, pp. 286–288.

mentioned, it was Deva Patirāja who carried out Parākramabāhu II's programme of meritorious works at Bentoṭa. And there are no valid grounds for assuming, as Mr. Bell has done, that Demaḷa-adhikāra Mindal of this record is the same as Deva Patirāja. 'Deva' and 'Mahinda' are two different names; and according to the *Attanagalu-vaṁsa* [1] Deva Patirāja was a scion of the Dunukēvatu family, whereas the family name of Mindal appears, from this record, to have been Kahambalkuḷu. In the thirtieth year of Parākramabāhu II, Deva Patirāja was, as is testified by the *Pujavalī* [2], the prime minister of the king; but in this record, which is dated in the thirtieth year of a Parākramabāhu, Kahambalkuḷu Mindal is referred to merely as the governor of the Pasyodun District, an officer lower in status than the prime minister. The other dignitaries figuring in this record are not mentioned in the accounts of the reign of Parākramabāhu II. The official titles such as Demaḷa-adhikāra, found in this document, are not known to have been in vogue in the Daṁbadeṇiya period, though of course we cannot definitely assert that they had then fallen into disuse.

The religious works of Parākramabāhu II and Deva Patirāja at Bentoṭa consisted of the celebration of a festival in honour of a reputed relic of Mahākassapa Thera, the laying out of fruit gardens, the construction of bridges, and gifts to the priesthood [3]. The present inscription, on the other hand, records the foundation of a monastery and shrines and their endowment. The religious works of Parākramabāhu II and Deva Patirāja have been described in great detail in the contemporary *Pūjāvalī* and *Cūḷavaṁsa* [4]; and if this king and his minister had really been instrumental in establishing and endowing a new monastery, the authors of these works, who missed no opportunity of glorifying the good deeds of these two personages, would not have contented themselves with stating that what the king, through his minister, effected, was only the usual type of benefaction to a religious establishment which was already in existence. When we consider the above facts, it becomes extremely doubtful whether this record is to be attributed to Parākramabāhu II.

Let us now consider whether there is evidence for assigning this epigraph to the reign of **Parākramabāhu I.** The chronicles do not mention a shrine at Bentoṭa as a work of that monarch; but it must be remembered that according

---

[1] Colombo edition of 1914, p. 45. [2] *Ibid*, 1922, p. 11.

[3] *Pūjāvalī*, 37th chapter, edited by B. Gunasekara, p. 44 and *Mahāvaṁsa*, chap. lxxxv, vv. 78–84 and chap. lxxxvi, vv. 16–17 and 44–47.

[4] *Mahāvaṁsa*, chap. lxxxv, vv. 78–84 and chap. lxxxvi, vv. 16–17 and 44–47.

to the record Galapāta Vihāra was not established by the king himself but by a local chief, though with the royal assent. Therefore, even if Galapāta Vihāra does date from the reign of Parākramabāhu I, it would not necessarily have been mentioned in the chronicle where the latter gives a list of that king's religious foundations.

The official title Demaḷa-adhikāra (P. *Damiḷādhikāri*) is known from the *Mahāvaṁsa*[1] to have been current in the reign of Parākramabāhu I; and names such as those of the dignitaries figuring in this epigraph were borne by personages who flourished in the reign of that monarch or in the decade or two which followed it. Three persons of the name of Mahinda are mentioned in the *Mahāvaṁsa* as having borne high office during the reign of Parākramabāhu I. Of these, one was a chieftain who fought on the side of Parākramabāhu I against Gajabāhu II in the civil war between these two princes[2]. The second, who had the title of Nagaragiri, was another general of Parākramabāhu I, and took part in the same campaign[3]. The third was a high dignitary who built a splendid shrine, for the Tooth Relic, at Poḷonnaruva[4]. It is not impossible that one of these Mahindas, towards the close of the reign of Parākramabāhu I, held the office of Demaḷa-adhikāra and was in charge of the Pasyodun District, and that he was identical with the Mahendra (Mahinda) of this epigraph.

Another of the donors in the present epigraph is named Vijayānāvan. In the Ruvanvälisāya inscription of Queen Kalyāṇavatī[5], which is twenty-one years later in date than the thirtieth year of Parākramabāhu I, a Vijayānāvan, who was the treasurer under a Parākramabāhu and other kings, is mentioned; but it is doubtful whether he was the same as the donor in the present record, for the family name of the Vijayānāvan of Kalyāṇavatī's inscription is given as Pirivatubim, whereas that of the Vijayānāvan of our record is Degalaturubim. Moreover, the Vijayānāvan of our inscription does not appear to have held the office of treasurer. In the Poḷonnaruva inscription of Vijayabāhu II, the successor of Parākramabāhu I, a high dignitary named Vijayā-yāntän-nāvan is mentioned[6]; and he may be identical with the Vijayānāvan of our record. *Yāntän* is the name of an office and according to the usage then prevailing it could have been added to the personal name of the dignitary if he had been appointed to that office. There is less likelihood that Kaṭuvitnā Devu of our inscription was the same as Koṭadanavu Deva of Kalyāṇavatī's record.

---

[1] Chap. lxxv, v. 117 and chap. lxxvi, v. 39.
[2] *Mv.*, chap. lxix, v. 13.
[3] *Ibid*, chap. lxx, vv. 89, 146, and 158.
[4] *Ibid.*, chap. lxxiii, v. 128.
[5] *J. R. A. S.*, C. B., vol. vii, p. 183.
[6] *E. Z.*, Vol. II, p. 184.

The inscription mentions a locality, near Galapāta Vihāra, named Niśśaṁka-gala; and it is possible that this place got its name from King Niśśaṁka Malla, who ascended the throne a year after the death of Parākramabāhu I, and whose connexion with Bentoṭa is attested by the chronicles[1]. This fact may perhaps be adduced as evidence against assigning the record to the reign of Parākrama-bāhu I. But one cannot be quite certain that the locality in question was not so named after some other personage called Niśśaṁka. It is also not unlikely that Niśśaṁka Malla, who hailed from Kāliṅga, was living in Ceylon towards the close of the reign of Parākramabāhu I; and a place may well have been named after him in the thirtieth year of that reign.

Taking all the facts into consideration, there is more reason for assigning this record to the reign of Parākramabāhu I than to that of the second; though it must be admitted that there is no evidence of a really decisive nature on this point.

The **historical information** supplied by this long epigraph is scanty, for the greater part of the document consists of a bare list of the lands and serfs dedicated to the monastery. In the text published by Mr. Bell that portion of the record containing the names of temple slaves has been purposely omitted as of no interest now-a-days. I have, however, included this portion, not only in order to have the complete text of the inscription, so far as it can be made out, but also because it tells us what the names of humble folk in Ceylon were like in the twelfth or thirteenth century. As Mr. Bell has observed, this is the only Sinhalese inscription giving a list of temple slaves. Some of the names of these slaves are Tamil or of Tamil origin; but no one who is familiar with the names of Sinhalese people to-day would, on that account, assume that the bearers of these Tamil names were Tamils by nationality.

As to the **geographical names** occurring in the record, Pasyodun-vaga is the modern Pasdun Kōraḷē and is mentioned in the *Mahāvaṁsa* as Pañcayojana-raṭṭha[2]. The chronicle also refers to Bentoṭa as a place which was within the limits of the Pañcayojana or Pasyodun District[3] in the reign of Parākrama-

[1] *Mv.*, chap. lxxxvi, v. 16 and *Pūjāvaliya*, *op. cit.*, p. 43.

[2] *Mv.*, chap. lvii, v. 71; chap. lxi, v. 35; chap. lxviii, v. 51; chap. lxxii, v. 57; chap. lxxv, v. 21; and chap. lxxxv, v. 81. The Pāli *pañcayojana* is a translation of S. *pas-yodun* and means 'five *yojanas*' (leagues). Possibly the district got its name from its extent. *Vaga* is P. *vagga* and names of districts ending in this word are found in the *Mahāvaṁsa*, e.g. Doṇi-vagga (chap. lxxv, v. 69) and Majjhima-vagga (chap. lxx, v. 21).

[3] *Mv.*, chap. lxxxv, v. 81.

bāhu II; but at present it is just outside the southern boundary of Pasdun Kōraḷē. Miyaṅguṇu is Mahiyaṅgaṇa of the chronicles, the modern Alutnuvara in the Ūva Province. Degalaturu is phonetically equivalent to Degaldoruva, but it cannot be ascertained whether it is the same as the place bearing that name near Kandy. Some of the names of localities in and around Bentoṭa figuring in this epigraph, are still known by the same, or similar, names. Mr. Bell has pointed out that Ṭiṅgavaṭu, Tiratenayāvatta, Boltuḍāva, and Niśśaṁkagala are known to-day as Timbavaṭuva or Timboṭuva, Tiritenayā-vatta, Boltuḍāva, and Nissaṅgala, respectively. The modern Kasagaltoṭa corresponds to Kasagalgoḍa of this inscription. Kakuḷuvāgala is probably the modern Käkulāgala and the Kaḷapuva (lagoon) is still known by the same name.

Velgammuḷa, the monastic institution to which the newly founded Galapāta Vihāra belonged, is possibly the same as Vilgammuḷa which, in the mediaeval period of Ceylon history, was an important college of monks [1]. Dharmarājan Pirivena is not known from other sources. Galapāta Vihāra is referred to, in the opening Sanskrit *śloka*, as Śailāntāyatana. This was an important religious establishment in the fifteenth century and the fame of the abbot who was at its head in the reign of Parākramabāhu VI has been sung by the Bengali Brahmin Rāmachandra Bhāratī in the Sanskrit poem *Vṛttamālā* [2].

The record opens with a Sanskrit *śloka* in the *Śārdūlavikrīḍita* metre; the rest of the document is in Sinhalese prose. Noteworthy words occurring in the document are *kaṭuvitnā* (l. 3), *sī-parapurā vä* (l. 5), and *koḷavel-aya* (l. 6). *Vidhi* in l. 8 is possibly an error for *vīdi* and *śāttunāvan* in l. 6 is incorrectly written with a palatal *ś*. In certain words occurring in this record, short vowels are substituted for long ones used in the standard forms; compare, for example, *vahanse* (l. 3), *nä* (l. 3), *mābo* (l. 4), *varundäla* (l. 5), *päḷa* (l. 7), *kere* (l. 11), and *me* (l. 12), which occur in literary works as *vahansē*, *nǟ*, *mābō*, *varundǟḷā*, *pǟḷa*, *kerē*, and *mē*, respectively. The forms *dagap* (l. 4), *pirivana* (l. 4), and *parilden* (l. 13), of which the usual forms are *dagäb*, *pirivena*, and *paridden*, are also noteworthy. In l. 8 occurs the form *ḥindavū*, which agrees with the standard usage, while in the same line and in l. 10 occur the variant forms, *hinduvu* and *hindivū*, of the same word. The style has a general resemblance to that of the documents dating from the Poḷonnaruva period.

---

[1] For this college of monks, see above, p. 86.

[2] Edited by the late Pandit Batuvantudave, 5th edition, Colombo, 1928.

TEXT.

1 ත්‍රිංශෙ භූමිභුජඃ **පරාක්‍රමභුජ[ස්‍යා]**බ්දෙ තදූර්ද්ධගත
ශුද්ධාචාරදධාධිකාරිවිභුනා නාම්නා **මංගලෙනාණි** තු [।*]
උත්තුංගාබ්ධිසසම්භවෙන විදුෂා කාන්තාය [සත්‍යාන්විනා]
ශෛලාගනායත[නාය දත්තවිච්ඡි]ත්‍යාමාදිසංබොධා[ච්‍ය]තෙ [॥*]
2 සිරිසඟබො **පරාක්‍රමබාහු** චක්‍රවර්ත්තිස්වාමීන්වහන්සෙට තිස්වනු වෙසගැ
පුර පොහොයැ පස්ලොදුන්විග කාරිය කොටැ සිටි දෙමළ[අධිකාර
කහඹල්කුළු මිඤල්]නා විජිහ අප හා අපගේ මෑ
3 ණියන් වහන්සෙ හා අපගේ බෑන මියගුණුකිම් **කොදනාවන්** හා දෙග
ලතුරුකිම් **විජයානාවන්** හා අපගේ නෑ **කවුම්ත්නා සෑතුමබ** හා .. .. ..
.. .. වූත් වෙල්ග
4 මිවුළට බද ච සධර්ම්මරාජත්පිරිවනට ඇතුළත් කොටැ රාජසම්මත ඇති වැ
දුගප් මාබො පිළිම පිහිටුවා අප කැරවූ **ගල්පාහාවිහාරයම** .. ..
කොටැ මෙමැ විහාර
5 යෙහි වැඩැ හිඳිනා වහන්සෙව්රුන්දූට ප්‍රත්‍යය පිණිසැ හා ලූ අප සිපරපු
රැ වැ වළඳ අ සියඹලාපය හා මෙහි මැ බද වියළ තැනු සුඹුළුපත්
හැල්ල ඇතු
6 ළුවූ තැනැ කුඹුරු හා මෙහි පොල් පුවක් ඇතුළුවූ කොළවෙල්අය කුස
ලාත් කොටැ හා කුත්රාමාශාතතුනාවත්ට රන් දිලා ගත් බෙම්තොටැ
නාවලඹට ඇතුළත් විගවටු
7 නාගයෙන් විහාරයට පැදුම්දිගින් කුඹුක් හිඳිවූ පොකුණ හා දකුණුදිගින්
කළපුව හා පැළදිගින් උඩයාදශපාලයන්ගේ චතුබඩැ පොකුණ හා
උතුරුදිගින් නම්සෙට්ටි
8 හිඳුවූ පොල්වතුභාගයෙහි වීඩි මහහිම් කොටැ මෙ අතුරෙහි කොළවෙල්
හා මෙහි බද කුඹුරු හා කෙවුළු මණකප්පම්බරාය[රු]ට විහාරයෙන්
රන් දිලා ගෙනැ පොල් පුවක් හිඳුවූ
9 මූඤල්කැමියා හුත් තිරතෙනයා[වත්ත] හා ඉසම්විටිවත්ත හා ඈවෙරියා
හුත් බෙරවාගමැ පනැස්පොල්වත්ත හා කසගලු(ගොඩ) හා මො .. ..
ගොඩ හා වල් කපා පවත් කළ .. ළග
10 න්නොටවත්ත හා කළපුමැඳැ (බම්)නඥනදුව හා මෙමැ අසැ මනො
නඥනදුව හා මෙමැ අසින් වල් කපා කොළවෙල් හිඳිවූ බොලුනුඩාව
හා මෙම අසැ බෙරවාගො[ඩ]
11 .. .. .. නිශ්ශංකගලට පැදුම්දිගින් කළපුව හා දකුණුදිගින් සුවවත්කැමි
යාගේ ගෙය කෙරෙ කෝන්ගස හා පැළදිගින් කකුළුවාගලැ අරම්බඩ
හා කිත්කෙවි
12 වෙන් පොල් හිඳිවූ දුලුබැස්ස හිම් කොටැ මෙ අතුරෙහි හිඳිවූ කොළ
වෙල් ඇතුළුවූ තැන් හා මෙ විහාරයට හා මෙ විහාරයෙහි වැඩැ හිඳිනා
වහන්සෙවරු

13 න්දෑම අත්පාමෙහෙ කරන පරිත්දෙන් අප අඬසාගතවහලින් හා රන් වහලින් හා මෙ විහාරයෙහි මුඳුකරඬුයෙන් රන් දිලා ගෙනෑ ලූ කොත්ත බොග

14 ත්ත හා මෙකු මවු උ(බ) හා මෙ(කු නං මි)ඳි හා මෙකු පිත් උයවඳ හා මෙකු මල් ගෙත්(කැමි) ලො(කො)යි හා මෙකු මල් පොත්වාණී මිඳ හා මෙකු මල් රකු හා මෙකු මල් (සුව) හා (මිඳල්කැඹියා) .. ..

15 රය හා මෙකු දූ ගොඬැලි දෙව .. .. නත්ත හා මෙකු බෑ පොරණ මණියා හා මෙකු මල් පොරණ බුදු හා දුඹ්දෙව හා මෙකු පුතු හා ගොඬැළී හෙළිලි රකගැ(ළී) සිනලිය හා මෙකු දූ සානි

16 ය හා මෙකු [පුතු] කරඬි .. .. .. හා මෙකු නං සෙ[ල්]ලිය හා [ගොඬලි] .. .. .. ය හා මෙකු දූ .. .. කැලිරක හා මානිය දූ සුව ගොඬලිය හා සෙ(නැ)න් කොත්තියං හා මෙකු දූ කොත්තිය හා මෙකු නං

17 රක හා මෙකු මල් .. .. හා මෙකු අඹු මිඳි හා මෙකු පිත් .. .. ණත්තු හා .. ලි දෙව හා මෙකු පුත් මත්දල සාතා හා මෙකු මල් පොරණ (ස)ලා හා මත්දල කොරල

18 දෙවු හා සාතන් සි .. .. මෙකු මල් ලොකෙයි හා මෙකු මල් .. .. .. හා මෙකු මල් ගොළු මිඳ හා මෙකු මල් බුදු හා බෙම්තොට කිත හා මෙකු පුත් සුවයා හා

19 .. .. .. දෙව හා මෙකු පුත් .. .. හා කළු කිතු හා එබෙර බොයි හා හෙ[ළි]ලි දෙව පුත් සුවයා හා කොර නාථා හා එනෑදි සානිය හා මෙකු නං සානිය හා මෙකු පු

20 ත් සුවයා හා මෙකු මල් .. . .. මෙකු මල් ලොකෙයි හා මෙකු නං රක හා මෙකු මල් .. .. (ඇවෙරි) දෙවු හා දෙමළ පයා හා මෙකු අඹු සුපනිය හා මෙකු දූ න(ඹ)ය හා මෙකු පුත් .. ..

21 හා කොර නම්බා හා මද්දළ .. .. යා හා කරඬ දෙවා හා අම්බලවා හා .. නියා හා කිළ .. .. කිතා හා ගගා හා ගැ .. ගයිය හා ල .. .. දිය හා නැවිය හා දෙමළ .. ..

22 සුඳ හා ජයව(ඳ) හා .. .. හා සෙලේ හා හෙළුලු රාමා හා කළු රාමා හා කුඩා රාමා හා සි(න්) .. දෙමැලි ගැඹ්ය හා බඩල් පෙරිය හා මෙකු දූ .. .. [මෙ]

23 කු පුත් .. .. යා හා .. .. හා මෙකු අඹු ආදිත්හිය හා මෙකු පුත් කොම්වා හා හෙළසරක් මිසරක් ඇතුළු[වූ] සියල්ලට තමන් තමන් විසින් .. .. (සල)

24 කමින් සංගීතාපවර්ගීත .. .. නොසලකා මෙයට හානියක් කළ එකෙක් ඇත් නම් කවුඩු බලු වූයේ යෑ කාවණුයෙහි ලූ බත් කෑයේ යෑ .. ..

25 කහම්බල්කුළු මිඳල්නා වම්හ කටුවිත්නා දෙවුම් මියගුණුකිම් කොදනා

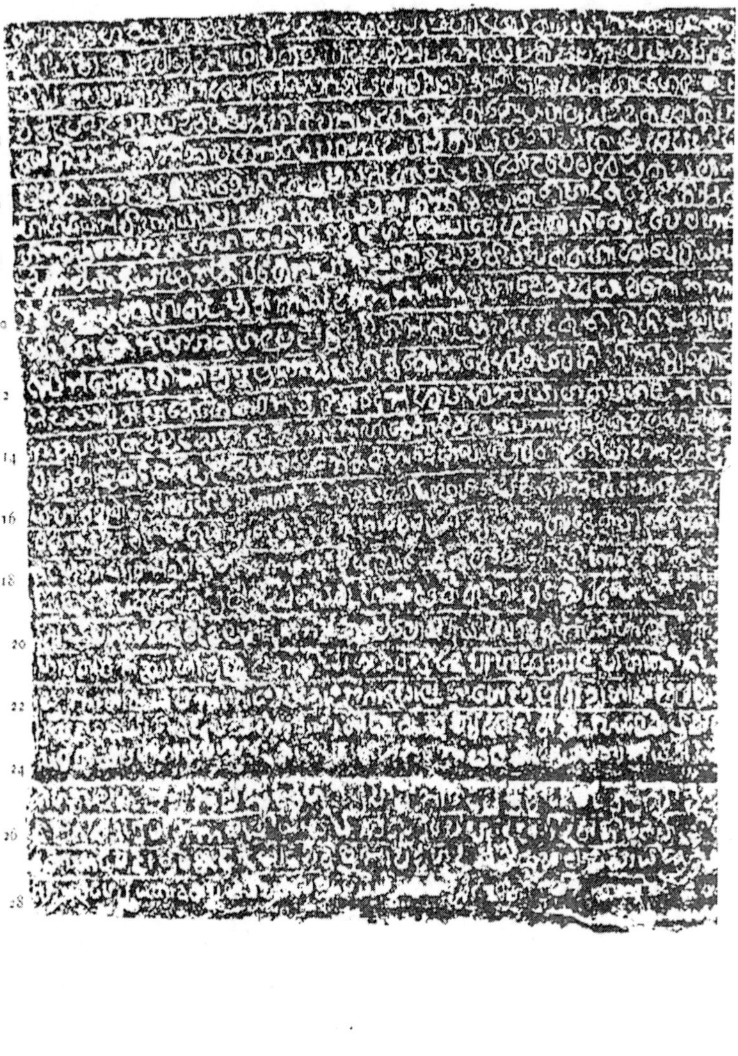

වම්හ දෙගලතුරුබිම් **විජයානා** වම්හ (දත්මි) රක්හැලි බුත් .. ..
26 (දත්මි) .. .. දෙවාමි දත්මි වත්කැමි
පෙදර නාථාමි දත්මි පෙදර විජයාමි දත්මි වත්කැමි රමුක්කඩු ද .. .. ..
දත්මි .. ..

27 * * * * * *

28 * * * * * *

TRANSCRIPT.

1 Triṁśe bhūmi-bhujaḥ **Parākrama-bhuja[sy** ā]bde [1] tad=ādeśataś=
Śraddhā=cāra-draḍādhikāri [2]-vibhunā nāmnā **Mahendreṇa** tu [।*]
Uttuṅg=ānvaya-sambhavena viduṣā kḷptāya [sat-kīrttinā] [3]
Śailānt=āyata[nāya datta-vividha]-grām=ādi-saṁkhy=o[cya]te [॥*]
2 Sirisaṅgabo **Parākramabāhu** cakravartti-svāmīn-vahanseṭa tis-vanu
Vesagä [4] pura pohoyä Pasyodun-vaga [5] kāriya koṭä siṭi Demaḷa-
[adhikāra **Kahambalkuḷu Mindal]-nā** vamha apa hā [6] apagē [7] mā-
3 -ṇiyan vahanse hā apagē bāna Miyaṅguṇubim **Kodā-nāvan** hā Degal-
aturu-bim **Vijayā-nāvan** hā apagē nä **Kaṭuvit-nā Sätumba** hā
.. .. vun [8] Velga-
4 -m-muḷaṭa bada va Saddharmma-rājan-pirivanaṭa ätuḷat koṭä rāja-sam-
mata äti vä dāgap [9] mā-bo piḷima pihiṭuvā apa kärävū [10] **Galpāta-
vihārayaṭa** .. .. [11] koṭä memä vihāra-
5 -yehi väḍä hindinā vahanse-varundäṭa [12] pratyaya piṇisä hā lū apa sī-
parapurā vä vaḷandā ā [13] Siyambalāpaya hā mehi mä bada viyaḷa
tänu [14] Sumbuḷupat-hälla ätu-
6 -ḷu-vū tänä kumburu hā mehi pol puvak ätuḷu-vū koḷavel-aya [15] kusalān
koṭä hā Kunrāmā-śättunāvanṭa ran dīlā gat Bemtoṭä tāvaḷamaṭa [16]
ätuḷat Ṭiṅgavaṭu-

---

[1] Bt. *-bhujaḥ śyābde.* [2] Bt. *dṛṣādhḷkāri.*
[3] Bt. *kālāpta-puṇyātmane.* [4] Bt. *Vesaṅgä.* [5] Bt. *raḷa.*
[6] Bt. *Keselä(na-bim Mahendra) maha (ämatiyā).*
[7] Bt. *apage.* [8] Bt. *Sätumba-delu (hā puda) nuva vun.*
[9] Bt. *dāgab.* [10] Bt. *käravū.*
[11] Mr. Bell conjecturally restores the missing letters as *pūjā-vastu*; but this conjecture is not supported by such traces of the letters as are still visible.
[12] Bt. *vahanse-varundäṭa.* [13] Bt. *Sisarasutā Värälanda ä.* [14] Bt. *viyahena.*
[15] Bt. *ayā.* [16] Bt. *tavalamaṭa.*

7 bhāgayen vihārayaṭa pädum-digin kumbuk hindivū pokuṇa hā dakuṇu-digin kaḷapuva hā päḷa[1]-digin Udayā-daśapālayangē vatu-baḍä[2] pokuṇa hā uturu-digin Nam-seṭṭi

8 hinduvu pol-vatu-bhāgayehi v(i)dhi[3] maha-him koṭä me aturehi koḷavel hā mehi bada kumburu hā kevuḷu Maṇakappambarāya[ru]ṭa[4] vihārayen ran dīlā genä pol puvak hindavū

9 Mundal[5]-kämiyā hun Tiratenayā-[vatta] hā Isamviṭi-vatta hā Äveriyā hun Beravā-gamä Panäspol-[6] vatta hā Kasagalu-(goḍa)[7] hā mo .. .. goḍa[8] hā val kapā pavat kaḷa .. ḷaga-

10 -ntoṭa-[9] vatta hā kaḷapu-mändä (Dharmma)-nandana-dūva[10] hā memä[11] asä Manonandana-[12]dūva hā memä[11] asin val kapā koḷavel hindivū Bolutuḍāva hā mema asä Beravā-go[ḍa]

11 .. .. ..[13] Niśśaṁka-galaṭa[14] pädum-digin kaḷapuva hā dakuṇu-digin Suva-vat-kämiyāgē geya[15] kere kōn-gasa hā päḷa[16]-digin Kakuḷuvā-galä[17] arama-baḍa hā[18] Kitkev-

12 -ven[19] pol hindivū Ilubässa him koṭä me aturehi hindivū koḷavel ätuḷu-vū tän hā me[20] vihārayaṭa hā me[20] vihārayehi väḍä[21] hindinā vahanse-varu-

13 -ndäṭa at-pā-mehe karana[22] paritden[23] apa anvayāgata-vahalin hā ran-vahalin hā me vihārayehi mundu-karaṇḍuyen[24] ran dīlā genä lū Konta Boga-

14 -nta[25] hā meku mavu[26] U(ba)[27] hā me(ku naṁ Mi)ndi[28] hā meku pit Uyavandā[29] hā meku mal Get(kämi)[30] Lo(ke)yi hā meku mal Ponvāṇī Mīndā hā meku mal Raku hā meku mal (Suva) hā (Mīndal-kämiyā) .. ..

15 -raya hā meku dū Goḍäli Deva .. .. natta hā meku bā Poraṇa Maṇiyā hā meku mal Poraṇa Budu hā Dämi-deva hā meku putu hā Goḍäḷi Heḷili Rakahäḷ(i) Sigaliya hā meku dū Sāti-

---

[1] Bt. *päla.* [2] Bt. *varubäsä.* [3] Perhaps to be corrected to *vidi.*
[4] Bt. *-kappambarāla.* [5] Bt. *mudal.* [6] Bt. *Panas-pol.* [7] *Kasagalu-toḷa.*
[8] Bt. *Mokusāgoḍa.* [9] Bt. *(rajagenarata)ḷa.* [10] Bt. *kaḷapu-mändäya Maḷandunan-dūva.*
[11] Bt. *mema.* [12] Bt. *Manobandana.*
[13] The second and third letters of this line have been read by Mr. Bell as *hā me.*
[14] Bt. *galäḷa.* [15] Bt. *Sujjita-kämiyä(ge yā)ya.* [16] Bt. *päḷa.* [17] Bt *Käkuḷuvā-gala.*
[18] Mr. Bell has added here *uturu-digin* which is not found on the stone.
[19] Bt. *Kikkevaven.* [20] Bt. *mema.* [21] Bt. *vāḍa.* [22] Bt. *karaṇa.*
[23] Bt. *paridden.* [24] Bt. *karaṇḍuven.* [25] Bt. *Konrābeg Rāma.* [26] Bt. *ambu.*
[27] Bt. *Umba.* [28] Bt. *duva Valindā.* [29] *Udaranda.* [30] Bt. *Ge(tta).*

16 -ya hā meku [putu] Karaḍi . . . . . hā meku naṁ Se[l]liya hā [Goḍali] . . . . . ya hā meku dū . . . Käliraka hā Māniya dū Suva Goḍaliya hā Se(nä)n Kottiya hā meku dū Kottiya hā meku naṁ

17 Raka hā meku mal . . . . hā meku ambu Mindi hā meku pit . . . ṇattu hā . . li Deva hā meku put Matdala Sätā hā meku mal Poraṇa (Sa)lā hā Matdaḷa Koraḷa

18 Devu hā Sātan Si . . . . meku mal Lokeyi hā meku mal . . . . . hā meku mal Goḷu Mindā hā meku mal Budu hā Bemtoṭa Kita hā meku put Suvayā hā

19 . . . . . Deva hā meku put . . . . hā Kaḷu Kitu hā Eṇḍera Boyi hā He[ḷi]li Deva put Suvayā hā Kora Nāthä hā e-nädi Sātiya hā meku naṁ Sātiya hā meku pu-

20 -t Suvayā hā meku mal . . . . . meku mal Lokeyi hā meku naṁ Raka hā meku mal . . . . (Äveri) Devu hā Demaḷa Payā hā meku ambu Supaniya hā meku dū Na(mbi)ya hā meku put . . . .

21 hā Kora Nambā hā Maddaḷa . . . yā hā Karaḍi Devā hā Ambalavā hā . . niyā hā Kiḷa . . . Kitā hā Gaṅgā hā Gä . . gaṅgiya hā La . . . . diya hā Näviya hā Demaḷa . . . .

22 Sundā hā Jayavand(ā) hā . . . . hā Selē hā Heḷulu Rāmā hā Kaḷu Rāmā hā Kuḍā Rāmā hā Sī(n) . . Demäli Gäviya hā Baḍal Periya hā meku dū . . . . [me]-

23 -ku put . . . . yā[1] hā . . . . hā meku ambu Ādittiya hā[2] meku put Kovivā[3] hā heḷa-sarak mī-sarak ätuḷu-[vū] siyallaṭa taman taman visin[4] . . . . (sala)-

24 -(kamin)[5] svargg=āpavargga . . . .[6] no-salakā ṁeyaṭa hāniyak kaḷa ekek ät nam kavuḍu balu vūyē yä[7] kāvaṇuyehi lū[8] bat käyē yä[9] . . . .

25 Kahambaḷkuḷu[10] **Mindal-nā** vamha Kaṭuvitnā[11] **Devumi**[12] Miyaṅguṇu-bim **Kodā-nā** vamha Degalaturu-bim **Vijayā-nā** vamha[13] (Datmi) Rak-häli But . . . . . .

---

[1] Bt. *Dilayā.* [2] Bt. *Rada-paṇḍarala-kaḷa hā Yäku dambudala Dittiya hā.*

[3] Bt. *Kovivā.* [4] Mr. Bell has omitted *taman visin.* [5] Bt. -*samin.*

[6] Mr. Bell fills the gap by (*iṣṭa säpa saha raja aṇa*).

[7] Bt. *baluhu yeyä.* [8] Bt. *kävanuye hala.* [9] Bt. *ba(t kävun samānayo)ya.*

[10] Bt. *Kahambaikula.* [11] Bt. *Kaṭuvitnā.* [12] *Deḷusa.*

[13] What Mr. Bell has made out of line 25 from this point and the first half of the next line is: *Āghara-Saṅgili Butu Pabandami Dakiṇa Moraṭāmändä Väliyā Saḍime Kuranavalu Devāmi Dathi Vatakaḍi-pedara Nāgāmi.*

26 (datmi) .. .. Devāmi datmi Vatkāmi Pedara Nāthāmi datmi Pedara Vijayāmi datmi Vat-kāmi Ramukkaḍu Da .. .. datmi .. ..

27 * * * * * *

28 * * * * * *

TRANSLATION.

[Line 1] In the thirtieth year of **Parākrama-bhuja**[1], the lord of the earth. (Herein) are enumerated the villages, &c., granted to the monastery of **Śailāntāyatana** which was established, at His Majesty's behest, by His Lordship the Dra[vi]ḍādhikārin[2] of pious conduct, by name **Mahendra**, who was born in high lineage, is wise and is of good repute.

[Lines 2–5] On the full-moon day of Vesaga[3] in the thirtieth year of His Majesty, the Emperor Sirisaṅgabo **Parākramabāhu**. We[4], **Kahambalkuḷu Mindalnā**[5], the Demaḷa-adhikāra[6], administering the Pasyodun-vaga. the lady our mother, our nephews, **Kodānā** of Miyaṅguṇu-bim and **Vijayānā** of Degalaturu-bim, and our kinsman, **Kaṭuvitnā Sätumba**[7], grant, as . . . . to the **Galpāta Vihāra** which we have founded with royal consent, making it connected with Velgammuḷa and included in the Saddharmmarājan Pirivana. and having established [therein] relic-shrines, great *bodhis* and images ; and for the things requisite for their lordships [the monks] who reside in this *vihāra*, the following lands which have been in the possession of our family[8].

[1] i.e. Parākramabāhu.

[2] *Draḍādhikāri*: The reading *draḍa* in this compound is free from doubt ; but it conveys no sense. In the corresponding Sinhalese portion of the epigraph occurs the title Demaḷa-adhikāra and it is therefore possible to conjecture that *draḍādhikāri* is a mistake for *draviḍādhikāri*, the Sanskrit rendering of the Sinhalese title. The word *draviḍādhikāri* contains one syllable too much for the metre ; and it is quite possible that the omission of the syllable *vi* was deliberate, being an expedient to satisfy the requirements of the metre. If so, it is a licence which cannot be justified on grammatical grounds.

[3] P. *Vesākha*, Skt. *Vaiśākha*. April-May.

[4] The original would read literally : We are Kahambalkuḷu . . . We, and the lady our mother . . .

[5] *Kahambalkuḷu*, appears to be a place name used as a family name. Such are *Miyaṅguṇu-bim* and *Degalaturu-bim* in the names of two other dignitaries occurring in this record. *Mindal* is the same as Pāli *Mahinda*.

[6] The officer who held the title of Demaḷa-adhikāra (the Superintendent of the Tamils) was most probably the Commander of the Tamil mercenaries who were in the service of the Sinhalese king.

[7] *Kaṭuvitnā*, in this name, appears to be an official title of which the significance is altogether obscure.

[8] *Sī-parapurā vä* is a phrase not found elsewhere ; but it is clear that it is connected with *siya-parapura* (Skt. *svīya-paramparā*) 'own lineage'.

[Lines 5-12] Siyambalāpaya and, appertaining thereto, the fields in the area included within Sumbulupat-hälla which has been made suitable for sowing[1]; the *kolavel-aya*[2] of this including coco-nut and areca (palms) given as religious donations[3]; the extent granted to the *vihāra* from the allotment of Ṭiṅgavaṭu, included in the *tāvaḷama*[4] of Bemtoṭa, which was bought by giving gold to the caravan leader[5] Kunrāmā, bounded, on the east by the pond (*pokuṇa*) at which *kumbuk* trees have been planted, on the south by the lagoon, on the west by the pond (*pokuṇa*) near the garden of Uḍayā Daśapālayā and on the north by the street[6] in the allotment of the coco-nut garden planted by Nam-seṭṭi; the *koḷavel* of this area and the fields appertaining to this; Tiratenayā-vatta which was bought by giving gold from the *vihāra* to the fisherman Maṇa-kappambarāyaru, which is planted with coco-nut and areca palms and in which Mundal-kämiyā[7] resides; Isamviṭi-vatta; Panäspol-vatta in Beravā-gama; in which Äveriyā resides; Kasagalu-goḍa; . . . . goḍa; . . . lagantoṭa-vatta which was prepared by having the jungle cleared; the island Dharmma-nandana in the

---

[1] *Viyaḷa tänu*: Compare the phrase *viyaḷa bahā tänu* in the Batalagoḍa-väva slab-inscription and see the remarks thereon, above pp. 80 and 82, n. 2.

[2] The word *koḷavel* has also been found in a document of Parākramabāhu VI, published by Mr. Codrington in *Vidyodaya*, I, p. 376. In l. 10 occurs the phrase *val kapā koḷavel hindi-vū* which shows that *koḷavel* is a term denoting some kind of cultivation. *Koḷavel-aya* would therefore signify the revenue due to the landlord or the state from this particular form of cultivation. *Koḷa* occurs in the compound *gaha-koḷa* which is used in colloquial Sinhalese, and may mean 'leaves' or 'shrubs'. *Vela* ordinarily means field. Mr. Codrington is of opinion that *koḷavel-aya* is the later *vatu-badda, i.e.* the tax on gardens.

[3] *Kusalān*: For this word, see *E. Z.*, Vol. III, p. 95.

[4] *Tāvaḷama* occurs nowhere else in Sinhalese literature or epigraphy. It seems to be the prototype of the modern Sinhalese word *tavaḷama* which means 'a number of oxen laden with merchandise' or 'a station on the frontier for the sale or exchange of commodities' (see Clough, *Sinhalese-English Dictionary, s.v.*). The first of these two meanings does not suit *tāvaḷama* in the context in which it occurs in this record; but the second seems to be applicable. The words *tāvaḷama* and *tavaḷama* both seem to be derived from T. *tāvaḷam* which means 'lodging or place of residence' or 'town or city in an agricultural tract' (see *Tamil Lexicon*, s.v.). In the compound *tāvaḷakkārar*, the Tamil word seems to have preserved the meaning which is found in its Sinhalese derivative, for it means 'traders from distant parts' or 'those who keep oxen for carrying burdens'. That part of mediaeval Bentoṭa designated by the word *tāvaḷama*, might have been so called because it contained a station for the exchange of goods, or from the fact of its being the centre of an agricultural tract.

[5] *Śāttunā*, wrongly written for *sāttunā*, Skt. *sārtthavāha-nāyaka*.

[6] This rendering is based on the correction of *vidhi*, occurring in the text, to *vīdi* (Skt. *vīthī*).

[7] *Mundal-kämiyā* means 'treasury official'. In olden times the custom of referring to, and addressing persons by, their official titles, in preference to their personal names, seems to have been prevalent among the Sinhalese as it is to-day.

middle of the lagoon; the island Manonandana in the same vicinity; Bolutuḍāva in which *koḷavel* has been planted after having had the jungle cleared; Niśśaṁka-gala, in Beravāgoḍa in the same vicinity, to which the boundaries are, on the eastern side the lagoon, on the southern side the *kōn* tree near the house of Suva Vatkämi, on the western side Aramboḍa of Kakuḷuvā-gala, and on the northern side[1] Ilubässa in Kitkevuva in which coco-nut palms have been planted; the *koḷavel* planted and the lands within these boundaries.

[Lines 12–23] And in order that they may perform services[2] to this *vihāra* and to their lordships [the monks] residing in this *vihāra*, the following [were granted] from among the slaves who have belonged hereditarily to our family, the purchased slaves[3] and those acquired by paying gold from the funds[4] of this *vihāra*:

Konta Boganta,[5] his mother Uba, his younger sister Mindi, his father Uyavandā, his younger brother Getkämi Lokeyi, his younger brother Ponvāṇī Mindā, his younger brother Raku, his younger brother Suva; Mindal-kämiyā . . . raya, his daughter Goḍäli Deva . . . natta, his elder brother Poraṇa Maṇiyā, his

[1] The words meaning 'on the northern side' (*uturu-digin*) which we should expect here, are omitted in the text.

[2] *At-pā-mehe-karana* means literally 'performing services by the hands and the feet'.

[3] *Ran-vahal*, literally 'gold slaves', may mean either slaves bought for money or those who were forced to slavery by debt.

[4] *Mundu-karaṇḍu*: This word occurs in the Mihintale tablets of Mahinda IV and has been translated by Dr. Wickremasinghe as 'a casket under lock and key'. *Mudu* is derived from Skt. *mudrā* and means 'seal' while *karaṇḍu* (Skt. *karaṇḍa*) means 'casket'. *Mundu-karaṇḍu* must therefore have been a sealed casket or box in which the small objects of value belonging to a monastery were kept. The term may well have been extended in use to the gold and jewels preserved in this place of safe deposit and seems to have been used in that sense in the present record.

[5] The method adopted by the writer of the epigraph in enumerating the slaves is to name one of them first and then to give the names of others related to him, the relationship being also stated. There is a certain amount of ambiguity regarding the relationships, as it is not always clear whether the pronoun *meku* 'of this' (translated by 'his') refers to the name immediately preceding it or to some other occurring previously. The writer of the epigraph seems to have had a certain sense of chivalry, for in enumerating the relatives of any person the womenfolk are generally given the precedence. The names of these humble folk are interesting in that they show us that, in the twelfth or thirteenth century, as to-day, ordinary persons had sobriquets, indicating some bodily characteristic of theirs, or their profession or residence, to distinguish them from their fellows of the same name. For instance we find in this inscription such names as Koraḷa Devu (Devu, the scaly), Goḷu Mindā (Mindā, the Dumb), Bemtoṭa Kita (Kita of Bemtoṭa), Kaḷu Kitu (Kitu, the Dark), Eṇḍera Boyi (Boyi, the Cowherd), Kora Nāthā (Nāthā the Lame), Heḷili Deva (Deva, the Fair), Demaḷa Payā (Payā, the Tamil), Heḷulu Rāmā (Rāmā, the Fair), Kaḷu Rāmā (Rāmā, the Dark), Kuḍā Rāmā (Rāmā, the Small), Baḍal Periya (Periya, the Goldsmith), and Getkämi Lokeyi (Lokeyi, the Tailor). Names of this type may be found in any Sinhalese village to-day.

younger brother Poraṇa Budu; Dämi Deva and his son; Goḍali, Heḷili, Raka-häla, and Sigiliya; his daughter Sātiya; his son Karaḍi . . . his younger sister Selliya; Goḍali . . . his daughter . . . kaḷi Raka; Suva Goḍaliya, daughter of Māniya; Senän Kottiya, her daughter Kottiya, her younger sister Raka, her younger brother . . . . . . his wife Mindi, his father . . . nattu; . . . li Deva, his son Matdaḷa Sātā, his younger brothers Poraṇa Salā and Matdaḷa Koraḷa Devu; Sātan Si. . ., his younger brother Lokeyi, his younger brother . . . ., his younger brother Goḷu Mindā, his younger brother Budu; Bemtoṭa Kita, his son Suva; . . . . Deva, his son . . . . .; Kaḷu Kitu, Eṇḍera Boyi, Suvayā son of Heḷili Deva; Kora Nāthā, his aunt Sātiya, his younger sister Sātiya, his son Suvayā, his younger brother . . . . . . his younger brother Lokeyi, his younger brother Raka, his younger brother . . . Äveri Devu; Demaḷa Payā, his wife Supaniya, his daughter Nambiya, his son . . . . . . Kora Nambā; Maddaḷa . . . . ya; Karaḍi Devā; Ambalavā; . . niyā; Kiḷa . . Kitā; Gaṅgā; Ga . . gaṅgiya; La . . . . diya; Näviya; Demaḷa . . . . . .; Sundā; Jayavandā; . . . . . Selē; Heḷalu Rāmā; Kaḷu Rāmā; Kuḍā Rāmā; Sīn . . .; Demäḷi Gäviya; Baḍal Periya, his daughter . . . . . .; his son . . . ya, ... his wife Ādittiya, and his son Kovivā.

[Lines 23–24] To all mentioned above, including neat cattle and buffaloes . . . . . . by one's own self . . . . . . considering . . . . . . heaven and final liberation. If there be any person who, not considering . . . . . ., does any harm to this [religious gift], may he become a crow or a dog; he is like one who has eaten the rice put in the *kävaṇu*[1].

[Lines 25–28] We[2] are **Kahambalkuḷu Mindal.** I am **Kaṭuvitnā Devu**, We are Miyaṅguṇu-bim **Kodānā.** We are Degalaturu-bim **Vijayānā.** I, Rak-häli But . . . . . know [this][3]. I, ... Deva, know [this] . . . . . . I, Vatkämi Pedara Nāthā, know [this]. I, Pedara Vijayā, know [this]. I, Vatkämi Ramukkaḍu Da . . . . . know [this] * * * * * * * * * * * *

[1] *Kävaṇuyehi lū bat käyē yä*: For this phrase, see above, p. 82, n. 4.

[2] Here, as well as in the beginning of the record, the dignitary named Mihindal or Mindal (Mahendra) refers to himself in the honorific plural which is also used by the other dignitaries, except Kaṭu itnā Devu, mentioned in the record.

[3] *Datmi, &c.*: With this formula used by the witnesses to this document, compare that occurring at the end of the Doraṭiyāva *sannasa* of Niśśaṁka Malla: for example, the phrase *dannam Kalyāṇa-mahādevīmha*, 'I, Kalyāṇa-mahādevī, know this' (see *J. R. A. S., C. B.*, vol. xxix, pp. 320 and 322). A similar formula is used by witnesses in Tamil inscriptions. Compare, for instance, the signature of a witness in an epigraph from the Sokkanātha Temple at Koliñjivāḍi: *ippāḍi aṟivēṉ Pallavarā-yarēṉ*, 'I, Pallavarāyar, know this (*S. I. I.*, vol. v, p. 95).